U.S. POLICY
IN THE CARIBBEAN

For God's sake, think of the West Indies. I have hitherto preached in vain; but any misfortune there will hurt you more than any other thing in the world.

—Horace Walpole to his brother Robert,
prime minister of England in 1735

America has a hemisphere to itself.

—Thomas Jefferson to Alexander von Humboldt,
December 6, 1813

U.S. POLICY IN THE CARIBBEAN

John Bartlow Martin

with a Foreword by M. J. Rossant

A Twentieth Century Fund Essay

Westview Press / Boulder, Colorado

Copyright © 1978 by the Twentieth Century Fund

Published in 1978 in the United States of America by
  Westview Press, Inc.
  5500 Central Avenue
  Boulder, Colorado 80301
  Frederick A. Praeger, Publisher and Editorial Director

Library of Congress Cataloging in Publication Data
Martin, John Bartlow, 1915-
  U.S. policy in the Caribbean
  "A Twentieth Century Fund essay."
  Bibliography: p.
  Includes index.
  1. Caribbean area—Foreign relations—United States. 2. United States—Foreign relations—Caribbean area. I. Twentieth Century Fund. II. Title.
F2178.U6M37   327.73'0729   78-52883
ISBN 0-89158-061-1

Printed and bound in the United States of America

The Twentieth Century Fund

The Twentieth Century Fund is an independent research foundation that undertakes policy studies of economic, political, and social institutions and issues. The Fund was founded in 1919 and endowed by Edward A. Filene.

Policymakers with limited time may wish to read only the first and last chapters. What lies between elaborates the first and supports the last.

—John Bartlow Martin

CONTENTS

FOREWORD

For some two hundred years, the United States has regarded the Caribbean as an American lake, vital to our security and generally profitable to our business interests. We have been accustomed to intervene freely in the affairs of the mini-states of the region, frequently with military force. The U.S. attitude toward the Caribbean began to change with the Good Neighbor policy of Franklin D. Roosevelt and went still further with the Alliance for Progress of John F. Kennedy, when the United States attempted to stimulate social reform by applying techniques of development assistance that had been successful in rebuilding Europe after World War II to the largely nonindustrial economies of Latin America and the Caribbean countries. The trustees of the The Twentieth Century Fund, which had sponsored a number of studies of economic development and international relations, saw that U.S. policy toward Latin America and the Caribbean was changing dramatically and demanded fresh evaluation.

In 1970, *The Alliance that Lost its Way*, by Jerome Levinson and Juan de Onís, was published as a Twentieth Century Fund Study. Levinson and de Onís produced a cogent analysis of the Alliance, but they did not deal with the countries of the Caribbean. The trustees considered that a comparable analysis of the Caribbean was urgently needed, although recognizing that it presented unusual problems for policy research. The region, as most observers define it, encompasses both islands and mainland countries—widely dispersed, varying considerably in size, terrain, natural resources, wealth, development level, population density, ethnic origin, language, and political system. After long and careful searching, the trustees chose John Bartlow Martin, former ambassador to the Dominican Republic, to undertake this difficult and demanding task. Martin himself perceived a special urgency in his assignment. Shortly before embarking on his research, he wrote:

> In our time, a revolutionary process has begun in the Caribbean, not the traditional nineteenth century Latin American "revolutions," which were actually nothing more than power struggles between rival generals, but a process bringing about profound change. Castro's military victory, Bosch's electoral victory, Betancourt's (and his successors') redistribution of wealth and moves to regain control of its own oil for Venezuela, and nationalistic protest at our ownership of the Panama Canal are manifestations of a revolutionary process which, having begun, is probably irreversible. For change is inevitable, and its velocity usually increases. What should our policy toward this change be? This study, which tries to answer that question, will have implications for our policy in Latin America as a whole and, indeed, for our policy toward the third world. If we cannot move effectively and helpfully in the Caribbean, we can hardly expect to do better in Asia or Africa.

More recently, in a continuation of the process that Martin had described, the countries of the Caribbean have joined other Third World countries in shifting the orientation of international organizations and in designing domestic institutional structures that owe little to the traditions of the advanced industrial democracies. One of John Bartlow Martin's achievements is an analysis that takes these changes into account and provides a sound basis for U.S. policy toward the complex region he has studied. The fund is grateful for his insight.

M. J. Rossant, Director
The Twentieth Century Fund
September 1977

ACKNOWLEDGMENTS

I owe thanks first of all to The Twentieth Century Fund. The board of the fund underwrote the considerable cost of the project, covering two years of research, travel, and writing. The director of the fund, Murray J. Rossant, and members of his staff guided the project and edited the manuscript. The book quite literally could not have been done without fund support; no commercial publisher could have undertaken it. For all this I am most grateful.

I owe thanks to Roxane Eberlein and J. Philip Rourk. Miss Eberlein, a free-lance researcher and editor, spent two years in Washington doing research for the book, especially the period before the Nixon-Ford administration. Phil Rourk, a retired foreign service officer with long experience in the Caribbean and now a consultant on tropical products to the Department of Agriculture, prepared several memorandums on the economics issues discussed in the book as well as the statistical studies.

For research, I myself traveled extensively in the Caribbean. In every country I visited, I received the unfailing cooperation of the United States ambassador and his staff. They extended courtesies, furnished information, helped arrange interviews with local leaders, and in every way were most helpful. To name the individual embassy officers here might embarrass them or hamper them in their important work; but I am most grateful to all of them. I do, however, wish to offer my thanks publicly to the following men, who were U.S. ambassadors or chargés d'affaires in the Caribbean while I was there: Diego C. Asencio in Venezuela, William J. Jorden in Panama, Max V. Krebs in Guyana, the late Francis E. Meloy, Jr., in Guatemala, Lloyd I. Miller in Trinidad-Tobago, Turner B. Shelton in Nicaragua, William B. Sowash in Honduras, Sumner Gerard in Jamaica, and Terence A. Todman in Costa Rica.

In Washington, I was fortunate to have the most helpful cooperation of the Department of State. Again, it seems best not to identify by name all the officers who helped me, but I do want to express special thanks to Joseph I. Sisco, William D. Rogers, and Harry W. Shlaudeman. In the Congress, I had the cooperation of Senators Hubert H. Humphrey and Edward M. Kennedy and Congressman Dante B. Fascell, together with members of their staffs and of their committee staffs, especially Pat M. Holt of the Senate Foreign Relations Committee and Michael Finley of the House Foreign Affairs Committee.

Several Caribbean ambassadors to the United States were most helpful. I want especially to thank Miguel Ángel Burelli of Venezuela, Douglas Fletcher of Jamaica, Livingston B. Johnson of the Bahamas, Victor McIntyre of Trinidad-Tobago, and Frederick Hilborn Talbot of Guyana, together with members of their staffs.

Apart from government officials, the following people in the United States gave me their time and thoughts: Francisco Aguirre, Milton Barrall, David Bell, Barry M. Blechman, Philip W. Bonsal, Luis F. V. Browne, Roy S. Bryce-Laporte, John Cates, Roland H. del Mar, Jorge Dominguez, Frederick Dutton, Richard Goodwin, Spencer M. King, Gordon Lewis (of Puerto Rico), Arnold Nachmanoff, Ben Stephansky, Tad Szulc, James D. Theberge, and Henry Wells. So did Galo Plaza of the OAS and Miguel Albornóz of the UN (in Venezuela).

In the Caribbean, I had the benefit of interviews with a great many people. I tried to seek out government leaders, opposition leaders, businessmen, labor leaders, intellectual leaders, editors and publishers, people of all sorts. Many of them would not wish to be identified here, but I am nonetheless grateful for their help. I do feel able to thank and want especially to thank for their thoughtful views the following: Jaime Benítez, Rubén Berríos, José Cabranes, Arturo Morales Carrión, Ángel Calderon Cruz, and Teodoro Moscoso of Puerto Rico; Alberto Cañas, Guido Fernández, Rodrigo Madrugal

Nieto, and Alfonso Carro Zuñega of Costa Rica; José Luís Cruz Salazar, René de León Schlotter, Jorge Skinner Klee, and Miguel Ydígoras Fuentes of Guatemala; Jorge Fidel Durón, Adolfo Facusse, Carlos Roberto Reina, and Mario Rietti of Honduras; Egerton Richardson, Edward Seaga, Theodore Sealey, and Philip Sherlock of Jamaica; Lloyd Best, Ellis Clark, and Cuthbert Joseph of Trinidad-Tobago; and Rómulo Betancourt, Alirio Parra, Arturo Uslar Pietri, and Luís Esteban Rey of Venezuela.

Finally, several people were good enough to read all or parts of the manuscript; they saved me many errors. Any errors of fact that remain are my own responsibility as, of course, are all matters of interpretation. I wish to thank the following for their most helpful reading: Philip W. Bonsal, Ellsworth Bunker, Dante Fascell, John Kenneth Galbraith, Max V. Krebs, Teodoro Moscoso, William D. Rogers, Arthur M. Schlesinger Jr., Harry W. Shlaudeman, and several foreign service officer experts better left unnamed.

Finally, I am grateful to Mrs. Joseph VanBogaert, who helped prepare and type the manuscript, and to my wife, Frances R. Martin, for her unfailing companionship, encouragement, and devotion.

J.B.M.

ABBREVIATIONS

AID: Agency for International Development
CACM: Central American Common Market
CARICOM: Caribbean Common Market
CECLA: Latin American Special Coordinating Commission
CIAP: Inter-American Committee, Alliance for Progress
ECLA: Economic Commission for Latin America
Exim: Export-Import Bank
GSP: Generalized System of Preferences
IADB: Inter-American Development Bank
IA-ECOSOC: Inter-American Economic and Social Council
IAF: Inter-American Fund
IBA: International Bauxite Association
ICA: International Cooperation Administration
IMF: International Monetary Fund
LAFTA: Latin American Free Trade Association
OAS: Organization of American States
OECD: Organization for Economic Cooperation and Development
OPEC: Organization of Petroleum Exporting Countries
ORIT: Inter-American Regional Association of Workers
SELA: Latin American Economic System
UNCTAD: United Nations Conference on Trade and Development

1
THE NEW CARIBBEAN

Few regions on earth are more complex, diverse, and unstable than the Caribbean, an area that stretches from the Bahamas south to the Panama Canal, and from the Mexican coast to Guyana. San Juan, Puerto Rico, is a thousand miles southeast of Miami, and Caracas, Venezuela, is five hundred miles south of Puerto Rico. Barbados is more than two thousand miles east of Belize; the Panama Canal is more than a thousand miles south of New Orleans. Here on thousands of islands, atolls, and closely related mainland nations live 52 million people—blacks, whites, native Indians, East Indians, and Orientals.

Varied though they are, these countries have a great influence on one another. Both Castro and Trujillo sent agents to assassinate Rómulo Betancourt of Venezuela. The Caribbean Legion helped Pepe Figueres take Costa Rica. Puerto Rico debates joining the Caribbean Development Bank. Jamaica, Venezuela, Trinidad, and Mexico are discussing joint aluminum production. In 1962, the leader of Nicaragua instigated the overthrow of the leader of Honduras.

Guatemala fears Mexican intervention in Belize. Cuba hopes to show all the others the way. So does Venezuela. We sometimes tend to lump the Caribbean nations in with South America, but they assert that they are different. Grey Lima has little in common with the gay Bahamas; Santiago, Chile, looks more like a northern European city than like hot, hysterical San Juan, Puerto Rico.

The Caribbean has been variously and always somewhat arbitrarily defined. We shall concentrate on the Greater Antilles (Puerto Rico, the Dominican Republic, Haiti, Jamaica, and Cuba); on Central America except for El Salvador (Guatemala, Honduras, Nicaragua, Costa Rica, and Panama); on Trinidad-Tobago; on two mainland countries, Venezuela and Guyana; and we shall also take note of Mexico and some of the smaller islands.

These place-names have a comfortable, familiar ring; they have been our friendly neighbors, our vacation spots, our business associates, and our trading partners. But they are no longer friendly; they resent our tourists; they do not want our traditional business enterprise; they reject our terms of trade. Almost unnoticed, over the last few years, they have slipped far closer to enmity toward us than to alliance with us. Yet our policies toward them have gone unchanged. We can no longer deal with this world in the old way; we must reexamine today's new Caribbean and adjust our policies toward it.

Some Caribbean territories are huge—Venezuela, with 352,000 square miles; some are infinitesimal—Montserrat with little more than 30 square miles. Some are becoming industrialized and show a relatively high (if misleading) per capita product—$1,834 in Puerto Rico; some are abysmally poor and backward—$145 in Haiti. Some like Venezuela are rich in natural resources, but the Bahamas can produce little but salt. Their political systems differ widely—two-party representative democracy in Venezuela and Jamaica, virtually one-party rule in Trinidad-Tobago, military rule in Guatemala and Honduras, one-family dynasties in Nicaragua and Haiti, and a peculiar form of guided democracy in Panama. Political instability is endemic; the history of the Caribbean is written in slave revolts, coups d'etat, assassinations, revolutions, riots, and armed interventions. Some of the islands are still under colonial rule; nearly all feel the influence of former colonial power.

Nor does the Caribbean have a homogeneous population; indeed, the population can be divided in half—the black and English-speaking Caribbean, consisting, for our purposes, of Jamaica, Trinidad-Tobago, and Guyana; and the mestizo and Spanish-speaking Caribbean, consisting of Puerto Rico, the Dominican Republic, Cuba, Central America, and Venezuela. (Haiti, black and French-speaking, stands isolated.) National unity and identity seem further advanced in the mestizo Spanish Caribbean than in the black English-speaking Caribbean states; they have been independent longer. In the black Caribbean, as Eric Williams makes clear, blackness, colonialism, and slavery are absolutely central to thought and politics.

Despite these differences, the Caribbean countries have certain things in common. They are what has been variously called backward, underdeveloped, less-developed, or developing nations. Let us simply call them poor nations. Few are highly industrialized; most are predominantly agricultural. They subsist on mining and plantation agriculture, much of it owned by foreign entrepreneurs. These nations argue that they have had to sell their natural resources and primary agricultural products to the industrialized nations cheap—and in return to buy manufactured products dear. That is their bitter complaint today—the unfair terms of trade, which, they say, are still widening the gap between the poor countries and the rich.

These nations share other afflictions. They cannot feed themselves despite their rich soils; their populations are growing with frightening rapidity; their wealth is distributed so inequitably that each of them contains a few very rich people and a great many very poor. Their exploding cities are becoming unfit for human habitation; some of their rural poor live entirely outside the money economy, often never seeing so much as $50 a year. In some of these countries, the classic Spanish-American power structure still prevails—the military, the church, and the oligarchy. In others, race is power. Their people have little education, few skills or trades; they have poor housing and little clothing; and they suffer from poor sanitation, poor medical care, and malnutrition. Many of them have no jobs; unemployment rates in the Caribbean run from 15 percent to 40 percent. The sons they send to the university often become more politicized than educated, and when they graduate (if they do), they often cannot find jobs and become alienated intellectuals who preach and, sometimes, attempt revolution.

It has become a cliché in recent years that in the Caribbean revolution is inevitable and, indeed, has already begun. It is not necessarily, however, the spectacular revolutions, such as Castro's, or the occasional tremendous effort by the United States, such as the Alliance for Progress, that has set broad currents in motion.

Twice in recent years the Caribbean world has been turned upside down. It happened first in the years around 1958, when the dictators Pérez Jiménez of Venezuela, Trujillo of the Dominican Republic (in 1961), Rojas Pinilla of Colombia, and Batista of Cuba were overthrown. At that time, what seemed in the balance was whether communism or democracy would follow them. Around that time, too, political parties arose in Jamaica and elsewhere in the colonial Caribbean. The Federation of the West Indies was formed, a first attempt to link the British colonies together. Rómulo Betancourt was elected President of Venezuela, becoming the first man in that position to serve out his term. Castro triumphed. Throughout the Caribbean, nationalism became the main current of political thought —and it has remained so to this day.

The Caribbean was stood on its head a second time in the early 1970s—1973, the year of the OPEC oil boycott, is as good a year as any to focus on the commodities revolution and the gathering storm of revolt against the terms of trade, a storm that still engulfs the Caribbean. The Caribbean nations drifted away from Washington and away from Moscow and toward the Third World. They struggled to regain control of their own natural resources. In so doing, they were driven toward statism, which greatly reinforced emerging nationalism. Call it what you will—socialism, nationalistic socialism, even national socialism (although sensitive leaders, remembering Hitler, shun that phrase)—the entire Caribbean region today, to a greater or lesser degree, has set sail on a leftward, statist, nationalist course with profound consequences for its relationship with the United States, the United Nations, the Organization of American States (OAS), and the rest of the world.

The first time the Caribbean was turned upside down, around 1958, it was a political earthquake. The second, around 1973, was an economic earthquake. The first forced the United States—long accustomed to a rather comfortable accommodation with a mixed bag of dictators and democrats—to readjust its entire policy. The second may force it into even more wrenching readjustments. Neither, however, was initiated by the United States; both were essentially Caribbean, in response to winds that swept the world.

Finally, these Caribbean countries share something else: the best winter climate on earth. And they are spectacularly beautiful— beaches and mountains and the fresh trade winds. So they are visited every year by hordes of northern tourists. This creates jobs. But it also creates problems, for the tourist sipping drinks beside the swimming pool is likely to be rich and white, while the waiter who brings the drinks is likely to be poor and black.

* * *

These Caribbean lands, then, are islands in the sun. They have been first the jewels, then the pawns, then the slums of empire. Do they matter to us—to the United States?

We have always thought so. Even before we were a nation, we, as colonies, traded with the French and Dutch West Indies, and Britain's attempt to tax that trade helped bring on our own revolution. Thomas Jefferson dreamed of a federation of all the Caribbean islands and hoped to obtain Napoleon's consent to the admission of Cuba into the Union. Indeed, a dozen presidents of the United States have found themselves deeply concerned with the Caribbean, and it is in the Caribbean that we have forged such cornerstones of our foreign policy as the Monroe Doctrine. We went to war with Spain over Cuba in 1898; we played out the prelude to World War I in the Caribbean; we fought the Cold War to apogee there and in Vietnam, risking a nuclear war with the Soviet Union over Cuba in 1962; and our reputation for imperialism, until Vietnam, rested largely on our military interventions in the Caribbean.

The importance we place on our relationship with the Caribbean rests on three interests.

First, our strategic, or national security, interest. From Monroe to Kennedy and Johnson, we have asserted before the world that the Caribbean is vital to our own defense. We have established bases in Puerto Rico, Cuba, and Panama. We have forbidden foreign powers to encroach. We have insisted on military control. To the U.S. Navy, the Caribbean has always been "Our Sea." Today, however, it is a frequently hostile sea, and in an age of jet bombers, nuclear missiles, and nuclear submarines (Soviet submarines lie off the Atlantic seaboard and visit the Caribbean), the importance of the Caribbean to our national defense is open to question.

Second, our economic interests. We are the dominant trading partner of the Caribbean nations. In the past, this has usually been put in terms of U.S. investment. Direct U.S. investment in the Caribbean has been estimated at $6.6 billion, about a third of the total for all of · Latin America. In varying degrees, depending upon who was in the White House, we have made it a primary purpose of our diplomacy to protect and even advance American private investment. But today our economic interest has suddenly shifted from the protection of private investment in foreign countries to assured access to their raw materials. In these days of shrinking natural resources, scarcities, cartels, and a determined effort by the Third World to bring about what it calls a new world economic order, we have suddenly become aware that we are critically dependent—at least for now—on the Caribbean. We get about 6.5 percent of our oil (18 percent of our oil imports) from Venezuela. We get virtually all our bauxite from the Caribbean. In addition, we obtain certain primary agricultural products from the Caribbean, including sugar, coffee, cacao, and bananas, and the countries that produce them are trying to cartelize them if they can, just as the oil countries cartelized oil.

Third, our political interests. These have also changed with the times. Jefferson envisioned the Caribbean as a territory to which we could extend our "empire for liberty," an idea echoed in John F. Kennedy's inaugural address. At varying times, we have sought to assist the Caribbean lands in establishing democratic constitutional systems patterned after our own, but at other times, we have remained indifferent to how they were governed; and at times, because we believed that the existence of the Panama Canal made the stability of this area of great concern to all nations, we have supported dictators as the price of that stability.

During the Cold War, we felt it necessary to prevent the extension of communism to the Caribbean. Under Kennedy's Alliance for Progress, we actively sought to help the Caribbean nations find a democratic alternative to the right-left extremes of military dictatorship and communist dictatorship. In so doing, we raised the question whether social justice and economic progress are consistent with freedom in the Caribbean—and the broader question: why does democracy find the soil of the Caribbean so stony? Beyond all this, we have another diplomatic stake in the Caribbean: what we do there affects our prestige in the rest of the hemisphere—and in the world. Great power flows not only from force—armadas of warships, fleets of bombers, showers of missiles—but also from prestige. And a democracy acquires prestige in many ways, among them by keeping its commitments to friends and allies and by remaining true to its own highest ideals (and sometimes these purposes come into conflict, as they did in Vietnam).

Because the Cold War is, if not ending, altering its shape, our political interests continue to shift. Rigid containment probably came to an end in Southeast Asia. The communist left in the Caribbean that so troubled us in the time of Eisenhower, Kennedy, and Johnson has been eroded or replaced by a New Left—a left of the Third World, of nationalism, of statism, of Black Power, and sometimes of terrorism and anarchy. The economic issues involved in raw materials have altered the political issues radically. In seeking to regain control over their natural resources, the Caribbean nations have declared war on the multinational corporations that exploit their natural resources. The question facing our own policymakers is no longer how to advance U.S. private enterprise; it is whether U.S. private investment will have any role at all to play in these emerging statist economies. And the Caribbean lands, seeking to make common cause with the Third World against the industrialized nations, are taking their case to the OAS and the United Nations, where with discouraging regularity they vote against the United States; they are political antagonists in our own backyard. Indeed, in the last twenty-five years, for the first time since Hamilton, we have learned that we could not make the Caribbean do as we wanted. We learned it in Guatemala, in Cuba, in the Dominican Republic, in Haiti, in Honduras, and elsewhere.

A dozen years ago, in the time of Kennedy and Johnson, the issues were predominantly military and political; today, they are predominantly social and economic. Social—a million and a half people have emigrated from the Caribbean, legally or illegally, to live in the United States, and because many of them are black, poor, unskilled, and ignorant of English, they create social problems inside the United States and diplomatic problems between the United States and their homelands. Economic—Caribbean governments, as they strike out on their own, trying to narrow the gap between the rich and poor countries and between rich and poor people in each country, find themselves in need of external capital, but they also find that external capital fears nationalization and statism. Thus, raw materials become important to us at the very time when it is becoming impossible, partly for racial and social reasons, for North American companies to extract them through mining and plantation agriculture.

All these social and economic issues may, sooner than we think, confront us with dangerous political issues. Caribbean governments, unable to solve their social and economic problems, may turn to irresponsible politics. At that point, such problems as the terms of trade may be overtaken by a political hurricane. It was, after all, ruinous inflation and deep depression that brought Hitler to power, but the political issues he raised soon eclipsed the economic and social conditions that produced him. It is not inconceivable that Caribbean governments, nationalizing their natural resources to increase their revenues and offset their oil costs and then pressed by the unemployed to distribute immediately the fruits of the resources, may be overwhelmed, throwing the United States back onto its concern over unstable governments in the Caribbean.

What, at bottom, makes the Caribbean important to the United States is proximity. The Caribbean, together with the Gulf of Mexico, comprises something like a fifth of our border—a great arc sweeping from Brownsville to Miami that is approximately equal to our Atlantic or our Pacific coastline. Today, across all three of our borders, where we are accustomed to seeing placidity, we see trouble—in Canada, in Mexico, and in the Caribbean. Despite jets and the computer-electronic age, geography still matters. The Caribbean people are part of our lives; we could not get rid of them if we would.

Not surprisingly, they nourish a love-hate relationship to us. They send their children to us to be educated, they regard us as the promised land of opportunity, they better themselves by working for our corporations, they seek to emulate our advanced industrial society. At the same time, they resent our economic and political domination, our tutelary or even colonialist attitude, our power and our arrogance, our Central Intelligence Agency (CIA), our violent television programs that corrupt their young, and our homogenized hotel chains and fast-food restaurants that threaten to turn their societies into carbon copies of everything that is shoddy in ours. If we pursue our relationships with them, they accuse us of intervention; if we ignore them, they accuse us of caring less about our neighbors than about Bangladesh. Nations of East Europe within the Soviet Union's sphere of influence resent and fear the Soviet Union; the Vietnamese resent and fear China; in much the same fashion, the Caribbean nations resent and fear us. Anti-Americanism of two kinds exists: that of the young radicals who were Castroites a few years ago and who are New Left today; and that of the cultured old aristocrats who disdain our materialist, moneygrubbing crudities.

We can escape neither our geographical location nor our enormous power and wealth. We cannot isolate ourselves. We are a world power and must behave like one. Whatever we do profoundly affects the Caribbean. Our slavery issue of the 1850s crucially affected our proposed annexation of Cuba; our Civil War helped produce the Cuban war of 1868; our interventions against Kaiserism early in the twentieth century and against communism in the middle of the twentieth century changed the history of several nations; the Great Depression of the 1930s and the Great Recession of the 1970s echoed disastrously in the Caribbean. Even what we do not do affects the Caribbean. No Caribbean policy is in itself a policy.

In the past, Latin American diplomats and politicians have been sensitive to our slightest gesture. They remember not only past U.S. ambassadors but such minor officials as consuls and—especially— military attachés, and each act by the U.S. embassy is viewed in purely local terms. But in large measure, U.S. policy toward the Caribbean has always been a part of our global concerns: the Monroe Doctrine flowed from our fear of European encroachment, the Spanish-American War from our expansion toward world power, the Roosevelt Corollary to the Monroe Doctrine from fear of Kaiserism, the Good Neighbor policy in part from FDR's need for hemispheric defense against the Axis powers, the Alliance for Progress in part from our struggle with communism. Thus, not only does Caribbean policy take second place to our broader interests; actually, for the most part, it moves only when prodded from afar.

Our recent Caribbean policy has varied from one presidential administration to another. In general, the United States has had two approaches: the activist policy of President Kennedy, which promoted economic progress and social justice in the Caribbean societies themselves; and the Nixon-Ford policy of neglect. But neither of these policies will work in the new Caribbean, an emerging world already almost unrecognizable. People who have never seen fifty dollars a year have caught a glimpse of what might be—television and, to an even greater extent, the transistor radio bring it to them daily—and they will not forever remain content. Nor will government leaders forever suffer foreign domination. A profound revolutionary process has already changed the Caribbean, a process visible in Castro's military victory; Juan Bosch's electoral victory; the heroic measures by Venezuela and Jamaica to regain control of their own natural resources; violent nationalist denunciation of our colonialism in Panama; Guyana's and Trinidad-Tobago's grasp at the Third World banners of Africa and Asia; the nationalization of U.S. private business; guerrillas in the hills and terrorists in the cities; the powerful magnetic pull of Cuba and Venezuela and Mexico on the Caribbean islands; efforts to form cartels and reform the terms of trade; efforts to forge new economic and even political groupings without the United States; Black Power and the New Left and student rebellion.

This new Caribbean is no longer our placid American sea. It is a seething cauldron, indifferent or even hostile to us. We can no longer neglect it; we can no longer patronize it; we must recognize its power as well as its problems. To meet the new realities of the new Caribbean, we must devise new policies—and we must devise them now.

The changes that have transformed the Caribbean in the last few years have gone almost wholly unnoticed by the U.S. public, for the U.S. press reports Caribbean news with woeful inadequacy. But even the executive and the Congress do not seem to understand the new Caribbean. We are probably the only country in the world that treats its near neighbors as unimportant. (In Afghanistan, our AID mission contains forty-four people; in Jamaica, seven.)

It is often said that if we cannot establish a good relationship with the Caribbean, we can hardly expect to do better in Africa or Asia. But because of our past close involvement, our difficulties may be greater in the Caribbean than anywhere else. Let us briefly review the historical legacy and then examine more closely the recent past, the years since World War II, for that will help show us how we got where we are today. Then let us look closely at our shifting interests in the Caribbean, the conditions that produced the changes, the conditions of today and probably tomorrow, and, finally, the policies we might pursue to deal with what is, essentially and suddenly, a wholly new Caribbean, a Caribbean of vital importance to us, and a Caribbean that may be heading today in directions potentially dangerous to us.

2
FROM JEFFERSON TO
EISENHOWER

The Monroe Doctrine

On December 2, 1823, President James Monroe sent Congress his annual message. It contained the statement known as the Monroe Doctrine—a declaration that we would regard any attempt by European powers to extend "their system" to any part of the Western Hemisphere "as dangerous to our peace and safety." The doctrine was an attempt to stop foreign powers from further colonizing the Americas or interfering in their affairs.

From the beginning, the Caribbean lands had been in dispute. During the English-French rivalry of the eighteenth and early nineteenth centuries, the Caribbean, and its sugar, was the critical prize. When the French were allowed by the Peace of Paris to retain the valuable sugar island, Guadeloupe, in return for what Voltaire called "a few acres of snow," Canada, they were delighted. Britain considered Barbados more valuable than its colonies of New York, Carolina, Pennsylvania, and New England together. The Dutch traded New York for Surinam. Trade between the United States and Latin America increased rapidly. After the Louisiana Purchase in 1803, however, it was our interest in Cuba's strategic position, not in its trade, that led Jefferson to hope that we could annex Cuba: "We should then have . . . such an empire for liberty as she has never surveyed since the creation; and I am persuaded that no constitution was ever before so well calculated as ours for extensive empire and self-government." Our urge to bring the blessings of democracy to the Caribbean has deep roots.

In the early nineteenth century, Spain's South American colonies rebelled; one result was that the monarchies of Europe viewed the young United States as a revolutionary people arrayed against the old order, exporting our revolution southward. During this period of revolution, Britain and France split over Spain; Russia demanded assurance of U.S. neutrality in South America, seeming to threaten encroachment on California. In 1823, the British foreign secretary, George Canning, suggested a joint British-American manifesto that would keep the New World free of European intervention and that, if accepted, would have bound both countries not to acquire Cuba or any other Spanish colony. This suggestion set off a round of consultations by President Monroe with his cabinet and his predecessors in the White House that eventually led to the Monroe Doctrine. Significantly, the doctrine left the United States free to acquire Cuba or any other Spanish possession that might come its way.

In the period after the Monroe Doctrine, southern expansion meant acquiring Cuba; and during the 1840s and 1850s, three Presidents—Polk in 1848, Pierce in 1854, and Buchanan in three separate messages to Congress—tried to buy and annex Cuba. Spain refused to sell. At the same time, romantic American adventurers called filibusters set forth for Cuba and Central America to fulfill what was thought of as America's manifest destiny—the belief that God intended Americans to spread their democratic institutions to those who needed them. The expansionist fever before the Civil War had two motives—to extend slave territory and to occupy the routes of a proposed interoceanic canal across Central America.

Toward the close of the century, a new interest came into play— U.S. private investment. Sugar had always been the central economic force in the Caribbean. The price of sugar in the world market meant economic life or death; and sugar was linked to race, slavery, and colonialism. By the 1880s, capital from the United States was involved in the Cuban sugar industry on a large scale, and soon it was invested in railroads, iron ore, and merchandising. In 1890, the United States eliminated tariffs on raw sugar and molasses, partly in response to the influence of the principal American producer of Cuban sugar—a beginning of private commercial influence on U.S.

Caribbean policy.

By 1890, the United States, with little unsettled territory, realized that further large-scale expansion would have to come elsewhere. Then in 1893, depression on the farm and panic in Wall Street caused many Americans to revise their estimate of the promise of inland empire and to look outward beyond the seas. It became clear that we would need overseas markets if we were to become the most powerful industrial nation on earth.

Our principal interest in the Caribbean, however, remained strategic. The ideas of Alfred Thayer Mahan, then a captain in the U.S. Navy, were catching hold. In 1890, he published his book, *The Influence of Sea Power on History,* which suggested that the key to national greatness was sea power. Theodore Roosevelt, appointed assistant secretary of the navy by President McKinley, agreed, and our navy, now considered vital to our national defense, continued to be expanded. The American people began to support the idea of an Isthmian Canal as well as more and bigger battleships.

The smell of empire was in the air. So, when Cuba rebelled against Spain, the Congress, the press, and such leaders as Theodore Roosevelt demanded that we go to war with Spain even after, as a result of our representations to Spain on Cuba's behalf, Spain had accepted nearly all of our demands. After the *Maine* blew up, hysteria swept the country; on April 25, 1898, the official congressional declaration of war was signed.

Although the war was to have been fought for Cuba's sake, we also attacked Spain in the Pacific. On Roosevelt's order, Dewey attacked the Spanish fleet in Manila Bay, and in seven hours, without losing a man, the United States became a world power. In the rush, Cuba was all but forgotten, just as Cuba was again forgotten in the missile crisis of 1962. Spain, its fleet destroyed, made peace on our terms: it got out of Cuba, gave us Puerto Rico and smaller islands in the Caribbean and Guam in the Pacific, and ceded the Philippines to us. Almost absent-mindedly, we took Hawaii, too. The war removed Spanish power from the Caribbean. And it made us a world power.

The treaty that ended the war freed Cuba at American insistence. Although awash with imperialist sentiment, we did not keep Cuba for our own for a number of reasons. Beet sugar growers in the United States feared cane sugar competition from Cuba. Populists sympathized with the Cuban rebels' goal of independence. Our whole history running back to our own revolution against colonial-ism spoke against our new imperialism. Congress's declaration of Cuban independence barred annexation. Annexing Cuba would have meant assuming a large Spanish debt. Philippine patriots were launching an insurrection against us, and so might Cuban patriots.

In the end, Senator Orville Platt of Connecticut devised the formula to resolve our dilemma. The Platt Amendment to the army appropriation bill of 1901 gave the United States the right to establish military bases in Cuba and the right to intervene in Cuban affairs. Cuba incorporated the amendment into its constitution under pressure from the United States, and it also became part of a treaty between Cuba and the United States. The amendment, coupled with large American private investments that quickly flooded into Cuba, enabled critics of U.S. policy to complain that Cuba was nothing but an imperial province. It might have been better had the United States taken full responsibility for Cuba for a time, as we did for Puerto Rico and the Philippines, and let it later move to statehood, commonwealth status, or full independence. In any case, once we had drawn the sword in Cuba, the Latin Americans, who had once admired us, came to hate and fear us. To this day, during periods when America pays little heed to the Caribbean, or even when its policy is benevolent and peaceable, they remain stubbornly con-vinced that one day the United States will reassert Mahan and Theodore Roosevelt, that the United States will declare its strategic interests imperiled, and that the dove will become the hawk.

In 1901, Theodore Roosevelt, a navy man and global strategist, became president. He had long had his mind fixed on the need for an interoceanic canal across the isthmus of Panama; now, with America's new naval ambitions and her new territories in the Pacific, a canal became essential. Two sites had been considered, Nicaragua and Panama, which was then a province of Colombia. A French company had tried to build a canal across Panama and had failed. Now, when Colombia balked at selling us a license to build a canal across Panama, a French adventurer, Philippe Bunau-Varilla, who was trying to salvage the French investment and who had access to President Roosevelt himself, fomented and financed a revolution in Panama; with the U.S.S. *Nashville* standing by, Panama declared its independence. Bunau-Varilla, having virtually appointed himself the new country's minister plenipotentiary, reached Secretary of State

John Hay before the official Panamanian delegation and offered our astonished secretary a treaty such as no sovereign nation had ever signed: It gave the United States rights "in perpetuity" over the Canal Zone in these terms: "The Republic of Panama grants to the United States all the rights, power and authority within the zone . . . which the United States would possess if it were the sovereign of the territory . . . to the entire exclusion of the exercise by the Republic of Panama of any such sovereign rights, power or authority." Secretary Hay told a senator, "You and I know too well how many points there are in this treaty to which Panaman patriots could object." Hay, however, signed the Hay-Varilla Treaty forthwith, on November 18, 1903, opening the door to more than seventy years of U.S. intervention and Panamanian resistance, of bitterness and bloodshed.

The Roosevelt Corollary

Although Theodore Roosevelt's name has become linked with "gunboat diplomacy," he does not fit the stereotype of an imperialist with basically economic aims. America's strategic, not its economic, interests were his primary concern. European capital had begun to build railroads and develop the natural resources of Latin America; Latin America in turn began to incur foreign debts. Latin American countries pledged their customs duties as security for debts, but foreigners found it hard to collect and requested help from their governments.

At first, Roosevelt believed that investors, Americans included, should handle their own problems. He also believed that foreign governments should be free to aid their citizens—as long as they had no territorial ambitions. Then, in 1902, England and Germany used force against Venezuela to secure payment of money owed their nationals; they seized gunboats, bombarded forts, and blockaded Venezuelan ports. To Roosevelt's surprise, the American press and Congress reacted violently. Roosevelt began to rethink American policy. Some years earlier, the British foreign secretary had complained that America claimed an interest in whatever befell any government in the hemisphere, yet accepted no responsibility for how those governments behaved. James Bryce had suggested a U.S. protectorate over Latin America to Roosevelt. Roosevelt began to feel that there might be merit in such a suggestion: "These wretched republics cause me a great deal of trouble. . . . I often think that a sort of protectorate over South and Central America is the only way out."

In this period, U.S. capital was entering the Caribbean, where the politicians in power were eager to attract foreign capital on almost any terms in order to develop their nations and enrich themselves. Each country was ruled by a small elite of politicians, generals, and oligarchs with whom an American capitalist arranged his loans and concessions. If a revolution overthrew them, the Americans tried to bribe the new leaders. If that failed, the Americans turned to their own government for protection, and usually the government came to the rescue. European investors operated the same way. The system was termed "economic imperialism."

By the end of 1903, the situation in the Dominican Republic had become explosive. The Dominican Republic, comprising the eastern two-thirds of the island of Hispaniola—Haiti has the western third—occupies a strategic location between Cuba and Puerto Rico, the linchpin in the arc of big islands that shields the Caribbean from the open Atlantic. For more than fifty years, it had fallen prey to incompetent, corrupt, and ruthless Dominican generals and politicians and foreign adventurers. As a result, civil strife was frequent and public debt huge. In October 1904, the Dominican government defaulted on its payments to an American financial company and, as agreed, turned over to a company agent the customs house at Puerto Plata; European governments whose nationals also had Dominican claims promptly protested. President Roosevelt decided to intervene and in May 1904 announced his policy: "Chronic wrongdoing, or an impotence which results in a general loosening of the ties of civilized society, may in America, as elsewhere, ultimately require intervention by some civilized nation, and in the Western Hemisphere the adherence of the United States to the Monroe Doctrine may force the United States, however reluctantly, in flagrant cases of such wrongdoing or impotence, to the exercise of an international police power."

This statement was the Roosevelt Corollary to the Monroe Doctrine. Under it, Roosevelt acted promptly: The United States and the Dominican Republic signed a protocol allowing the U.S. government to take over all customs collections and distribute them equitably among the various claimants. Although the Senate stalled ratification, Roosevelt acted. By executive agreement, he took over the customs houses, and while his agent collected and distributed the Dominican customs receipts, Roosevelt kept the U.S. Navy in Dominican waters to impress German, Italian, and French units there.

The executive agreement, used extensively by Roosevelt, was an erosion of congressional power over foreign policy. Roosevelt said, "It is evident that the Senate is a very poor body to have as part of the treaty-making power." The Senate complained that the executive agreement amounted to a protectorate, especially when Roosevelt made it clear that American warships in Dominican waters were under orders to maintain the present government in office. In his 1905 message to Congress, Roosevelt explained his policy, carefully relating it to the Monroe Doctrine.

Roosevelt's interest in the Caribbean had always been primarily strategic. In a speech delivered in 1913, Roosevelt emphasized that the underlying purpose of the corollary had indeed been strategic: "I [had] learned that no less than three Old-World powers intended to land troops and seize ports. . . . If this had been done, San Domingo as a nation would have disappeared, and those Old-World powers would have been in practical possession of the island today. This I did not intend to permit; and I did not permit it."

Toward the end of his administration, Roosevelt, still concerned about maintaining stability close to the Canal, attempted to settle quarrels that had led to intermittent warfare among the Central American states. Conventions were signed at Washington in 1907 that were the forerunners of a system of inter-American settlement of disputes. By the time Roosevelt left office, though, the Central American nations, especially Nicaragua and Honduras, were torn by civil strife and burdened by heavy foreign debts, just as the Dominican Republic had been. Roosevelt's successor, William Howard Taft, and Taft's secretary of state, Philander C. Knox, favored a different solution to Latin American problems. By actively encouraging U.S. private investment in Latin America, Taft attempted to "substitute dollars for bullets." He and Secretary Knox seemed to think that the remedy for revolution, instability, and fiscal irresponsibility in the Caribbean was a large infusion of private U.S. investment with U.S. government support. It is hard to say whether the Taft-Knox policy, which was based on the Roosevelt Corollary, resulted from pressure from private business or *on* private business.

Of course, Taft and Knox also professed concern for U.S. strategic interests, especially near the Panama Canal.

Taft's policy was implemented in Honduras and Nicaragua. When revolution in Nicaragua led to default on foreign debts, an agreement was made for customs duties to be collected by a receiver-general to be appointed by the president of the United States and for the U.S. government to provide protection for the arrangement. When the Nicaraguan Senate balked, and a revolution seemed possible, we sent a warship. No warship, however, could influence the U.S. Senate, and the Senate, in a mood to rebel and assert itself in foreign policy, as it was in the 1970s at the end of the Nixon administration, rejected the treaty.

Woodrow Wilson

President Wilson and his first secretary of state, William Jennings Bryan, inherited a Caribbean policy designed by Roosevelt to safeguard U.S. strategic interests and modified by Taft to safeguard U.S. financial interests. Wilson and Bryan found "dollar diplomacy" abhorrent and imperialism even more abhorrent. Yet in the end, they extended U.S. control of the Caribbean by military force.

Like President Kennedy and President Nixon later, Wilson addressed himself to Latin America almost immediately after taking office. In a statement circulated to U.S. diplomats in Latin America, he said: "One of the chief objects of my Administration will be to cultivate the friendship and deserve the confidence of our sister republics in Central and South America and to promote in every proper and honorable way the interests which are common to the peoples of the two continents. . . . We can have no sympathy with those who seek to seize the power of government to advance their own personal interests or ambition. . . . As friends . . . we shall prefer those who act in the interest of peace and honor, who protect private rights and respect the restraints of constitutional provision."

Within that bland prose lurked a new policy. Wilson was making clear that he did not approve of those who seized power by force (previously we had followed traditional diplomatic practice of recognizing any government that was in control of the national territory and honored its international obligations); he was making clear that he preferred governments that dealt justly with their own citizens (previously we had thought it proper to concern ourselves only with how they treated *our* citizens); and he was making clear that he preferred governments that took and exercised power in accordance with constitutional processes.

Wilson and Bryan believed fervently in the triumph of democracy throughout the world. They considered our system best and wanted to share it with—or impose it on—Latin America.[1] The new administration was brimming with good intentions; it was determined to protect America's strategic interests and to extend the blessings of democracy to our benighted neighbors. Knowing little about Latin America, fired with moral zeal but lacking experienced diplomats (they had replaced what they regarded as the Republican elite in the State Department with personal friends and Democratic hacks), Wilson and Bryan set sail upon the stormy Caribbean. On its treacherous shoals their policy foundered, and they ended disgraced before the world as apostles of the very imperialism they opposed.

When Bryan began grappling with Central American affairs, he told President Wilson, "it is pathetic to see Nicaragua struggling in the grip of an oppressive financial agreement." Bryan intended to reverse the Republicans' dollar diplomacy and free Latin America by using the financial power of the U.S. government itself to break the bankers' grip. Because the bankers charged excessive interest on the ground that they must be paid to run risks and then proceeded to demand that the U.S. government eliminate the risks, the policy was in itself unexceptionable. Yet in the realities of politics—U.S. and Caribbean—it failed.

Bryan negotiated a treaty with Nicaragua under which the U.S. government would give Nicaragua $3 million to rearrange its finances in return for an option on an alternative canal route, certain base rights, and the right to intervene under the Platt Amendment. But the U.S. Senate rejected the treaty. Bryan then suggested that the U.S. government loan money directly to Nicaragua at an interest rate lower than that charged by private bankers—a precursor of modern foreign aid. This time Wilson refused. Bryan was forced to choose between withdrawing his support from the Nicaraguan regime, which would have meant civil war, or coming to terms with the bankers. He reluctantly endorsed a new loan agreement between Nicaragua and the bankers.

Bryan was also involved with the problems presented by Haiti and the Dominican Republic. Then as now, Haiti, poor even by African or Asian standards, had been ravaged for years by violence, plunder, and assassination. The threat of European intervention was great; France and Germany were pressing for control of Haitian customs to service Haitian debts. Because Haiti lay athwart the strategic approaches to the Panama Canal, Bryan wanted a naval base in Haiti, but Haiti refused to sell us the necessary land. As war began in Europe, Bryan told Wilson that it was imperative that American bankers buy out European interests; however, because they would do so only if the U.S. government took over Haitian customs, he recommended sending Haiti an ultimatum backed up by a warship. Wilson approved. When a new wave of violence broke out in Haiti, the United States landed marines, settled down to a long occupation, and installed a pro-American regime that signed a treaty establishing a virtual U.S. protectorate over Haiti. The U.S. Senate concurred because of the war in Europe.

President Wilson, perturbed by seemingly endless revolutions in the Dominican Republic, called for new and supervised elections and declared that, once a constitutional government had thus been established, the United States would insist that revolution cease and governments be changed only by peaceful constitutional process. Wilson seems to have assumed that a democratically elected government, if shielded from violence by American power, would govern well, safeguard American strategic interests, provide for a better life for the Dominican people, and protect them from foreign financial domination. Bryan even proposed that the United States not only supervise Dominican revenue collection but also decide what to spend it on. Never before had we intervened so deeply. The Dominicans refused to agree; so in the spring of 1916, after prolonged stalemate and another revolution, the marines landed. Resistance developed, and when the Dominican president called for congressional elections, the United States, fearing those elections would produce domination of the Dominican Congress by a pro-German politician, proclaimed a full American military government; Wilson said privately that he did so "with the deepest reluctance." The American military occupation of the Dominican Republic lasted until 1924.

American control in the Caribbean reached its peaks with the military occupation of Nicaragua, Haiti, and the Dominican Republic. Of 199 U.S. military hostilities abroad without a declaration of war between 1798 and 1972, no fewer than 81 took place in the Caribbean. We never intervened south of the Canal. Kaiserism was to Theodore Roosevelt, Taft, and Wilson what communism would be to Eisenhower, Kennedy, and Johnson. To defeat it, they intervened deeply; because of it, Congress sanctioned interventions of which it would otherwise have disapproved. Once again, our Caribbean policy was fixed by our larger European interests—and by our strategic interests.

The Republican 1920s

Although U.S. policy for a brief period after World War I seemed to be continuing on the course set by Wilson, Warren G. Harding, when campaigning for president, had renounced U.S. interference in Caribbean countries' affairs. Events were pushing for a shift in policy. Such American liberals as Oswald Garrison Villard of the *Nation* were exposing abuses by the marines in the Dominican Republic. Dominican nationalists were demanding Dominican sovereignty, our fear of Kaiserism had abated, the world seemed to be moving toward naval disarmament, and the importance of the Canal appeared to lessen. The old predatory European empires no longer appeared to threaten our hemisphere, and it seemed to many people that our interventions in the Caribbean had brought us much trouble and had failed to set those countries on the road to freedom, prosperity, and political maturity.

In 1923, Washington had summoned the Central American states to a conference to reaffirm in even stronger terms than those of 1907 its determination to preserve peace and condemn governments established by force. But a few years later, Washington found that this laudable move was causing trouble: Henry L. Stimson, sent to Nicaragua by President Coolidge in 1927, discovered that the 1907 and 1923 conferences had made free elections the "very heart" of the Central American problem—in each country, the government in power controlled the election machinery, and so the opposition saw no way to win except by revolution (and those out of power hated the United States for making control by the party in power permanent).

The spirit of postwar isolationism was dominant in the United States. We had exhausted ourselves in the Caribbean through strenuous exertions ever since the Spanish-American War, and now we were not so much deliberately withdrawing as subsiding. In the Caribbean, no less than elsewhere, under Harding and Coolidge, the business of the United States appeared to be business.

In 1900, U.S. exports to Latin America had amounted to only $132 million, less than 10 percent of our total exports. But during World War I, the situation began to change. Between 1913 and 1919, the U.S. share of total annual Latin American imports jumped from 25.03 percent to 47.9 percent, and U.S. investment capital began to crowd out European capital. After the war, U.S. private investment in Latin America grew steadily. By 1925, the American stake in Cuba had risen to more than $1.25 billion. Americans controlled not only sugar mills but half the railways and the major utilities. By 1927, probably 40 percent of Cuba's total land area was controlled by a few U.S. corporations.

This development led U.S. policy toward the Caribbean to be designed to protect U.S. property owners. The Cuban economy went through the wringer and came out in U.S. hands. President Machado visited Washington, and President Coolidge embraced him; New York bankers and utility executives gave luncheons for him; and Coolidge went to Havana and announced that the Cuban people were "independent, free, prosperous, peaceful, and enjoying the advantages of self-government." It did not matter that Machado was a crook and a butcher. The Republican administrations were indifferent to the character of the Cuban government—Wilsonian policy had been revised.

The next step in the new policy was to extricate ourselves from the Dominican Republic and Nicaragua. In the Dominican Republic, the process took four years. After skillful and firm political intervention by Sumner Welles, a free election was held on March 15, 1924, and the last marines left.

Getting out of Nicaragua proved more difficult. The marines left in 1924; but when another revolution began with Mexican support, Secretary Kellogg stretched the Monroe Doctrine to cover the danger of "Mexican-fostered Bolshevik hegemony between the United States and the Panama Canal," and we sent the marines back to Nicaragua. It was a reversion to the old Roosevelt-Wilson fear of kaiserism near the Canal, only now kaiserism had become bolshevism.

This second full-scale marine occupation of Nicaragua created more difficulties. A Nicaraguan general, Augusto Sandino, took to the hills, and for years, he and his followers carried on guerrilla warfare against both Nicaraguan and American troops. Sandino, denounced as a "bandit" by Washington, was hailed as a "patriot" by many Nicaraguans. The continuing warfare convinced Stimson and the State Department that intervention got us into all sorts of unwelcome activities, including fighting revolutionary patriots. Finally, in 1932, elections were held, and when the new president was inaugurated the following January, the last marines left.

Perhaps influenced by Secretary Stimson, President Hoover took steps to reverse the interventionist policy that had begun with Theodore Roosevelt. In 1932, Hoover and Stimson tried to make arrangements to withdraw the U.S. Marines from Haiti, two years before the date originally agreed upon. (The marines did not actually leave until 1934, however.) The administration showed restraint when the Dominican Republic and El Salvador defaulted on U.S. loans. Nor did it intervene in Panama to thwart a revolution at the very site of the Canal. Instead, the administration seemed to adopt as policy a memorandum saying that the Monroe Doctrine's original purpose had been solely the defense of the Western Hemisphere from European aggression and did not justify the Roosevelt Corollary.

Hoover, as president-elect, had made a goodwill tour of Latin America. In a speech delivered in Honduras, he had said, "I come to pay a call of friendship. . . . I would wish to symbolize the friendly visit of one good neighbor to another." But all Hoover's good intentions in Latin America fell in ruins with the enactment in 1930 of the Smoot-Hawley tariff. That tariff set such high rates on imports that it nearly ruined the Central American economies. It was left to Franklin Roosevelt's reciprocal trade agreements to rescue the Central American economies. And it was left to FDR to attach the word *policy* to *good neighbor*.

Good Neighbors

Surely no other U.S. policy was ever received with such unanimous enthusiasm in Latin America as FDR's Good Neighbor policy. It was his attempt to reverse the picture of the United States as dominant in the Caribbean. Roosevelt was more interested in Latin America than any U.S. president except Theodore Roosevelt and Kennedy. His liberal structural reform of American society was widely admired and copied by liberals in Latin America—indeed, the New Deal's social security system was adopted throughout Latin

America. Furthermore, Roosevelt, opposed to the abuse of power by big business, refused to give American private investment in Latin America the all-out support it had enjoyed under Republican administrations.

To Latin American nations, the Good Neighbor policy meant, above all, that the United States had declared them its equal and would henceforth treat them as such, sending diplomats, not troops, to resolve differences. The Good Neighbor policy had no economic content except for the Export-Import Bank and the Reciprocal Trade Agreement Amendment to the Tariff Act of 1930, which gave the president power to reduce existing rates up to half. The policy lacked concrete programs for structural reform, such as those sought by the Alliance for Progress. Its heart was nonintervention.

Nevertheless, only a few months after his inauguration, Roosevelt intervened in Cuba. By then, the price of Cuban sugar was disastrously low, and the dictator Machado had brutally repressed protest.

Roosevelt sent Sumner Wells to Havana as ambassador. Welles, intervening politically as he had earlier in the Dominican Republic, helped bring down Machado and put together a new government, which was soon overthrown by the so-called Sergeant's Revolt led by Sergeant Fulgencio Batista. Welles, deeply disappointed, called for U.S. troops, but Roosevelt and Hull refused his request. With time, however, Welles came to see Batista as Cuba's best hope. As a result, when Batista put a popular opposition leader in power, we promptly recognized his government. Roosevelt gave Cuba a share in the American sugar market, a reciprocal trade agreement that cut the sugar duty by more than half, and a credit to purchase surplus foodstuffs; and he abrogated, by treaty, the hated Platt Amendment. The hemisphere concluded that the Good Neighbor policy had turned its back on armed intervention for good; it overlooked our political and economic intervention.

Sumner Welles, who became under secretary of state in the Roosevelt administration, influenced U.S. policy in Latin America at that time more than any other man. The administration anguished over interference short of force—particularly interference in the domestic affairs of Central American countries. In 1936, the U.S. minister to El Salvador, warning Washington that would-be dictators were saying that the Good Neighbor policy gave them a free hand to get rid of constitutionalism and go back to the old rule of force, suggested "possible preventive steps." The suggestion revealed fundamental differences of opinion. Welles, noting that he had been "unhappy" about this for some time, wrote that "the personal influence of the American Minister, if exerted tactfully, quietly, and without publicity, and with regard to matters that affect the general relations between the Central American republics, and, inferentially, their individual or joint relations with the United States, should be of the utmost value." He also said that noninterference should not rule out "helpful and friendly advice" on matters in which the Central American republics and the United States all had "a legitimate interest."

Welles's view was opposed by Laurence Duggan, the only other State Department official with influence on our Latin American policy at that time. Duggan argued that in some situations no action at all was better than action whose precise consequences could not be foreseen, that even the personal opinion of a U.S. minister was taken as the considered judgment of his government and so given great weight, and that to give ministers discretion was unwise because their abilities varied widely. Duggan apparently persuaded Welles, for Welles asked him to prepare an instruction, telling ministers in Central America to conduct themselves exactly as if they were dealing with one of the great nations of South America or with any non-American power—that is, they should "religiously abstain from offering advice as regards any domestic question," even if asked. Welles did not want the language of the instruction to suggest that the United States was assuming "a sterile policy of aloofness" but, rather, to show that the United States was aiming at "a policy of constructive and effective friendship solely provided that neither this government nor its representatives are drawn into any domestic concerns" of the Central American countries. The instruction went out to our ministers in the five Central American countries on April 30, 1936; later, it was extended to Mexico, Cuba, the Dominican Republic, Haiti, and Panama. Under it, despite appeals, we refused to exert any influence on the process that brought Somoza to power in Nicaragua. Indeed, not long before Pearl Harbor, Welles took the extreme view that the United States should not intervene in any Latin American country even though its government was under the influence of the Axis; it was a curious reversal for a man who had intervened so deeply in the Dominican Republic and Cuba.

The real test of the administration's nonintervention policy came in 1938, when Mexico expropriated the properties of U.S. oil companies. The companies pressed claims for huge compensation and sought the support of the U.S. government. The administration took the position that Mexico had the right to expropriate the properties, provided that it paid for them. The administration persuaded the companies, who eventually received only about 10 percent of their original claims, that the national interest overrode their financial interest, a view that became increasingly plausible as World War II began in Europe.

World War II

The Good Neighbor policy, which initially had little or nothing to do directly with the defense of the United States, came to be seen as having forged an inter-American system that was, with the exception of Argentina, united with the United States against the Axis. When Secretary of State Cordell Hull, at a Havana conference on World War II, emphasized the importance of "orderly and stable governments," he was uttering the new watchwords of our Latin American policy. The remark attributed to Roosevelt that Trujillo "may be a son of a bitch but he's our son of a bitch" is to this day quoted widely in the Caribbean. Today, young Caribbean leftists are inclined to view the Good Neighbor policy as nothing more than America's way of guarding its back while it faced the Axis.

Despite the ideals of the Good Neighbor policy, in 1940-1941 Roosevelt approached the British with the idea that U.S. bases in their Caribbean island colonies were essential to continental defense, and he seems even to have entertained thoughts of taking over the islands outright. But he sent an envoy to inquire into conditions there and learned that between 1935 and 1938 widespread strikes and riots had been put down only by British troops and warships, that poverty was widespread, and that new trade unions and new political parties were creating instability—the islands might prove a burden. In the end, he merely offered to give Britain fifty overage destroyers in exchange for ninety-nine-year leases on bases in Antigua, St. Lucia, Jamaica, British Guiana, and Trinidad. Representatives of the colonial governments objected strenuously. But the British government, with its back to the wall, was not in a position to plead the colonies' case, although it thought the colonies might well resent the changes in their way of life that were bound to, and indeed did, occur. After the war, the United States gave up these bases.

The war had profound and direct effects on other underdeveloped areas of the world, but in the Caribbean, except for the winding down of British colonialism in the black English-speaking islands, the war's effect was less dramatic. President Roosevelt, a staunch antiimperialist, had tried to reverse the imperial policies we had pursued in the Caribbean from McKinley's time to his own. During the war, France, Great Britain, Italy, Germany, and Japan had been forced to relinquish their roles in the Caribbean, and the United States had consolidated its dominant position. We had given the Latin American countries preferential treatment, and they had become accustomed to close economic cooperation. Even more important, perhaps, were the great expectations raised in Latin America as elsewhere during the war. FDR's Four Freedoms, the Atlantic Charter, and all the other magnificent promises were taken seriously by the politicians and the peoples of Latin America. After the war, they looked to us.

When Harry Truman assumed the presidency, he faced the reconstruction of Western Europe, the unfolding of the Cold War, and the war in Korea. Although he said he intended to carry forward Roosevelt's policies, and although he never renounced the Good Neighbor policy, he paid little attention to Latin America. In some respects, his approach was similar to that of Lyndon Johnson. Johnson never renounced his dead predecessor's Alliance for Progress; indeed, he explicitly reaffirmed it. But Johnson became preoccupied with Vietnam.

During Truman's administration, the State Department had no high-ranking official like Sumner Welles with a deep interest in Latin America. And although it was undoubtedly not Truman's intention, Latin American leaders came to feel that he had abandoned the Good Neighbor policy and neglected them. Nevertheless, Nelson Rockefeller, as FDR's coordinator of inter-American affairs, had begun the creative programs of economic and technical assistance to Latin America that flowered much later under the Alliance for Progress.

Just before the war, Roosevelt had commenced a program of loans, grants, and technical assistance to Latin America. Under Truman (and later under Eisenhower), Latin America received technical assistance, Export-Import Bank loans, and military aid. But in the first ten years after the war, Latin America's share of direct dollar grants and credits was the smallest of any major area in the world except Eastern Europe. The Truman administration relied on private capital investment, which was seen by liberal Latin Americans as abandoning government loans and handing matters over to Wall Street bankers.

Truman's actions were motivated by the Cold War. He even mended relations with the neofascist Perón regime in Argentina in order to make possible the signing of the Rio Treaty (1947), which committed its signatories to collective action in defense of any signer suffering "extracontinental" aggression. And in 1948, the Charter of the Organization of American States was agreed to in Bogotá at the Ninth International Conference of American States. What pleased Latin Americans was that no OAS member possessed a veto, not even the United States; this was thought to restore the Good Neighbor principle. What pleased us was the prospect of hemispheric solidarity against communism.

At the Bogotá Conference, Secretary of State Marshall explained that the United States could not provide massive aid to the underdeveloped world at the same time that it was undertaking the economic reconstruction of Europe, but he promised a later economic conference. Thus, during the Truman and Eisenhower years, as so often in the past, our Caribbean policy was a mere appendage of our larger concerns, neglected when we were occupied elsewhere, attended to when we thought our strategic interests were threatened. In the end, it took the extension of the Cold War to Cuba and Guatemala during the Eisenhower administration to revive U.S. interest in the Caribbean.

3
THE EISENHOWER YEARS

The Rule of George Humphrey

We have the word of John Foster Dulles that when President Eisenhower took office he was concerned about Latin America—he felt that the United States was not doing enough to develop the hemisphere and was worried about "the advance of the international communist conspiracy" in the hemisphere. In June 1953, the president sent his brother Milton to South America to survey conditions there. Milton Eisenhower's report emphasized economic issues and failed entirely to address the urgent social and political questions later addressed by the Alliance for Progress. Although the report placed heavy emphasis on the role of private capital, it advocated development lending by the Export-Import Bank as well as by the World Bank and proposed stockpiling raw materials to support their prices. Milton Eisenhower's report was a solitary beacon of liberating light, but Eisenhower's secretary of the treasury, George M. Humphrey, surely the ablest, most effective, and one of the most ideological of Eisenhower cabinet members, made certain that the report would come to nothing whatever.

For many years, Latin Americans had wanted to set up an Inter-American Development Bank. The United States had repeatedly put them off, most recently when Secretary Marshall told them at Bogotá that they would have to await European recovery. He had

promised them an economic conference at a later date. Now the
Eisenhower administration brushed aside such a conference.

At the very beginning of the Eisenhower administration,
Humphrey got his hands on the Export-Import Bank (Exim), which
he did not want used for development loans lest it compete with
private enterprise. Over the years, Exim had won great respect
among Latin Americans, who regarded it as far more sympathetic to
their development problems and far more generous in its lending
terms than most international bankers. The effect of Humphrey's
policies at Exim was felt quickly: in 1952, Exim had loaned $261
million spread over twenty-one projects: in 1953, it loaned only $5
million for two projects.

Then, at the Tenth Inter-American Conference in Caracas in
March 1954, Dulles seemed to be reversing policy when he said that
henceforth Exim would consider applications for certain kinds of
development loans "on their merits." He may have done it because he
wanted to push an anticommunist resolution through the conference.
Indeed, in order to get his anticommunist resolution, he agreed
finally to hold the Inter-American Economic Conference so long
desired by Latin Americans. A little later, legislation restored some
freedom to the Exim Bank.

The Economic Conference was attended by most of the intelligent,
sophisticated young economists and political leaders of Latin America. Their liberal views, developed under the guidance of Raúl
Prebisch of the United Nations Economic Commission for Latin
America (ECLA), were presented in a paper that argued that, as a
consequence of the communications revolution, the Latin American
masses were no longer content to do without a better life, that
political instability and social tensions were bound to increase, and
that the economic prospects of Latin Americans were poor because
they were receiving less and less for their primary commodities but
paying more and more for our manufactured goods—the "terms of
trade" complaint that exploded twenty years later in the Third
World commodity revolution. They held that, while the key to
development lay in an aggressive industrialization policy for import
substitution, their immediate need was for an assured flow of foreign
exchange to make the transition to industrialization—and that meant
stabilization of commodity prices and long-term low-interest loans.
They drew up a program of both international cooperation and

domestic Latin American self-help that prefigured the Alliance for Progress: annual foreign investment of $1 billion for ten years ($600-650 million from the World Bank and Exim Bank, $50-100 million from an Inter-American Fund, and $300-500 million from investment); national planning; and commodity price stabilization agreements.

The Latin Americans, presenting a common position on external assistance for the first time, had high hopes. After all, their politicians had given Secretary Dulles his anticommunist resolution; now, they thought, they would receive their economic reward. But George Humphrey continued in command. Much of what they had in mind ran contrary to administration doctrine, which held that we should rely on private investment, should be most cautious about diverting government funds into schemes overseas, and must prevent any tampering with the free play of market forces and capital movement. Secretary Humphrey urged the Latin American finance ministers to go home and get inflation under control and maintain realistic exchange rates in order to attract more private foreign investments, for in private investment lay their salvation. To their proposal of an inter-American development bank or fund, he said no. To their proposals that the United States participate in commodity stabilization schemes and national planning, he said no. To everything else, no.

Guatemala, Arbenz, and the CIA

President Eisenhower's major concerns about Latin America were that we were not "doing our part" economically and that, politically, communism was spreading to our hemisphere. Secretary of State John Foster Dulles and his brother Allen at the Central Intelligence Agency (CIA) hatched a scheme to manage the political side of the problem. They would stop communism in the hemisphere by overthrowing its protagonist, the president of Guatemala, Jacobo Arbenz Guzmán.

Guatemala, a country of some 2 million impoverished Indians in the highlands ruled by a few mestizos in the capital, was in colonial days the proud seat of the Captaincy General of all Central America. In the twentieth century, Guatemala became almost a fiefdom of U.S. corporations, especially the United Fruit Company. For the sake of its bananas—and its profits—the United Fruit Company made and unmade Guatemalan leaders for many years.

Then in 1944, the people freely and overwhelmingly elected a university professor president, Juan José Arévalo. Arévalo's program of genuine social and economic reform set him in conflict with the old oligarchy and, eventually, the middle class. Arévalo's base of support was the labor unions—and communists controlled the unions.

In 1951, Arbenz was elected to succeed Arévalo, and on February 25, 1953, the Arbenz government announced the expropriation of 234,000 uncultivated acres owned by United Fruit. The Eisenhower administration demanded compensation for the United Fruit Company; Guatemala refused. The Eisenhower administration decided that Arbenz had to be removed from power. Although it is widely assumed today that the United States plotted Arbenz's overthrow because of the expropriation of the United Fruit Company's land, it is more likely that the Eisenhower administration, thoroughly involved in the Cold War, saw the Arbenz regime as the beachhead in the Western Hemisphere of what was then called the Sino-Soviet bloc. The new ambassador to Guatemala City had reported to Secretary Dulles that Arbenz "thought like a Communist and talked like a Communist, and if not actually one, would do until one came along," and he predicted that unless communist forces were stopped, they would take full control of Guatemala within six months. The CIA then began helping train and equip troops in Honduras under Carlos Castillo Armas, an exiled Guatemalan military man. The administration sent a new ambassador to Honduras to persuade the Honduran government to permit the training and signed mutual security treaties with Honduras and Nicaragua. It was at this point that Secretary Dulles mounted his major effort to push an anticommunist resolution through the OAS.

When Guatemala received a shipload of arms originating in Czechoslovakia, the U.S. government, amid uproar, announced that it was flying several planeloads of small arms to Honduras and Nicaragua in line with the treaty just signed. At press conferences and in speeches, Eisenhower and Dulles repeatedly found the situation "disturbing" and hinted at action.

On June 18, Castillo Armas and his small force—about 300 to 500 men—crossed the border into Guatemala. They proceeded only about twenty miles, then bogged down. The Guatemalan army, although it numbered 6,000 men, showed little taste for battle. Arbenz fell a few days later, say Guatemalans who were involved, not because of the CIA and Castillo Armas but because the Guatemalan military, itself fearful of communism, overthrew him. Eisenhower and Dulles maintained at the time that Guatemalans themselves had thrown off the yoke of communism; later, however, they took credit for the CIA role. The overthrow of Arbenz came to be considered a great new triumph for democracy and the CIA.

The coup had long-lasting effects. Castillo Armas—who returned the expropriated lands for a reward of some $90 million in aid—launched a purge of communists and their sympathizers, including labor union and peasant league leaders, killing hundreds and imprisoning thousands. Before the overthrow of Arbenz, Guatemala had seemed to be heading leftward—toward communism, according to the Eisenhower administration; toward liberal democracy or socialism, according to Guatemalan liberals. Ever since then, Guatemala has been one of the most conservative countries in the Caribbean. Guatemalan politicians take it as axiomatic that they need the support of the CIA to win an election. When the United States decided to use the CIA to arm and train a brigade of Cuban exiles for what became the Bay of Pigs invasion, President Ydígoras Fuentes offered Guatemala as the training site; then, when a military revolt threatened Ydígoras—an unpopular leader—the CIA came to his rescue. Still later, when President Kennedy began his program of counterinsurgency training to counteract Castroite guerrilla movements, the counterinsurgency movement in Guatemala was accompanied by a terrorist campaign conducted by right-wing Guatemalan extremists, and many Guatemalans believe they were aided by U.S. Special Forces.

By its actions, the CIA revived a Central American tradition of military intervention in one another's affairs. Fairly or not, many Guatemalans identify the United States with repressive regimes. Armed intervention, or its encouragement, by the United States is a highly serious step, likely to have long-lasting and not always foreseeable results.

Nixon and Eisenhower to the Caribbean

In the first years of the Eisenhower administration, while the Soviet Union was attempting to improve relations with Latin America, the United States' attempt along the same line consisted of two trips. Early in 1955, Richard Nixon, Eisenhower's vice-president, went to the Caribbean. In Cuba, he embraced the dictator

Batista; in Guatemala, he gave the impression that aid to Castillo Armas would be forthcoming; in Haiti, he emphasized U.S. trade; in the Dominican Republic, he toasted Trujillo. The trip accomplished little of substance.

In July 1956, Eisenhower journeyed to Panama to meet with sixteen Latin American chiefs of state and was photographed shaking hands and conversing in a friendly way with some of the most odious tyrants in the hemisphere.

In 1953, the Soviet Union announced that it would participate in the United Nations' expanded program of technical assistance to underdeveloped countries. It was seeking close ties with the neutralists of Asia, Africa, the Arab world, and Latin America— what later came to be called the Third World. The Eisenhower administration was slow to respond to the Soviet initiative. Eisenhower appointed an isolationist to head the International Cooperation Administration (ICA), a forerunner of AID, and he reinforced Secretary Humphrey's policy, as did Budget Director and Under Secretary of State Herbert Hoover, Jr. By 1955, Latin American trade with communist countries had risen to almost half a billion, from $70 million in 1943, while U.S.–Latin American trade had barely held its own. Eisenhower's message to Congress in 1956 reflected no concern, and Senator Mike Mansfield (D.-Mont.) tried to nudge the Congress into responding to the Soviet threat. But Congress, then as later, found it hard to initiate policy.

The Caribbean Earthquake

The year 1957 marked the beginning of a series of events that fundamentally altered the Caribbean and its relationship to the United States. Those events occurred in the Caribbean. And in response to them, and for its own internal reasons, the Eisenhower adminstration shifted policy.

In 1956 and 1957, several conservative administration leaders resigned, including Secretary Humphrey. In 1957, President Eisenhower appointed C. Douglas Dillon deputy under secretary of state for economic affairs, and that same year Dillon, along with Humphrey's successor at Treasury, Robert B. Anderson, led the U.S. delegation to the Inter-American Economic Conference at Buenos Aires. Although the United States maintained its earlier position, Dillon, a Republican Wall Street banker of liberal bent and internationalist outlook, was greatly impressed by the views of the Latin Americans at Buenos Aires.

At the same time, the pace of change in the Caribbean itself accelerated, especially in Venezuela and Cuba.

* * *

U.S. oil companies had been in Venezuela since the 1920s, enjoying the protection of the terrible Venezuelan dictator, Juan Vicente Gómez. Reformist agitation after his death in 1935 had culminated in a coup in October 1945, perpetrated by a strange alliance of young army officers and Acción Democrática (AD), a labor-based political party with a socialist program led by Rómulo Betancourt. The AD pushed through legislation providing for a 50-50 division of all oil profits between the companies and the Venezuelan government, encouraged labor unions, proposed agrarian reform, and undertook programs to aid the neglected countryside. The government established the *Corporación de Fomento* to increase national production, develop new industries, and improve old ones. Venezuelan private interests and opposition parties as well as the oil companies were unhappy with the ideas of the AD, and in 1948, the army overthrew the AD government. Marcos Pérez Jiménez, who became dictator, reversed AD policy, collaborated with the oil companies, abandoned the AD's plan to conserve petroleum, rejected labor's demands, provided incentives to U.S. mining companies to open Venezuela's iron ore deposits, neglected the countryside, built Caracas—and its slums—extravagantly, and embarked on a grandiose program of public works. For his efforts—or, as his detractors had it, for the new leases he gave the oil companies—the Eisenhower administration gave him the U.S. Legion of Merit. By 1958, direct private U.S. investment in Venezuela was estimated at more than $2 billion, greater than in any other foreign country in the world, save Canada, and Pérez Jiménez seemed as secure as his fellow dictators—Trujillo of the Dominican Republic, Somoza of Nicaragua, Batista of Cuba, and Rojas Pinilla of Colombia. But suddenly, one after another, they all fell: Somoza was assassinated in 1956 (but his family retained control), Rojas Pinilla was overthrown in 1957, Pérez Jiménez was overthrown in 1958 and replaced by Betancourt, Batista was defeated by Castro in 1958-1959, and Trujillo was assassinated in 1961. It was truly a Caribbean political earthquake.

At this time, early 1958, the Reciprocal Trade Bill was struggling through Congress; it passed only after the administration granted concessions to various special interests, including the oil companies, which wanted and got further restrictions on Venezuelan oil. That and other provisions affecting commodities helped to undermine the hemispheric goodwill that the Trade Bill was intended to generate. (And so, later, the Trade Act of 1974 caused an explosion in the Caribbean.) Secretary Dulles tried to smooth feelings by offering the Latin Americans consultation on the violent price swings of their commodities; the Latin Americans were unimpressed. Under Secretary Dillon had been trying for some time to persuade the U.S. government to discuss with Latin America the serious problem of declining commodity prices, but he was told that such discussions would inevitably lead to proposals that we get into international price fixing, which the Commerce Department flatly opposed. Again, the divided Eisenhower administration had reached a policy stalemate, and again, as a substitute for policy, it sent Vice-President Nixon on a goodwill tour of Latin America.

Mr. and Mrs. Nixon and their party left Washington April 27, 1958. They visited Uruguay, Argentina, Paraguay, Bolivia, Peru, Ecuador, and Colombia before arriving in Venezuela on May 13. For several weeks, the press, labor, and students in Venezuela had agitated against Nixon's visit—not only had the Congress just passed a trade act that hurt Venezuelan oil; even worse, the United States had just granted residence to Pérez Jiménez, the hated fallen dictator. Caracas had been plastered with *"Fuera Nixon"* signs, which in the last days before his arrival were changed, chillingly, to *"Muera Nixon."* When he stepped from his plane, a crowd of hecklers hooted and jeered and, as he started for his car, spat and screamed at him. En route to the U.S. embassy, his car was trapped in a traffic jam, and immediately a gang of men attacked it, but Nixon escaped to the embassy unhurt. Hostile mobs continued to roam the city, however, and violence broke out at the government palace. That night, Eisenhower, angered and alarmed, ordered four companies of marines and paratroopers flown to the Caribbean bases for use if requested by the Venezuelan government. Nixon cut his visit short and the next night drove to the airport through streets empty but for tanks and troops. Nixon's experience in Caracas shook the Eisenhower administration badly, and when Nixon returned, he made seven recommendations:

1. American government personnel abroad must do a more effective job of reaching the opinion-makers of Latin America. . . . Students, teachers, newspaper editors, reporters, labor leaders. . . .

2. We must develop an economic program for Latin America which is distinctly its own. . . .

3. We should not appear to give dictators . . . the same moral approval that we gave to leaders who were trying to build free and democratic institutions. But we must not go overboard the other way.

4. We cannot expect that U.S.-style, democratic institutions will work without modifications in countries . . . [without such] traditions or experience.

5. Support of adequate military and security forces must continue so that free governments will have the strength to maintain stability. . . .

6. The people of Latin America . . . respect courage. . . .

7. We must show proper respect for [Latin American] traditions, customs, and culture.

Castro

A number of events were taking place at about the same time. Betancourt was elected president of Venezuela in 1958, and his progressive regime began Venezuela's determined effort to regain control of its own natural resources. Betancourt served his full five-year term, during which he became the major leader of the noncommunist left in the Caribbean. In 1958, all the Caribbean islands except Puerto Rico, the Dominican Republic, Haiti, and Cuba were colonies of European powers, and so were the three mainland Guianas. Britain, striving to arrange some sort of future for its colonies, which were soon to become independent, formed them into the Federation of the West Indies. In British Guiana, the two major political leaders, Cheddi Jagan and Forbes Burnham, had split, thus setting the pattern of Guyanese politics for years to come. In Honduras, the army took over power from the banana companies. The next year, in Nicaragua, rebels from Costa Rica attacked the

Somoza regime, but they failed.

These events, following Nixon's Caracas trip and recommendations, called for change in U.S. policy. But what finally pushed the Eisenhower administration into a new policy was the success of Fidel Castro.

Castro had landed on Cuba's coast with a small band of followers at the end of 1956; they took to the mountains and, by 1958, seemed about to prevail. The United States' total embargo on the shipment of arms and ammunition to both sides in Cuba had little effect except to erode morale among Batista's troops, many of whom were about to abandon him anyway. The actions of the United States were probably not aimed at any specific outcome, although it is possible that at some point the CIA, in the course of aiding noncommunist leftists in the Caribbean, gave aid to Castro. For at that time, Castro enjoyed considerable sympathy and popularity in the United States, and, so far as we knew, he was not a communist nor supported by the Soviet Union. Indeed, not until midsummer of 1958 did the Cuban Communist party join him.

On the morning of New Year's Day 1959, Batista fled Havana. The Eisenhower administration promptly recognized Castro's government and sent Philip Bonsal to Havana as ambassador. Plainly, the president and the State Department intended to try to reach an accommodation with Castro. This was evident in the choice of Bonsal, who had been U.S. ambassador to Bolivia at a time when there was a substantial (for those days) aid program to the revolutionary government, which had nationalized its tin mines. Bonsal had had no love for Batista, and he recognized that much of U.S. public opinion could only applaud Castro's promise to restore democracy to the Cuban people. Bonsal's policy was to accept Castro's power; he believed the Cuban people could influence and modify the direction of the revolution and therefore was determined to pursue the inter-American doctrine of nonintervention. Bonsal thought economics offered the best opportunity for getting along with the new regime: the sugar quota, tariff arrangements, a friendly U.S. attitude toward Cuban application for emergency financial aid to the International Monetary Fund, and, if possible, equitable formulas for compensation should Castro take over United Fruit Company lands and U.S.-owned public utilities.

Not everybody agreed with Bonsal's approach. Robert Hill, U.S.

ambassador to Mexico, wanted the United States to submit to the OAS the evidence that had convinced Hill—this was in April 1959—that Castro was a tool of Moscow and Peking. Bonsal's two immediate predecessors in Havana as well as numerous conservatives agreed that Castro was a communist, but Bonsal remained convinced that sufficient evidence to prove such a judgment did not exist, and at the time he was almost surely correct.

In April, Castro went to Washington to address a group of American editors, and Vice-President Nixon undertook to advise him to avoid the toils of international communism; the meeting did not go well. Castro went on to Buenos Aires, where he monopolized attention at an inter-American conference, the only one he ever attended, by proposing that the United States supply $30 billion over ten years to support development in Latin America; the proposal was rejected.

Bonsal considered Castro's proposal an early indication of his "sense of continental mission." Indeed, while he was away, his followers dispatched an expedition to overthrow the government of Panama; it failed. Then, not long after he returned, while denouncing any hint of intervention in Cuban affairs by the United States, Castro began to welcome, arm, and train in Cuba exiles from the Dominican Republic, Nicaragua, Guatemala, and other countries and to send arms and supplies to guerrilla bands in some of those countries. In June, he actually sent expeditions to try to overthrow the governments of the Dominican Republic, Nicaragua, and Haiti; he failed. At a meeting of foreign ministers, who were generally opposed to any form of intervention, the United States hoped to persuade them to condemn Cuba's behavior. This was our first effort to restrain Castro or, failing that, to isolate him in the hemisphere. After a long wrangle, the ministers adopted an innocuous resolution setting out the democratic principles of OAS membership.

When Bonsal went to Washington in September, he found opposition to Castro building. Although the State Department had not yet made a firm policy decision, other agencies of government were taking a harder line. Bonsal was aware of the possibility that the CIA was engaging in activities of which he was ignorant. What he did not know and would have found hard to believe was that, contrary to our treaty obligations and the policy Bonsal was trying to help execute, Vice-President Nixon had, since June, been urging that the CIA be instructed to recruit, arm, and train Cuban exiles who had fled the Castro regime. CIA involvement eventually led to the Bay of Pigs.

At the United Nations, Cuba reversed its former pro-Western position and abstained on the vote to seat the People's Republic of China. At home, Castro seized on several minor terrorist acts to launch a propaganda attack against American efforts to destroy him. By the end of the week of October 19, 1959, Bonsal had lost any hope of establishing a rational relationship between Cuba and the United States. During that week, Castro arrested his comrade-in-arms, Hubert O. Matos, who was, after a trial at which Castro spoke, condemned to twenty years in prison. The same week, Castro's antiaircraft guns, attempting to stop an airplane from dropping leaflets, fired at the plane causing projectile fragments to fall into Havana streets; three people were killed and over forty were wounded. Castro denounced it as a bombardment of Havana perpetrated by the U.S. government. (American authorities had indeed failed to prevent the flight, which was in violation of U.S. law, but they took the pilot into custody when he returned to Florida.) Castro also went on to announce he would create a people's armed militia in order to repel invaders, and he led the mob to cry out for the execution of Matos and other traitors. Bonsal thought Castro had taken leave of his senses. Thus ended Bonsal's hopes. In ensuing weeks, Castro purged other noncommunist leftists in his government. Bonsal did not think any of this proved any rational plan on Castro's part to lead Cuba into the Soviet orbit. Rather, he thought, it happened because of the dynamics of Castro's lust for power—the airplane leaflet dropping simply provided Castro with a convenient way to distract attention from the potentially dangerous Matos affair by whipping up the mobs with cries of external aggression. Bonsal has never believed Castro deliberately "betrayed" his revolution into the hands of the Soviet Union. Rather, he considers that what drove Castrol basically was not ideology but a lust for absolute personal power. Castro operated by intuition, drawing sustenance and even policy from the reactions of the mobs he harangued. To this might be added the notion that he needed the United States as enemy in order to consolidate his revolution. The enemy without gave him cause to build up his state security system within. And he was always par excellence the agitator in power. If the United States had not existed, he would have had to invent it.

In the first week of December, Bonsal told the State Department that so long as Castro ruled Cuba, "productive diplomacy" was out of the question. He and the department agreed, however, to try to maintain diplomatic relations for the sake of U.S. property in Cuba, U.S. tourists and journalists who were still coming to Cuba, Cubans who wanted to leave for the United States, trade, and Guantánamo. In January 1960, President Eisenhower issued a policy statement expressing concern at the deterioration of relations with Cuba, reasserting our nonintervention, declaring his intention to restrain illegal private activities in the United States, expressing concern at Castro's increasing tendency to create "the illusion of aggressive acts and conspiratorial activities," recognizing Cuba's sovereign right to reform its system, promising to bring to the Cuban government's attention any violation of U.S. citizens' rights under Cuban and international law, and expressing confidence in the ability of the Cuban people "to recognize and defeat the intrigues of International Communism." It was an admirable document reflecting Bonsal's views, but it was not followed. After Soviet Deputy Premier Anastas Mikoyan visited Havana in February to arrange for the Soviet Union to purchase Cuban sugar, and after the explosion of a French munition ship in Havana harbor—an incident Castro blamed on the U.S. government—the Eisenhower adminstration abandoned nonintervention and secretly adopted a policy of overthrowing Castro by any means short of openly sending U.S. forces to Cuba. President Eisenhower, late in March, decided to adopt the policy of Vice-President Nixon and authorize the CIA to recruit and train anti-Castro Cubans residing in the United States for military service against Cuba. Castro's intelligence services learned about this program soon after it got under way, but Ambassador Bonsal in Havana and even the State Department in Washington were not informed of the decision.

The administration had changed its policy for a number of reasons. U.S. public opinion was swinging against Castro because of his show trials, his extremism, and his anti-U.S. fulminations. The Mikoyan sugar deal raised the specter of a serious Soviet presence in the Caribbean—a threat to our strategic interests. And perhaps most important of all, 1960 was an American presidential election year, and the Republican administration, always sensitive to its party's right wing, feared being called soft on Cuban communism.

In June and July, the administration adopted economic measures intended to bring about Castro's downfall. Instead, they strengthened his hand. Ché Guevara, in charge of Cuba's economy since late 1959, told two U.S. oil companies in Cuba that they would have to import, refine, and sell Soviet crude oil. The companies were advised to refuse Guevara's request by Secretary of the Treasury Anderson. Bonsal, when informed of this advice by an executive of one of the companies—not the State Department—told the department he hoped it "knew what it was doing." The result was that the Soviets hauled Soviet crude oil from the Black Sea to Cuba; the Cuban government took over the three refineries and refined the Soviet crude itself; and there was no oil or gasoline shortage in Cuba. "The Cuban Revolution," Bonsal concluded, "had won a great victory and had had a powerful ally thrust into its arms." A week later, President Eisenhower suspended Cuba's American sugar quota. Bonsal objected, "With this action I contend that the United States turned its back on thirty years of statesmanship in the Latin American field."

The result of all this was not to "drive Castro into Russia's arms," as some have said, but, rather, to drive the Soviet Union into Castro's arms. At that time, the Soviet Union was not eager to take on Castro as a client. The Soviets were not sure they wanted someone they considered an erratic adventurer to (in effect) represent them in the Western Hemisphere. Nor did they intend to replace us as Cuba's major trading partner. Although they were no doubt happy to have him harass the United States and denounce our imperialism, they had no wish to confront the United States themselves. They might even have preferred that Castro remain neutral. But between them, Eisenhower and Castro forced Russia's hand. Events moved rapidly thereafter. Within three months, all private property in Cuba was expropriated. On October 19, 1960 the U.S. government prohibited all imports from Cuba and all exports to Cuba except for nonsubsidized food, medicines, and medical supplies (which would also be banned in a few months). Ambassador Bonsal went home for good. On January 2, 1961, Castro demanded that our embassy staff in Havana be reduced to eleven; the Eisenhower administration broke off diplomatic relations; and Castro ordered full-scale mobilization of his armed forces.

The Policy Shift

The Eisenhower administration's policy toward the rest of the Caribbean in this period after 1957 was also changing. Under Secretary Dillon, responding to Latin American views, began working to realign policy and turn it in a new direction, a direction that led, under President Kennedy, to the Alliance for Progress. Dillon gained control of administration tariff and trade policy, the operations of a revivified Exim Bank, relations with the World Bank and International Monetary Fund (IMF), the farm surplus disposal program—and negotiations with Congress on most of these matters. Under him, the United States, after half a decade of talk, at last had come to favor larger contributions to the World Bank and IMF; Exim had been bailing out such countries in trouble as Brazil, Colombia, Britain, the Philippines, Chile, and India; the United States had announced it was willing at least to discuss commodity agreements, including one on coffee; and the administration had abandoned its rigid bankers' principles and recommended a subsidy and stockpiling scheme for the domestic mining industry rather than raise tariffs on lead, zinc, and possibly copper at the expense of Chile, Peru, and Mexico. Moreover, under Dillon's prodding, Congress had passed the largest extension of the reciprocal trade program in history and a $3.3 billion foreign aid bill and had added $4.2 billion to the Exim Bank and farm surplus disposal program. In all this, Dillon, who was convinced that the most important economic issue of the time was what economic system would be adopted by the poor countries of the world, had the help of Secretary of the Treasury Anderson.

Not long after the Nixon incident in Caracas, President Juscelino Kubitschek of Brazil proposed "Operation Pan America," an ambitious program for economic development, commodity market stabilization, and expansion of existing international financial institutions. Dillon promptly announced that the United States was "prepared to consider the establishment of an inter-American regional development" bank. The following spring, an OAS committee agreed on terms for creating such a bank: total capital of $1 billion, of which $450 million was to come from the United States; 15 percent of total resources to be used to make soft loans for projects not necessarily self-liquidating.

In February 1960, seven South American countries signed the

Montevideo Treaty establishing a Latin American Free Trade Area and Latin American Free Trade Association (LAFTA). Shortly thereafter, President Eisenhower left on a two-week goodwill visit to Brazil, Argentina, Chile, and Uruguay. After the trip, Eisenhower, although insisting that social reform in Latin America was an internal matter, sent a special message to Congress, asking it to authorize an expenditure of $600 million for Latin America over and above the current mutual security estimates, most of it to be earmarked for projects designed to help build a better life for individuals in Latin America. He asked for the money before the OAS committee began its climactic meeting at Bogotá on September 5. Congress, although not enthusiastic, agreed; it realized that a refusal would put the United States in awkward position at Bogotá and, furthermore, felt that it could reconsider when the time came actually to appropriate the money. Castro was forcing even Congress to pay heed to Latin America.

Events were moving rapidly in the Caribbean. On August 16, near the height of the Cuban-American crisis and only weeks before Bogotá, the OAS called a meeting of foreign ministers in San José, Costa Rica, at the request of President Betancourt of Venezuela. Betancourt wanted the OAS to move against Trujillo, who had, on June 24, 1960, sent his secret police to assassinate Betancourt. Trujillo had apparently come to believe that President Betancourt of Venezuela had aided an attempted invasion of the Dominican Republic by some fifty exiled Dominicans.

The United States was not unsympathetic to Betancourt's complaint against Trujillo, but it was more interested in persuading the OAS to move against Castro. Eisenhower appointed Thomas C. Mann, a Texan and conservative career diplomat, assistant secretary for ARA.[1] At San José, the meeting of foreign ministers found that "high officials" of the Dominican government had aided the attempt to murder Betancourt, declared the Dominican Republic an aggressor nation, and imposed diplomatic and economic sanctions. As for Cuba, the U.S. delegation had hoped for a resolution condemning the Cuban government for having denied representative democracy to the Cuban people and for having encouraged Cuba's penetration by international communism. But the other ministers, knowing Castro still enjoyed considerable popularity in their own countries, and convinced that the United States had helped precipitate Soviet involvement by its economic warfare against Castro, passed a resolution merely reasserting that "any form of totalitarianism" was incompatible with the inter-American system and condemning "energetically" the intervention or threat of intervention by "an extra-continental power" in hemisphere affairs. The United States probably got that resolution only because the ministers hoped for guarantees of aid from the United States at the forthcoming Bogotá meeting.

The Bogotá OAS meeting was an important turning point in U.S.-Caribbean relations. Under Secretary Dillon proposed an attack on Latin America's social problems through improvement of rural life, housing, communications, and education; tax, credit, and land use reforms by Latin American governments; and a social progress trust fund, authorized by Congress to make soft loans for a program of social development projects never before eligible for U.S. aid, to be financed by half a billion dollars from the United States and administered largely by the Inter-American Development Bank (IADB). All this was to be in addition to aid for basic economic and industrial development. The Act of Bogotá approved the special fund for social development and called for prompt action on industrialization and commodity prices. The Inter-American Development Bank began operations October 1; two weeks later, John F. Kennedy, in Florida, nearing the end of his campaign for president, released his speech calling for a new Alliance for Progress. The modern relationship between the United States and the Caribbean was about to begin.

4
THE KENNEDY YEARS

The Alliance Conceived

The 1960s were revolutionary years—in the United States, years of campus rebels and Black Panthers, in the world, years of Nkrumah and Sekou Touré, of Lumumba and Sukarno and Castro. World War II had let loose new revolutionary currents everywhere as old empires crumbled and the Axis tide receded. Independence and freedom—and later development—became the watchwords of a good part of the world. In an eloquent statement on the aspirations of the developing world, John F. Kennedy said a year before he became president:

> If the title deeds of history applied, it is we, the American people, who should be marching at the head of this worldwide revolution . . . for whenever a local patriot emerges in Asia, the Middle East, Africa, or Latin America to give form and focus to the forces of ferment, he most often quotes the great watchwords we once proclaimed to the world: the watchwords of personal and national liberty, of the natural equality of all souls, of the dignity of labor, of economic development broadly shared. Yet we have allowed the Communists to evict us from our rightful estate at the head of this worldwide revolution. We have been made to appear as the defenders of the *status quo*.

Nearly every time a foreign issue becomes entangled in a presidential campaign, it is distorted: 1960 was no exception. The Eisenhower administration was obliged to try to realign its Latin American policy in the uproar of the presidential campaign. Kennedy made Latin America an issue, and he focused his attack on the administration's handling of Cuba. At one time, Kennedy had seen Castro as the heir of Bolívar, as one of the world's flaming young revolutionaries; but now, he denounced Castro. He did not attack the administration for its unwise policies of economic warfare against Castro; instead, he criticized the administration for not opposing Castro vigorously enough. He said we must assist the anti-Castro Cubans in exile. Vice-President Nixon, who knew (as Kennedy did not) that the CIA, at his own suggestion, was already secretly training anti-Castro exiles, criticized Kennedy's suggestion as "dangerously irresponsible."

As soon as he was elected, Kennedy set up a task force on Latin America headed by Adolf A. Berle, Jr., a New Deal Democrat with ties to such new democratic left Caribbean leaders as Rómulo Betancourt of Venezuela, Luís Muñoz Marín of Puerto Rico, José Figueres of Costa Rico, and Lleras Camargo of Colombia. Among its members were Lincoln Gordon, an economics professor at the Harvard Business School, later assistant secretary for ARA; two associates of Governor Muñoz Marín of Puerto Rico, whose thinking was to influence the new administration's policy, Arturo Morales-Carríon and, especially, Teodoro Moscoso; and Richard N. Goodwin, an able, young, and at that time somewhat abrasive Kennedy speech-writer who had invented the phrase "Alliance for Progress."

On January 6, Berle gave the task force report to Kennedy. The report said that there was a full-scale cold war under way in Latin America, that the bloody guerrilla phase of the war was threatening to spread throughout the Caribbean, and that U.S. policy must maintain a "quiet quarantine" of Cuba while strongly supporting such key democratic strongpoints as Venezuela. The report stressed the need to stabilize the revolutionary movement at the left of center—essentially the Betancourt plan for Venezuela, which was modeled on Muñoz Marín's program in Puerto Rico. Berle's report suggested that we should no longer support such "dying dictatorships" as those in the Dominican Republic, Haiti, and Nicaragua. The report's program called for an inter-American development fund and stabilization of commodity prices through "buffer stocks."

On January 20, 1961, from the frozen steps of the Capitol, President Kennedy delivered his inaugural address. It included these passages:

> To those peoples in the huts and villages of half the globe struggling to break the bonds of mass misery, we pledge our best efforts to help them help themselves, for whatever period is required, not because the Communists may be doing it, not because we seek their votes, but because it is right. If a free society cannot help the many who are poor, it cannot save the few who are rich.
>
> To our sister republics south of our border, we offer a special pledge: to convert our good words into good deeds, in a new alliance for progress, to assist free men and free governments in casting off the chains of poverty. But this peaceful revolution of hope cannot become the prey of hostile powers. Let all our neighbors know that we shall join with them to oppose aggression or subversion anywhere in the Americas. And let every other power know that this Hemisphere intends to remain the master of its own house.

In that passage, Kennedy set out, perhaps unwittingly, a double policy that plagued the Alliance from the outset. On the one hand, he declared that we would help the poor nations restructure their societies not because of communism but because it was right. On the other hand, having been briefed on the CIA's Cuban exile training, he was no longer (as earlier) thinking only of containing "this revolution in Cuba itself" but would utilize other means offered him to ensure that "this Hemisphere" remained "the master of its own house."

In the late 1970s, it is hard to recall the spirit of boundless hope that John F. Kennedy brought to Washington in 1961. In part it was owing to his youth and the youth of so many around him, especially after eight years of Eisenhower and his elderly bankers. But it was more. In part, it was rhetoric, golden words of hope after the flabby prose of Eisenhower. And in part, of course he was asserting the leadership not only of America but also of what was then called the whole free world in the struggle against communism, surely a unifying cause. Beyond all that, however, did not he kindle boundless hope because he spoke to the best in the American people and to their finest traditions and most deeply held beliefs? That—and a conviction he seemed to hold and surely imparted that for America, anything was possible. In those days, nothing better symbolized the Kennedy hope than the Alliance for Progress—unless it was the Peace Corps. (And to some of us in the field, it sometimes seemed that the Peace Corps youngsters were giving the peasants of the Caribbean more tangible help than the Alliance and its money could.) "Anything was possible"—all this, of course, was before we learned the lessons of the Bay of Pigs, before the stubborn resistance to the Alliance for Progress, before Vietnam.

The Alliance was not implemented immediately. When Kennedy took office, he had not yet chosen an assistant secretary for ARA. Thomas C. Mann, whom he inherited from Eisenhower, would go on to become ambassador to Mexico; he was not the man to head a new Alliance containing numerous political and social reforms. Berle would not take the job unless it was upgraded to the rank of under secretary. Kennedy did not appoint an assistant secretary for several months, and when he did, he chose a career diplomat, Robert F. Woodward, not a particularly inspiring leader. Indeed, the men who were to be most influential in shaping the new Latin American policy were Douglas Dillon, now Kennedy's secretary of the treasury; Berle; Goodwin; Arthur Schlesinger, Jr., and, a little later, Ralph Dungan, both of the White House staff. (Dungan, who handled ambassadorial appointments and other high-level patronage for Kennedy, gradually took over Latin American affairs for the White House.)

When Kennedy came to power, left democrats were scattered around the Caribbean—Betancourt, Lleras Camargo, Muñoz Marín, Villeda Morales (of Honduras). But in the center lay trouble— Trujillo's "dying dictatorship" in the Dominican Republic; Haiti, where Duvalier's tyranny might dissolve into communism or anarchy; and Cuba. Throughout Berle's diary of these months rang the phrase "the Caribbean crisis," the most urgent matter in all Latin America. In the first eight months of his administration, President

Kennedy had to deal with the Bay of Pigs invasion of Cuba, the assassination of Trujillo, an election in a Guyana torn by racial conflict, Jamaica's fatal withdrawal from the West Indies Federation, shaky democratic left governments in Venezuela and Honduras, a continuing political crisis in Guatemala, and a meeting at Punta del Este to establish the Alliance for Progress. But it was "the everlasting question of Cuba," as Berle called it, that absorbed everyone's attention. The CIA was concentrating on Cuba, not only mounting the Bay of Pigs expedition but bending its efforts throughout the hemisphere to undermine Castro's influence. Cuba made the headlines that spring. But our policy toward other countries was more important.

To emphasize the change in U.S. policy toward Latin America, Kennedy made his administration's speech to Latin America himself. On March 13, he addressed the Latin American diplomatic corps assembled in the East Room of the White House. He had done his preparation well, soliciting—and accepting—the suggestions of Venezuela's ambassador, José Antonio Mayobre. Mayobre, aware of a major opportunity, had invited nine prominent Latin American economists to join him in replying. Among them were Raúl Prebisch of the United Nations' Economic Commission for Latin America (ECLA); Felipe Pazos, who had been Castro's first president of the Central Bank of Cuba but had defected; Felipe Herrera, president of the Inter-American Development Bank; and Jorge Sol Castellanos, executive secretary of the Inter-American Economic and Social Council. Their memo was based on the proposals rejected in 1957 at Buenos Aires by the Eisenhower administration. Kennedy accepted nearly all. The speech contained solid substance and specific structural reforms. Kennedy said that he had asked Congress for $500 million to implement the Act of Bogotá, that he would support economic integration, and that he would seriously examine commodity problems "case by case." He said the Alliance must work to eliminate tyranny from the hemisphere and expressed hope that the people of both Cuba and the Dominican Republic would soon "rejoin the society of free men." He placed his heaviest emphasis on political freedom and social reforms, including land and tax reform, and he harked back to our revolutionary beginnings. Furthermore, he called for a meeting of the Inter-American Economic and Social Council, which would begin planning for the Alliance. Never before had

Latin American ambassadors heard such a speech—and such concrete proposals—from a U.S. president.

On the following day, Kennedy sent a special message to Congress. He asked it to appropriate the $500 million promised by the Act of Bogotá; he proposed that $394 million be assigned to the Inter-American Development Bank, which would be administered under a special trust agreement and be used mainly for loans on flexible terms to promote land settlement and improved land use, housing, water supply, and sanitation. Six million dollars would go to the OAS to help strengthen it. The remaining $100 million would be administered by the International Cooperation Administration (ICA)—the ICA was a predecessor to the Agency for International Development (AID)—for education, training, health, and other economic and social development. Ideally, projects would be undertaken only after a country developed an integrated overall plan. But Latin America was "seething with discontent and unrest"; the IADB and the aid agency needed the money immediately.

Although Kennedy and the others who shaped the Alliance understood that economic aid was necessary, the heart of the Alliance was not money; the heart of the Alliance lay in a determination to strengthen political democracy throughout the hemisphere and to bring about revolutionary social and economic change—to do nothing less than guarantee freedom and end poverty and injustice.

* * *

In memory, the Alliance was instantly and universally acclaimed. In truth, it was not. Kennedy had expected Latin Americans to respond to the Alliance as Europeans had responded to the Marshall Plan. But instead, nothing happened. Embarrassed, Moscoso asked Betancourt, Figueres, and other leaders of the democratic left to send telegrams to Kennedy. After a week or so, they did.

American editorials politely applauded the Alliance, but the public at large remained indifferent. On Capitol Hill, when a House subcommittee opened hearings on Kennedy's request for the $500 million, Chairman Otto Passman denounced it as "a blank check." The hearings went on and on, and Passman relented, but only after the Bay of Pigs disaster—that was about the only benefit the administration derived from the Bay of Pigs.

The Bay of Pigs

On April 17, 1961, only a month after Kennedy's speech to the Latin American ambassadors, the CIA under his orders launched the disastrous Bay of Pigs invasion. Although responsibility for the invasion, as Kennedy himself said, was inescapably his, there are conflicting accounts of the origin of the plan. Historians of the Kennedy administration have reported that the invasion was prepared by the Eisenhower administration and presented to Kennedy by the CIA as something he was already committed to. More recently, officials of the Eisenhower administration have recalled that, although a Cuban exile force existed, the invasion plan as such did not. Whatever the plan's origin, it appears unrealistic to have expected 1,500 exiled patriots to defeat more than 100,000 well-trained and well-armed troops—or to have expected the Cuban people to rise against Castro. President Kennedy was criticized by some for not sending American forces to aid the expedition, but if he had, he might well have become bogged down in a long guerrilla war or, if the invasion succeeded, found himself having to support, possibly militarily, whatever government replaced Castro's. Kennedy's mistake was not his failure to support the invasion; his mistake was authorizing it.

Reactions to the Bay of Pigs invasion varied. Although Latin American diplomats officially deplored intervention, privately they were shocked to learn how well-armed Castro's troops were and were surprised that the United States had not sent its own troops in to finish the job. For Castro, who had economic difficulties, the Bay of Pigs was a welcome diversion, and he brought the matter before the United Nations. Honduras broke diplomatic relations with Cuba as Guatemala, Haiti, and Nicaragua had already done. In the press, in the United States, criticism of Kennedy was surprisingly mild, but far less mild elsewhere. In Guatemala City, Mexico City, Caracas, and elsewhere, pro-Castro and anti-Castro demonstrators fought.

Immediately after the invasion, U.S. political leaders, including Republicans, rallied around the president, but soon Republican senators were criticizing Kennedy, saying he should have been tougher. When Dean Rusk testified before a Senate committee on behalf of a new foreign aid bill, he said it would provide a new means to counter growing threats to the internal security of freely elected Latin American governments (existing law forbade the use of U.S.

military aid for internal security).[1]

Punta del Este

The meeting of the Inter-American Economic and Social Council called for by Kennedy in his March 13 speech took place at Punta del Este, Uruguay, from August 5 to August 17, 1961. The meeting resulted in the Charter of Punta del Este, which established the Alliance for Progress. The charter, signed by the United States and all Latin American nations except Cuba, demanded structural changes in Latin American societies of unprecedented breadth and depth. Its objectives were economic progress and social justice with political liberty. Its objectives were extremely ambitious—a rate of economic growth within each Latin American country of at least 2.5 percent per capita per year; "a more equitable distribution of national income"; economic diversification; accelerated industrialization and agricultural production; agrarian reform to transform "unjust structures and systems of land tenure and use"; an end to illiteracy; increased life expectancy; low-cost housing; stable price levels; and support for economic integration. It called for the strengthening of labor unions; cooperatives; and commercial, industrial, and financial institutions. It called for "the social reforms necessary to permit a fair distribution of economic and social progress" achieved under the Alliance. And it called for tax reform, "including fair and adequate taxation of large incomes and real estate." The charter recognized that Latin American nations would need outside capital—at least $20 billion in public development funds in the next ten years.

In response to the claim by Latin Americans that they sold their raw materials cheaply to industrialized countries but paid high prices for those countries' manufactured products, the charter provided that all countries should "eliminate as soon as possible undue protection of the production of basic products," should "seek to end" the special preferences enjoyed by former colonies of the European Common Market countries and Great Britain and by the Soviet bloc (all of which limited Latin America's access to world markets), should promote the processing of their own raw materials by the poor countries, and should work together to stabilize commodity markets. The United States committed itself to participate in an international coffee agreement and to help police it by imposing import quotas.

In addition to the charter, the delegates at Punta del Este signed a separate "Declaration to the Peoples of America." It contained a passage stating that the goals of the Alliance could best be achieved by "free men working through the institution of representative democracy." The United States appears to have insisted on this in order to prevent Cuba from participating in the Alliance. In return, the United States obligated itself to provide "a major part of the minimum of $20 billion, principally in public funds," that Latin America would require over the next ten years.[2]

Punta del Este was regarded, both in the United States and in Latin America outside Cuba, as a triumph. For the first time, the United States had met Latin American demands for help. For the first time, Latin Americans had agreed radically to alter their societies. If implemented fully, the Alliance would forever change, if not end, Latin America's ancient burdens of injustice and inequality, oligarchical landownership and impoverished peasants, repressive and unresponsive government.

But in an institutional sense, the Alliance did not exist; it was not a separate entity like the Peace Corps. Instead, President Kennedy incorporated it into the structure of his new Agency for International Development (AID), which in turn was under the jurisdiction of the State Department; indeed, AID possessed regional and country desk officers parallel to those of State. The Alliance had no director or administrator; instead, it had a coordinator, Ted Moscoso. Moscoso, a man of furious energy, had operated Puerto Rico's remarkably successful Fomento, an agency for industrial development, for Governor Muñoz Marín. His new task was staggering, and so were his difficulties. Few Latin American nations possessed coherent development plans. Many of their statistics were, as the saying went, poetry. Many governments, with money and technical help suddenly available, did not know what to ask for first. Nearly every project, and there were a bewildering variety of them, required feasibility studies. AID policy was constantly being debated inside AID. Should it approve money to meet the payroll of a democratic government, thus propping up democracy? Or build a needed dam in a country ruled by a dictator? Or build low-cost housing, thereby risking an increase in the flow of people to the cities, which were already badly overcrowded? Or create immediate jobs by digging sewers? Or help set up an agrarian reform institute in a nation where agrarian reform was opposed by every powerful segment of society?

Moreover, other arms of the U.S. government created difficulties: the Treasury Department insisted on applying bankers' tests to what Moscoso saw as a social revolution; the Department of Agriculture was eager to look after U.S. beet-sugar producers; the Commerce Department was concerned about U.S. textile mills; the Labor Department opposed "exporting jobs." The Exim Bank, with long experience, tended to stand aside and view the free-for-all with detachment. Many members of Congress were deeply suspicious of the whole enterprise (though, of course, some, like Senator Humphrey, supported it valiantly)—and Congress had to vote the money.

Moscoso's greatest difficulties seemed to be inherent in his position. He felt he needed autonomy. But if Kennedy had given it to him as he requested, Moscoso might have found himself running a foreign policy program of his own and one that might not always coincide with that of the State Department. Secretary Rusk and Under Secretary Ball insisted that Moscoso remain under State's jurisdiction, but neither had much time or attention to devote to Latin American affairs. Moscoso had many confrontations with Rusk and Ball, and his middle-level officers inevitably came into frequent conflict with the middle-level officers of State. Moscoso, facing these many difficulties in an atmosphere of desperate urgency and crisis, frequently found himself repeating Pepe Figueres: "It is one minute to midnight."

*   *   *

President Kennedy's activist policies and activist diplomacy, including the most constantly interventionist Alliance and his frequently interventionist ambassadors, probably helped precipitate and sharpen crises. Indeed, his administration seemed to live in an almost constant series of crises—Guyana, Venezuela, Haiti, the Dominican Republic, Guatemala, Honduras, and, always, Cuba. Moreover, he never resolved the central dilemma of the Alliance for Progress: how to promote rapid change and deal satisfactorily with its consequences. But in his short presidency, he attempted more and accomplished more in that part of the world than any U.S. president since FDR.

Muñoz's Puerto Rico

In many ways, the prototype of President Kennedy's Alliance for Progress was Puerto Rico, which had made enormous economic progress under liberal democracy. The modern history of Puerto Rico began on October 18, 1898, when the Spanish flag was hauled down and the American flag was raised above El Morro, commanding San Juan harbor. In 1900, the U.S. Congress passed the Organic Act of Puerto Rico, providing for a republican form of government with a freely elected legislature and a governor appointed by the president of the United States. In 1917, the U.S. Congress conferred U.S. citizenship upon Puerto Ricans. During the Great Depression, Puerto Rico, with 65 percent of its labor force out of work, became known as "the poorhouse of the Caribbean." President Roosevelt's New Deal programs, extended to Puerto Rico, helped set the country on its feet.

In 1938, a new political organization arose in Puerto Rico led by Luis Muñoz Marín. Muñoz was a shrewd politician, a strong leader, and a liberal who as a young man leaned toward socialism. He had lived in Washington and New York, and he knew many New Dealers, who informed him in advance of grants to Puerto Rico; he was thus able to announce in the Puerto Rican Senate what his friend FDR was giving Puerto Rico. Muñoz and his party dominated Puerto Rican politics from 1940, and when the U.S. Congress amended the Organic Act (1947) to permit Puerto Ricans to elect their own governor, Muñoz became the first elected governor. He launched what he called Operation Bootstrap—a major effort to modernize and develop the Puerto Rican economy—with Teodoro Moscoso as his principal economic advisor. At first, they emphasized land reform and public investment in new industry, a program leaning toward socialism. About 1946, however, they reversed themselves, emphasizing industrialization instead of land reform, and began promoting private, instead of public, investment in industry. The results were phenomenal. Attracted by such incentives as ten-year tax exemptions and cheap labor, U.S. factories and luxury hotels rushed to Puerto Rico. Between 1940 and 1964, net income from manufacturing rose from $27 million to $486 million, trade and commerce from

$26 million to $375 million, and contract construction from $3 million to $144 million.

Despite its name, Operation Bootstrap was not entirely a self-help program. It benefited from the wartime industry boom; the expansion of the world's economy after the war; America's break with Castro's Cuba, which shifted both American tourists and rum production from Cuba to Puerto Rico; the fruition of many long-range New Deal programs; and the expansion of welfare payments and other social programs on the mainland. And, of course, the fact that its goods enter the U.S. mainland duty-free also helped transform Puerto Rico from a sugar plantation colony of the United States into an economy officially designated by the World Bank as a developed economy.[3] Muñoz became an authentic folk hero.

In 1950, Muñoz proposed that the U.S. Congress establish Puerto Rico's status as that of the *Estado Libre Asociado de Puerto Rico*—the "Free Associated State of Puerto Rico"—but it became known in English as the Commonwealth, an unfortunate mistranslation. Congress adopted a compact enabling the people of Puerto Rico to organize a government under a constitution of their own choosing. Under it and accompanying legislation, Puerto Ricans are citizens of the United States. They elect their own governor and legislature; they pay no federal taxes; they receive federal subsidies and substantial other federal revenues from customs duties and excise taxes; they are not subject to compulsory U.S. military service; and they share with the United States a common market, a common defense, a common currency, as well as common citizenship. But they have no voting representation on the floor of the U.S. Congress, and they are subject to most federal laws of general application (although much political and legal controversy surrounds that provision). Theirs is a unique status in the American federal system.

For many years, public opinion in Puerto Rico has been divided on Puerto Rico's status. Muñoz and his party were the preeminent champions of commonwealth. The principal opposition party favored statehood. A small minority preferred independence.

Muñoz maintained that commonwealth preserved political dignity, cultural integrity, and juridical equality; that it gave Puerto Rico substantial economic advantages, authority to manage its own taxes and public spending, as well as U.S. citizensip with all its advantages and protections, including the right to emigrate freely to the mainland. Under commonwealth status, he argued, Puerto Rico had the best of both worlds—national independence and U.S. statehood.

Those in favor of statehood are for the most part conservatives, and those that favor independence are mostly leftists. Muñoz and his party occupy the center-left. But both the statehood and independence parties denounce commonwealth status as nothing more than colonial status. The statehood advocates go on to argue that only statehood can irrevocably guarantee U.S. citizenship, ensure Puerto Rico's continued economic growth through private investment, and give Puerto Rico representation in Congress. The independence advocates simply demand a sovereign republic of Puerto Rico, equal in dignity to any nation on earth.

Muñoz had always argued that commonwealth status enabled Puerto Rico to serve as a bridge between the United States and Latin America. President Kennedy agreed and saw its progress as an ideal model for the Alliance for Progress. Therefore, he put Moscoso at the head of the Alliance and brought other Muñoz men into his administration. Today, in retrospect, many thoughtful Puerto Ricans consider Moscoso's appointment (and those of other Puerto Ricans) a mistake. Other Latin Americans did not like it, regarding Puerto Ricans as colonials; and it gave Puerto Ricans themselves an unreal sense of their importance; it smacked of tokenism.

Beyond that lay more serious flaws in thinking of Puerto Rico's development as a model for the hemisphere. The other nations of the hemisphere did not enjoy Puerto Rico's advantages. They pay tariff duties on goods entering the United States; they bear the burden of their own defense; they pay for their own welfare systems; their unemployed cannot emigrate freely to the U.S.; and so on—as sovereign nations, they differed so greatly from Puerto Rico that comparisons were almost meaningless. Trinidad-Tobago carried out a program between 1950 and 1956 modeled on Puerto Rico's; it did not work. Indeed, if anything, it increased the visible unemployment, for it drew workers from farm to city, thereby raising the welfare load. (Officially, unemployment increased from 6 percent in 1956 to 15 percent in 1966.) As a result, officials in Trinidad-Tobago—and Jamaica and other Caribbean countries—concluded that the Puerto Rican system was useless.

Furthermore, as more time passed, it has become clear that

Operation Bootstrap really was not a magic cure-all even for Puerto Rico. Most of the new industries are capital-intensive; they must automate in order to compete in world markets and, therefore, create relatively few jobs. And having put its emphasis on industry, not agriculture, Puerto Rico has large numbers of unemployed unskilled workers for whom factories have no use. Puerto Rico suffers high chronic unemployment (nearly 30 percent in 1975). Nearly half the population is eligible for food stamps. And about a million Puerto Ricans have moved to the mainland, a third as many as live on the island.

In 1962, Muñoz Marín proposed certain changes in the commonwealth relationship: a plebiscite to end accusations that commonwealth was not the free choice of the Puerto Rican people and an end to any restrictions on Puerto Rico's complete governmental power that were not indispensable. President Kennedy was receptive, and Congress created a thirteen-member U.S.-Puerto Rico Commission on the Status of Puerto Rico. The commission's most important conclusion was that all three status alternatives— commonwealth, statehood, independence—"are valid and confer upon the people of Puerto Rico equal dignity." The commission expressed no preference among them but said the choice belonged to the people of Puerto Rico.

Over objections of the statehood and independence leaders, a plebiscite was held on July 23, 1967. Commonwealth won with 60.5 percent of the vote. Statehood got 38.9 percent. Independence leaders had instructed their followers to boycott the election. (Most authorities at the time guessed that independence would have received about 10 percent or 12 percent without the boycott.) After the plebiscite, Muñoz said that "the century-long debate about political status has ended." Nobody took him seriously. They were right—status is the overriding issue in Puerto Rico to this day, and agitation over it is increasing if anything. Although previous presidents had consistently taken the position that the Puerto Ricans' status was theirs to decide, President Ford, shortly before leaving office, issued an unexpected unilateral statement favoring statehood. It angered about half the Puerto Rican political leaders and embarrassed the other half. It might prove to be a mischievous statement, for it could destroy the centrist commonwealth position and polarize Puerto Rico between statehooders and *independentistas,* two groups not known for their moderation. If things were to go in that direction, one could not even rule out the possibility that what has been essentially a peaceable people living together could be transformed into two hostile and even violent camps.

Guyana, Jagan, and Burnham

U.S. Caribbean policy, which had dealt primarily with Spanish-speaking mestizo nations during Kennedy's administration, had to begin to deal also with the English-speaking black nations—British colonies now gaining independence. The British Commonwealth Caribbean, covering 105,000 square miles and containing about 4.5 million people, was bounded by the Bahamas on the north, Guyana on the south (on the South American mainland), Barbados on the east, and British Honduras, or Belize, on the west. The area was dominated by Jamaica, the largest British island, just ninety miles below Castro's Cuba, and by Trinidad-Tobago, only ten miles north of Venezuela, and it also included a number of islands in the Lesser Antilles—Antigua, Dominica, Grenada, St. Lucia, Montserrat, and so on. These countries vary greatly in size, population, and natural resources—Jamaica was rich with bauxite, the Bahamas produced little but salt. Nearly all depended heavily on the tourist industry. And most were poor.

The native political leaders who arose as the colonial period drew to a close were by and large leftist—socialists—many of them educated at the London School of Economics, men whose power base lay in the local trade union movement. Manley and Bustamante of Jamaica, Jagan and Burnham of Guyana, and Eric Williams of Trinidad-Tobago gained political leadership while their countries were still colonies, gained political power after independence, and were on hand in Kennedy's time (and some are still in power).

During and after World War II, Great Britain gave the Caribbean commonwealth countries increasing amounts of self-government. In 1958, it formed most of them into the West Indies Federation, which was supported by the United States. But in 1961, Jamaica pulled out; the federation collapsed and with it collapsed U.S. policy toward the black English-speaking Caribbean. Neither Kennedy nor any of his successors ever devised a coherent policy toward the area, which was moving toward independence at an uneven pace. Jamaica and Trinidad-Tobago became independent in 1962 without difficulty;

but Guyana stumbled toward independence amid violence. It was to Guyana that President Kennedy had to address himself in 1961 and to the end of his life.

Guyana is a huge (83,000 square miles), thinly populated country. It is situated on the north coast of South America, but it faces the Caribbean. It has no land route from its capital to its southern neighbor Brazil, its trade and political ties are to the Caribbean nations, its leaders went to school with theirs, and it is in fact a sugar-and-bauxite island surrounded on three sides by land. Most Guyanese live in or near Georgetown, the capital, on a narrow swampy coastal plain protected from the sea only by a leaky dike. The hinterland is vast jungle and savannah, nearly empty. The Guyanese economy was until the 1970s run on the ancient plantation system—absentee-owned sugar plantations run from London, and absentee-owned bauxite mines run from North America. Before independence, it was British Guiana, one of the three Guianas; the others are French Guiana, known mainly for its infamous Devil's Island, and Surinam, formerly Dutch Guiana, which borders Guyana on the east and claims certain Guyanese territory. Guyana's neighbor on the west is Venezuela, which has for years claimed about five-eighths of Guyana's territory.

A Guyanese poet once wrote, "I come from the nigger yard of yesterday." The issues of race and slavery are central to the politics of Guyana. Guyana was a slave nation; one of its national heroes was the leader of a slave rebellion in 1763 (before Haiti's). After Britain abolished the slave trade, Caribbean planters began importing indentured workers from India. Between 1838 and 1924, 238,000 Indians were shipped into Guyana; and to them were added other Asiatics. Today, the population of Guyana is about 50 percent East Indian, 30 percent Negro, and the rest other or mixed (including about 4 percent aboriginal Amerindians in the jungle).

In 1953, Britain gave Guyana not independence but an advanced constitution including universal adult suffrage. In the election that year, the People's Progressive party emerged as the dominant party; it was led by Cheddi Jagan, an East Indian dentist educated in the United States, who became premier, and Forbes Burnham, a Negro lawyer educated in England and usually considered a socialist, who became minister of education. Britain expected colonial politicians to behave in a nationalist and leftist manner, to win power under new constitutions, then, upon assuming the burdens of office, to become moderates and cooperate with British officials and business-men. This was the road taken by Bustamante and Manley in Jamaica, Grantley Adams in Barbados, and Nkrumah in Ghana. But Jagan and Burnham rejected it and, from the outset, employed the rhetoric of Marxism, denouncing imperialism and proclaiming themselves revolutionaries. The British government became alarmed, and so did the Eisenhower administration. When Jagan and Burnham were elected, the Eisenhower administration, already wondering what to do about the Arbenz regime in Guatemala, began to press the British to act against the Jagan-Burnham government. The administration feared interference with U.S.-owned bauxite operations, and even more, it feared the specter of a communist state in the Caribbean. After six months, when the Jagan-Burnham government seemed clearly turning far left, the British landed troops and expelled the government, saying it planned to turn British Guiana into "a totalitarian state dominated by communist ideas." Looking back, Jagan said he had been guilty of "deviations to the left," had overestimated his party's revolutionary power; and he quoted Stalin and Mao to sustain that analysis.

As joint party leaders, Jagan and Burnham had complemented each other: Jagan commanded the loyalty of the East Indian majority, many of them rural field workers, and Burnham commanded the loyalty of the black—and urban—minority. Out of power, they split and became rivals. From that time to the present, Guyana politics has divided dangerously along almost rigid racial lines.

On August 21, 1961, seven months after President Kennedy was inaugurated, elections were to be held in Guyana. As the day approached, interest—and concern—rose in the United States. Jagan won twenty of the thirty-five seats in the lower house but only narrowly defeated Burnham in the popular vote. After the election, Jagan announced that, although he would seek development aid from the United States and Britain, he would accept aid from the Soviet Union.

The Kennedy administration was anticolonialist and sympathetic to national aspirations to independence, even to young revolution-aries. State Department specialists felt that aid might keep Jagan out of the Soviet orbit and provided tentatively for about $5 million in aid for Guyana. But at the same time, the Kennedy administration recognized the strategic danger to the United States and the domestic political danger to Kennedy if Jagan later turned out to be a disciplined communist.

Jagan came to the United States, and in public appearances refused to deny he was a communist, refused to say anything critical about the Soviet Union, but said that socialism was a better system than capitalism for Guyana and that "active neutralism" was Guyana's best foreign policy. Later, when Jagan and Kennedy met, Jagan outlined his plans for industrializing Guyana under socialism. He claimed to be committed to parliamentary government and nationalism—and asked for about $40 million in aid, a huge sum. Pressed on communism, he dissembled. Kennedy told him we were not crusading for private enterprise, that the primary purpose of our aid was national independence, and that its secondary purpose, where possible, was to encourage individual and political freedom. Kennedy explained that our only condition for nationalization was compensation. Jagan asked whether the United States would regard a trade agreement with the Soviet Union as an unfriendly act; Kennedy said a simple trade agreement was one thing but a relationship that resulted in economic dependence was another. Kennedy refused to give him an aid commitment. Privately, Kennedy thought that Jagan, faced with racial tensions and high unemployment and a stagnant economy, could not develop his country through a parliamentary system. Jagan went home and reported to his legislature that the United States had refused his request for aid, a move some Washington officials thought was inspired by the hope of offers of communist help. Although the British urged cooperation and forbearance—they preferred Jagan to Burnham—Kennedy, fearing that support for Jagan might endanger the whole aid program in Congress, turned his back on Jagan.

In Guyana, Jagan launched an economic program intended to mobilize Guyana's own resources to develop the nation. It quickly resulted in disaster. Prices skyrocketed, business firms cut wages and laid off workers, and unemployment soared. The trade unions led by Burnham denounced his program as "a scheme to tax the poor" and launched a general strike. Rioting broke out, spread, and polarized racially, leaving several people dead and many injured and Georgetown burned. Jagan asked for British troops. They came and temporarily restored order, but frequently, over the next two years, rioting flared up, and at times Guyana seemed on the brink of racial civil war. The result was a cynical political alliance between Burnham and a right-wing party to gain a plurality.

The United States, searching for an alternative to Jagan, nervously began urging Britain to delay Guyana's independence (to the amusement of the British, whom Washington had been prodding to grant independence everywhere ever since the war). The alternative was obvious—Burnham. He visited Washington in May 1962 (one may surmise he was secretly invited), and met with Arthur Schlesinger. Schlesinger reported to Kennedy that Burnham belonged firmly to the noncommunist left. Schlesinger felt that Burnham would cause us far fewer problems than Jagan, especially if he would adopt a multiracial policy. The United States set sail with Burnham.

Long before President Kennedy took office, the AFL-CIO had been active in Latin America through its Inter-American Regional Organization of Workers (ORIT) and its American Institute for Free Labor Development (AIFLD). AIFLD became an important arm of the Alliance for Progress and received foreign aid money from the U.S. government. In some countries, it also became a conduit and front for the CIA. Now, in Guyana, it launched a campaign to overthrow Cheddi Jagan. It worked closely with Burnham's party and with its ORIT affiliate in Guyana, largely urban and black. When Jagan introduced a labor relations bill, the ORIT affiliate denounced it as a "blueprint for the end of trade union freedom" and called a general strike. Burnham declared that Jagan was trying to turn Guyana into a "Soviet satellite." Race riots began again. Jagan blamed Burnham, his rightist ally, big business, the press, British intelligence, and the CIA.

The CIA probably paid out about $1.2 million in strike pay to bring down Jagan; the AFL-CIO openly boasted of its role. Kennedy and his advisers were no different in some respects from other presidents and their staffs: they feared that a communist takeover in Guyana could defeat Kennedy in his reelection bid. Prime Minister Macmillan, as a result of a visit by President Kennedy, agreed to delay Guyana's independence beyond the American election, using the general strike as an excuse. That fall, the British government, at America's urging, gave Burnham what he wanted: a new election based on proportional representation so rigged that it almost ensured Jagan's defeat. Sure enough, although Jagan's party received nearly

46 percent of the popular vote, Burnham became prime minister in a coalition with the right-wing party. When Guyana finally became independent in 1966, Burnham was prime minister; and he has remained prime minister to this day. He has kept power by electoral fraud and by pursuit of an independent left, nationalist course.

The history of the Kennedy administration's actions in Guyana was not too different from that of earlier administrations elsewhere that had earned us enmity. It was a history of intervention: intervention in behalf of liberal Guyanese democracy, in behalf of our own national political-strategic interests as the Kennedy administration saw them, and in behalf of the domestic political interests of the administration. Thus, although we were attempting to build a new relationship with the Caribbean nations through the Alliance, we were jeopardizing that relationship by acting in old ways.

Betancourt and Venezuela

Liberal democracy, always in short supply in the Caribbean, appeared to be gaining a foothold in 1961. Such British Commonwealth territories as Guyana and Jamaica seemed to be developing two-party systems. Honduras had elected a Liberal party president to a six-year term in 1957. Colombian politicians had worked out a system of rotating the presidency. Puerto Rico had a stable working democratic system, as did Costa Rica. Costa Rica, indeed, has long been considered the most fertile soil in the Caribbean for democracy, largely because of its high rate of literacy and its historical legacy: it lay outside the mainstream of the Spanish Captaincy General, contained no large Indian population the Spaniards could enslave, and no gold or silver Spanish captains could exploit. It was settled by Spanish farmers. Later, when they began to export coffee, the English came, bringing with them British traditions, instead of the authoritarian Spanish tradition of a powerful military. The Costa Ricans held no slaves. They spent public money on education, not the military, and small parcels of land were standard. Thus, Costa Rica had no abysmally deprived class that needed to be repressed to maintain the power of the wealthy. A Costa Rican saying has it: "The bigger the *fincas,* the bigger the army"—the Latin American army exists to protect the large landowners from the dispossessed. When Pepe Figueres came to power, he abolished the army and turned the *fortaleza* into a museum. Costa Rica became almost aggressive about its democracy and enjoyed honoring a visiting foreign military man with a parade of schoolchildren carrying flowers. Figueres and the Costa Rican ambassador to the United States maintained unusually close ties with the Kennedy administration.

But Costa Rica is an exception. When Trujillo was assassinated in May 1961, Kennedy decided to try to establish a democratic system in the stony soil of the Dominican Republic. After all, democracy was what the Alliance for Progress was all about. And in the view of the Kennedy administration, the major testing ground for democracy in the Caribbean was Venezuela.

Venezuela, the biggest and richest country in the Caribbean, had been governed during most of this century by military dictators. Its modern political history began in the late 1930s and early 1940s, after the death of the tyrant Gómez, when COPEI and AD, the two parties that have dominated modern Venezuela, arose.[4] Rómulo Betancourt of AD was elected to a five-year term in 1958. Betancourt had learned from earlier experience not to move so fast as to alarm the military. Aside from putting an end to foreign oil concessions—a liberal gesture that was rather meaningless since the dictators had already given away most of the country's oil—he tried to steer a left-center gradualist course. About once a week, he visited a military barracks and, in general, did as much as he could to cultivate the military. He was a liberal and a democrat but not a rigid ideologue. Rather, he was a pragmatic, tough, and shrewd politician and, in his later years, a statesman of great stature.

Betancourt had been in office nearly two years when President Kennedy came to power. He was governing by means of an uneasy coalition. In 1960, both Castro and Trujillo had sent armed agents to kill him. The Declaration of San José that year, which, even though it did not condemn Cuba, reaffirmed that the inter-American system was "incompatible with any form of totalitarianism," made serious trouble in Venezuela—street riots began in Caracas, leftists contrasted the slow pace of Betancourt's social reforms to Castro's and denounced Betancourt for his move to attract foreign capital, and his foreign minister resigned, taking his leftist party out of Betancourt's coalition. At the same time, foreign investors, fearing Betancourt's socialist principles, were taking capital out of the country. The result was a recession that coincided with a slump in the world market for oil. Betancourt's program of school, housing, and road construction, while too modest to please the left, was adding to inflationary pressures.

Betancourt called out the troops to stop the riots, warned that the "era of leniency" was over, partially suspended constitutional guarantees, and appealed for help, indicating Venezuela needed an immediate loan from the United States of $300 million. Venezuela had had a low loan priority because of its oil riches; but now, with Kennedy coming to power, Venezuela was seen as the keystone of Caribbean democracy, crucial in the effort to stop the spread of Castro's influence. Therefore, in May 1961, the IADB approved the first development loan to Venezuela; more followed. During the three years between 1962 and 1965, the Caribbean countries in our study received a total of $1,206.6 million (compared to $712.8 million in the *eight* years from 1953 to 1961); of that, $450.6 million went to Venezuela (compared to $114.1 million from 1953 to 1961).

President Kennedy appointed Teodoro Moscoso his first ambassador to Venezuela. At the time, it was considered a brilliant appointment and clear evidence of the importance Kennedy attached to Betancourt's success, for Moscoso enjoyed great prestige in the Caribbean. Only later did we realize that much of Latin America felt Puerto Ricans were nothing more than our colonial lackeys.

When after the Bay of Pigs Kennedy sent Adlai Stevenson, his ambassador to the United Nations, to Latin America to repair our reputation, Stevenson stopped in Caracas. Not even Kennedy stood higher in Latin American esteem than Stevenson. Moscoso planned a cocktail party for Stevenson, and Betancourt, missing no opportunity, asked Moscoso to invite General Antonio Briceno Linares, Betancourt's defense minister, saying that Briceno worshipped Stevenson. Moscoso invited Briceno to arrive an hour before the other guests. Stevenson charmed Briceno, and, briefed by Moscoso, told Briceno that, as military commander, he and he alone stood sentinel at the gate of Venezuelan democracy. Subsequently, Stevenson sent a letter to Briceno, putting it all in writing. A year or two later, the general told Moscoso that he still carried Stevenson's letter next to this heart, and he pulled it out of his pocket, tattered and worn, and displayed it proudly. It may be taken as a sample of Kennedy's skill, of Stevenson's effectiveness, of Betancourt's and Moscoso's political sagacity, and of the importance of personal gestures in Latin American diplomacy. At the same time, one should not overestimate the importance of symbolism—or, for that matter the importance of Kennedy's role in propping up Betancourt. Local political events occur largely for local reasons, and what the United States can do to influence their course and outcome is severely limited. True, General Briceno treasured Stevenson's letter; but had subsequent Venezuelan political events made him feel obliged to overthrow Betancourt, he would have done it and, albeit regretfully, ceased to carry Stevenson's letter next to his heart. Just so, in 1962 the present author, as Kennedy's ambassador to the Dominican Republic, enjoyed excellent relations with the provisional government and its wholehearted cooperation with the Alliance for Progress; but when a shift in Kennedy's worldwide sugar policy had the unintended effect of threatening the preferential U.S. quota for Dominican sugar, the provisional government instantly announced a strike against the Alliance, shut down all its projects, and threatened to return its loans.

* * *

By the fall of 1961, Betancourt's success in putting down leftist disturbances encouraged him to take a stronger stand on Cuba. He expressed support for collective action on Cuba, and Venezuela became the tenth Latin American country to break diplomatic relations with Cuba. Panama and Colombia did so a little later, and Colombia called for a meeting of foreign ministers. American leaders did not agree on a course of action: deLesseps Morrison, our ambassador to the OAS, believed U.S. public opinion demanded strong action against Castro; thus he was determined to press for a meeting under the Rio Treaty. Adlai Stevenson feared that invoking the Rio Treaty would divide the hemisphere and favored invoking the milder Act of Bogotá. The State Department sided with Stevenson. But at a preliminary OAS meeting, Morrison exceeded his instructions and managed to push through a Rio Treaty resolution—which cost the support of three of the most important powers in Latin America: Argentina, Brazil, and Mexico. The incident illustrates the two pressures pushing the U.S. hemisphere policy in opposite directions. On the one hand, domestic public opinion inside the United States demanded strong action against Castro (at least in the view of Morrison and other politicians), and, on the other hand, domestic public opinion in Latin American nations sympathized with Castro (at least in the view of *their* political leaders).

On December 5, 1961, the day after the OAS vote, the State Department announced that President and Mrs. Kennedy would visit Venezuela and Colombia, stopping in Puerto Rico to "dramatize and spotlight" the Alliance for Progress. Undoubtedly, those countries were chosen because they best represented the Alliance's purposes—economic and social progress under democracy, plus a firm political stand against Castro.

In Caracas, encouraged by Castro, leftists demonstrated against the visit, and a student was shot. Leftists scrawled on walls, "Kennedy, No," to which their opponents replied by scrawling on the walls, "Jackie, Sí." Terrorists seized a radio station briefly and broadcast a protest against the visit. The Venezuelan government jailed some 2,000 as possible troublemakers. The State Department worried about the risk to the Kennedys and ordered unusual security precautions. When the Kennedys drove through the streets of Caracas, a double cordon of soldiers stood with guns turned on the spectators. The precautions proved unnecessary. Kennedy spoke at a ceremony distributing land to eighty-six families, and Mrs. Kennedy said a few words in Spanish. Kennedy and Betancourt issued a joint communiqué, which barely mentioned Cuba ("confidence that freedom will prevail in all American countries") but which enlarged upon Venezuela's economic needs and plans for development. When the Kennedys' motorcade departed for the airport, people lined the streets and waved goodbye from the same places from which they had mobbed Nixon three years earlier. In Colombia, where enthusiastic crowds also lined the streets, President Lleras Camargo told Kennedy, "Do you know why those workers and *campesinos* are cheering you like that? It's because they believe you are on their side." The trip was a triumph, as was his trip the next year to Mexico City and his trip the following year—the last of his life—to Costa Rica. Always he spoke of the democratic revolution; in private, he often wondered how he could help strengthen democratic governments.

Punta II (Cuba)

The meeting of foreign ministers on Cuba was to convene on January 22, 1962, at Punta del Este. The United States thought the economic conference at Punta del Este (Punta I), which established the Alliance, was a necessary preliminary to collective political action against Cuba. But even with the successful outcome of Punta I, the administration's soundings before Punta II were not encouraging. Moreover, Kennedy's advisers were once more divided. DeLesseps Morrison and others favored a hard line: OAS diplomatic and economic sanctions against Castro at least as stringent as those of the OAS had imposed on Trujillo. Stevenson had come back from his tour after the Bay of Pigs convinced that collective action against Castro would be meaningless unless supported by two of the three biggest powers—Argentina, Brazil, and Mexico. Morrison pushed the hard line at a policy meeting; he had fourteen votes in support of such sanctions—a bare two-thirds. Kennedy wanted more support and agreed with Richard Goodwin, who argued we should not sacrifice substantial consensus for hard symbolic action.

At Punta del Este, the big Latin American delegations maintained their opposition to punitive action against Cuba, but Colombia and the Central American states asked for, at least, Cuba's suspension from the OAS. The U.S. delegation soon abandoned all hope of getting a mandatory break in diplomatic and economic relations, but the American congressional delegates let it be known that Congress could hardly be expected to look favorably on Alliance aid for countries that refused to face up squarely to Castro. The United States, however, did not issue ultimatums, and it showed flexibility in negotiation. At a critical point, the United States (perhaps acting through Rusk himself and at least with his approval) bought Haiti's vote with a promise of $6 million to enlarge the airport at Port-au-Prince.

The resolution that was finally adopted fourteen to one, with Argentina, Bolivia, Brazil, Chile, Ecuador, and Mexico abstaining, declared that Cuba by its acts had "voluntarily placed itself outside the inter-American system" and went on to resolve that any member's adherence to Marxism-Leninism was "incompatible with the inter-American system." Cuba was, therefore, excluded. The expulsion satisfied the American public and, therefore, the congressional members of the delegation, who went home filled with praise for Rusk. It was a good example of how executive branch policymakers must constantly take into account the Congress, whose members, in turn, take into account domestic public opinion.

Trujillo's Heirs

The odious tyranny of Generalissimo Rafael Leonidas Trujillo y Molina came to an end the night of May 30, 1961. The Dominican dictator was assassinated four months after President Kennedy came to power. Rumors in the Dominican Republic then, and more recently in the United States, said that the CIA had had him killed, but that was not true, so far as this author knows.[5] The rumors had a certain plausibility—the United States supported the OAS sanctions, which hurt Trujillo politically; the Kennedy administration seemed intent on ending the period symbolized by Vice-President Nixon's public embrace of Trujillo; Kennedy had publicly expressed the hope that the Dominican people would soon rejoin the society of the free; certain high CIA officials concerned with Latin America were anti-Trujillo liberals; and the philosophy behind the Alliance for Progress, with its emphasis on democracy and reform, was contrary to Trujillo's. During the months before the assassination, there had been several plots to kill Trujillo, and the CIA may have been involved in one or more of them. But the men who killed Trujillo had no need of such help; some of them were officers in Trujillo's own military, and one was chief of his armed forces. Whatever the CIA may have attempted, the men who actually killed Trujillo, and those who plotted with them, did it themselves.[6]

Trujillo came to power in 1930. Critics of the United States believe he came to power because of the United States occupation of the Dominican Republic in the 1920s, and it is true that Trujillo was part of the U.S.-controlled Dominican Constabulary and that, after the marines departed, he became commandant of the Constabulary and then the nation's dictator—just as, in Nicaragua, Somoza emerged from our occupation. But Trujillo became dictator through a failure of Dominican politics, not through our intervention. And he remained in power for thirty-one years, longer than any other modern dictator except Salazar of Portugal. The Dominican Republic under Trujillo was a totalitarian state complete with torture chambers, population checkpoints, concentration camps, wiretaps, and murder factories. When he died, he left a looted treasury, thousands of dead enemies, and a whole generation that had never known any other system. Indeed, the Dominican Republic has enjoyed only about a dozen years of representative democracy. The country had been occupied by Haiti from 1822 to 1844, and, as noted, by the United States Marines from 1916 to 1924. Its history between occupations was little more than a series of coups, countercoups, dictatorships, and revolutions. It had 123 rulers before Trujillo, nearly all tyrannical. It was not a promising soil for democracy.

The United States had long had a special relationship with the Dominican Republic. It was close to us geographically and heavily dependent on us economically; we had occupied it militarily; and only the U.S. Senate had prevented the Grant administration from annexing it. At times, we had smiled on Trujillo (during World War II, for the sake of wartime hemispheric unity), and at times, we had frowned on him (after his kidnap and murder of a professor exiled in New York and after his attempt to murder Betancourt).

After Trujillo's fall, the Kennedy administration saw three possible directions for Dominican government to take: a communist takeover; a continuation of the dictatorship by Trujillo's son, brothers, and other heirs; or some form of representative democracy. From Kennedy's standpoint, the worst would be communist takeover and the best representative democracy. If left alone, however, it seemed likely that there would be a restoration of Trujillo family power, with a possibility of a later communist takeover. Thus, President Kennedy decided to try to help establish representative democracy. He sent an emissary to try to negotiate the Trujillos out, and when that met with only partial success, he sent the U.S. fleet to throw them out; then his emissaries helped set up a seven-man provisional government called the Council of State. Kennedy was demonstrating America's support for freedom after Trujillo's tyranny. He wanted to help build a "showcase for democracy" next door to Castro's Cuba.

But although, as far as one could tell, the Dominican people wanted democracy, they had no experience of democracy, and the seven members of the Council of State had almost no experience in government. They had but a single civil servant to aid them, and they did not have a popular mandate. The council wanted to act as if it were a caretaker government and hang on until elections could be held rather than govern. But in the wake of Trujillo's fall, a political hurricane was sweeping the Dominican Republic—caretaking was impossible.

Under President Kennedy, our diplomats generally were activist (or, in the view of more traditional diplomats, outrageously interventionist), and nowhere were they more so than in the Dominican Republic. We went well beyond giving the Republic money (though our loans and grants far exceeded previous U.S. aid to Trujillo). The Republic contained a number of trained communist agents financed by the Soviet Union or Cuba. They organized and paid thieves and thugs to riot; we organized counterriots. They infiltrated the nascent Dominican labor movement: we also infiltrated it. They tried to subvert political parties; so did we. But we did more than match the communist moves. We trained the Dominican police to control rioters.[7] We worked with and advised the political parties that were emerging. We gave advice to the Council of State, helped it develop AID programs, and then showed it how to run them. We invented public works programs to reduce unemployment, which approached 30 percent, and thus to quiet unrest. We pressed the Council of State, some of whose members were related to the landed oligarchy of the Dominican Republic, to undertake far-reaching social, political, and economic reforms. When an agrarian reform measure divided the council three to three with one abstention, President Kennedy's press secretary, on a holiday in the Republic, was asked to take the swing vote man aside at a cocktail party and tell him, "President Kennedy wants this bill." He got it. We repeatedly warned the Dominican military, growing restless at all this democracy and reform and threatening to overthrow the council and take power for itself, that the United States "would find it extremely difficult to recognize and almost impossible to assist any regime which took power by force or threats of force." To emphasize our position, we brought, at various times, aircraft carriers or high-ranking U.S. generals to the Republic to impress upon the Dominican military our support of the civilian Council of State. We persuaded the council to invite the OAS to supervise, or at least observe, the elections, and we pressed the council to hold elections on schedule.

The council never became a strong government, but it gave the Dominican people a year of peace and personal freedom, laying the groundwork for structural reform. On December 20, 1962, the first free election in the Dominican Republic in thirty-eight years was held. Juan Bosch, a noncommunist leftist, was overwhelmingly elected president.

During the year of the Council of State, we had pursued three policy objectives: to help keep the council in power, to help hold free elections, and to help get the winner into the palace alive. We accomplished all three. After Bosch's election, our policy objectives were to help him complete the peaceful democratic revolution he had promised and to help him serve out his elected term. We failed in both. Bosch was overthrown by a military coup after only seven months. It was a serious blow to American prestige, and we were powerless to prevent it. Its causes lay in Dominican politics.

Bosch took office with many things in his favor. He had been given a mandate to make a peaceful revolution; he was supported by a powerful party machine and enormous international goodwill— Betancourt, Figueres, Muñoz Marín, Villeda Morales of Honduras, Bustamante of Jamaica; indeed, he had a chance to become the leader of the noncommunist left of the Caribbean. And he had the wholehearted support of the U.S. government. But he also had great handicaps: the history of the Dominican Republic, which had no democratic traditions and the terrible legacy of Trujillo, as well as all the problems the Council of State had not tried to deal with, such as serious economic difficulties. He also faced the intransigent opposition of the political leaders he had defeated, of much of the oligarchy, and nearly all the rising middle-class business people, as well as the grave suspicions of elements of the church and military. That is, he faced the intransigent opposition or grave suspicion of virtually the entire Dominican power structure, for between elections the support of the Dominican masses counts for little. Furthermore, his landslide had destroyed the opposition political parties, making the military the most likely opposition.

Some of Bosch's problems were personal. The twenty-odd years he had spent in the conspiratorial world of exile politics had ill prepared him for the presidency; he entered the palace without plans or program. Bosch, a writer by profession, was difficult, moody, sometimes reckless, and vain. Moreover, he was obliged to govern almost single-handedly—for his election had been truly revolutionary. It had brought to rule a group of people who had no experience at governing. Finally, he made mistakes. He spent his first six weeks in office trying vainly to balance the budget. He wasted more than a month in almost going to war with Haiti. Under leftist pressure, he permitted Dominicans to travel to Castro's Cuba, and he refused to close a school run by a communist. Although those activities were of little real importance, they did give Bosch's enemies on the right a pretext to attack him.

At the end of his first hundred days, the voters who had elected him were asking: where's the revolution? Unemployment was, if anything, worse. His agrarian reform was stalled. He had no money, no programs, almost no government. By the end of June 1962, it appeared he would fail.

Until then, he had not asked us for help because he wished to maintain his independence, but now he asked. We responded with $8 million in surplus rice and corn, a commitment to bring in experts to start planning a vast river-valley development, public statements reaffirming our support of his government (thus putting President Kennedy's own prestige on the line), and private and repeated warnings to the Dominican military not to attempt to overthrow him.

By the end of summer, he has lost the support of everyone but a few members of the oligarchy, the small, Moscow-directed Communist party, and the U.S. embassy. The business middle class had been galvanized into open opposition (along with the political right) by two land reform bills he introduced that threatened property rights; they now began a general strike against him. The military, judging that Bosch had lost his broad base of popular support, overthrew him on September 25, 1963. The military had judged correctly: nobody went into the streets to object to the coup.

President Kennedy took a hard line against the coup. Then, a few days later, in Honduras, the military overthrew the liberal, elected president, Villeda Morales, to prevent a forthcoming election. Kennedy, fearing a chain reaction throughout Latin America, especially in Venezuela, where Betancourt's term was ending and new elections were scheduled, instructed Rusk to issue a statement:

> We view the recent military *coups* in the Dominican Republic and Honduras with the utmost gravity. The establishment and maintenance of representative and constitutional government is an essential element of the Alliance for Progress. Stable and effective government, responsive to the popular will, is a critical factor in the attainment of social and economic

progress.

Under existing conditions in the Dominican Republic and Honduras there is no opportunity for effective collaboration by the United States under the Alliance for Progress or for normalization of diplomatic relations. Accordingly, we have stopped all economic and military aid to these countries and have commenced an orderly reassignment of the personnel involved.

Some congressmen appeared pleased by the coup against Bosch, thinking it might have forestalled a communist takeover in the Republic. On the other hand, such senators as Hubert Humphrey (D.-Minn.) and Jacob Javits (R.-N.Y.) denounced the coup, Senator Ernest Gruening (D.-Alaska) proposed that the United States send a destroyer to intercept the Dominican ship carrying Bosch into exile and take him back to the palace, and Senator Wayne Morse (D.-Ore.) urged that we call an immediate meeting of foreign ministers of the OAS to consider collective measures, not excluding military measures, to restore Bosch to power.

The Dominican and Honduran military coups, the fifth and sixth against governments cooperating with the Alliance for Progress, called into question the workability, if not the wisdom, of the Alliance. Edwin Martin, assistant secretary for ARA, wrote, "By tradition and conviction as well as a matter of policy, the United States opposes the overthrow of constitutional and popular democratic governments anywhere," especially Latin America. But, he went on, sometimes the military overthrew dictators, such as Perón; sometimes military-controlled governments were "reform" governments; and the United States could not, as a practical matter, "create effective democracy by keeping a man in office through use of economic pressure or even military force when his own people are not willing to fight to defend him." Senator Morse said this view "undercuts and destroys" the Alliance's basic premise. President Kennedy, however, denied that Martin's views represented a policy reversal and said flatly that "we are opposed to military coups." Furthermore, he said he was satisfied we had done everything possible short of using force to prevent the Dominican and Honduran coups.

In the ensuing weeks, the Kennedy administration withheld

diplomatic recognition from the civilian triumvirate installed by the Dominican military. It tried to persuade other countries to do the same and, by other means, tried to pressure the regime to return to at least some semblance of constitutionality. The regime defied us. When we looked at the situation more closely, we began to fear that a collapse of the triumvirate might bring back a harsh military dictatorship; we feared a communist uprising; and we feared we might encourage young noncommunist leftists to fight and die uselessly. Other nations, including Great Britain, were pressing us to recognize the triumvirate. We began to fear that we would suffer a diplomatic defeat and have to recognize the government. The triumvirate, feeling its own prestige committed and facing the military's guns, grew increasingly stubborn. Our power was narrowly limited. A polarization process had begun in the Republic, with leftist opponents of the regime taking to the hills and the military hunting them down. This seemed to be leading to guerrilla warfare and military dictatorship. President Kennedy prepared to grant recognition if the regime would establish a timetable for new elections, but he was assassinated before he could do so. President Johnson's advisors feared that if he made Dominican recognition his first act, it might be misunderstood as a policy shift to the right. He therefore did not recognize the new regime until December 12.

In retrospect, it appears that in the Dominican Republic the United States undertook tasks beyond its power. We could not establish a lasting democratic system from the ruins of tyranny, and we could not maintain in office an elected president who had lost the support of his own people. We might have been wiser, when Trujillo fell, to have asked the OAS to put the Dominican Republic into some sort of OAS trusteeship until free elections could be held. But the OAS had to be persuaded even to observe the 1962 Dominican elections; it would almost surely have recoiled with horror from the prospect of trusteeship.

United States policy toward the Dominican Republic during the last months of the Eisenhower administration and throughout the Kennedy administration should hearten those American liberals who complain that the United States always supports dictators. Under Eisenhower, we supported the OAS sanctions against Trujillo, sanctions that caused him many problems. Under Kennedy, we sent the fleet to intervene against a continuation of his dictatorship, and we supported the Council of State and President Bosch against threats from both left and right, all at considerable cost in effort, money, and political risk. Liberals complain that we invariably support such men as Chiang, Batista, Diem, Thieu, Rhee, Trujillo, and Duvalier. They are wrong. At times, we do support such people, perhaps all too often, but by no means invariably. Our policies in the Dominican Republic in those years may have been too interventionist, and ultimately they failed. Yet they did the United States much credit. And so did our policies during those same years toward the dictator of Haiti, François Duvalier.

Duvalier of Haiti

Haiti, which shares the doomed island of Hispaniola with the Dominican Republic, possesses a people even more wretched, a landscape even more impoverished, and a history of despotism even more awful. Black and French-speaking, the Haitian people have always been isolated. While in their arts they show great creativity, in other respects they live half-savage lives of hunger, disease, ignorance, and voodoo superstition that make theirs the only lives in the Western Hemisphere comparable to the worst in Africa.

Throughout its history Haiti's politics has been almost without exception a politics of terror and murder. François Duvalier, called "Papa Doc," became president in 1957. He ruled absolutely until he died of natural causes in 1971.

The Kennedy administration, trying to demonstrate that good things happened to the Dominicans when they built a showcase of democracy under the Alliance, seemed to be trying to use Haiti to build a showcase in reverse—an example of the bad things that happen when a nation fails to live up to the standards of Alliance democracy. Unlike Castro, Duvalier stood up to this pressure alone, without Soviet or other outside help.

The Duvalier problem preoccupied the Kennedy people even before Kennedy's inauguration. As early as mid-1960, Adolf Berle feared that Duvalier might patch together a working agreement with Castro, thereby giving the Soviet Union control of both sides of the Windward Passage. Berle's task force recommended that we work with Haitian politicians in exile to plan a transition government after Duvalier's term expired, as it was supposed to, in the spring of 1961. Duvalier, however, surprised everyone by having his name illegally printed at the top of ballots used in a parliamentary election and then declaring himself reelected. We adopted what we called "cool and correct" relations. At almost the same time, Trujillo was assassinated. Duvalier's dictatorial rule had been unchallenged while Trujillo ruled next door, but Trujillo's death changed everything. Now, while the Dominicans were struggling through turmoil and confusion, Haiti too had problems.

The nature and "correctness" of U.S.-Haitian relations in the months following Duvalier's takeover are hard to evaluate. We tried to pressure him into political reform: we told him he would get no large-scale Alliance aid until he freed political prisoners, ended rule by decree, published his secret budget, called a presidential election, and disbanded his irregular security force, the thugs called the Ton-Ton Macoutes. When he refused, we suspended economic aid. We continued military aid, however, for the head of our military mission considered the regular Haitian army the strongest democratic force in Haiti and the only counterweight to the Ton-Ton Macoutes. Our military mission openly sided with the Haitian army against its own president. As a result, in 1963 Duvalier threw it out.

At the start of the Punta del Este Conference on Cuba, Duvalier's foreign minister had announced that Haiti would not take sides because it opposed all intervention. The United States, needing Haiti's vote against Cuba, began to negotiate, offering a loan to expand its airport to accommodate tourist jets. A newspaper at Punta del Este reported: "Ambassador [deLesseps] Morrison turned in his expense account for the day: Breakfast, $1.50; Taxi in the morning, $2; Lunch, $2.50; Afternoon taxis, $3; Dinner with foreign minister of Haiti, $5,000,000."

In April, the U.S. ambassador announced that the United States had allocated $7.25 million to the 1962 program of aid to Haiti. Duvalier informed the Haitian legislature of the allocation in a speech that, as Senator Stephen M. Young (D.-Ohio) said, "seemed to equate American economic aid with support of his regime." The State Department suspended aid "for technical reasons." The Kennedy administration was still internally debating the airport loan when Haiti supported our quarantine of Cuba during the Cuban missile crisis of October, offering the use of its harbors and airfields to the United States. The United States then signed the airport loan agreement. Over the next few years, the airport project went through numerous on-again, off-again cycles in response to many pressures—criticism of Duvalier in Congress and in the liberal U.S. press, such urgent and overriding policy requirements of the U.S. government as the missile crisis, the progress of the CIA in searching for an alternative to Duvalier, the prospects of exile opposition groups that might offer an alternative, events in the Dominican Republic, and Duvalier's own capricious actions inside Haiti. Duvalier did not have State Department support; indeed, George W. Ball had a special aversion to him, and, as Ball rose from under secretary of state for economic affairs to become *the* under secretary—second only to Rusk—the activists who wanted to bring about Duvalier's downfall gained ground. United States policy cannot be designed or carried out in a vacuum; the Haitian airport was only one example of how policy can be pushed first in one direction, then another. Haitian events moved toward crisis in the spring of 1963, which was to mark the end of Duvalier's legal presidency. Although there was pressure within the Kennedy administration to try to force Duvalier out when his legal term ended, the members of the administration were not sure how to do it.

The members of this administration had forgotten—as we usually do in this country—that we were not the only ones with an interest in Haiti. The Caribbean nations are interrelated—and none more so than Haiti and the Dominican Republic. Ever since Haiti conquered the Dominican Republic in the nineteenth century, relations between the two countries, for the most part, had been bad. Now President Bosch began plotting against Duvalier. His reasons for doing so are varied: he hoped to become the leader of a democratic Caribbean; he viewed Duvalier as one of the last of the old-line dictators; he knew that Duvalier had tried to have him assassinated; and he hoped to distract his own people's attention from their troubles, thus ensuring his ability to remain in power. Bosch encouraged the half-dozen or so groups of anti-Duvalier Haitian exiles in the Dominican Republic and the United States, and the five underground groups that were operating inside Haiti. Toward the end of April, gunmen fired on a car containing Duvalier's children. In response, Duvalier's gunmen began rounding up oppositionists, some of whom took asylum in the Dominican embassy in Port-au-Prince; Duvalier's gunmen "invaded" the embassy. Bosch then sent an ultimatum to Duvalier threatening an air and ground invasion;

at the same time, he appealed to the OAS for assistance. When Duvalier filled Port-au-Prince with troops and tanks, the U.S. government sent the aircraft carrier *Boxer* and four other ships to waters off Port-au-Prince and prepared to evacuate Americans if necessary.

The U.S. government thought that if Bosch handled himself well he might obtain OAS action against Duvalier or even be able to apply enough pressure to force Duvalier to flee the country. But Bosch overplayed his hand. His utterances were so belligerent that opinion in the OAS, which initially agreed with him, turned against him, and for a time, it appeared the OAS might accuse Bosch, not Duvalier, of being the aggressor. Wild rumors abounded—that the Trujillos were en route to Port-au-Prince, that Duvalier was preparing to flee the country, that Duvalier had signed a secret agreement with Czecho-slovakia. The U.S. government moved the *Boxer,* with 2,000 marines aboard, closer to Port-au-Prince and, fearing that communists might seize power and ask for recognition by Cuba and the Soviet Union if Duvalier fled, made contingency plans: the U.S. ambassador and other OAS ambassadors in Port-au-Prince would help set up a temporary government that would seek provisional recognition from other nations, ask OAS help in keeping order, and later give way to a broadly based provisional government formed by exile and other opposition groups.

But Duvalier did not leave. For several months, Haiti continued to have problems: gun battles in the streets as the Ton-Ton Macoutes hunted down Duvalier's enemies, bombings and executions, small uprisings, and small invasions. The United States suspended diplomatic relations; the CIA gave clandestine aid to rebel groups. But it all came to nothing. Duvalier's hold on his own people was simply too strong to break without using massive armed force against him. Sometimes, the United States finds that it cannot control or even strongly influence events, public opinion, foreign presidents, and foreign political currents. The outcome of the Haitian crisis—a weakening of Bosch's power and a strengthening of Duvalier's—was exactly the opposite of what we wanted.

After President Kennedy was killed (Duvalier told his people that he had put a voodoo death curse on Kennedy), Johnson's men in charge of Latin American affairs sought to restore a more correct relationship with Haiti. Our new ambassador established friendly contacts with officials and broke many contacts with the opposition. We began to encourage the return of private investment and tourism to Haiti. The long-awaited jet airport finally was built, though not with U.S. government money. When Duvalier died, his son succeeded him.

The Cuban Missile Crisis

The Cuban missile crisis of October 1962 was not a U.S.-Cuban crisis but a U.S.-Soviet crisis—the first nuclear confrontation in history—yet it affected our relations with the Caribbean. The OAS, convoked in emergency session, unanimously supported our quarantine of Cuba. But in the Caribbean, voices of dissent were raised, albeit mostly by students, and sporadic rioting occurred. Governments, however, put down dissent, not only rightist military-dominated governments but liberal democratic governments: Betancourt mobilized the Venezuelan armed forces. Venezuela, the Dominican Republic, and Costa Rica offered the United States the use of their airfields and harbors, and the Dominicans sent ships to join ours on the quarantine line. Nations that had long resisted our lead in condemning Castro joined us now. In several countries, such as the Dominican Republic, where feelings about the United States were mixed, people rallied around their government and, thereby, the United States.

The crisis, however, set in motion new relationships and policies. On the one hand, Caribbean countries, for the first time directly involved in missile threats, feared Castro's Cuba as a forward base of Soviet power. On the other hand, some of them, seeing Soviet-American rivalry as a direct threat, began to search for a third way, a nonaligned way. Until then, neutralism had not seemed possible in the Caribbean; in another decade, it would be a fact (though the missile crisis, as we shall see, was only a small factor in bringing it about). On balance, the crisis was a serious blow to Castro's prestige in the Caribbean. When Mikoyan went to Cuba and told Castro he must relinquish his missiles, the other Caribbean countries began to see Castro not as the master of a brave, indigenous revolution but as Moscow's puppet. If Castro had not previously realized the full extent of his dependence on Russia, he did now; and so did his neighbors. And this realization in turn had two major effects. Since the Soviet Union's treatment of Castro hurt his prestige in the

Caribbean, some Caribbean leaders felt less need to establish a democratic alternative to Castroism. In the United States, as the Castro threat faded, Congress felt less compelled to vote large appropriations for the Alliance for Progress.

In their memoirs, members and observers of the Kennedy administration concluded that the crisis was a textbook example of good crisis management. Kennedy had quickly assembled his principal advisors, and over the next twelve days, they debated what action the president should take in response to the presence of the missiles. A number of important decisions were made at the outset: (1) to keep the group small in order to maintain secrecy; (2) to have the members of the group maintain their normal routines as much as possible to keep from rousing the press corps' suspicions; and (3) to let the group debate without Kennedy present in order to encourage a free exchange of opinions.[8]

The debate ranged over numerous possibilities—all the way from doing nothing, through quiet diplomacy with the Soviets (or an appeal to the UN or both), through a blockade or "quarantine," to a so-called surgical air strike against the missiles, and even to an all-out invasion of Cuba. No alternative seemed really satisfactory, and as the principals debated, their views of the narrow limits within which U.S. power moves became evident. The United States could not remain aloof—the danger to our national security was real, and, moreover, so was the political danger to President Kennedy inside the United States. We could hope for little from quiet diplomacy since we already knew the Soviets were not being aboveboard in this matter (and an appeal to the UN would be useless because the UN cannot act in matters directly affecting the vital security interests of a great power). We could not employ an air strike; it might not succeed, and if it did it might kill Soviet technicians, thus risking World War III. Moreover, Robert Kennedy argued, we must act with a decent respect for the opinion of mankind, which still believed that the United States was not only a great power but a moral power and would not rain death on the people of a small nation. (Vietnam still lay ahead of us.) An all-out invasion had all the disadvantages of an air strike—and the prospect of heavy U.S. casualties. In the end, the Executive Committee recommended, and the president adopted, the blockade (calling it a "quarantine" since, in international law, a blockade is an act of war). The blockade offered a number of advantages: it applied pressure but showed restraint, it left the military alternative in reserve, and it was likely to be approved by the OAS, the UN, NATO, and domestic and world opinion. Kennedy announced the decision to the nation in a television broadcast on October 22.

Muted criticism arose. Some Europeans feared a worldwide holocaust; some thought Kennedy should have used the crisis to put an end to the Cuban-Russian connection; Dean Acheson thought Kennedy should have used his initial advantage to gain more concessions from Khrushchev; Adlai Stevenson thought Kennedy should have tried to get a broader settlement with the Soviets, including not only the complete demilitarization of Cuba (we would give up Guantánamo; the Soviets would give up the missiles) but even its neutralization (which might entail the removal of Castro himself). On the whole, however, the early Western reaction to Kennedy's policy was favorable. In more recent years, revisionists have attacked it as amateurish, irresponsible, and dangerous.

The executive machinery that carried out the policy functioned brilliantly. Acheson, despite his reservations, went to Europe and ensured the support of the United States' friends and allies. The Defense Department expertly deployed men, ships, and planes. The State Department guided well U.S. ambassadors in their effort to gain the support of the hemisphere. Adlai Stevenson, by his powerful advocacy of a policy in which he did not wholly believe, carried the day in the United Nations. It is worth noting that although Congress supported the president, it was not consulted in advance, and thus the already great power of the president was even further advanced.

The crisis had an effect on Soviet naval thought that bears directly on Caribbean affairs. During World War II, the Soviet navy had nothing more than a coastal defense force and a naval infantry. After the war, the Soviets concluded that a great power needed a powerful navy, and they began building one, eventually developing guided missiles and nuclear-powered submarines. But for the most part, they still operated in waters close to their own shores. The Cuban missile crisis of 1962 made them aware of what it took to control the sea or deny its use to an enemy. By 1966, their navy was operating on the high seas. They went on to send their submarines into the Caribbean, as we shall see. The navy became more influential in the Soviet military establishment, and Sergei G. Gorshkov, commander of the

Soviet navy, an advocate of challenging Western naval supremacy, gained power. He has since taken his navy to sea—to the Mediterranean-Suez-Arabian seas, Southeast Asia-Straits of Malacca, and the Caribbean. He has set up permanent stations in the Mediterranean and the Indian Ocean, regular patrols off the west coast of Africa, nuclear submarines off the eastern seaboard of the United States, and visits to Havana and to a Soviet submarine base on the southern coast of Cuba.

JFK and Central America: The Final Move

Shortly after the Cuban missile crisis, President Kennedy decided to go to Costa Rica to meet with the presidents of the five Central American countries and Panama. (Costa Rica was chosen because it made a good showcase for the Alliance for Progress and for President Kennedy.) A formal announcement emphasized the economic purposes of his trip—to review progress and problems of the Alliance and to discuss how the United States might promote Central American economic integration. But clearly, Castro would also be on the agenda. Central American leaders wanted stronger action against Castro—economic development was impossible with Cuba stirring up trouble, helping Central American guerrillas, and thereby frightening off the private investment that development required. The Kennedy administration at this time, however, seemed somewhat reluctant to move against Castro: perhaps because of negotiations with the Soviets at the UN about removal of Soviet troops and equipment from Cuba; perhaps because of negotiations for release of the Bay of Pigs prisoners; perhaps because Kennedy was determined, in view of his larger interests in accommodation with Khrushchev, to do nothing to further humiliate him; perhaps because CIA officials were secretly plotting Castro's overthrow or even assassination, as the Church committee contended much later; or perhaps because Kennedy hoped to normalize relations with Castro, a possibility that he instructed an emissary to explore the following autumn.[9] Nevertheless, in his opening speech to the meeting of presidents on March 18, Kennedy tried to reassure them: "I am hopeful that at this meeting we will again increase our capacity to prevent the infiltration of Cuban agents, money, and propaganda." The Declaration of Central America, issued two days later at the meeting's end, said little about Castro and emphasized economic matters. The

Central Americans had hoped for a joint call for strong OAS action against Castro but apparently settled for U.S. aid. It was almost a direct reversal of the roles of the United States and the Caribbean in Eisenhower's time.

President Kennedy's trip to Costa Rica was a personal triumph. Thousands of Costa Ricans lined the streets and cheered him with warmth and affection whenever he appeared. Such receptions are more than personal triumphs; they promote goodwill toward the United States, and, to the extent that they do, they promote its cause. Kennedy, who had done more for Latin Americans than any president since FDR, aroused Latin American emotions as had no president since FDR. It was presumably during this trip that, according to Richard Goodwin, Kennedy in private pointed to a cable he had just received on Southeast Asia and said, "Think of the effort we're making over there, and they don't even like us. This is where we really need to make an effort. The whole thing's going to be won or lost right here, in Latin America." Indeed, one is tempted to wonder what might have happened had we expended half our subsequent Vietnam effort on Latin America. But President Kennedy's influence did not have long to live; a new policy, Lyndon Johnson's, would soon replace it.

THE JOHNSON YEARS

"Let Us Continue"

Like any successor president, Lyndon Johnson said he would continue his predecessor's policies, but he worked quickly to put his own stamp on them. Nowhere was this clearer than in his Latin American policy. Johnson assumed the presidency on November 22, 1963; five days later, in an address to a joint session of Congress, he spoke the words that set the mood of the early days of his administration: "Let us continue." He publicly asked the Kennedy cabinet, the Kennedy staff, and the Kennedy ambassadors not to resign. Then, on December 14, the White House announced the appointment of Thomas C. Mann as assistant secretary of state for ARA (replacing Ed Martin); on December 18, it announced Mann's appointment as the special assistant to the president on Latin American affairs (replacing Ralph Dungan); and on December 27, it announced Mann's appointment as administrator of the Alliance for Progress (replacing Teodoro Moscoso). At the press conference, the president said, "We expect to speak with one voice on all matters affecting the hemisphere. Mr. Mann . . . will be that voice." It was a major turn in Latin American policy. Mann, a career officer then ambassador to Mexico, was a conservative, a Cold War hard-liner, a believer in the role of private investment in developing Latin America, and, in his own view, a "realist." Somewhat old-fashioned, himself a Texan, he took a Texan's amused, tolerant, patronizing view of Latin Americans.

Under Kennedy, Martin, Moscoso, and Dungan, the administration of Latin American affairs had been somewhat chaotic. Mann merged the Alliance for Progress and ARA and began to establish order: clearances on cables could be obtained far more rapidly; competition between AID and ARA diminished; technical issues could be resolved at a low level. Shortly after taking office, Mann brought his ambassadors together in a closed meeting and set forth the new U.S. policy: cooperation with Latin American governments no matter how they attained power (and as long as they were not communist-controlled or in danger of becoming so); promotion of economic growth; neutrality on social and political reform; and protection of U.S. private investment. A little later, the United States promptly recognized a Brazilian regime installed by a military coup. When Johnson sent the marines to the Dominican Republic Mann was viewed by liberals as the incarnation of reaction, but although he had chosen the ambassador whose mistakes helped make the decision to send the Marines necessary, he had not made that decision.

A week after Mann was sworn in as Alliance administrator, he was plunged into his first crisis: anti-U.S. rioting began in Panama.

Panama

The Republic of Panama was conceived in intervention and born in revolution. In the sixty-seven years between 1904 and 1971, the government in power changed fifty-nine times. The political rivalry was bitter but meaningless; the government—no matter who was president—was controlled by a few powerful families. During those years of turmoil, the United States repeatedly intervened—sometimes with troops, as was its right under the 1903 treaty and the Panamanian constitution until Franklin Roosevelt renounced the right of intervention.

Panama had gained its independence from Colombia with U.S. aid; it paid for the aid with the 1903 Hay-Bunau-Varilla Treaty, which gave the United States "in perpetuity" all rights that it would possess "if it were sovereign." That treaty led to the building of the Panama Canal and the creation of the Canal Zone, which divides Panama in half.

The Canal Zone, where Panama has no jurisdiction, is run by the U.S. Army; Panamanians who enter the Zone are subject to American, not Panamanian, law. Some 44,000 people, about 37,000 of them Americans, many second-generation and third-generation Zonians, live in the Canal Zone; they live in government-owned housing and shop at government commissaries. The Canal Zone is a subsidized socialist paradise in which there is no private enterprise or private property. The sharp contrast between the comfortable lives of the Americans and the poverty of nearby Panamanians is clear for Panamanians to see.

Over the years, Panamanian demands for a new treaty became more and more vehement. In 1962, President Kennedy and President Robert F. Chiari set up a joint commission to discuss differences; they also agreed to arrange for the flying of Panamanian flags in the Canal Zone. After four months of discussion, the joint commission issued a communiqué that outlined a formula for flying flags. But the formula created so much controversy, giving rise to a lawsuit, that officials decided not to fly any flags at all over schools. In January 1964, however, American students raised an American flag over a high school. Americans then rushed to buy flags at the commissary, and soon American flags were flying everywhere. A few days later, about two-hundred Panamanian students entered the Zone, saying they wished to fly their flag alongside the American flag at the high school and to sing their general rioting—snipers, Molotov cocktails, attacks on American business buildings and the embassy. In the three days before order was restored, some twenty Panamanians and four Americans died.

Panama broke off diplomatic relations with the United States, and President Chiari, accusing the United States of "unprovoked aggression," requested a meeting of the UN Security Council. President Johnson, amid reports that the rioting was at least encouraged by pro-Castro Panamanians and that "another Cuba" might be in the making, personally telephoned President Chiari. Chiari, facing an election, wanted Johnson to agree to "negotiate" the situation. Johnson, also facing an election, wanted merely to "discuss" it; he gave ground slowly and ended by promising an entirely new treaty. Panama thought it had finally won. But for ten years, fruitless negotiations continued. During that period, in 1968, a left nationalist military man overthrew the ancient oligarchy and set about mobilizing world opinion to drive the Americans out of the Canal Zone.

Cuba Again

Castro was a continuing problem in the Caribbean. Privately, some Caribbean diplomats urged using force against him, but Johnson counseled restraint, as Kennedy had in his last years. But in the fall of 1963, Castro, seeking to smash the elections in Venezuela, supported a guerrilla band there. Because of the successful agrarian reform initiated by Betancourt (who could not succeed himself), the guerrillas found no sanctuary in the countryside; they were forced to flee to the cities, where they fell into the hands of the police. Betancourt announced proof of Cuban aggression—a cache of three tons of Cuban weapons buried on a beach—and demanded OAS action against Castro. The OAS Council voted to investigate. Castro dropped hints he might be interested in normalizing relations with the United States. The State Department continued to insist that two "elements"—Castro's ties to the Soviet Union and Castro's continuing promotion of subversion in the hemisphere—were not negotiable. The OAS meeting of foreign ministers in July 1964 adopted a resolution condemning Cuba for aggression against Venezuela and voted to apply sanctions: to end diplomatic and consular relations with Cuba, to suspend all trade (except food and medicine) and all sea transportation (except for humanitarian purposes). All the Caribbean countries voted for the resolution, and although Bolivia, Chile, and Uruguay voted against, they eventually broke relations. Only Mexico, traditionally noninterventionist, maintained diplomatic relations and air travel. Thus, five years after he came to power, Castro was officially isolated in the hemisphere.

The Dominican Republic Again

On April 24, 1965, in Santo Domingo, political supporters of Juan Bosch, defecting military men, and leaders of communist and Castroite groups rose in armed revolt against the triumvirate that the Dominican military had installed when they overthrew President Bosch. Four days later, on the recommendation of his ambassador there, W. Tapley Bennett, President Johnson sent in the marines and followed them with airborne troops. In a few days, we had about as many troops (some 22,000) in the Dominican Republic as in Vietnam.

At first, President Johnson said he was sending the troops to protect U.S. lives and property. Later, it became clear he wanted to prevent the rise of another Castro in the Caribbean. The U.S. troops interposed themselves between the rebel and loyalist forces; the OAS called for a cease-fire; mediators succeeded in getting one. The OAS voted to send an inter-American peace-keeping force to the Republic. Brazil sent 1,300 troops; Honduras, Costa Rica, Nicaragua, and Paraguay sent token forces, although the effective military presence remained American. After long and difficult negotiations, OAS mediators, chiefly Ellsworth Bunker of the United States, succeeded in establishing a provisional government that held office until the following June, when Joaquín Balaguer, who had been Trujillo's last puppet president, was elected president over Juan Bosch.

The story of our Dominican intervention is too well known to need retelling here.[1] Critics accused Johnson of violating the Rio Treaty and the OAS Charter by intervening unilaterally with military force, of overreacting, of stifling a democratic movement against a military-backed regime, of abandoning the Kennedy policy for the hard-nosed policy of Tom Mann, of exaggerating or even inventing the danger of a communist takeover, and of promulgating, as a further extension of the Monroe Doctrine, the Johnson Doctrine: the United States has a right to intervene militarily in the hemisphere to prevent communism from establishing itself. All this, it may be, need not have come about. True, the assassination of Trujillo after thirty-one years had probably made a bloodbath of some sort inevitable. And, to be sure, the overthrow of Bosch had destroyed the political system and created a left-right polarization that culminated in civil war. Nevertheless, had we, the United States, involved ourselves deeply in Dominican affairs between the fall of Bosch and the rebellion, we might have been able to guide dissension into peaceful channels. And had Ambassador Bennett seized an opportunity offered him at the rebellion's outset to mediate between rebels and government, he might have settled the entire thing without troops. But the polarization did occur, Bennett did keep hands off, and communists and other extremists did take over political leadership of the rebellion. President Johnson felt he had no choice but to send the troops—the Dominican government had ceased to exist, it could no longer guarantee American lives or property, what government remained wanted our military assistance, his own ambassador asked for troops, and there appeared to be a real danger of a communist takeover.

The Dominican intervention cost the United States slightly more than $35 million in Defense Department expenditures alone (and a great deal more in conscience money: between 1962 and 1965, we had loaned or given the Dominican Republic $108.9 million; after our intervention, we nearly doubled that figure in a comparable period). It cost us much in goodwill throughout the hemisphere, although probably less than one might expect—Latin Americans simply assume that when we think our strategic interests are threatened in our own sphere of influence, we will use force if necessary. And they understand that at that time, no president—at least no Democratic president, after all the McCarthy years—dared, for reasons of domestic politics, permit another Castro to arise so close to home.

The intervention divided U.S. policy-makers, political leaders, and journalists bitterly.

At the outset of the Dominican Republic venture, most members of Congress supported Johnson. But after he acknowledged that his primary purpose had been to prevent the rise of another Castro, Senate opposition emerged, especially among liberal Democrats. Senator Wayne Morse, for example, introduced an amendment reducing loan funds for the Alliance for Progress by $100 million, saying the Alliance by now more closely resembled the pro-dictator policies of Eisenhower than the Alliance under Kennedy. It was the Dominican intervention that touched off the revolt of liberal Democratic senators against President Johnson's foreign policy. In a two-hour speech, Senator William Fulbright argued that any reform movement was likely to attract communist support and that if we automatically opposed such movements we would end by opposing every reform movement, thus becoming the defenders of an unjust status quo. Fulbright thought the future in Latin America belonged to social revolution, with only the nature of the revolution—communist or democratic—in doubt. The OAS Charter forbade intervention. We were currently fighting in Vietnam because, we said, the United States must honor its word. How, then, could we not honor our word to the OAS Charter? Fulbright thought the Dominican intervention had shaken if not shattered the confidence in the United States that had been built up over the thirty years since the Good Neighbor policy. He proposed that "a new and healthier relationship" between the United States and Latin America must be a "freer" relationship than before. To the United States, the inter-American system represented a way of maintaining law and order close to home, thus leaving us free to conduct our global policies. But to Latin Americans, the system locked them into the Western Hemisphere, leaving them no way to escape the perhaps well-meaning, but often stifling, embrace of the United States. (Small nations have difficulty living comfortably in the shadow of large neighbors—Ireland with England, Belgium with Germany and France, Eastern Europe with Russia.) Perhaps we should seek looser, not closer, ties with our near neighbors. They should feel free to maintain or sever existing ties as they see fit and to establish new arrangements, both among themselves and with outside nations, in which the United States would not participate. The strongest bonds, after all, are voluntary.

It was a prescient speech, and it signaled the end of the bipartisan hard-line Cold War consensus. After it, President Johnson never again consulted Senator Fulbright. Soon Fulbright attacked what he called "the arrogance of power" and continued to elaborate his idea that we should loosen our ties to Latin America. Something similar was proposed later in a different context when a member of the Nixon administration suggested a policy of "benign neglect."

Actually, the Dominican intervention had few political implications beyond the one most people assumed—that the United States would use force if necessary when it felt its strategic interests were threatened in its own sphere of influence. That we had intervened there did not necessarily mean we would intervene everywhere in Latin America. The Dominican Republic in 1965 was a special case, just as it had been in 1961, when Trujillo died; in 1962, when Bosch was elected; and in 1963, when Bosch was overthrown. Because of its history and because of Trujillo's long tyranny, it was unlike any other nation; we treated it so; and it would be a mistake to think that everything we did there between Trujillo's death and our intervention flowed from an overall Latin American policy design. It does appear, however, that Vietnam and the Dominican intervention marked the high-water mark of the rimland stage of the Cold War. After World War II, we had adopted George Kennan's policy of containment. The containment of Soviet expansion had been wise and essential in the European heartland shortly after World War II, and that was what it was designed for. But when the Soviet-U.S. struggle shifted away from the European heartland to the rimlands of the world, we extrapolated containment and applied it there—something its architects never intended—and there it sometimes obliged us to align ourselves with the status quo against revolution and seemed about to lead us into an effort to police the world. Thus, we got into Vietnam and the Dominican Republic. The Cold War distorted our policy in many ways.

The End of the Johnson Administration

During the last three years of the Johnson presidency, the OAS was trying to remake itself. As the British colonies became independent, they were admitted to OAS membership, unless they were engaged in a territorial dispute, despite their ties to the British commonwealth. This admitted Trinidad-Tobago, Barbados, and Jamaica but not Guyana and Belize; Canada did not apply for membership, although it was eligible. The OAS was examining a proposal for a permanent multilateral peace-keeping force. The United States supported the proposal, but Chile, Argentina, Mexico, and Venezuela opposed it; and in the end, we could not even get a committee appointed to study it. What the Latin Americans really wanted was what they had wanted at least since Eisenhower's time—better terms of trade. They wanted the United States to reduce or limit its tariffs and other trade barriers on articles manufactured in Latin America and to pay higher prices for Latin American primary export commodities, such as bauxite and coffee. They opened a strong drive to incorporate those matters into the OAS Charter itself. The United States flatly refused.

While the OAS was involved in those matters, the first Tri-Continental Conference met at Havana on January 2, 1966. It was the biggest gathering of procommunist and anti-American forces ever, with delegates from Latin America, Africa, and Asia. The delegates to the conference, dominated by Moscow, called for the violent overthrow of governments they disapproved of and chose Havana as headquarters for international subversion and guerrilla operations. Although Soviet diplomats in the United States claimed the conference was just a tactical move in the contest for Third World leadership between Moscow and Peking, its domination by Moscow was the principal concern of the United States at the time. In retrospect, the conference may be seen as a beginning of the Caribbean political shift toward the Third World.

After the Dominican intervention, President Johnson attempted to better relations with Latin America by personal diplomacy: he visited Mexico twice, sent Vice-President Humphrey to sign a treaty to prohibit nuclear weapons in Latin America, helped forestall a rightist coup in Guatemala, and agreed to attend a conference of American chiefs of state at Punta del Este in April 1967. He hoped to arrive with an additional $1.5 billion for Latin America, but was rebuffed by Congress. Unable to make specific commitments, he still diligently courted the Latin Americans, held private talks with each Latin American president, and stressed that he was there to listen, not to talk. It was an impressive performance. The conference issued a Declaration of the Presidents of America, which resolved to "create progressively, beginning in 1970," a Latin American common market and to get it into operation within fifteen years. The presidents agreed to lay the foundation for economic integration through multinational projects, to eliminate unnecessary military expenditures, and to try harder in the fields of agricultural production, education, health, and science. The declaration lacked the passion of the original Alliance Charter and contained no reference to political development or basic structural and social change. It was, however, a personal triumph for President Johnson, for he exuded a warmth of spirit they had not seen. A little more than a year later, in July 1968, he met with the five Central American presidents in an atmosphere of crisis caused by balance-of-payments deficits and brought with him tangible evidence of his concern—approval of $35 million in loans to Guatemala, Nicaragua, Honduras, and Costa Rica.

Judgment on the Alliance

Although during the eight years of the Nixon-Ford administration the assistant secretary for ARA still bore the additional title of "Coordinator of the Alliance for Progress," the Alliance as originally conceived died during President Johnson's term—indeed, its partisans feel it died with President Kennedy. Johnson and Tom Mann (and Mann's successors) continued to make speeches about the Alliance, but they realigned its actual policy: they cut out its social and political heart, emphasized money, and turned it into just another foreign aid program.[2] And it was a foreign aid program influenced by our own political affairs: we tended to give aid to countries that voted with us in the United Nations and in other ways supported us.

An oil company executive said, "Not until Tom Mann came back in 1964 did the business community feel that it was 'in' again with the United States government." Mann stopped aid to the reformist government of Peru in the hope of forcing it to make a favorable settlement with a Standard Oil of New Jersey subsidiary. Partisans of the Alliance maintain that Johnson and Nixon allowed it to die in part because they were out of sympathy with its reformist heart, in part because they wanted nothing to do with a program so intimately associated with President Kennedy. Senator Robert F. Kennedy tried to revive his brother's Alliance, to no avail.

The death of the original Alliance, however, may have been due not entirely to Kennedy's death but, rather, to its own inherent defects, to Johnson's preoccupation with Vietnam, and to broad changes that swept the hemisphere, especially the drift in the Caribbean toward the Third World. One of its principal defects was that many Latin Americans who praised the Alliance did not really believe in its reformist goals—they simply wanted U.S. money. We built into the Alliance our Anglo-Saxon preference for peaceful change. It may be that change in Latin America inevitably will be sudden, wrenching, violent, even bloody.

Even before Johnson and Mann took over, the big shift from political and social reform to economic progress had already begun. The Kennedy administration began backing away from its emphasis on reforms when it became clear after two years of the Alliance that the ruling class could not be expected to give up power and riches, that military coups had overthrown the very governments attempting reform, and that the United States had been unable to reverse the coups by withholding diplomatic recognition.

Even during its first year, the Alliance was subject to constant criticism. Congressional hearings on foreign aid produced complaints about the flight of capital from Latin America, the shortfall of U.S. private investment, the lag in development planning and self-help, and the absence of real reform. Dean Acheson said, "We can't have the Latin American countries screaming for worms like a bunch of young robins in a nest. We must see some progress from them first." (He also said he did not think the new emerging nations could make any contribution to international politics nor did he care if they made a bargain with the Soviets.) Rodman Rockefeller told the Joint Economic Committee that the Alliance, in its first year, had done little more than create a new bureaucracy and try to allocate $1 billion in loans. In the press, the Alliance was described as "a patchwork that satisfies almost nobody," and journalists reported that much of the money obtained through the Alliance had gone to pay off past Latin American government debts. Editorials complained that the United States was not insisting that governments reform themselves before receiving aid. The Alliance was also under attack by powerful political and economic interests, and by extreme leftists.

President Kennedy had been aware of these problems. On the first anniversary of his original proposal, he again spoke to Latin American diplomats gathered in the White House. The Alliance's "most impressive achievement" to date, he said, was the "dramatic shift in thinking and attitude" throughout the hemisphere; success, he went on, depended on the Latin American nations themselves. The fight for basic reforms would have to be led by men of wealth and power: "Those who make peaceful revolution impossible will make violent revolutions inevitable." At a news conference on June 14, 1962, he warned against expecting too much too soon and said the Alliance was probably the most difficult task the United States had ever undertaken. On December 14, 1962, when asked about Latin America's progress at a question-and-answer period after his address to the Economic Club of New York, Kennedy said, "We have made some progress in some countries. But tax reform is very difficult." And later in December, in a television interview, he concluded that "there are greater limitations upon our ability to bring about favorable results than I had imagined."

Fidel Castro once explained why Kennedy's "good ideas" would come to nothing: big business saw its interests damaged; the Pentagon thought its strategic bases were in danger; the Latin American power groups sabotaged the Alliance—"in short, Kennedy has everyone against him." Sometimes it seemed so. The poor were apathetic and skeptical; the rich and the rising middle class, fearing they would bear the burden of any gains made by the poor, regarded Kennedy as a traitor to his class and resisted basic reforms. Student radicals considered the Alliance nothing but U.S. imperialism in new disguise. Most government officials, who came from the class that stood to lose the most, considered the Alliance nothing but an anticommunist program to which they had to pay lip service in order to keep the U.S. cash flowing.

The few individuals who were really dedicated to the Alliance— often young, U.S.-educated, and idealistic—were not in power. Perhaps in the early 1960s we were misled by the prospects of such men as Betancourt, Bosch, Lleras, Frei, Belaúnde, and Haya. Of that group, only Betancourt succeeded in doing approximately what the Alliance set out to do. Perhaps what really went wrong with the Alliance was that it came ten years too late—ten years after we might have persuaded young leftist nationalists to join with us. If the United States had presented the idea of the Alliance right after World War II, we might have had a new hemisphere today. Instead, we created the Marshall Plan and built a new Europe. That was the choice, conscious or not. As a result, it may have been true, as Marxists said, that only bloodshed could bring about real change.

In the mid-1970s, in the Caribbean, the most frequent answer to the question, "What did the Alliance for Progress accomplish here?" would have been "not much." A Venezuelan deputy: "The Alliance was not a success but it had positive aspects—at least it showed your interest." A U.S. diplomat in Guyana: "The Alliance did quite a good deal here—roads, potable water, the airport." A Honduran manufacturer: "The Alliance helped us build this mill. But on the whole, not much effect. It raised more expectations than anything else. It was pushing social development on us faster than we could absorb it. The Alliance required a commitment we couldn't give." A Honduran politician: "The Alliance—mainly spiritual benefits. A big moral help. A little material benefits, like houses for the workers." A Honduran banker: "I was on the planning commission here. We couldn't respond to the Alliance. Oh, we made plans; but we couldn't translate them into action." A Nicaraguan educator: "The gap between the rich and the poor is still the same." A Costa Rican politician (emotionally): "The only United States policy with vision was President Kennedy and the Alliance for Progress." A Costa Rican publisher: "All the good intentions, all the money spent, ten years of effort, ended in one thing—he made the structure of the government in Costa Rica bigger, stronger, and less efficient. Your intervention in Vietnam is very much like the Alliance for Progress. You have a model society you'd like to impose on both. Why is it no one wants it?''

Ted Moscoso, looking back, says the Alliance accomplished some things that in the long run will be helpful: for example, national planning and family planning. But when asked, "Did it help the common man?" he said, "Not much. But more than if there had been no Alliance. And we built some stuff—bridges, roads, dams, schools—which probably would have been built anyway, although that's not certain." Talking with him, one gets the feeling that, although in the end the Alliance failed, it was good that we tried. Although few Caribbean leaders in the mid-70s mourned the demise of the Alliance for Progress, without exception they mourned the loss of President Kennedy. And so did the poor—they put up shrines to his memory in their huts. Something about him captured the Latin American imagination as had no other U.S. president—and held it a dozen years later. It was not just that Johnson and Mann redirected the Alliance; it was also that they simply were not Kennedy.

In 1969, at the beginning of the first Nixon administration, the House Subcommittee on Inter-American Affairs, after four months of hearings, concluded that the Alliance's performance in promoting both reform and development had been disappointing. After nearly eight years of effort, the peaceful revolution was "only beginning to take hold": the $8.3 billion contributed by the United States had produced "only modest visible development gains." The subcommittee found that, although economic growth had averaged about 5 percent per year, the highest rate of population increase in the world (between 2.5 percent and 3.5 percent) had eroded economic growth to 1.5 percent per year per person.

Latin America's export earnings, during all but one of the eight years since the Alliance, rose at the rate of more than 5 percent per year. But development had been undercut by trends in international trade: Latin America's exports dropped from 21 percent of U.S. imports to only 13 percent; its share of European markets shrank because Europe gave preferential treatment to its own former African colonies; and its foreign exchange earnings were lowered and terms of trade worsened because primary commodity prices fluctuated widely, mostly downward. Prospects for improving its position in the world seemed poor. Although 12 million children had been added to the elementary school rolls, only 10 of every 1,000 students who enrolled in primary schools finished high school, and only one graduated from college. Accordingly, the prospects for building a modern technological society did not look favorable. Some countries had begun far-reaching reforms; land and tax reforms, although planned, had not, in most cases, been implemented; tax collections and public administration generally had been improved. But overall, help from abroad had not measured up to expectations; its terms had become increasingly stringent; and Latin America was building a huge debt for the future, a debt it would be hard pressed to service. Already in 1967 debt repayments, interest, repatriated earnings of foreign corporations, and other capital outflows exceeded all forms of foreign aid and private investments by more than $500 million. Everywhere entrenched interests resisted change, and sometimes they called out the army to halt it—sixteen coups in eight years had discouraged reformers and dampened the enthusiasm of private investors.

What went wrong?

It is fashionable to say the Alliance promised too much—was launched with too much fanfare and exaggerated rhetoric, set goals impossibly high, promising to reverse four-hundred years of history in only ten years. Arthur Schlesinger has concluded in retrospect that some of Kennedy's language "seems extravagant"—"yet there are moments when there is no substitute for eloquence. Rhetoric, it might be added, was the coin of political discourse in Latin America."

The Alliance contained inherent flaws and contradictions.

First, some of its supporters imagined that a massive infusion of loans and grants could work the same miracle in Latin America that the Marshall Plan had in postwar Europe. But the cases were very different. Although the war had destroyed the cities and the industrial plants of the Western European democracies, they still possessed relatively stable governments with democratic traditions, a large, well-trained corps of experienced government servants, diversified economies, advanced technology, ample resources for planning, and an educated citizenry that formed a huge pool of highly skilled labor (perhaps most important of all). Latin America lacked those resources and many more.

Second, the United States misperceived certain Latin American problems and assumed greater democratic reformist sentiment than actually existed. For example, we thought that a few changes in the structure of Latin American societies, such as breaking the stranglehold of the landed oligarchy, would be sufficient to bring about revolutionary change. But although in some countries the oligarchy's stranglehold is sometimes the cause of inequitable and inadequate economic growth, the real cause is usually the oligarchy's inefficient use of its land, the country's dependence on a few commodities subject to wild price swings, and low productivity and low income, which keep almost everybody poor, thus preventing the country from making the capital investments in industries and schools and health that are essential to growth. The Kennedy men had little firsthand information about Latin America. They hoped to strengthen the democratic left by proposed reforms that aroused such fierce reaction they actually strengthened the military right; at the same time, they did not get the support of the left because of their insistence on antiinflationary fiscal policies. Moreover, they overrated the demand for change in Latin America. Their call for revolution went unanswered—the masses were inert, the ruling classes had no enthusiasm for cooperating in their own demise, and the democratic left had little real power. Kennedy greatly overestimated the capacity of the democratic left, which when in power was under constant attack by both the far right and far left, could not itself govern effectively, failed to inspire the labor unions and the masses, and so built no base of its own; in country after country, the democratic left went the way of Juan Bosch. It is possible that such revolutionary change as we demanded could come in only one of two ways—either through a ruthless dictatorship forcing change against all opposition, as had happened in Cuba, or through a genuine understanding and acceptance on the part of the populace of the sacrifices demanded. The Kennedy administration feared—as Castro hoped—that a mighty tide of Castroite revolutions would sweep the southern half of the hemisphere, but both of them were wrong—Cuba was the exception, not the rule. Latin America is, after all, a conservative region; church, military, and landed oligarchy resist change, as do the middle classes, even with success in sight. Even the poor are "too mired in traditional ways," as Schlesinger has put it, "too underfed and apathetic or too brutalized to act against the existing order."

Third, the Alliance was based on proposals that had been advanced by Latin Americans and was launched as a joint U.S.—Latin

American undertaking, but it never really became a joint enterprise. McGeorge Bundy once asked, questioning its origins, "Was there not a paradox, right from the beginning, in announcing an Alliance, whose mainspring must be in South America, in a White House speech?" In the beginning, the Latin Americans, used to having the United States lead, expected the United States to lead the Alliance; only later did resentment of the United States come to the surface. Moreover, all too often, Alliance projects were developed not in response to what the people of a country needed and asked for but, instead, in response to what the Washington bureaucracy decided they needed. And so a project became not a local one carried out with some U.S. assistance but, rather, a U.S. project with a little local help and sometimes a good deal of local hostility. Starting in 1963, Moscoso, Averell Harriman, and others launched a plan through IA-ECOSOC to provide the Alliance with a Latin American facade—it would be guided by "the nine wise men" of the Inter-American Committee, Alliance for Progress (CIAP). Harriman even proposed that the United States keep out of it, although Moscoso disagreed. Then, at the last minute, President Johnson refused to appoint the man chosen to head CIAP—Raúl Prebisch, the eminent economist—because word of his appointment had leaked to the *New York Times*. The CIAP never accomplished its purpose.

Fourth, the Alliance presented the State Department bureaucracy and its traditional diplomacy with many difficulties. It involved the United States deeply in the internal affairs of foreign nations. Every U.S. ambassador, as William D. Rogers has pointed out, found himself consulting with not only the foreign minister but also with ministers of finance, education, public works, agriculture, industry, health, interior; with leaders of cooperatives, labor unions, and business groups. Each ambassador had to concern himself not only with matters of protocol and relations with the OAS and the United Nations, but also with the national budget, the agrarian reform law, tax reform, river-valley development, and a thousand other issues alien to traditional diplomacy. Few foreign service officers were trained for the new tasks or were comfortable with them; those who favored peace and harmony were asked to aid wrenching change. Secretary Rusk did little to resolve the tensions that arose; he became involved with Latin America only at times of extreme crisis. Ted Moscoso's flamboyant dedication unnerved department career officers, who viewed the new Kennedy program with disdain. For example, Ellis Briggs, a career ambassador with much experience, denounced the Alliance as a "blueprint for upheaval throughout Latin America" and as a "pernicious doctrine" akin to throwing lighted gasoline into a neighbor's woodshed. Other problems developed because some of AID's own people were ignorant of Latin American realities and tended to think that what worked in Iowa would surely work in, say, Guatemala. In general, the Alliance was pulled and pushed from all directions of the vast government bureaucracy—the Treasury Department feared the impact of its program on the U.S. balance of payments, the Commerce Department wanted to use it to expand exports and promote U.S. business profits, and the Agriculture Department wanted to make sure that no aid was given to produce commodities competing with U.S. exports.

Fifth, Latin American governments presented the Alliance with yet another set of problems. In Latin America, bureaucracies often did not exist; and when they did, they had no plans and were run by people with little education or training. Throughout the Caribbean, little or nothing existed between the president-minister level and laborers. In the Dominican Republic, we used to talk of bringing promising Caribbean government workers to Washington for intensive training, but we could never spare the handful of prospects from their jobs in the palace. National plans were essential to the Alliance, but most countries lacked even the statistics to base them on. So Alliance funds went to establish bureaucracies; the cause of reform languished.

Sixth, there was the U.S. Congress: some members, such as Senators Morse and Gruening, supported the Alliance enthusiastically; but Representative Otto Passman kept slashing away at appropriations, and he was by no means alone. Like many other programs of the 1950s and 1960s, the Alliance was sold to the Congress—and the nation—out of fear of communism. But this created problems. After the Cuban missile crisis and the defeat of Castro's guerrillas elsewhere, our fear of communism in the hemisphere abated. Moreover, in Latin America itself, constant headlines about congressional cuts made Latin Americans suspect that the Alliance had been only a reaction to Castro and not a binding commitment to Latin American development; AID sought five-year authorizations, with a carryover of unspent funds into future fiscal years; but Congressman Passman insisted on rigid annual appropriations. In addition, Congress, over the years, burdened its assistance authorizations with restrictions: no assistance to "the present government of Cuba," none to a government that aids Cuba, none to a government whose ships trade with Cuba, none to any country "controlled by the international communist conspiracy," none to any enterprise that would compete with a U.S. business, none to governments that break contracts or seize U.S. fishing vessels or expropriate U.S. property without compensation. In spite of all this, however, and remembering that the Alliance provided members of Congress with little for their constituents, the Alliance, on the whole, enjoyed a surprising amount of support in Congress.

Seventh, the economic structures of the Alliance were based on the assumption, which soon proved erroneous, that much of the money for development would come from private investment. Private investors were frightened by the social and economic goals of the Alliance, which seemed to promote instability. Although some new capital went to Latin America, it was offset by outflows of service on past debts and remitted profits. Between 1961 and 1969, transactions of the Export-Import Bank with Latin America yielded note repayments of $437 million, including interest, to the United States. Debt service in Latin America sometimes absorbed as much as 90 percent of monies obtained through the Alliance, leaving little for the work of the Alliance. Oddly enough, the Alliance probably benefited U.S. private investors inordinately, for by the end of its second year, the private investment guarantee program, established earlier, came into widespread use. This program, in effect, meant that the Alliance paid U.S. investors money that had been provided, for a very different purpose, by U.S. taxpayers. The Latin American leftists who accused the Alliance of being just another scheme to advance Yankee imperialism were not without a point (although they usually stated it wrongly). In 1962, Brazil expropriated International Telephone and Telegraph's subsidiary; ITT's president, Harold Geneen, declared that the United States must be persuaded not to give aid to countries that expropriate private U.S. investments without fair and prompt compensation. The result of such complaints by Geneen and other big business leaders was the Hickenlooper Amendment, requiring the United States to suspend economic aid to any Latin American government that takes strong measures against

U.S. corporations, including nationalization without compensation and even discriminatory taxation. Ever since, liberals have attacked the Hickenlooper Amendment and other related legislation. They overlook one point, however: ambassadors have sometimes found it useful to have Hickenlooper in reserve during difficult negotiations with a Latin American government. And ambassadors have often wished the investment guarantee program did not exist—they have sometimes found a U.S. corporation facing a takeover by a Latin American government wholly inflexible in the negotiations because it is safe in the knowledge that if worse comes to worst its property is protected by the investment guarantee program. Still other U.S. congressional restrictions on the Alliance aroused Latin American suspicions—tied aid, for example, and requirements that 50 percent of all government aid shipped to a Latin American country must be hauled in U.S.-flag ships.[3] Thus did the shining Alliance become encrusted with barnacles.

*   *   *

The surest way for the Alliance to reach the masses was to bring about agrarian reform. Traditionally, throughout most of Latin America, a few families and a few foreign planters owned nearly all the arable land, and the vast majority of those living in rural areas either worked for them almost as serfs or tried to scratch out a subsistence on tiny patches of earth far too small to be farmed economically. Because this system of land tenure lay at the very heart of Latin American society, agrarian reform, as John Kenneth Galbraith has pointed out, was a revolutionary step that would shift power, property, and status from one group to another. And such a step was necessary if the Alliance was to change the social structure and work its revolution. It failed. Faced with a choice between the equitable redistribution of landholdings and increased agricultural production, the Alliance seemed confused about which to choose. In the early years, the Alliance emphasized redistribution of holdings, but it may have underestimated the difficulties of redistribution. If the government broke up a large estate and gave pieces of it to small farmers, it had to give them more than land—to succeed, they needed credit, technology, education, management experience, marketing skill, even access to the nearest highway. Moreover, because small farmers are more likely to be mired in the past, and so be more deeply conservative in skills and practices than big landowners, the small, newly landed farmer was almost certain to be inefficient. Therefore, if land tenure reform was attempted at a single stroke, agricultural production was almost certain to decline steeply (the break up of estates that followed Mexico's 1910 revolution produced a drop in agricultural production that was not fully made up until about 1935). But agricultural production was central to these countries' very existence. In country after country, jobs, foreign exchange, and much more depended on a single commodity such as coffee or sugar. To gamble with its production was to gamble with the nation's economic fate for years to come. And so many governments dragged their feet, not only because landed oligarchs opposed reform but also because governments understandably feared to gamble. They went through the motions of agrarian reform to satisfy the Americans, but they did not undertake deep change—and perhaps they could not, short of violent revolution. The U.S. Congress was also nervous about land redistribution; a subcommittee of the Joint Economic Committee warned that redistribution was a "dangerous aspect of a program for the improvement of agriculture." Congress also opposed using U.S. aid money to buy land for redistribution or even to guarantee Latin American agrarian reform bonds.

Toward the end of the Kennedy administration and during the Johnson administration, the Alliance shifted its emphasis from redistribution of land toward increasing agricultural production and efficiency, seeking to stimulate output by injections of funds for improved seed strains, fertilizer, better irrigation, and better farm management.[4] The Alliance made governments throughout the hemisphere conscious of the need for agrarian reform of some sort. The ideas if not the actual reform have trickled down; if it did nothing else, the Alliance focused attention on the problem, which differs in each country. In somewhat the same way, the Alliance brought to the fore government planning, tax reform, and better tax collection.

*   *   *

Today in the Caribbean, the emerging issues of importance are not military and political, as in Kennedy's time, but economic and social. Perhaps they are emerging now precisely because the Alliance failed to achieve its dual goals: social justice and economic progress.

The Alliance was by no means a disaster. It met or came close to meeting its targeted economic growth rates. It built schools, hospitals, cheap housing, roads, sewage disposal systems, irrigation, electric power—and helped with population control, perhaps the most critical problem of all. The Alliance worked best where the local government made it work—in Venezuela, the shining example. If the nascent democracies it tried to encourage did not always succeed, the Alliance did raise the democratic standard, and its ideas permeated even some of the military regimes that replaced democracies. It also led to the creation of the technocratic bureaucracies that today increasingly play central roles in Latin American governments, whether of the right or of the left; and these nationalistic bureaucracies have come to be confident of their own abilities to pursue national interest without outside advice or interference and determined to take charge of their nations' futures.

Could—and should—the Alliance for Progress be reborn?

Some of the Alliance's early friends have concluded that the whole thing was a bad idea. Perhaps influenced by Vietnam, Senator Frank Church in 1971 called the Alliance "the high-water mark of our innocence in supposing that we could liberate traditional societies from their centuries-long legacy of tyranny and stagnation with a little bit of seed capital and some stirring rhetoric." Despite our enormous power and all our good intentions, Church thought, some undertakings are beyond our strength. We cannot go around promoting revolution—to do so would violate the UN Charter and all diplomatic standards. We should, however, stop promoting counterrevolution; to Church, that meant ending all our bilateral aid except for technical assistance. He too favored "loosening our embrace." By 1974, he had concluded that, without revolution, foreign aid was harmful and, with revolution, it was unnecessary.

Arthur Schlesinger, arguing that the Alliance was "never really tried," that is, tried only during Kennedy's truncated presidency, still believes its formula right and thinks it might yet be revived successfully, provided that four things happen simultaneously: a strong progressive democratic revival takes place in Latin America, a strong liberal administration comes to power in Washington, the

6
THE NIXON-FORD YEARS

Nixon Begins

Richard Nixon did not mention the Western Hemisphere in his inaugural address. But one of the first callers he received in the White House was Galo Plaza, secretary-general of the OAS, who told him the hemisphere was in disarray. Nixon asked what the Latin Americans wanted from us, and Galo Plaza asked permission to ask them. The Chileans proposed that instead of working through the OAS the Latin American leaders meet by themselves, without the United States.

The meeting at a Chilean resort produced the Consensus of Viña del Mar, a document that some specialists consider the most important Latin American declaration in thirty or forty years. (In 1964, Latin American leaders had formed CECLA, the Latin American Special Coordinating Commission, the first purely Latin American body.)

Nixon took other early initiatives. He announced that he was sending Nelson Rockefeller around the hemisphere; he asked Congress to elevate the assistant secretary of state for ARA to under secretary rank; he said at a press conference he considered Latin

America "an area of top priority"; and said that he hoped to visit Latin America himself. These statements raised high hopes among Latin Americans, who had viewed Nixon's election with misgivings. (Many Latin Americans have come to believe that they fare better with a Democratic than with a Republican president.)

The Consensus of Viña del Mar declared that the Alliance for Progress, which had set out to promote profound changes in economic and trade relations between the United States and Latin America, had never been properly implemented; as a result of the failure of the Alliance, the gap between rich and poor nations was still widening. The consensus presented the United States with detailed and far-reaching proposals that added up to better terms of trade (including a U.S. system of generalized nonreciprocal trade preferences for the manufactured and semimanufactured goods of poor countries), easier credit terms, an end of tied aid, and a bigger voice in shaping their own destinies and world affairs.[1]

But what was perhaps most significant about the consensus was its tone. The Latin Americans were not asking—they were demanding. It was a new way of talking to the United States.

Gabriel Valdez Subercaseaux, an aristocratic left nationalist Chilean, presented the consensus to President Nixon in June 1969. Employing the tone of the consensus, he spoke of the need for a "constructive dialogue" between equals, rather than a "monologue." He declared that the interests of Latin America and the United States were not identical. He referred to "so-called assistance" and asserted that far from receiving aid, Latin America was actually contributing to U.S. development, for private American investors took out profits "many times" larger than their investments. The meetings at Viña del Mar stated principles that "must be respected" and specific measures that "should" be implemented. He told President Nixon, "I am not afraid to address Your Excellency in such a clear way, because I know that one of your virtues is frankness."

The presentation, which was regarded as acrimonious by the administration, played squarely into President Nixon's hands. His Nixon Doctrine said that "the United States will participate in the defense and development of allies and friends, but . . . America cannot—and will not—conceive *all* the plans, design *all* the programs, execute *all* the decisions, and undertake *all* the defense of the free nations of the world." The State Department interpreted it thus: "The Nixon Doctrine, as it applies to Latin America, seeks the strengthening of our relations with nations of the Hemisphere on the basis of a mature partnership in which rights and responsibilities are shared by a community of independent states. . . . Our profile has been lowered." President Nixon was only too willing to let the Latin Americans have the initiative. And as we have seen, such influential senators as Fulbright and Church were already skeptical of aid to Latin American countries and wondering if we would not do better in the long run if we loosened our ties with them, removed our suffocating embrace, and encouraged them to turn to Europe and elsewhere.

President Nixon responded to the consensus the following October in an address to the Inter-American Press Association. After indirectly criticizing the Alliance for Progress,[2] he offered "a more mature partnership" between the United States and Latin America. Proposing multilateral assistance and support of Latin American initiatives, he promised to help Latin Americans expand their exports of manufactured and semimanufactured products by leading an effort to reduce nontariff barriers to trade maintained by nearly all industrialized countries. He also promised to support increased technical and financial assistance, to promote procedures for advance consultation on trade policy, and—most important—to "press for a liberal system of generalized tariff preferences for all developing countries." The Generalized System of Preferences (GSP), as it was called, was something the Latin Americans had been wanting since the first United Nations Conference on Trade and Development (UNCTAD) in 1964, when the seventy-seven "less-developed" countries met to see what they could do to improve the terms of their trade with the rich industrialized nations. It called on all rich countries to eliminate or reduce tariffs on all manufactured exports of poor countries. The United States had been committed to the idea at least since 1967, but Congress had not acted on it. Nixon also announced that henceforward aid to Latin America could be spent not only in the United States (tied aid) but anywhere in Latin America. (This meant little.) He said that the United States was ready to help in regional economic integration. Then he stressed the "vital" role of private foreign investment in Latin America and warned that it would dry up if "local conditions face it with unwarranted risks." He responded only with rhetoric to the consensus request that the U.S. share its technology. He said we hoped that eventually all nations would share "the blessings" of democracy, but in the meanwhile, we would deal "realistically with governments . . . as they are." Finally, he denounced Cuba for exporting revolution. In closing, he took note of the feeling that the United States "really 'no longer cares' " about Latin America and said, "We do care. I care."

Official State Department spokesmen hailed it as a major speech that "sets the United States on a new course" in Latin America. Latin Americans, however, regarded it as a signal that the United States was washing its hands of Latin America. "Mature partnership" was regarded as code language for "benign neglect" (or, as one put it, "malign neglect"). Even those State Department specialists who thought it time that we end our hemispheric hegemony and our tutelary role thought we were moving too fast.

Nothing came of the Nixon speech except for a partial loosening of tied aid; nothing came of the Rockefeller report; nothing came of the proposal to elevate the assistant secretary to under secretary. Loans from the Social Progress Trust Fund had already stopped. Soft loans from the IADB made in dollars would now have to be repaid in dollars. Nixon's secretary of the treasury, on leave from a Chicago bank, told IADB that "the multilateral banking approach to development . . . is sound and deserves further emphasis. I underscore *banking* here, with the emphasis on high standards and economic performance by borrowing countries that the term implies." He went on to stress the perils of inflation and the virtues of private enterprise. Five years passed, and with the United States sliding into a deep recession, Congress was still unwilling to enact GSP or to increase financial aid; the administration seemed reluctant to expand commodity agreements in order to protect Latin America from commodity price swings; Latin America continued to bear a debt-service burden of about one-sixth of its total export earnings; and in 1970, the United States enjoyed a net annual flow of funds *from* Latin America of about $500 million—"a condition," as one observer put it, "which prompted some Latin Americans to wonder precisely who was aiding whom."

Nixon destroyed the autonomy of the Peace Corps and radically altered its direction. Under President Kennedy, Peace Corps volunteers had tended to be idealistic young people with liberal arts educations; under Nixon, they tended to be retired plumbers who took their families abroad with them. The Nixon administration viewed the giant multinational corporations, so widely criticized in Latin America, as "an important positive factor." A thoughtful Jamaican observed, "The Nixon Administration has no policy toward Latin America—except when a big U.S. corporation is threatened." Charles Meyer, Nixon's assistant secretary for ARA, an amiable man on leave from Sears Roebuck, showed considerable skill in bantering with congressional committees, but sometimes he seemed somewhat muddleheaded. Nixon appointed his share of political, noncareer ambassadors. His ambassador to Jamaica harbored antiblack sentiments, intervened clumsily in Jamaican politics, and ended by being declared persona non grata, something unheard of in the Caribbean.

After the initiatives of Nixon's first ten months, Secretary Rogers, Assistant Secretary Meyer, and his cautious successor, Jack Kubisch, as well as President Nixon himself, made innumerable speeches on Latin America and answered innumerable questions about it at press conferences; but nothing happened. Often the speeches were clad in the soaring rhetoric of the Alliance for Progress, filled with phrases about "the legitimate aspirations" of the underprivileged masses of Latin America; but nothing lay behind the rhetoric.[3] Year after year, Secretary of State William Pierce Rogers trudged up to Capitol Hill and, in a short paragraph in a long policy statement, promised congressional committees that we were in truth developing "a more mature partnership" with Latin America, regretted that he had paid less heed to it last year than he had hoped, and promised to do better next year; but he never did. Once a congressman asked if the policy of cooperating with governments regardless of their internal policies meant that the Alliance's objective of strengthening democracy was dead; Meyer's answer was vague. Nixon, in a message to Congress, acknowledged the widespread feeling that we were neglecting Latin America and said it resulted from his deliberate decision to reduce "our visibility" and encourage Latin Americans to "play more active roles" themselves.

Latin Americans had liked some of Nixon's early initiatives. He seemed to have been saying that Latin Americans have grown up, that we are going to stop preaching to them. But that soon deteriorated into a low profile, they felt, and before long, the low profile became, as one said, *no* profile. Foreign policy is permeable and is dominated by our security interests, and when our security interests decline—as they seemed to in the Caribbean after the Cuban missile crisis and the death of Ché Guevara—other interests, such as big business, big labor, or emotional domestic public or political opinion, invade policy.

In 1961, President Kennedy had invited the suggestions of Latin American leaders and then had adopted those suggestions into the Alliance for Progress. In 1969, President Nixon had invited the suggestions of Latin American leaders. In response, they had produced the Consensus of Viña del Mar, but he almost completely ignored it. In the long sweep of history, the Consensus of Viña del Mar may turn out to have been the last chance the Latin Americans gave us before going their own way. It not only gave Latin American demands a sharp new edge, it also began the shift in the Caribbean from political-strategic issues to social-economic issues, the leading issues to this day.

Kissinger, State, and Congress

Latin Americans who had learned to expect little from President Nixon expected little from his appointed successor, Gerald Ford, and they got little. In fairness, it should be said that no president coming to the White House in the wake of Vietnam and Watergate could be expected to devote much time to Latin America.

Latin Americans did, however, briefly hope for better times when in 1973 Secretary Rogers was replaced by Henry Kissinger, a jaunty, bouncy academician with whom Latin Americans felt comfortable. Kissinger's prestige was enormous at that time, the time of Vietnam and Watergate. President Nixon was reeling, the whole U.S. system seemed to be collapsing, and virtually the only thing standing between the American people and the abyss was Kissinger. On October 5, 1973, only a few days after being sworn into office, Kissinger gave a lunch for Latin American delegates to the UN General Assembly. At the lunch, he said, "I am grateful . . . for this opportunity to tell you that we are serious about starting a new dialogue with our friends in the Americas." (Valdez, in presenting the consensus, had urged a "dialogue.") Then five months later, in February, Kissinger went to Mexico City to attend a meeting of

Latin American foreign ministers—the Conference of Tlatelolco. At the conference, he reiterated his "new dialogue" idea and proposed that the nations of the hemisphere "avoid both condescension and confrontation." The Nixon administration, he said, was prepared to give strong support to congressional enactment of GSP, to participate in a new inter-American commission on technology, to share our research on energy sources and explore ways of financing oil deficits, to maintain present U.S. aid levels, and to participate in reshaping the inter-American system. The conference was acclaimed a great success, and hopes were high for "the spirit of Tlatelolco" and the "new dialogue." But nothing resulted. Before long, Caribbean leaders were saying, "We are talking more about the new dialogue than we are dialoguing." Some Caribbean leaders took to calling it "a hoax." The conference, like Nixon's initial moves, raised then dashed hopes. Kissinger scheduled a number of trips to the Caribbean or South America, but each time he canceled. It was 1976 before he finally made a quick trip there. The most charitable Caribbean leaders simply concluded that Kissinger, like Nixon and Ford, had no interest in Latin America. A cynical bureaucrat in ARA said, "This disaster of the new dialogue was like the Dominican intervention—it was mercifully short."

Kissinger, preoccupied with the Middle East, the Soviet Union, Western Europe, and China—not to mention Vietnam and the rest of Southeast Asia—had little time for Latin America. This has been true of every secretary of state at least since Acheson. But although Secretary Rusk had been unable to devote time to Latin America, President Kennedy had been interested in it. Nixon and Ford were not. Without interest at the top, there is no hope. In their time, it would have taken an explosion in the Caribbean to get our attention. After Kissinger became secretary, the men in ARA made a determined effort to get his ear, and they felt they were making some progress. Then war broke out in the Middle East, and Kissinger attempted to end it by personal diplomacy. After he made his first visit to the Middle East, he found that other rulers, fearful for their prestige, refused to deal with anyone else; he spread himself too thin. He had entered the department intending to institutionalize foreign policy; instead, he personalized it. Dean Acheson once said that policy does not trickle down from above, it bubbles up from below.[4] But Kissinger made policy himself, on high, and only later informed the ARA bureau. This changed in 1974, when William Dill Rogers was appointed assistant secretary. Rogers, an able, experienced man of liberal bent who had been Moscoso's deputy in the Alliance under Kennedy, had refused the assistant secretary's job under Nixon but, at Kissinger's urging, accepted it under Ford. Since the 1966 escalation in Vietnam, ARA had had inadequate leadership on high, and the ARA assistant secretaries had been unable or unwilling to make policy themselves. Rogers, who had a certain political base of his own, was willing to make policy declarations without clearing them with Kissinger. He was surely the best and strongest ARA assistant secretary at least since Ed Martin in Kennedy's time. Before Rogers' appointment, Kissinger had attempted to handle only two Caribbean issues: he had taken steps to get the Panama Canal negotiations moving, and he had attempted to get our relationship with Cuba moving. Rogers no doubt would have liked to have pushed both, but they faced strong opposition in Congress, and without active support from President Ford or Secretary Kissinger—unlikely in an election year—Rogers could do little. He had taken the job hoping to change our indifference toward Latin America, but events conspired against him. In mid-1976, Rogers became under secretary for economic affairs—the first time since Sumner Welles that we had an able man deeply interested in Latin America at the under secretary level (although Rogers was not the first deputy to Kissinger). Moreover, Rogers was replaced at ARA by Harry W. Shlaudeman, a liberal-minded career officer experienced in Latin American affairs and one of the ablest men in the State Department. Thus, the State Department was prepared to handle new initiatives whenever the White House desired.

Although the secretary of state is the senior member of a president's cabinet, he often does not control foreign policy. The Rockefeller report estimated that the State Department controlled less than half the decisions relating to the Western Hemisphere—the rest were scattered among Treasury, Commerce, Agriculture, and Defense. The Nixon Doctrine, which sought to substitute increased foreign military assistance for American troops, often gave control of foreign policy to the Pentagon and the Armed Services committees of Congress. Under Nixon, the secretary of the treasury was chairman of the committee that developed U.S. positions on loan applications to the IADB and the World Bank. Congressman Fascell, told that

World Bank and IADB policies were under review, once remarked, "Does that mean that somebody has decided that the Secretary of the Treasury ought not to be making foreign policy decisions?" Kissinger has said that in the last three administrations, State's policymaking role had declined partly because internally the department was more geared to clearing cables than to making long-range policy and partly because no one higher than assistant secretary had time to think. Power in the department is in the hands of the middle bureaucracy—the geographical assistant secretaries and their immediate deputies. At times, the president's national security advisor carries more weight than the secretary of state. Dean Acheson had warned against permitting any presidential assistant to direct cabinet officers, for then power "becomes anonymous" and "there can be no more dangerous situation" in our system. Averell Harriman once opposed creating a White House staff for policy planning—policy should be made in the department, which commanded specialized skills and day-to-day contact with operations, whereas White House planning ran the risk of producing "ivory tower policies." The secretary's relationship to the president—and to the Congress—is of the utmost importance. If it becomes clear that in 90 percent of interdepartmental disputes the president will support his secretary of state, the secretary will not have to carry most disputes to him. But if it is clear that the secretary of the treasury will prevail, foreign policy's limits will be fixed by budgetary considerations. Acheson advised the secretary to join the White House group when it gathered to draft a foreign policy speech for the president, for that is where high policy usually is made. Senator Mansfield adjured Kissinger to see to it that CIA and military attachés at embassies owed their first loyalty to State as they had under Kennedy. "What this committee wants to see is the supremacy of the Department of State restored," Mansfield said. He went on to note that the State Department has by far the smallest budget of any regular department of government.

Many varied forces influence foreign policy: big business, big labor, the CIA, the Pentagon, other government departments, the political parties, the press, the academic comunity, and more. And when the president and secretary of state pay little heed to an area, outside influences tend to override State Department policy, as they did in the Caribbean during the Nixon-Ford years.

It is often asserted that "politics stops at the water's edge."

Actually, that is often where politics begins. Some hold that domestic public opinion and domestic political considerations should have no place in foreign policymaking. A long line of scholars—from de Tocqueville through Lippmann and Kennan and Acheson—has concluded that mass opinion is incapable of deciding questions of foreign policy wisely. James Reston has said that the Senate almost invariably gets into trouble when it tries to direct U.S. foreign policy. All this raises an ultimate question: is democracy well suited to conduct foreign affairs? Kennan once acknowledged a "distaste amounting almost to horror for the chaotic disorder of the American political process." Acheson once groaned that after 1949 he was obliged to spend one-sixth of his time as secretary in preparing for or attending meetings with Congress. Every secretary of state and every foreign service officer has probably, at one time or another, privately damned the press. Certainly, the men in the Kremlin who make Soviet foreign policy have little need to consider Soviet public opinion. But in an open society such as ours, it is hard to see how the State Department could possibly ignore American public opinion.

The relationship between the State Department and the Congress is essentially an adversary relationship: Congress has the power to raise armies, declare war, and appropriate money; the president is commander in chief of the armed forces and head of foreign affairs. The balance of power between the executive and the Congress is constantly shifting. Congress reacted to the interventionism of Theodore Roosevelt and Woodrow Wilson by rejecting the Treaty of Versailles and leading American foreign policy into isolationism. Under FDR, foreign policy leadership passed back to the White House, where it stayed through the Kennedy administration, reaching its peak under President Johnson in Vietnam. But Johnson went too far, and Nixon tried to go too far: the country and the Congress rebelled. By the time Nixon was driven from office, Congress had the bit in its teeth on foreign policy, and it stayed that way under President Ford. Moreover, whereas during Nixon's last years in office Secretary Kissinger seemed to be a miracle worker and Congress deferred to his judgment, in Ford's time Congress began asserting itself against Kissinger. Members of Congress, determined to avoid another Vietnam, forbade American involvement in Angola. Repeatedly, Congress intervened in foreign affairs; repeatedly, Kissinger warned it not to. But he was no longer trusted, and demands for his resignation were made. He became a controversial issue early in the 1976 campaign. His policies—détente with the Soviet Union, shuttle diplomacy to the Arabs and Israelis, aid to an Angola faction, negotiations with Panama, and talk of negotiations with Castro—were attacked from all sides. Congress seemed determined to get control of foreign policy. As the attacks mounted, everyone lost sight of the basic reality that all the awful problems of foreign policy are intractable, that many are not capable of solution, and that, as often as not, all the alternative policies are bad.

Congress usually influences foreign policy by appropriating or refusing to appropriate money, by ratifying treaties, by investigating and holding committee hearings, by approving executive appointments, and by passing resolutions expressing the sense of the Congress. Sometimes it goes further, as in Senator Jackson's effort to make Soviet-American relations contingent on the Soviet Union's liberalizing its emigration policies for Jews. State tends to resent such initiatives. Many foreign service officers—and secretaries—are convinced that members of Congress are ill prepared to deal with foreign policy questions and are interested only in matters that directly affect their own constituents. Neither State nor Congress thinks highly of the other. State thinks that the members of Congress engage in sordid politics and drink too much. Congress considers the department elitist, unable to comprehend political realities. State is constantly appalled at the amendments Congress tacks onto bills, limiting State's maneuverability; Congress thinks State wants to give money away.

All too often, the assistant secretary of state for congressional relations does little more than handle congressional mail, usually involving a constituent's complaint. Although he is all too often a bureaucrat with little political insight, occasionally he is an experienced politician with White House connections. Fred Dutton was a member of the White House staff when he became assistant secretary under Kennedy and therefore had considerable influence. At his suggestion, Secretary Rusk ordered returning foreign service officers to visit their home political districts. Dutton also arranged meetings between members of Congress and foreign service officers, and he made a point of trying to warn Congress privately of foreign policy crises anticipated by the geographical bureaus.

Some Latin American diplomats are convinced that big U.S.

corporations, and not the State Department, really make U.S. foreign policy by having their lobbyists put pressure on Congress. And one can find instances that justify that conviction, for example, the successful lobby for the Hickenlooper Amendment by the head of ITT. Nonetheless, only a handful of Latin American ambassadors in Washington cultivate congressmen and senators. Some avoid them because they are discouraged, some because they are disorganized, and some because they consider that cultivating them would be an unacceptable intervention in domestic American affairs.

Although Congress supported the Alliance for Progress under President Kennedy, more recently it has been reluctant to vote appropriations for foreign aid, and it has been pressing to eliminate foreign military aid to Latin America entirely. The influence of domestic politics and of Congress on foreign policy has seldom been clearer than it was near the end of the Nixon presidency. At that time, two big Caribbean issues were surfacing—a new Panama Canal treaty and normalizing relations with Cuba. Although the issues differed, roughly about a third of the Senate and a third or more of the House opposed both—and they belonged to the same right wing of both parties that Nixon was counting on to block his conviction if he were impeached. Thus impeachment effectively blocked movement toward a policy shift. After Nixon left office, the Ford administration, eyeing right-wing Republican support for Ronald Reagan, was loathe to deal with either issue until after the 1976 election.

Shortly after Nixon became president, the House subcommittee on Latin America held extensive hearings on strategy for inter-American development. Congressman Fascell (D.-Fla.), the chairman, expressed doubt that Congress could do anything to improve our relations with Latin America because of economic nationalism—expropriation of American properties was the order of the day. Congressman H. R. Gross (R.-Iowa) complained of having been misled into thinking that the Alliance would make U.S. investments safer, whereas in fact it had made them riskier. Nevertheless, the subcommittee issued a report that called for "a renewed commitment" to the objectives of the Alliance for Progress; the report was issued at a time when the Nixon administration sounded as if it intended to do exactly that. But the administration reversed direction and went backward. And as the administration's interest in Latin America waned, so did most congressmen's interest, except for two issues—the Canal and Cuba. As relations between President Nixon and Congress worsened, exchanges between members of Congress and the executive became increasingly sharp. During a Senate Foreign Relations Committee hearing in 1973, Senator Fulbright asked the assistant secretary of state for economic affairs, who was testifying, "Why do you shy away from the reason? . . . Why are you so reluctant to be truthful about it?" In 1970, Fascell and others on his subcommittee complained bitterly that the White House was willing to brief the press about rumors that Soviet submarines had a base in Cuba but was unwilling to send witnesses to tell the subcommittee about it or even to make its press briefing available to the subcommittee. In August 1969, Senator Fulbright said that "our relations in Latin America are in a deplorable state," and he denounced administration secrecy. Fulbright also complained because the military outvoted the Senate Foreign Relations Committee in Congress. Criticizing the proliferation of the intelligence community, he voiced a widely held congressional view when he said, "I have a feeling . . . that for twenty-five years we assumed we had to save the world from itself. We have become an international busybody." In 1975, Senator Gail W. McGee (D.-Wyo.), recalling that almost exactly a year earlier the hemisphere was filled with "the spirit of Tlatelolco" and "the new dialogue," said the first anniversary of Tlatelolco was "more like a wake than a celebration." He hoped rather wistfully that Secretary Kissinger would be able to find time to testify before his subcommittee. But Kissinger did not.

* * *

During the Nixon-Ford years, while the U.S. government was ignoring it, the Caribbean itself was undergoing radical and wrenching change. Let us now depart Washington and look closely at what has been going on inside the Caribbean states themselves. And let us see how our policies look to them.

Black Power and the Black Caribbean

The Haitian constitution of 1805 destroyed color distinction and decreed that henceforward all Haitians would be known as blacks. The term became popular in the United States about 1967, the

same time that the civil rights movement became a black revolution—one aspect of which was the Black Power movement. The
Black Power movement reached the Caribbean about 1968, the year
Martin Luther King was assassinated, blacks burned American cities,
and Nixon was elected president. But Black Power was to some
extent indigenous in the Caribbean: Marcus Garvey, Jamaica's
national hero, was a black nationalist of the 1920s; C. L. R. James of
Trinidad tried to organize black pan-Caribbean nationalism in the
1920s; and Stokely Carmichael came from Trinidad-Tobago. Caribbean blacks had always looked to blacks in the United States, and
beginning in 1968, some of them began to wear sandals, beads, exotic
clothes, and African hairstyles. The Black Power movement in the
Caribbean was not anti-American per se, although it sometimes took
that form; rather, it was antiestablishment. It began on university
campuses and was, as in the United States, to some extent linked to
the youth revolt and protest over Vietnam. Walter Rodney, a young
Guyanese historian, lecturing on Black Power at the University of
the West Indies in Jamaica, said, "The Caribbean is predominantly a
black nation, and as such the blacks have a right to power
commensurate with their own numbers." In the fall of 1968, Jamaica
deported him, and protesters rioted all over the black commonwealth
Caribbean. Lloyd Best, an economist who was a Black Power leader
in Trinidad, has said that the Rodney incident "revealed the powder
keg."

People in the Caribbean like to think they are without race
prejudice. But the Dominican Republic has few black physicians or
generals; Costa Rica for years forbade blacks to ride its trains;
Guyana was nearly torn to pieces by racial rioting; and people in the
Caribbean are quick to categorize a man's color, noting that the
Caribbean leadership is predominantly brown. A high-ranking
brown Jamaican diplomat maintains almost belligerently, "We are a
black nation," but Prime Minister Manley of Jamaica looks to be of
mixed ancestry. Although Prime Minister Williams of Trinidad-
Tobago and Prime Minister Burnham of Guyana are black, their
ministers are of mixed blood.

On campuses, Black Power tends to be associated with the New
Left. In the streets, it has tried with little success to ally itself with
labor unions; almost without exception the establishment politicians
whom Black Power opposes themselves sprang from the labor move-

ment and maintain their bases there. The Black Power movement is a separatist movement that favors separate but equal black and white societies. Some think Black Power is declining in the Caribbean, just as radicalism in general has declined throughout the world. Others think it will not decline because of its links to nationalism. The movement helped force governments into expropriating American property and reclaiming their countries' natural resources, and it has put pressure on Manley of Jamaica, Williams of Trinidad-Tobago, and Burnham of Guyana to move to the left. When Black Power radicals from the United States tried to establish a base in Guyana, Burnham got rid of them. Manley has attempted to contain Black Power in Jamaica by preaching socialism and egalitarianism and by identifying himself with "the sufferers," as he calls the poor in Jamaica's shantytowns.

In 1970, in Trinidad-Tobago, the Black Power movement nearly overthrew the government. Beginning with a small demonstration by nine men against the white power structure, it mobilized 10,000 in a week, and for eight weeks they paralyzed Trinidad, marching in African robes and raising clenched fists, looting, burning, and throwing bombs. White middle-class Trinidadians began to leave for Barbados. Then, a demonstrator was killed by the police, and 30,000 people went to his funeral. They called a general strike, and Prime Minister Williams imposed martial law, which led to military mutiny. The Williams government asked the United States for help. The Nixon administration responded with a planeload of arms and ammunition and a six-ship squadron to evacuate American nationals if necessary, but announced it would not intervene because it considered the problem Britain's, not ours. Venezuela, only ten miles south of Trinidad, prepared to intervene and sent planes into Trinidad airspace and ships into Trinidad waters. Government troops finally put down the revolt. A few demonstrators briefly turned terrorist, emulating the *tupamaros,* but the police broke them brutally. As a result, the governments of smaller islands took steps to suppress or deport Black Power leaders—Barbados banned all Black Power spokesmen; Grenada nearly doubled its police force; St. Vincent got up a list of "undesirable aliens."

Traditionally, tensions have existed between the black English-speaking Caribbean and the mestizo Spanish-speaking Caribbean; it has been easier for Guyana to relate to Jamaica than to the Dominican

Republic. When Trinidad applied for OAS membership, Prime Minister Williams felt some OAS members seemed cool to it because of race prejudice. But the OAS countries had other reasons: they feared that the English-speaking states would form a bloc that could be manipulated by the United States and Great Britain and would reduce the Spanish-speaking countries' share of U.S. financial aid. Their British tradition—and their leaders' British educations—has tended to make them more democratic, more liberal, and less militaristic than the Spanish Caribbean.

A high Trinidad official believes, however, that a new regrouping of Caribbean nations may emerge now that the metropolitan powers have all but departed and new economic issues have arisen. Haiti and the Dominican Republic have shown an interest in joining the Caribbean Common Market (CARICOM); Trinidad wants to bring Cuba into it and consistently voted to end OAS sanctions against Cuba. Both Spanish-speaking and English-speaking nations are in ferment today, and both are to some extent hostile to the United States. They tend, therefore, to make common cause against us on economic issues. Those shared interests may be able to bring them together as never before.

Black Caribbean leaders, many of whom have been knighted, tend to be well-educated, moderate leftists, able leaders—notably better than those in most Spanish-speaking Caribbean countries. But the new leaders who will emerge from the campuses and the unions may be far more radical and less well educated. This may be the last generation of trained men; the day of the wild man may yet arrive in the English-speaking Caribbean. Wealthy white residents of Tobago, which has been free of the Black Power movement that afflicted Trinidad, say, "We may have a few more years of peace." The potential future leaders are being educated, not in England, as today's leaders were, but at the University of the West Indies and other local institutions and at Howard University in Washington, a black university that is a product of U.S. segregation. Recently, members of the black caucus in our Congress have shown an interest in the black Caribbean. Their interest, as well as an incredible number of immigrants from the black Caribbean now living in the United States, may someday force the U.S. government to develop a policy for the black Caribbean; today, it has none.

Jamaica. Jamaica, a British Crown Colony until 1944, is probably the most advanced of the English-speaking Caribbean nations. In 1938, riots spawned a mass trade union movement (led by Alexander Bustamante) and a mass political party (led by Norman Manley) demanding political independence and social and economic reform. Before long, Bustamante, the union leader, formed a political party, and Manley, the political leader, formed a trade union. Bustamante's party and his union became the more conservative of the two. The result was the most effective two-party system in the English-speaking Caribbean. As a Jamaican diplomat put it, "We have a working commitment to democracy." Jamaica made probably the most serene and sophisticated transition from colony to independent state in our time—so orderly, in fact, that Prime Minister Michael Manley (son of Norman Manley) once said that many young Jamaicans today feel themselves "cheated by history," that is, deprived of heroism in the birth of liberty.

But although Jamaica gained political independence, some Jamaican leaders contend that it did not gain economic independence. Until recently, the bauxite industry was entirely owned by North Americans and much of its tourist and sugar industries are still owned by foreigners. Agriculture has stagnated—and half the population depends on agriculture. As a consequence of all this, more than 20 percent of the work force is unemployed, and young people, who suffer the highest unemployment rates, are close to angry rebellion. In Prime Minister Manley's view, the economy must be restructured: land reform, tax reform, nationalization and industrialization, and interindustry linkages. Jamaica exports J$62 million of sugar, bananas, citrus, and coffee, but it imports J$60 million worth of food. As part of his agrarian reform program, the government would buy back all sugarland from big foreign corporations and convert at least some into cooperatives. His programs also include mobilization of Jamaica's young people for national service. Because he seeks joint foreign-Jamaican ownership and control of new industry, he refuses to grant tax incentives indiscriminately to foreign capital.

In politics, the trade union movement is all-important. Everything is unionized, and both the major parties are labor-based. Each party has its own union—and its own thugs. Running a labor-based government is not easy; it is hard for a prime minister to discipline his own union while the opposition union is behaving militantly. In the 1950s, Manley's Bauxite Workers' Union pursued an aggressive wage policy against the giants of the bauxite industry—Alcoa, Kaiser, and Reynolds of the United States, and Alcan of Canada. When the companies began quoting wage rates in Guyana and Surinam to counter Jamaican union claims, the Jamaican union formed the pan-Caribbean Bauxite, Mining, and Metalworkers Federation, with Manley at its head; the union made huge gains in wages and fringe benefits.

Bauxite dominates U.S.-Jamaican relations. (So often in the Caribbean a single commodity controls.) The Manley government's proposed takeover of the bauxite industry more closely resembled President Frei's negotiated nationalization of Chilean copper than Allende's or Castro's outright expropriations. Manley wanted to gain a controlling interest in the American and Canadian companies and wanted to relate the price of bauxite to the price of finished aluminum ingots. The U.S. aluminum companies had about $600 million invested in Jamaica, most of it covered by OPIC guarantees, at the time. Therefore, when Manley went to Washington to ask the State Department to stay out of the negotiations, State replied that it could not because of the policy on investment disputes. Asked whether the U.S. government "leaned on" the Jamaican Embassy in Washington, a Jamaican diplomat said, "No—but they told us the consequences of failure to agree. I'd say tilt, not lean." The State Department, afraid of Alcoa's lobby on Capitol Hill, slowed down an AID loan to Jamaica. The initial negotiations failed, and in March 1974, Jamaica unilaterally imposed a direct tax on bauxite, which raised the government's revenues by nearly 700 percent. The United States contends that the tax raised the price of bauxite from $2.50 to $14, raised the price of aluminum in the United States from 25¢ to 39¢ a pound, but did not affect the companies' earnings (because they passed the increase on to consumers). A Jamaican diplomat has said that U.S. government grants and loans from 1945 to 1973 came to a total of only $97 million, and in one year, the new bauxite tax will give Jamaica twice that amount. Sir Egerton Richardson, the preeminent Jamaican bauxite negotiator, has said, "Up until now the companies have got the ore for the cost of getting it out of the ground. Now they have to pay for its intrinsic value plus a tax on profits made in mining. Formerly, the United States Internal Revenue Service actually got more tax money than the Jamaican Government from bauxite mining.'' The U.S. Treasury Department was unhappy, the companies screamed in anguish about government intervention, and their lobbyists marched up to Capitol Hill and may have been responsible for a punitive proviso in the Trade Act of 1974. Then the Jamaican government, a self-proclaimed socialist government, set out to reclaim ownership of its own bauxite resources and to participate in the equity and profits of the six foreign companies. (Kaiser and Reynolds separately agreed to sell all their bauxite and agricultural lands, all their livestock, and 51 percent of their mining assets to the Jamaican government; the government leased the bauxite lands back to the companies but retained title.) Negotiations continued.

Jamaican planners realized that if they were to take full advantage of their new bauxite riches, industries would have to be developed to take the place of bauxite when the bauxite reserves were exhausted. Although Jamaica possessed trained and talented people for such a project, allocating funds for it is difficult politically when food prices are rising rapidly and unemployment is high. One Jamaican planner said that the best use of the money for the next twenty-five years would be education: for five or ten years, development of aluminum and other industries; for today, get the unemployed off the streets. Because politicians must think about today, the Manley government raised public employees' salaries and spent millions on a massive politically administered make-work program—sweeping streets and patching roads by hand. Manley felt that if he had not taken the unemployed off the streets, Jamaica would have exploded in riots.

Pressed hard by Black Power and the New Left, Manley set out to restructure society along socialist lines, a redistribution of wealth that fell most heavily on the middle class. He tried to set up a sophisticated, highly technological state without the mechanisms for production, marketing, or price control. For example, the government built beautiful new supermarkets but could not stock them. Inflation and unemployment remained high. Agriculture declined and imports increased. Gangsters from the United States began flying to Jamaica in planes loaded with guns and trading them in Jamaica for marijuana grown there; street crime became widespread; armed bank robbery, unheard of a half-dozen years earlier, became commonplace. Racism rose. The slums seethed with violence. Soon, people feared even the main streets after dark. As a result, tourism declined, and many upper-class and middle-class Jamaicans, frightened by the violence and fearing Manley's socialism, fled to the United States and Canada, taking large amounts of capital with them. Dissatisfaction became widespread.

In 1975, the opposition party headed by Edward Seaga began demanding new elections. Seaga, a leftist who for tactical reasons turned right, courted the middle class, spoke out for private initiative, and denounced Manley's socialism. For a time, the United States seemed tempted to favor him, but many people who regard him as an opportunist and a violent man likely to wage a McCarthyesque campaign thought it would be a mistake. Elections were held in 1976, and Manley won.

Jamaica faces many problems. It has a free press, educated worldly lawyers, impressive economists, an entrenched establishment loyal to the queen; yet it also has a destitute rural population and city slums wracked with violence. A change to better the lot of the masses is imperative. Manley, despite his moves toward nationalization, land reform, and mass mobilization, insists that socialism, two-party democracy, egalitarianism, personal and political freedom, and a mixed economy are compatible and will bring about the most peaceful and constitutional revolution in history. If his program were to fail, and if a Marxist-Leninist leader appeared, a real Marxist-Leninist movement might arise.

In 1962, Khrushchev proposed to Bustamante that the Soviet Union and Jamaica exchange ambassadors. Bustamante replied, "Not just yet." An exchange was finally worked out under Manley in 1975. A PRC trade fair opened in Kingston. Jamaica began air service to Cuba. Manley began to move in tandem with the Third World and with Venezuela and Mexico. Under Manley, Jamaica is no longer automatically "with the West," as Bustamante put it in the 1960s. Its attitude toward the United States is ambivalent. It has many ties to us: many of its young people went, and are going, to college in the United States; many Jamaicans come here to work; Jamaicans respect our power. But the black revolution in the United States evoked sympathy in Jamaica. And Vietnam soured everything. Although Vietnam did not arouse the masses as Black Power aroused them, it alienated the educated classes. It became fashionable to denounce the multinational corporations. Some resented the affluence of American tourists even while they encouraged tourism. "Admiration of you yet resentment," said a Jamaican. "Esteem yet distrust and suspicion." It is not uncommon throughout the Caribbean today.

Trinidad-Tobago. Trinidad entered its modern era after World War I, when oil was discovered, indentured servitude abolished, and the Trinidad Labour Party established. Oil and sugar workers rioted in 1937 because of low wages and high unemployment. Soon demands began for independence. Eric Williams assumed political leadership in 1956, and when in 1962 Trinidad became independent, he was elected prime minister. He has been prime minister ever since. An eccentric, unpredictable man given to criticizing his own party and threatening to resign, a serious historian and lively writer and speaker, Williams confides in no one and often appears to be a prisoner of the anticolonialist past, not a leader of the future, as Manley of Jamaica may turn out to be. Williams, a skillful politician, had used patronage to build up his party's machine at subdistrict levels and has strengthened his position by paving streets and improving water supplies in villages. Originally a charismatic leader, in recent years he has become aloof and remote. He has been in power so long that he has become accustomed to making all decisions—his cabinet only discusses. Some believe he has recently shown a tendency to authoritarianism. The press detects hints of government control.

Unlike Jamaica, Trinidad has only one real political party: Williams's party. In Jamaica, opposition takes the normal channels of parliament and the labor movement, but in Trinidad, Williams has all but destroyed parliament, and Trinidad's unions are far less free than Jamaica's. All governments work on narrow margins, but the margin would seem to be unduly narrow in Trinidad. Sooner or later, Trinidad will face the difficult problem of the transfer of power. The principal opposition to Williams comes from the Tapia House Group, a faculty association with socialist overtones at the University of the West Indies in Port-of-Spain; this group is led by Lloyd Best, earlier a Black Power leader. Both the orthodox Marxist left and Black Power would exclude elites; yet Tapia is an elite.

The ambassador of Trinidad-Tobago to Washington once said, "Our three-letter foreign policy is OIL." Trinidad grows such export crops as sugar and cocoa, but its economic base is petroleum, which it both produces and refines. At first, Williams and his party proposed only that the government promote further development of natural resources in the fashion of Puerto Rico. This effort failed. In 1971, Williams reversed policy and proposed that the government take control of its natural resources—that the government buy outright or buy an even 50 percent share or buy a controlling 51 percent share in the oil companies, principally Shell and Texaco, and in the big, British-owned sugar company. Since then, the government has acquired a controlling interest in the sugar company, complete control of the Shell holdings, about a 63 percent share of production in a new oil field, and it has entered negotiation with Texaco over its operations. It has gained participation in or outright ownership of various other enterprises. No 100 percent foreign-owned company will be allowed to enter the country. Trinidad-Tobago has undertaken all this with the help of Canada, the World Bank, the IADB, and perhaps the Shah of Iran—not the United States. The United States loaned Trinidad-Tobago $29 million and granted it $40 million between the end of World War II and 1966, when AID pulled out entirely. The Trinidad-Tobago ambassador to Washington has said, "We don't want aid, we don't like handouts, we are proud." Trinidad-Tobago regarded our grants as "reparations" for damage it claims from our wartime base. "Americans don't realize they are dealing with a small country and a sensitive people," the ambassador said. "We feel more British than American—but we're not British either," and he spoke at length about his people. The question of identity—it is a besetting problem for the black and independent Caribbean.

The government derived $350 million from oil in 1974—over half its total revenue. What has it done with its oil money? It has loaned some $25 million to Jamaica and $20 million to Guyana and subscribed $7.7 million to the Caribbean Development Bank. It has undertaken public works to reduce unemployment, officially at 15 percent but actually much higher. It has been trying to establish ammonia plants and plants manufacturing petrochemicals from oil. It hopes to build an aluminum smelter, using its own natural gas for power and processing alumina from Guyana, Jamaica, and possibly Surinam. It hopes to create joint public-private ventures to develop industries based on oil. It has published ads in newspapers as far away as Chicago, calling trained Trinidadian experts home. But in Trinidad, as in Jamaica, political pressures and unemployment have forced the government to waste some of its new riches. In 1974, it raised the pay of civil servants 45 percent, raised the pay of its oil field workers by some 40 percent, cut taxes, and, in order to reduce the cost of living, paid government subsidies on certain products. Foreign diplomats were inclined to doubt that the government's development program would succeed, and even if it did, they felt it would do little to reduce unemployment.

Port-of-Spain, the capital of Trinidad-Tobago, is, like Kingston, essentially a small town living at a leisurely pace, quite unlike the bustle of Caracas or Chicago. Again like Jamaica, Trinidad has had increasing street crime and violence. Beneath the surface lie serious political tensions. Strikes in sugar and oil have become increasingly political since the government took over; they are, in effect, strikes against the government, and they bear racial overtones. Some foreign diplomats believe that leftist pressure is forcing Williams toward socialism, though not so fast as Manley of Jamaica or Burnham of Guyana. In 1960, Williams went out of his way to make it clear that Trinidad-Tobago was west of the Iron Curtain and would take its place in the OAS. Some Trinidad-Tobago politicians criticized him, saying he had thrown away Trinidad-Tobago's independence and turned its back on Africa. Later, Williams began to work to repeal the OAS sanctions against Cuba, and he took various steps to strengthen Trinidad-Tobago's ties to Africa, including sending an ambassador to Addis Ababa (which also obliged him to send one to India). In 1972, the Williams government resisted U.S. pressure and voted against us to admit the People's Republic of China to the United Nations. The first governor-general of Trinidad was Chinese.

Guyana. In 1968, only a few weeks after Richard Nixon was first elected president, the party of Prime Minister Forbes Burnham won outright the first election after Guyana's independence. During the campaign, the party of Cheddi Jagan had openly declared for Marxism-Leninism. Although Burnham had publicly rejected Marxism-Leninism in Washington, his opponents say he had secretly been a communist since his student days in London, where along with Kenyatta and Nkrumah he was trained by a member of the Comintern. Most people, however, consider Burnham an opportunist rather than an ideologue, a shrewd and nimble politician. (One former high U.S. official has said that Burnham agreed to help the CIA get rid of Jagan "for a price.") Although his black party contains only a minority of Guyana's divided black-Indian population, Burnham has won reelection—through fraud and with the help of the military. He still has vestiges of the common touch, but as he remains in power, he seems increasingly arrogant. He constantly reiterates, "We have come from a slave society." When Martin Luther King was assassinated, Burnham ordered an official day of mourning and led 10,000 people in a candlelight procession through the streets of Georgetown. In his oration, he quoted King, "I have a dream. . . ."

Since independence, Burnham's development plans have accomplished little. Unemployment hovers around 30 percent. In 1970, Burnham proclaimed Guyana the first "Cooperative Republic" on earth, but despite a stream of speeches and papers, the meaning of "Cooperative Republic" is not clear. Under President Johnson, the United States gave Burnham large quantities of AID, but after our fear of Jagan subsided and Nixon came to power, no major new loan or grant agreements were signed. Subsequently, Burnham denounced foreign aid. Nor did he seem to like private foreign investment. Spurred in part by Jagan's taunt that he is a U.S. puppet, Burnham has moved further and further left. He declared Guyana a socialist and a nationalist state determined to create an egalitarian society and specified his ruling party as a Marxist-Leninist party. (As a consequence, he reached an accommodation of sorts with Jagan— having first weakened him.) Burnham has nationalized the entire bauxite industry, which was developed and owned by Alcan of Canada and Reynolds Metals of the United States and which is by far Guyana's biggest industry. His government has taken control of rice, sugar, public utilities, meat-packing, most dairying, much timbering, ferryboats—virtually all important means of production. He is increasingly turning Guyana into a repressive one-party state. The Burnham government has ordained "national service" for young people; taken over both daily newspapers and all but one radio station; and controls prices and wages. Increasingly, Burnham's base of power seems to be the military. Unemployment is high, crime and misery are widespread, gangs of young thugs roam Georgetown streets, and few people venture into the streets by night.

The Guyana government, in addition to mining bauxite, makes alumina out of the raw bauxite (as does Jamaica). The next step, making aluminum itself, requires heavy capital investment and large quantities of power. Guyana, Jamaica, and Trinidad-Tobago have discussed building a smelter in Trinidad that would make use of its oil and natural gas to produce aluminum from Guyanese and Jamaican bauxite and alumina, a project with dubious prospects. Guyana and Jamaica collaborate closely because Burnham and Manley have been friends since Burnham went to Oxford and Manley went to the London School of Economics. Guyana collaborates less closely with Trinidad-Tobago.

When a poor country nationalizes an industry, the question always arises: can it run it? Burnham's government has operated its bauxite and alumina properties reasonably well, for Reynolds and Alcan had trained a local staff. It has managed one of four government banks well, the other three poorly. In other industries, its record has been mixed.

Burnham has sought to make himself a Third World leader. He intended to "reintegrate" Guyana into the Caribbean and at the same time develop relations with the communist bloc and the Afro-Asians. As early as 1959, he was denouncing white racism in Africa, and he did so again when Lumumba was murdered in the Congo. After 1970, when, in Burnham's view, the United States refused to support him in his border dispute with Venezuela, he moved Guyana into the Third World camp of the nonaligned. Then, a little more than a year after he was elected, he attended a Third World summit meeting, along with such neutral leaders as Nyerere of Tanzania, Kaunda of Zambia, Mrs. Gandhi of India, and Tito of Yugoslavia. Heady stuff. Burnham warned publicly that the neutrals possessed most of the world's resources. His able foreign minister was widely respected at the United Nations, and Guyana began to assume the role of leader of the neutralist bloc. If Venezuela or Surinam were to attempt to take the Guyanese territory they claim by force, Guyana could probably count on strong support at the UN. (The UN is more important to Guyana than to many Latin American countries because its border dispute with Venezuela keeps it out of the OAS.) Burnham has made an extremely successful visit to Africa, and such African leaders as Nyerere and Kaunda have come to Guyana. A Burnham cabinet minister visited Zambia and Algeria. Burnham sent aid to the Organization of African Unity to support African "liberation" forces that fought Portuguese rule in Mozambique and Angola (though some of his countrymen grumbled, "We're hungry here in Guyana").

Burnham has good relations with the communist bloc. The Soviet

Union maintains a diplomatic mission headed by an ambassador in Georgetown. Guyana has probably sent more young people to study in the Soviet Union than any other Caribbean country save Cuba. Guyana and Cuba enjoy cordial diplomatic, economic, and military relations. Burnham established diplomatic, trade, and cultural relations with the PRC, and the PRC gave Guyana soft loans totaling about $37 million for development, built a huge pavilion for an exposition in Guyana, and maintains a mission in Georgetown at least as big as ours. (The president of Guyana is Chinese.) Despite his own neutralism and his country's large Indian population, Burnham has been closer to China than to India, no doubt because India was close to Jagan. Nonetheless, Guyana's president has visited India, and India has given Guyana technical assistance. Guyana is a member of CARICOM, the Caribbean Common Market, but has probably benefited less from it than Jamaica and Trinidad-Tobago have.

Although Burnham in power has gone further left and become far more anti-American in his speeches than we had expected when we chose him over Jagan, we are stuck with him. No real alternative is in sight.

Our Strategic Interests in the Caribbean

A Soviet geopolitician once observed that the importance of the Caribbean to the United States "can hardly be exaggerated. In military-strategic terms, it is a sort of hinterland on whose stability freedom of United States action in other parts of the globe depends." The Caribbean Sea, together with the Gulf of Mexico, has been called "the American Mediterranean" and "our inland sea." It is larger than the Mediterranean, covering an area of 1.5 million square miles; indeed, it is the fifth largest body of water in the world. And it can be defended as the broad Atlantic or Pacific cannot. It is strategically important in four ways: (1) As a potential base from which a hostile power might launch military operations against the United States. If a Caribbean country fell to a hostile power, the security of the United States itself (and other countries of the area) would be endangered. Cuba under Castro, with its military ties to Russia, already requires constant surveillance and ties down U.S. military and intelligence forces. (2) As a source of strategic raw materials. Virtually all our bauxite, vital to airplane manufacture, comes from the Caribbean. Over a quarter of our oil imports and one fifth of our iron ore and ore concentrates imports come from Venezuela. A good share of our total imports of graphite, sulphur, barium, fluorspar, and zinc comes from Mexico and the Caribbean. (3) As the location of American territories and military installations. We are bound by our own laws and constitution to defend Puerto Rico, the Virgin Islands, and the Panama Canal Zone; we are bound by treaty to defend many Caribbean nations. (4) As a major seaborne logistic route. In the Caribbean, major trade routes of the world converge. Through the Caribbean and the Panama Canal, we ship goods to our own West Coast and the west coast of South America. Cargo vessels cross the Caribbean to carry such bulk commodities as grain, coal, crude oil, petroleum products, and lumber, as well as general cargo between the main production and consumption areas of Europe, Asia, South America, and the United States.[5]

James D. Theberge, a student of the subject, has said, "The defense of the U.S. mainland and the Western Hemisphere requires that the United States have unimpeded access to Caribbean waters, certain territories, bases, and the Panama Canal." The presence of Soviet strategic and conventional forces in the Caribbean would not alter the world military balance, he believes, but it would have adverse political and psychological effects on our position in the hemisphere. And if we failed to resist such a change in the status quo, we would risk eroding our credibility elsewhere.[6] We maintain military bases in Puerto Rico (about 6,000 military personnel), the Canal Zone (about 10,000), Guantánamo, Cuba (about 3,000), and small installations in Bermuda and the Bahamas. We keep the Second Fleet in the Caribbean. We have a naval air station in Bermuda. In the Canal Zone, headquarters of the Southern Command, the Army has six forts and one other installation; the Navy has a naval station, a ship repair facility, and a communications station; and the Air Force has two bases. At Guantánamo, we have a naval base complex. The headquarters of COMCARIBSEAFRON—the Commander of the Caribbean Sea Frontier—under CINCLANT is in Puerto Rico, where the Navy and Air Force also have other important facilities. In addition, we have missile tracking stations along the Cape Kennedy firing range. And important parts of our continental early-warning system are the submarine detecting devices in the Atlantic, which register at ground stations in Bermuda and the Bahamas.

Authorities differ on the importance of all these installations.

Some contend, for example, that although the Bahamas are more important to us than Guantánamo, even the Bahamas would be of little use in time of war—a nuclear war might be over before we could find and destroy a submarine detected by our mid-Atlantic hydrophones. They argue that although Guantánamo, today only a training base though once needed as a coaling station for the Navy, is virtually obsolete, yet some admirals hang onto it "like grim death." One student of the subject feels that since the next general war will almost surely be nuclear, Guantánamo has only political, not military, importance and that even the Canal is not vital. On the other hand, a different expert has pointed out that it is unsafe to write off bases because weapons systems change rapidly: "You may say that today we have aircraft carriers and nuclear submarines and missiles and so it doesn't matter to us if the Soviet Union controls every island in the Caribbean; but that's today, and tomorrow someone may invent a whole new weapons system that will once again make geographic proximity vital."

The peacetime Navy is an important instrument of diplomacy. We sent the fleet to Dominican waters as part of our program to force out Trujillo's heirs. Later, on a number of occasions, we sent a carrier to pay a "courtesy call" at Santo Domingo, thereby pointedly rein- forcing our political support for the shaky provisional government. Our purpose here is not to decide whether we should do such things; the purpose is to note our ability to do them.

Soviet strategists say that the United States, with its Sixth Fleet in the Mediterranean and its Seventh Fleet in the waters of Southeast Asia, is using its "pet instrument of foreign policy—the Navy— against the progressive forces" everywhere. In the past, the British, Dutch, and French kept naval forces in the Caribbean; today, the Caribbean naval defense burden falls entirely on the United States. No Caribbean nation possesses an effective fleet or air force. "Who's going to defend them?" a retired general asked. "The Russians could walk ashore." (Of course, we do not know whether they want to walk ashore.)

Another aspect of our Caribbean military presence is our military aid program, our military training groups, and the military attachés in our embassies. It is hard to remember that in 1940 Nazi Germany held an important position with the military throughout Latin America—in training, equipment, and political influence. One of

FDR's policy aims was to undermine that position, and he succeeded in part through military aid. When we give—or sell—military equipment to a Caribbean country, it becomes dependent on us to train its troops in the use of the equipment and for replacements and spare parts. Our military missions and attachés gain access to the country's military in order to gather intelligence about it and exert political influence—and in many Caribbean countries, the key to politics is the military. In the early 1960s, our military aid and training programs in the Caribbean were both extensive and important to our diplomacy. But after a time, Congress became disillusioned with military aid and even with military sales abroad—in part because of the cost to U.S. taxpayers; in part because of a feeling that we ought not encourage arms races, which tend to further militarize Latin America; and in part because we feel poor countries ought not waste money needed for development on arms. A suspicion arose, in large part unfounded, that our military missions were encouraging military coups in Latin America. However, by 1971, we were no longer the leading arms supplier in Latin America. The Nixon administration preferred to sell equipment rather than make grants, and to some extent, it tried to limit sales, advising Latin Americans to spend their money in other ways. Latin Americans resented this advice and bought in Europe what we refused to sell. No matter what our aim, it would seem unwise for us to withdraw entirely from training and advising the Caribbean military or from giving or selling it equipment. If we get out, somebody else will go in—and we may not like that "somebody."

The Cuban missile crisis gave Admiral Gorshkov the victory he sought inside the Kremlin. As a result, today the Soviet navy is global, and the United States is no longer the undisputed master of the seas. The Soviet Union uses its Navy as an instrument of state policy, as, in Engels' phrase, "the political force at sea." Between 1969 and 1972, some 1,000 Soviet warships visited the ports of sixty nations in Europe, Asia, Africa, and Latin America. (In recent years, Admiral Gorshkov has pointed out that navies have acquired a new significance, for the bottoms of the oceans and the oceans themselves have been found to contain almost inexhaustible natural resources—minerals, food, and energy. Although the United States is by no means so dependent on foreign sources of raw materials, as, say, Japan, neither are we so self-sufficient as the Soviet Union.)

In 1963—a year after the Cuban missile crisis—Soviet hydrographic ships began to operate in Cuban waters, doing research for later use by Soviet submarines. Then, early in July 1969, only six months after Nixon took office, the United States again faced the issue of Cuba as a forward base for Soviet arms: a seven-ship Soviet squadron sailed into the Gulf of Mexico and the Caribbean Sea. For the first time since we destroyed the Spanish fleet off Cuba in 1898, the naval force of a rival power from outside the hemisphere entered the Caribbean. The Soviet flotilla of 1969 included three surface warships, two diesel-powered attack submarines, and a nuclear-powered attack submarine.[7] All but the nuclear-powered submarine visited Havana between July 20 and 27. The flotilla included some of the most modern ships afloat, and they carried missiles, including missiles capable of delivering nuclear warheads. Such missions are regularly undertaken by all major navies in areas where they may be obliged to operate. Ten months later, in May-June 1970, the Soviets sent a second seven-ship flotilla to the Caribbean, including a missile cruiser and two diesel-powered attack submarines; but this time, instead of the nuclear-powered submarine of the first visit that carried only torpedoes, it included a submarine that carried cruise missiles—and this one did put into port.

In 1970, 1971, and 1972, the Soviet Union sent at least eight more naval squadrons to the Caribbean. Each squadron was about equally divided between surface ships and submarines. They called at nine Cuban ports, including Havana and Cienfuegos. The submarine sent in May 1972 was a GOLF-II submarine, the first strategic missile submarine the Soviet Union ever sent, a submarine that carries three SERB solid-fuel ballistic missiles, each fitted with a one-megaton nuclear warhead that can be launched while submerged and with a range of 650 miles. In April 1973 and again in April 1974, the Soviets sent another GOLF-class strategic submarine to Cuba. Both visits took place on April 29; they were probably timed to join the celebration of the anniversary of the Bay of Pigs. Castro made heavily publicized visits to the ships.

When a Soviet squadron that went to Cienfuegos in September 1970 included a submarine tender and a vessel carrying two large barges for nuclear submarine support, it became clear that Moscow intended to use the sheltered deepwater port at Cienfuegos to replenish its nuclear-powered submarines. The United States was convinced that the Soviets were developing their own base by the appearance on photographs of two barracks and a recreational area, including a soccer field—Cubans do not play soccer, but Russians do. On September 25, Kissinger, then the president's assistant for national security affairs, reminded the Kremlin of Khrushchev's pledge to Kennedy at the time of the missile crisis to keep "all weapons systems capable of offensive use" out of Cuba. He went on to say, "The Soviet Union can be under no doubt that we would view the establishment of a strategic base in the Caribbean with the utmost seriousness." A confusing exchange between Moscow and Washington ensued, and the impression arose that the Nixon administration had reached some sort of tacit "understanding" with the Kremlin. If so, it is still secret.

Most people tend to think of a forward submarine base in pre-World War II terms—a fixed, massive, expensive, and politically difficult installation. Today, a forward base needs only an airstrip and a sheltered deepwater anchorage. The support is afloat in ships. Just what were the Soviets up to? Assuredly, part of their purpose was political: to visibly reinforce foreign policy, to reassure Castro that they would defend Cuba, and to enlarge their influence in the Caribbean. They seem to intend to establish some sort of continuing naval presence in the Caribbean. And while they have moved cautiously, testing U.S. reaction, they have continued to inch forward, moving, since 1970, from diesel attack submarines to nuclear-powered submarines carrying guided missiles with nuclear warheads (GOLF-class). They have probably hoped that this incremental strategy will finally lead to our acceptance of a YANKEE-class submarine fitted with missiles like our Polaris. A base at Cienfuegos would double the time that Soviet submarines could stay on station off the East Coast of the United States.

In any case, the Soviet naval presence has changed the political-psychological climate of the Caribbean. Our Caribbean bases may have seemed unnecessary before 1969; now perhaps they are needed. If we are entering a period of low-key U.S.-USSR rivalry, the Caribbean becomes an important arena for political influence close to home. For example, should the Caribbean states themselves become increasingly radicalized and anti-American, they might encourage a larger Soviet naval presence. Would we be comfortable with that? One view of Soviet intentions holds that the Soviets will fill any vacuum anywhere. A different view is that they intend to match us ship for ship in the Mediterranean and Indian Ocean but not in the Caribbean or the South Atlantic. In this view, the U.S. Navy has no real mission in the South Atlantic in wartime, and in peacetime the Soviets have no desire to acquire another expensive client-state such as Cuba. If the latter view holds, the strategic importance of the Caribbean depends in part on what kind of war one thinks is coming. If a long conventional war is expected, the Caribbean matters greatly—we could not resupply our own West Coast, let alone the west coast of South America, without the Panama Canal; and we could not get oil, bauxite, and other raw materials without control of the Caribbean. In World War II, German submarines sank U.S. ships in the Caribbean, cut off Puerto Rico and Barbados, and attacked the refineries at Curaçao; the Soviet Union today could do far more. On the other hand, in the event of a short nuclear war, the Caribbean would matter little. Those who say that our Caribbean bases are not vital to our defense argue that if an enemy were to try to interdict our Caribbean supply routes anything we would do to prevent him we could do as easily from Florida as from Guantánamo, Roosevelt Roads, or the Canal Zone. They think that generals and admirals who insist on the importance of our Caribbean bases are still fighting the last war. They say that what is really important is the way in which we withdraw from our bases—if we are forced out, our reputation is damaged; if we withdraw voluntarily and gracefully, we gain prestige; and so, they argue, if the political cost of clinging to our bases outweighs the military advantage, we would be wise to leave soon.

The Panama Canal

On October 11, 1968, just a few weeks before Richard Nixon was first elected president, Colonel Omar Torrijos, head of the Panamanian National Guard (Panama's only military establishment), overthrew the elected president of Panama. Torrijos has ruled ever since.

A young, good-looking, forceful man given to wearing khakis and drinking hard, Torrijos does not come from a wealthy family; his parents were schoolteachers in a provincial capital. He is not highly educated and is in many ways a primitive, but he is a shrewd judge of men and politics, he absorbs information hungrily, he has probably spent more time in the villages than any other Caribbean leader, and he has surely done more for the villagers than any other Panamanian leader. He is revolutionary, nationalist, leftist, militarist. He has tried to improve schools, health, and sanitation in the villages and has attempted agrarian reform; at the same time, he has been developing Panama into the biggest banking center in the hemisphere outside the United States and the Bahamas. Panama's geographical location is almost its only natural resource, and its leadership wants to make Panama "the bridge of the world"—a center for transit and transshipment, a big free-trade zone, a big import-export center for trade brokers. Panama permits easy ship registry and today ranks second among nations in which ships are registered. It has low taxes and no foreign exchange controls. Bananas are still the country's major foreign exchange earner, but increasingly Panama's economy is becoming one of banking, tourism, and gambling (which is owned by the government and growing rapidly).

Torrijos has developed a novel political system, one that might be called a form of guided democracy. He flies around the country a great deal, talking to peasants, and an informal system of consultation has developed between him and them. His new constitution provides for a four-layered governmental structure: national, provincial, municipal, and ward. Each ward has a five-man board that cannot pass laws but can give guidance in such matters as marriages, minor disputes, development, and business operation. Small amounts of government money go to the boards for such community projects as wells. The purpose is to teach the peasants not to look to the central government but to each other. The ward board elects one of its members to a municipal council that has the power to enact legislation. The next higher layer of government, the provincial coordinating council, meets once a month with members of whatever national government agencies are running programs in the province. The municipal councils send representatives to the National Assembly, which meets for a month each year. The National Assembly questions the ministers in the national government and censures or approves what they have been doing. Such censure is not binding, but the national government must take note of it. In addition, the system contains a nine-member national legislative commission that reviews legislative proposals that come from the ministers and from the provincial councils, takes them to the country to get the people's reaction, enacts laws, and submits them to the national government, whose chief is Torrijos. It is an odd system. It is clearly not pure democracy—political parties are forbidden, the press is not really free, unions cannot strike against the government, and no political institution can check Torrijos. At the same time, it is far from absolutist dictatorship. As one diplomat has said, "In a way, the Torrijos revolution is what the Alliance for Progress was all about." But of course, ultimate power resides where it always has—with the national guard.

Before Torrijos took power, Panama's capital budget was only $27 million a year; in 1975, it was $395 million. Torrijos has made a start at redistributing income by increasing the tax on large incomes. Torrijos seems to want the government or his friends to compete with the traditional oligarchic private sector. He has nationalized utilities and is taking over United Brands' (formerly United Fruit's) banana production; he paid United Brands compensation and concluded operating arrangements with it. The PRC brought its traveling industrial exhibit to Panama. Some specialists seem to think Torrijos will pursue a socialist course.

But the overriding issue in Panama is not socialism, not the economy, not even Torrijos himself. In Panama, the obsessive and primordial issue is the Canal.

The Panamanians hate the 1903 Canal Treaty and are demanding an entirely new treaty. As things stand, the United States occupies a ten-mile-wide strip of land that cuts Panama in two. The Panamanians resent the fact that we monopolize Panama's principal natural resource, that we rule in the Canal Zone as if sovereign, and, worst of all, that we can stay forever.

Opposition to relinquishing the Canal Zone is perhaps not so widespread among the American people as is, say, opposition to gun control. But the two have similar overtones. Opponents of changing the Canal Treaty turn up in odd places. The American Legion strongly opposes such change. Bumper stickers reading "Give Away Henry—Keep the Canal" have been spotted in a remote logging town in the Upper Peninsula of Michigan. A Mississippi congressman has said, "When I am home in my district, there is only one thing I can say that invariably makes them cheer. I say that if we can keep the striped-pants boys out of it and leave the Canal to the Corps of Engineers, then things will work out fine." In the Senate, opposition is led by Strom Thurmond (R.-S.C.) and John McClellan (D.-Ark.), whose daughter lives in the Canal Zone. To hard-liners, the Canal is a patriotic issue involving nothing less than the national honor.

Those in the U.S. Congress opposed to a new treaty continue to argue simplistically along this line: we bought it; we built it; we paid for it; why give it away? They often assert the Canal's strategic importance. Today, most experts agree that the Canal is still strategically important, but they consider it less so than formerly. Years ago, we had only a one-ocean Navy and needed the Canal to move ships from ocean to ocean; today, we do not. Moreover, missiles and aircraft have tended to make the Canal obsolete. Today's large aircraft carriers and supertankers cannot get through the Canal—and much of U.S. naval strategy is organized around task forces, which are organized around carriers. Our access to the Canal during the Vietnam and Korean wars was more convenient than essential. Nevertheless, the Canal still enables us to move big tonnage of bulk cargo cheaply and quickly among our three coastlines, and in the event of a long war, such mobility might become critically important. In sum, the Canal is likely to have little or no strategic importance in case of nuclear war, but it saves us money and time in a war like the one in Vietnam. In a long conventional war, it might be extremely important. Of course, nobody is proposing that we give up use of the Canal; we would insist on guaranteed access in any new treaty. Panama would gain nothing by closing the Canal to us; the Canal will almost certainly always be neutral; and we, as the closest big power, can always control it. Panama can defend it against local sabotage as well as or better than we; we can defend it against distant attack as well from the mainland as from the Zone. At present, the primary physical threat to the Canal is posed by nationalistic saboteurs; hence, the Canal probably would be physically safer if Panamanians knew it was theirs. Apart from the Canal itself, the Canal Zone is of vital importance mainly to the Southern Command officers and the residents of the Zone, those favored Americans who live cheaply in the Zone, in part at the American taxpayers' expense. The military training we conduct in the Zone could be undertaken elsewhere.

At the outset, the Nixon administration appeared cool to the idea of negotiating a new treaty. In 1970, when the administration

indicated that it was ready to reopen talks with Panama, no fewer
than eighty-eight members of the House of Representatives introduced no fewer than forty-two resolutions to express the sense of the
House that the United States should maintain its "sovereignty" and
jurisdiction over the Canal Zone. (It would appear at first glance that
only the Senate, not the House, would have to ratify any new treaty.
But members of the House argue that the Constitution requires the
agreement of both houses of Congress to proposals to dispose of any
territory belonging to the United States, and they maintain that this
clause covers the Canal Zone. This last is disputed.)

Congressman Fascell's subcommittee held hearings on the resolutions. The principal opponent of change was (and is) Congressman
Daniel J. Flood (D.-Pa.). Flood's constituents would seem to have
little interest in the Canal, but the congressman has explained that
President Theodore Roosevelt used to be an occasional house guest of
Flood's grandfather and spent hours regaling his hosts (and their
young grandson) with heroic tales of the building of the Canal. Flood
presented the Fascell committee with a long history of the Canal,
denouncing every event in the last sixty-eight years that in any way
"weakened" the U.S. position. He referred, for example, to the
"massive Red led mob invasion" of the Zone in 1964, to the "miners
and sappers" from the State Department who had persuaded
President Johnson to agree to negotiate a new treaty, and to the "fly-
by-night sanguinary revolutionary" government of Torrijos.

Faced with so much opposition, the Nixon administration did not
push the issue. Torrijos evidently concluded that he would have to
organize pressure on the United States to force change. With great
skill, his foreign minister, Juan Antonio Tack, began rounding up
support for Panama's cause in the OAS and among Third World
countries at the United Nations. Just as Venezuela and Jamaica and
many other Third World countries were striving to recover their
own natural resources, he said, so was Panama trying to recover
sovereignty over its own territory. His efforts bore fruit at the UN in
1973, when, after an intensive Panamanian diplomatic campaign, the
Security Council moved its deliberations to Panama City for an
extraordinary session. The subject of these deliberations was a
resolution, sponsored by Panama and Guinea, India, Indonesia,
Kenya, Peru, Sudan, and Yugoslavia, stressing Panama's sovereignty
and urging the United States and Panama to continue negotiations

in order to conclude "without delay" a new treaty. The Security Council met for a bitter week. We alone vetoed the resolution. The United Kingdom abstained, and all other thirteen nations voted yes.[8] Congressman Donald M. Fraser (D.-Minn.) saw in this vote a message: we were wrong on this issue; we should conclude the negotiation.

Panama's pressure strategy succeeded, at least in part, for in the fall of 1973, shortly after being sworn into office and proposing his "new dialogue," Secretary Kissinger appointed Ambassador Ellsworth Bunker to take over the Canal negotiation and get it moving. Kissinger and President Nixon probably took this step because they recognized that the issue was undermining our position in Latin America and the world at large, a position already severely eroded by Vietnam, and that the negotiations had languished long enough. Bunker, an elderly diplomat of great skill and long experience, succeeded where earlier negotiators had failed. He and Tack were able to agree on a set of "principles for negotiation" of a new treaty, and Kissinger and Tack initialed them. (Tlatelolco was just ahead.) The principles responded to features of the 1903 treaty that Panamanians found most objectionable: perpetuity and sovereignty.[9]

In June 1974, Bunker and the Panamanians began substantive talks. They reached agreement rather quickly on several important points: (1) Jurisdiction: jurisdiction over the Canal Zone would pass to Panama gradually during the life of the treaty. The United States would retain the right to use those areas necessary for the operation, maintenance, and defense of the Canal. (2) Operation: during the treaty's lifetime, the United States would have the primary responsibility for operating the Canal. Panama's participation in day-to-day operations would grow gradually in preparation for its assumption of full responsibility upon expiration of the treaty. (3) Defense: the United States would have primary responsibility for the defense of the Canal during the life of the treaty, though Panama would participate.

Other problems would take longer: the amount of compensation to be paid to Panama during the life of the treaty; the right of the United States to expand the Canal if it wishes; the size and location of the land and water areas needed for operation and defense; a mutually acceptable formula for the Canal's neutrality and the nondiscriminatory operation of the Canal after the treaty ends; and, probably hardest of all, the duration of the new treaty (during the negotiation, Torrijos announced that the longest time period he could accept was twenty-five years, that is, expiration by the year 2000; the Pentagon wanted the treaty to have a longer life).

Early in the negotiations, Bunker convinced Torrijos that we really wanted a new treaty, and so Torrijos behaved more flexibly than formerly. But as time went on and no treaty was initialed (let alone signed and ratified), and as U.S. domestic political obstacles to the new treaty arose, Torrijos's position appeared to stiffen a bit. The White House had problems with the Hill and the conservative wing of the Republican party, but Torrijos had his own problems with students and leftists inside his own country and feared that intense nationalism might begin to erode even the strong political base he had built for himself. Underlying the negotiations, of course, was the reality that Panama's long-range overall interests lie with the United States, a matter that Torrijos seemed to understand. But he felt obligated to escalate his rhetoric, a dangerous game. Violence would cost Panama dearly. Its tourists would evaporate, and even banking has been known to disappear almost overnight. But those arguments are logical, and this issue is not logical but emotional. Nationalism is a powerful force, and Panamanians' feelings on this issue are at least as deep as Americans'. Torrijos has been restraining the students and extremists. But he has said that if the issue is not resolved, Panamanians will invade the Canal Zone, that he will have to decide whether to shoot them or lead them, and that he will not shoot them.

Meanwhile, the treaty became entangled first with Watergate and then with the 1976 presidential election. In 1974, Senators Thurmond and McClellan introduced a resolution opposing change. The resolution had thirty-five cosponsors—about a third of the Senate, the number that Nixon would need to escape conviction of impeachment, which then seemed imminent. State Department officers believed that many of those senators would vote otherwise on actual ratification of a treaty; the resolution contained language forbidding any change without due constitutional process—something no one had ever proposed. But a senator or congressman could not hope to make as many votes back home by voting for a new treaty as by voting against it, and the State Department was slow to lay the groundwork with Congress.

In the spring of 1976, former Governor Reagan, running against

Ford in the presidential primaries, made a blatant appeal to public sentiment against changing the Canal treaty. President Ford fumbled his response. The new Canal treaty would have to wait until after the 1976 presidential election. In the summer of 1977 Ambassador Bunker and the Panamanian negotiators announced they had reached "agreement in principle" on "the basic elements" of a treaty and that legal specialists would hone the language of the formal treaty. One of the key "basic elements" was agreement to turn the Canal over to Panama by the year 2000, Torrijos's deadline. A side agreement would give the United States the right to defend the Canal for an indefinite period of time, something that Congress was likely to insist on.

The politics surrounding the Canal negotiations provides an excellent example of the role of Congress in, and the influence of domestic politics on, U.S. foreign policy.

But these maneuvers have had serious consequences for hemispheric relations. At present, all Latin America feels neglected; all Latin America views the Canal as a colonial enclave; and all Latin America views our Canal policy as a supreme test of our good faith. Panama and Cuba, along with the Trade Act of 1974, are the major points of political conflict between the United States and the Caribbean nations. It will be impossible for us to evolve a sensible relationship with the Third World at large until we resolve the Canal issue.

By the time we ratify a new treaty, Panama may have become so deeply indebted to the Third World that it will have to vote in the Security Council against us on other issues. Panama and the United States are inextricably linked by economics and history and tradition. It is probably unfortunate for everybody that we and Panama and the OAS did not adopt an idea put forward several years ago to internationalize the Canal Zone and move OAS headquarters there. Now it is too late—Panama will settle for nothing less than the new treaty. Early in 1978 its fate in the Senate was in some doubt.

The Third World

By 1973, the lines of political force had for several years been pulling the Caribbean toward the Third World. The reasons for this attraction were several: United States neglect, Black Power radicalism, the sympathy of black delegates to the United Nations with

Africans oppressed by white minorities, the natural kinship of Caribbean governments drifting toward socialism with established socialist regimes elsewhere, the failures of democracy in Latin America, the abatement of the Cold War and efforts at East-West détente, the changing position of the PRC in the world, the changing role of Cuba in the Caribbean, economic discussions at UNCTAD, purely political meetings such as the Tri-Continental Conference at Havana, nationalism and the nationalization of natural resources, disillusionment with the slow rate of development under private enterprise capitalism and Western tutelage, increasing dissatisfaction with what Caribbean leaders regarded as the unjust terms of trade with the rich nations, and much more. But in 1973, economics suddenly made political chimeras a reality. For 1973 was the year of the oil embargo, the year of OPEC. And in the stunning success of the oil-producing countries, Caribbean leaders thought they saw a lever the Third World could use to move the First: cartel. The Caribbean and its relationship to the United States would never be the same again—or at least not if Caribbean leaders had their way.

Oil and the Caribbean. "Islam has reversed the Crusades," Prime Minister Williams of Trinidad-Tobago said in effect in 1974. Similarly, when returning from a trip to Peking, which he made at the invitation of Premier Chou En-lai, he went on to denounce the Magna Carta ("the most backward, obnoxious, and repressive document ever framed") and to praise revolutionary China and the oil nations of the Third World. Trinidad-Tobago is not a member of OPEC; it applied for admission but was vetoed by Iraq. Of all the Caribbean countries, only Venezuela is a member of OPEC (as is one other South American country, Ecuador). But Trinidad-Tobago has taken advantage of the OPEC-rigged price rise.

For the other countries of the Caribbean, without oil of their own, OPEC has been an economic disaster. Its price rise has bled their foreign exchange white. Without outside help, Honduras could not have got through even one year of post-embargo oil prices. The rest of Central America is not much better off. The Dominican Republic's oil purchases drained away the nation's windfall profits from increases in the price of sugar. The oil price rise disrupted CARICOM. It siphoned off one-seventh of Puerto Rico's entire gross national product. Jamaica, already watching its foreign exchange drain away as inflation tripled the price of wheat and doubled the price of manufactured products—which it had to import—was, in early 1974, within three weeks of exhausting its foreign exchange reserves entirely. It was desperation that prompted Jamaica's unilateral imposition of the new levy on bauxite.

Given the financial hardships that results from quintupling the price of oil, the Caribbean countries might reasonably have been expected to respond to the price increase with vigorous opposition. But they did not. In fact, relations of the Caribbean nations with Middle East nations, which had hardly existed, suddenly blossomed: Arab delegations showed up in the Caribbean; Caribbean leaders went to the Middle East. Despite all that they are suffering from high oil prices, the Caribbean countries and the rest of the Third World have so far maintained almost perfect solidarity with the oil states. The oil price rise cost Jamaica almost $100 million in the first year alone, yet Jamaica is stoutly supporting OPEC. Sir Egerton Richardson of Jamaica has explained: "President Nyerere of Tanzania made a speech. He said, 'Ten years ago it took ten bales of our cotton to buy a tractor. Five years ago ten bales would buy only half a tractor. Now it'll buy only one-third. Soon it will buy only one wheel.' That is what the economc power of the industrialized nations can do. They can demand what they please. *Now,* for the first time, a group of countries—the oil-producing states—has decided to prove *its* power. And we *all* support them." Even Assistant Secretary Rogers of ARA was surprised: "It is astonishing, the unanimity of the Third World, even those countries that are hurt the most by OPEC."

Nearly every nation in the Caribbean is trying hard to find oil in its own territory; at present world prices, it is profitable to explore areas that were formerly neglected. When the minister in the Ministry of External Affairs of Trinidad-Tobago drives along the waterfront of the narrow channel separating Trinidad from Venezuela, he murmurs, his eyes gleaming, "It's all shallow and we don't know what lies under it." (The Law of the Sea issue has come to the fore in part because of offshore oil.) If the Caribbean nations find their own oil, such fresh supplies may well break OPEC's price, which, by encouraging exploration, may yet prove to be the cartel's undoing. Caribbean countries also are talking about finding alternative sources of energy. But they are doing little about developing such alternative sources, although if solar energy has practical application anywhere, it should be in the perpetually warm Caribbean. Hydroelectric development requires suitable rivers, not abundant in Caribbean countries; moreover, hydroelectric development is initially enormously expensive and probably beyond the means of any but a few countries, such as Venezuela. Oil shale and coal gasification probably will be developed only if the United States guarantees a long-term high price for oil (as has been proposed). Caribbean countries can do relatively little more than watch uneasily while the United States tries to arrive at some sort of rational energy policy.

Venezuela. The originator of OPEC was not an Arab but a Venezuelan. Juan Pablo Pérez Alonzo, one of Betancourt's collaborators in founding AD and his minister of mines and hydrocarbons, believed that the oil-producing nations should organize themselves and should own their own oil, the national patrimony. He founded OPEC in 1960, but for more than ten years, it amounted to little because he could not persuade the Arabs to cooperate; they thought it was some Venezuelan scheme to cheat them. But then in 1973 came war in the Middle East, the oil embargo—and the chance to cartelize the oil and raise its price. OPEC acted, and it has kept the price up ever since. Venezuela did not participate in the embargo, but it did participate fully in the price rise. In the first year of the OPEC-initiated price increase, Venezuela, whose total gross national product was only about $18 billion, found its oil revenues increased by nearly $4 billion. Its government increased its 1974 national budget by 200 percent. Some years earlier, Venezuela had asked the United States to buy its oil at a preferential price above the world market. We refused. Had we agreed, OPEC might not have succeeded, or at least Venezuela might have stayed out of it.

In 1973, too, Venezuelans elected by a big majority the AD candidate for president, Carlos Andrés Pérez. Pérez, a striking man with a high forehead, straight black hair, and the countenance of an Indian, comes from an Andean state far out in Venezuela's west—an impoverished area with rough, frontier traditions. Pérez joined the AD when still in his teens. He spent part of the years of the Pérez Jiménez dictatorship with Betancourt in exile in Costa Rica; there he met Figueres and Gonzalo Facio. He went home when Pérez Jiménez fell and went into the AD politics that Betancourt led, first as a deputy and then as minister of interior, where he ran the toughest and most effective campaign in all Latin America against Castroite guerrillas. He campaigned for president for two years. The two Venezuelan presidents who followed Betancourt had governed well but quietly. Pérez campaigned on the slogan "Democracy with energy" and promised excitement. "He came in with a bang and hasn't stopped running yet," a U.S. diplomat has said. The observation is more than a figure of speech. Pérez literally walks fast and dives into crowds. A tough, able, practical politician rather than an ideologue, he arises at 5:30 A.M. and works far into the night, driving his cabinet ministers wild with his peremptory phone calls.

In the 1973 election, Pérez won something not even Betancourt had had: control of both the presidency and the two houses of Congress. Taking office with a clear mandate from a constitutional democracy in time of peace, political stability, and more oil prosperity than anyone had dreamed of, Pérez realized that he could do what he chose—within certain limits set by the military. (Mindful of what happened to Betancourt when he first held power, he keeps the military fat and content.) He recognized the great opportunity he had and resolved to make Venezuela great. He seemed to see himself as a modern Bolívar; he even wore his sideburns like Bolívar's.

Within his first two years in office he nationalized Venezuela's iron ore and oil, formerly exploited by big American companies (and Royal Dutch/Shell); he began trying to redistribute income justly; he gave across-the-board increases in wages and salaries; and he thrust out in foreign affairs, taking half a dozen initiatives in the Caribbean and seeking to become the leader of all Latin America before the OAS and the UN. He seemed driven by the conviction that the things he sought to do should have been done long ago, that only he could do them, and that if they were not done Venezuelan democracy would perish and give way to dictatorship of the right or left.

On March 12, 1975, before a joint session of Congress, "Citizen President" Pérez delivered an account of his first year in office and set out his future plans. The speech was filled with urgency—"We have lost two decades"—and shot through with nationalism: "Venezuelan nationalism," he declared, "is antagonistic toward no country, is Latin American, and is in solidarity with the Third World." He also spoke of "the new economic order" and "a new road for Venezuela." No longer would North American oil companies make Venezuelan decisions in the interests of the United

States, he said; now Venezuela controlled its own destiny. Oil must not be used to enrich privileged groups or places. The government would prohibit any new industrial plants in overcrowded Caracas and would ask for tax reform to redistribute wealth more equitably. Venezuela had long been too dependent on oil; he proposed new directions. He had stopped the export of iron ore and planned to build a steel industry, announcing as his policy "full development of heavy national industry." His ministers were studying other mineral riches: coal, gold, diamonds. He proposed to develop a nickel industry run by the state. He suggested an energy policy that would utilize hydroelectric, coal, oil, and gas resources. He said, briefly, that private enterprise would play "an important part," for Venezuela would need foreign technology and even multinational corporations, but he insisted on "safeguarding the State's control over the basic industries and a majority control over the mixed"—state enterprise would occupy the "preeminent position." Turning to foreign affairs, he made it clear that Venezuela was undertaking a new leadership role. He disclaimed any ambition toward Venezuelan hegemony in Latin America, but he quoted Simon Bolívar: "Let our motto be unity in South America. . . . For us the Fatherland is America." He noted, however, that Venezuela had the "most active ties" with Asian and African countries of the Third World.

Pérez included in his speech a report on his trip to Algeria to a meeting of the chiefs of state of the OPEC nations; they had discussed not only oil but all the common problems of the poor countries of the world and had agreed to continue to fight for the Third World's right to economic independence. It was imperative to create a new world economic order—"a just and new balance in the world." Therefore, he reported, he had told President Ford that Venezuela's views did not always coincide with those of the United States, he had asserted to him Venezuela's right to conserve its nonrenewable resources and to use them to raise its people's living standard, and he had made known to him his views of the rights of poor countries and the obligations of the rich.

The OAS, Pérez continued, had been important in the past but now needed "restructuring." He intended to promote a purely Latin American organization, excluding the United States. He also wanted to strengthen Venezuela's ties to its neighbors in the Caribbean. To that end, he and his ministers and commissioners had traveled widely throughout the hemisphere during his first year. But, he added, Venezuela also wanted relations with the industrialized countries of Europe and also with "the socialist countries." (Much had happened since Venezuela led the move to throw Cuba out of the inter-American system. When, as minister of interior, Pérez was combating Cuban guerrillas, he declared that as long as Castro was in power Venezuela would "never" recognize Cuba. But after he became president, he established diplomatic relations with Cuba.) Pérez recounted his administration's achievements in this area. Venezuela had established diplomatic relations with the PRC. Venezuelan officials had gone to Spain, France, Great Britain, and Italy; Venezuela had established diplomatic relations with Bulgaria; a Venezuelan mission had gone to the Soviet Union. As to Asia and Africa, a Venezuelan mission had visited Iraq, Iran, Kuwait, Qatar, Saudi Arabia, and Lebanon; a Venezuelan mission had visited Japan. The chancellor of Lebanon, a mission from "the Khmer Republic," the deputy foreign minister of North Korea, and the president of Gambia had all visited Venezuela. Moreover, Venezuela had demonstrated its "definite anticolonialist position" at the UN and had recognized the new Republic of Guinea-Bissau. Under Pérez, Venezuela would be host to the Third UN Conference on the Law of the Sea. Venezuela would attend many other international meetings —and at every one repeat its demand for a new world economic order. Throughout the speech, Pérez asserted Venezuela's dignity, leadership, and independence.

Meanwhile, it was becoming apparent that Venezuela could not absorb its new oil riches, that unless the government acted effectively inflation would destroy the national economy. The government accordingly set up a special Investment Fund to loan money to Caribbean countries injured by the oil price rise; to buy bonds of the World Bank and other multilateral lending agencies; and to help develop steel, petrochemical, and other Venezuelan industries. It set up another fund for agricultural infrastructure development, such as farm-to-market roads, and a third fund for industrial development. It would spend the rest on education, sanitation, and housing. It launched an ambitious shipbuilding program and planned a subway for crowded, sprawling Caracas. Many years ago, Mexico had nationalized its oil industry and made it the central growth point in its economy; now Venezuela would try to do likewise. (This emulation of the Mexican example contributed to the closeness of Pérez of Venezuela and Luis Echeverría Álvarez of Mexico.)

But it took months to establish the Investment Fund because of a political quarrel. And despite all the planning, a good deal of the oil money was used to satisfy consumers. To slow down the import of luxury goods, the government imposed outrageous tariffs; for example, it levied an import duty of 110 percent on foreign automobiles. But so great were the oil riches that the streets of Caracas were filled with American-made cars costing $23,000. In Caracas's luxury hotels, tourists drank French cognac at $75 a bottle. With too much money around, inflation rose rapidly. As one expert observed, those who talked about doubling or tripling steel production did not stop to wonder where it would be marketed or how to move it without trucks and with highways that could not withstand heavy trucking anyway. It might be years before any substantial change occurred in the creation of wealth aside from oil. Venezuela's political freedom exposed the government to attack. Statesmen might aver that oil is too precious to burn, that it is better to have oil underground than money in the bank; but great political pressures would be placed on the government to stop lending money abroad and, instead, to use it at home to create jobs. Another observer, an elderly Venezuelan intellectual, pointed out that not many years ago, Venezuela was a rural country integrated around agriculture, where people lived at a modest level with what little wealth they had. The advent of oil distorted the economy, agriculture declined, people rushed to the city, and a newly affluent class arose, profiting from the sale of the nation's resources. But the old integrated society was fractured. Now, 90 percent of Venezuela's foreign exchange and 80 percent of its revenues come from oil, produced by only 25,000 workers; everybody else lives on government handouts and produces no wealth. Nonetheless, of all the oil-rich countries in the world, Venezuela is the most developed and the best equipped to use the new riches wisely. It is under some pressure to do so. At today's production rate, Venezuela's known oil reserves are expected to last about twenty years. Venezuela has until about 1995 to use its oil wealth to develop industries that will provide jobs and create wealth in place of oil. "It's a big gamble," one expert said, "it looks so easy." Another remarked, "It's now or never. We have maybe ten years." To date, the oil windfall has done little to improve the lot of the ordinary man. Pérez is said to be hag-ridden by fear that if his government does not satisfy the aspirations of the poor—1 million Venezuelans live in the terrible slums of Caracas alone—Venezuelan democracy is doomed. And his term is running out. Tax reform is urgent, for taxes have always fallen most heavily on the poor; but efforts to distribute the burden more equitably have failed in the past and probably will fail again. If the government moves too rapidly to tax the rich, it may provoke their opposition and that of the Venezuelan military.

In the rush to use its oil money for development, Venezuela has resorted increasingly to a centrally planned economy. Basic industries are now almost entirely government-controlled. The government has been planning for mixed private-state control in the later stages of production. United States–owned automobile assembly plants remain in private hands as long as companies sell their cars only in Venezuela, but if they decide to export to other Andean countries, they will have to sell 51 percent of their stock to the state. The government is planning an aluminum development joint venture with a foreign company; the company is to own 20 percent and the state 80 percent. Such large commercial establishments as Sears Roebuck have been obliged to sell 80 percent of their equity to the state. The state seems about to take over the few remaining private utilities and all communications, including television. Both political parties favor public ownership of enterprise, and U.S. companies appear to be offering less resistance than Venezuelan private enterprise (no doubt because they have less direct political influence). American private investment has turned cautious. Uncertainties lie ahead, and the question of how to mesh private American enterprise with a centrally controlled economy remains to be answered.

Central to Venezuela's future was another unanswered question: having nationalized oil and iron, can the government run them? Like most, if not all, Caribbean countries, Venezuela lacks a large pool of skilled manpower and experienced managers. Of the personnel employed by the foreign oil companies, 98 percent were Venezuelans —but the remaining 2 percent were top management. Venezuela intended to contract with the American and British Dutch companies for management assistance and overseas markets—highly important matters—at least for a time.

The Venezuelan ambassador in Washington once said that

Venezuela needed U.S. brains more than U.S. trade. In the summer of 1974, Pérez suddenly decided to send 10,000 students a year abroad, most of them to the United States, to study, starting in September. (The program, hastily thrown together, was only partly successful.) Again as throughout the Caribbean, Venezuela has a limited number of people experienced in government—and half of them are cast aside after every election. To date, the government's management of the Guyana Corporation, set up to develop natural resources in the eastern part of the country, has been successful.

In other countries, when government took over an industry, it frequently rewarded political friends and bought off opposition agitators by putting them on the industry payroll. In the Dominican Republic, when the weak provisional government inherited Trujillo's sugar mills, it was totally unable to resist pressure to pad the sugar mills' payrolls with political workers. Elsewhere, the opportunities for massive graft and corruption in large government-run industries have proved irresistible. And government ownership raises questions of a different sort. Shortly after the Venezuelan government took over the oil industry, its workers threatened to strike. Pérez persuaded them to go back to work. Although the incident was trivial in itself, it was also a manifestation of a basic problem: workers striking against a privately owned factory are conducting a purely economic operation; but workers striking against a government-owned factory are conducting a highly political operation, and, unlike a private owner, a government must react in a political manner. Moreover, in the old days, if times were hard and jobs were scarce and wages low, and if demonstrators took to the streets to protest, the government had only to make sympathetic noises and blame all misery on the remote multinational companies, to whom the corrupt dictators of the past had unscrupulously handed over the national patrimony, leaving the present government helpless. Today, with government ownership, the government cannot escape responsibility. If times are hard and jobs are scarce and wages are low, the government is the only culprit; it stands naked before the people. Like other Caribbean countries, Venezuela took an enormous risk in going statist. Furthermore, should OPEC fail owing to circumstances beyond Venezuela's control, Pérez's whole policy would collapse. No wonder an expert said, "It scares me. It scares a lot of people."

Until the 1960s, Venezuela did not amount to much, even as

a colony, relative to other colonies. Venezuelans feel this lack of distinction keenly. And so they are all the more nationalistic and expansionist now that their country has suddenly emerged rich and powerful. Under Pérez, Venezuela has moved rapidly to extend its influence. Central America, the Dominican Republic, and others have swung toward its orbit. A Dominican newspaper said that historians will cite 1974 as the year when the economic and political dependence of the Dominican Republic moved from north—the United States—to south—Venezuela. Pérez has the money and the expansionist ambition to make Venezuela a middle-class world power; the question is whether Venezuela has the human resources.

When one of Pérez's cabinet minsters declared in a speech in Brazil, "Venezuela's oil is at the disposition of the Western Hemisphere," a voice from the back of the room called out, "At what price?" Venezuela launched its own foreign aid program. The Venezuelans saw from the beginning that OPEC could succeed only if the oil-producing nations took up the cause of the Third World and its other commodities. If Guyana, for example, saw itself going bankrupt because of the high price of cartel oil, it would turn on Venezuela in hatred—unless Venezuela helped it to organize a bauxite cartel. This notion, plus anticolonialism, lies at the heart of Third World solidarity. Recognizing that the oil price worked serious hardship on Venezuela's neighbors, President Pérez convened the presidents of the five Central American countries and Torrijos of Panama and offered them a refund of $6 a barrel on oil purchases (about half price) in the form of five-year loans (thus virtually guaranteeing a Central American market for its oil) and, in addition, offered to finance Central American coffee stockpiling to keep prices high. Venezuela was making this effort to help the Central American countries create a coffee cartel similar to OPEC and drive the price of coffee up; it failed, and the loans will end up as pure budgetary-support loans. Unlike the Arab nations, which have invested much of their surplus oil revenues in rich industrialized countries, Venezuela has invested much of its surplus in poor countries. Venezuela has loaned money to the World Bank, the Inter-American Development Bank, and the Central American Development Bank. It subscribed $4.5 million to the Caribbean Development Bank. It has made loans to Bolivia, Uruguay, Peru, Ecuador, Paraguay, and Chile at or just below the commercial money market rates.

In its present expansionist mood, Venezuela probably believes that when the Dutch leave the Caribbean their islands off the Venezuelan coast, including Curaçao, will gravitate to Venezuela. When in 1969, riots broke out in Curaçao, Venezuela was poised to send troops there to protect the refineries, as it was during the Black Power riots in Trinidad-Tobago. Venezuela's expansionism may tend to erode CARICOM—already such nations as Jamaica appear to be looking more toward Venezuela and Mexico than toward CARICOM. Venezuela arrayed itself with Panama on the Canal issue. (Panama is looking increasingly to Venezuela for leadership.) Pérez strongly supported Echeverría's proposal of a Latin American Economic System (SELA), and on October 17, 1975, Venezuela and Mexico, together with twenty-three other Latin American nations, including Cuba, endorsed SELA's charter. The United States was excluded. The aims of the new organization, which happens to have its headquarters in Caracas, are the defense of regional economic interests and solidarity in international forums. At its first meeting, President Pérez, citing the success of OPEC, urged that similar cartels be created for other commodities. Some experts view SELA as a rival or even an alternative to the OAS.

One other nation is emerging as an expanding Caribbean power— Mexico. President Echeverría was criticized as a socialist ideologue and as an opportunist who spent the final months of his term promoting himself for secretary-general of the United Nations. He and Pérez exchanged visits and worked to expand their influence in the Caribbean. They had much in common; both were flamboyant leaders employing fiery Third World rhetoric.

Former ministers of the interior, they were known for their forceful attack on guerrillas some years ago; as presidents, they seemed determined to prove that they were leftists and not lackeys of the United States. When Pérez visited Mexico in 1975, he and Echeverría toured the nation together, and Pérez's speeches were more strongly pro-Third World and anti-rich nation than usual. No doubt, Venezuela and Mexico have no intention of taking on real responsibility, but they do see economic and political opportunities in the Caribbean. Mexico has held discussions with Jamaica about building a smelter in Mexico to make aluminum from Jamaica's bauxite and alumina, using Mexico's hydroelectric power and oil. Mexico may be willing to put money into developing additional alumina facilities in Jamaica on a minority basis. Jamaica sees Mexico and Venezuela emerging as Caribbean powers and wants to join with them. Confronted with the choice of accepting an investment from a Third World nation or from the United States, it would undoubtedly take Third World capital. Venezuela and Mexico, joined by Cuba, have proposed to establish a multinational Caribbean shipping line. Costa Rica, Panama, Jamaica, Guyana, and Nicaragua agreed to join; Guatemala, Honduras, and the Dominican Republic balked. A Mexican cabinet minister recently announced that Mexico, Venezuela, Cuba, and the Soviet Union would form a trading company to sell oil. When Mexico made a big new oil strike, it announced that Cuba would be the first country given an opportunity to buy its export petroleum and added that Latin American countries, rather than the United States, would get special treatment. Although not an OPEC member, Mexico has not undercut OPEC prices. But despite the rhetoric, Mexico still sells almost all its exportable oil to the United States and very little to Cuba.

American liberals hoped for a new democratic left in the Caribbean allied with a liberal administration in Washington and led by Puerto Rico, Costa Rica, and Venezuela. But Governor Hernández Colón of Puerto Rico was no Muñoz, President Oduber of Costa Rica is no Figueres, and Pérez is far different from Betancourt. Today, Venezuela, Mexico, and Cuba are the three powerful magnets pulling on the Caribbean, and if anything, they are pulling the Caribbean away from, not toward, the United States. They have real economic power: Venezuela with its oil, Mexico with oil and hydroelectric power, and Cuba with its sugar (although the recent decline in the price of sugar has hurt Cuba badly). Of course, Venezuela, Mexico, and Cuba—especially the first two—may yet become not allies but rivals. In any case, in the Caribbean, the United States is no longer alone as a source of leadership.

In Central America, Venezuela's initiatives have been welcomed wholeheartedly only by Costa Rica (and Mexico's not at all). Somoza of Nicaragua sees Venezuela as a positive threat. And throughout the Caribbean, a real fear of Venezuela's economic power and political ambitions hangs in the Caribbean air. At diplomatic cocktail parties the talk is about Venezuela's "new imperialism." "Bolívar Diplomacy" is no more popular than "Dollar Diplomacy." Although some Caribbean leaders welcome Venezuela's power as a countervailing force to U.S. power, Prime Minister Williams has made it clear he would not go to Caracas hat in hand. Lloyd Best of Trinidad sees a need to speed up economic integration of the English-speaking Caribbean lest Venezuela gobble it up. Guatemalans feel crushed between Venezuela and Mexico. Hondurans complain that Venezuela has driven a hard bargain with its loans, charging 8 percent interest. If other Caribbean countries find Venezuela's loans burdensome and become reluctant to repay them, or even if the OPEC oil price slips, the opposition parties in Venezuela will accuse Pérez of wasting Venezuela's riches on grandiose foreign adventures instead of spending the money at home. Many people in the Caribbean consider Venezuelans new-rich and boorish and their president as aggressively expansionist. Not even all Venezuelans support Pérez's ambition. His wide-ranging travels have thrilled some Venezuelans, but others grumble that he ought to stay home and solve his own country's serious problems.

Venezuela has such common Caribbean problems as untrained and unemployed masses, a shortage of skilled workers, and highly skewed distribution of income, plus the added strains of rapid, helter-skelter growth and change. People in booming Caracas, built crazily over the hills and valleys of a spur of the Andes, with its towering office buildings and looping expressways and grand hotels and awesome slums, say, "More will happen here in the next five years than in the last fifteen years; more happened in the last fifteen years than in the last forty; and more in that forty than in the last four hundred." The prospect of Venezuelan leadership in the Caribbean should excite and hearten us, for, more than any other Caribbean country save Costa Rica and Puerto Rico, Venezuela's modern political tradition is democratic. Venezuela may well prove to be the key to a whole new policy and power arrangement in the Caribbean. The Venezuelan ambassador to Washington may not have been wrong when he said, "These other countries, from Mexico to Argentina, all speak the same language and belong to the same race, but they are not important either financially or militarily, but we—" with outflung arm, "we Venezuelans are the future." Yet, at least until very recently, for at least ten years, the United States had no policy toward Venezuela.

Third World Politics. What is today called the Third World is the product of three major changes since World War II: the end of colonialism, a new craving for development, and the Cold War. The Third World is difficult to define. If it consists of the nonwhite peoples of the earth, then it does not include Yugoslavia and many Latin American countries. If it consists of poor countries, it might have to exclude Puerto Rico by the standards of many of Asia's and Africa's poor. If it consists of the countries not aligned politically with either of the two major blocs, then it includes very little of Latin America. Chad and Argentina appear to have little in common, but nearly all Third World countries have at least two things in common: they are relatively poor and they depend heavily on the export of primary commodities.

In recent years, the Caribbean nations have been increasingly drawn to the African and Asian countries of the Third World. The poor countries can have greater influence at the UN if they are united. They seek to exact similar economic concession from the rich nations (although during and after the oil boycott and price rise the Caribbean countries also used Third World solidarity as a means of obtaining access to the Arab nations). Moreover, Africa is the ancestral home of a great many of today's Caribbean peoples, and they feel a strong emotional attachment to Africa and South Asia on the basis of race. On such racial issues as South African apartheid, most of the Caribbean votes almost automatically with the Afro-Asian bloc at the UN. They feel a certain duty toward each other. In the early 1960s, the black Caribbean was sending aid to Angolans fighting Portuguese rule. The Caribbean countries opposed our policy in Vietnam. Interestingly, as détente improves East-West relations, North-South relations deteriorate.

Of course, the current denunciations of U.S. trade policy and declarations of economic independence from the United States under a new world economic order may amount to little more than a rhetorical updating of the anti-Americanism that numerous Latin American politicians have invoked for domestic political purposes through the years.

The frequent expressions of concern on the part of Caribbean leaders about injustice in Africa, and their almost incessant travels to each other's countries and to Africa and Asia, may also contain an element of escapism; it is always easier to solve some other country's problems than one's own. And running off to Mexico or Zambia is certainly more exciting than trying to cope with the slums of

Caracas or Georgetown. The Caribbean does share real economic interests with other Third World countries. At the same time, it may share more basic political, economic, and strategic interests with the United States than with, say, Tanzania. The Caribbean countries might derive more benefit from money spent at home than from money sent to African guerrillas. (This is not to question their motives but their practicality.) The Caribbean countries may ultimately find the African economies an unsatisfactory model; Nyerere, a political hero to so many Caribbean leaders, has virtually ruined the economy of Tanzania. And while Caribbean oratory praises African freedom and black renascence, the sad fact is that the political realities of African freedom today are military dictatorship, government by assassination, and tribal warfare.

People who have been to Peking recently note striking similarities in the directions development has taken there and in the Third World nations of the Caribbean. China has made a successful all-out attack on illiteracy as has Castro's Cuba; China is driving toward an egalitarian society, as is Manley of Jamaica (he says); China lays heavy emphasis on improving health and sanitation among the rural peasantry, as does Torrijos of Panama; in China as in Cuba everybody works for the state; and so on. Like much of the rest of the Third World, the Caribbean seems more closely akin to Peking than to Moscow.

Manley has deliberately and assiduously sought Third World connections, even though trade and capital flow in other directions. He does so primarily for political and emotional reasons rooted in race. He brought Nyerere to Jamaica with great fanfare. His critics say he has spent too much time on the Third World and that he sees himself, unrealistically, as some sort of spokesman for the Third World. Jamaica and Trinidad-Tobago were once firmly with the West, but today, they, especially Jamaica, are nonaligned. Prime Minister Williams of Trinidad-Tobago wants to move closer to the Soviet bloc but is restrained by his own people. The New Left suspects that Manley and Williams, in sending aid to African guerrillas, are merely making gestures to their electorates and trying to preempt the Third World rhetoric of New Left and Black Power groups. Of all Caribbean nations save Cuba, Guyana under Prime Minister Burnham has probably gone furthest toward alignment with the Third World countries of Asia and Africa. Central America, a conservative area, has had relatively little to do with the Third World.

All the Caribbean countries are related in one way or another. Puerto Rico wants to join the Caribbean Development Bank and maintains communication with Cuba. Trinidad-Tobago lends oil to Jamaica, and Guyana wants to bring Cuba into CARICOM. Haiti and the Dominican Republic want to join CARICOM. The Dominican Republic tried (without success) to work out close economic ties to Puerto Rico. The common interests and projects of Venezuela and Mexico are of particular economic importance, but the whole Caribbean is virtually seething with such new projects. Jamaica admires Cuba. CARICOM leaders dream of a link to the Central American Common Market. Some people think that the dominant power in the Caribbean will be Cuba. Although Bahamas remains relatively isolated, and is almost unique in that respect, it must deal with Cuba, its closest neighbor and one that fishes in its waters.

Like Venezuela, the commonwealth countries, especially Jamaica, consider themselves the leaders of the Caribbean; they regard Puerto Rico, the Dominican Republic, and the French and Dutch islands with disdain, although they sympathize with Cuba in its struggle with the United States. They want economic and technical help from the United States without political involvement. The United States is reluctant to give help with no strings attached, especially to the smallest islands; but if the United States continues to hang back, Venezuela and Mexico may move in—and Cuba seems almost sure to do likewise.

Third World rhetoric generally regards capitalism as imperialistic and socialism as nationalistic. In 1971, Congressman Fascell observed, "An epidemic of economic nationalism is sweeping Latin America. The message seems clear: 'We don't want U.S. business.'" Some Caribbean countries look to Peru as a model of assertive nationalism and technocratic leadership. Some consider Castro's Cuba a better model for them than Puerto Rico. Country after country has nationalized its natural resources and partly or wholly nationalized foreign enterprises. Technocrats are taking over; U.S. companies can no longer walk into a ministry and, through bribery, obtain a favorable mineral concession; even in Haiti, the recent bauxite negotiation was difficult for the company. To a considerable extent, the sophistication of national planning and the importance of technocrats in the governments of the Caribbean countries are a result of the Alliance for Progress and may prove the Alliance's most lasting effect. Caribbean politics may swing even further to the left; some leftists agree with Frantz Fanon of Martinique that the national elites of the Third World countries have lost touch with the people; they oppose the leadership of men like Williams. The Caribbean has produced two strains of radicalism; that of Garvey, Manley, and Burnham, oriented toward Black Power and Africa, and that of Alberto Campos of Puerto Rico and Fidel Castro of Cuba, who identify with Hispanic America. What is clearly emerging in the Caribbean is the combination of nationalism and socialism. It is not international socialism in the classic European sense; Caribbean politics is far too proudly nationalistic for that. Rather it is a pragmatic system of statism—a mixed economy with strong central government planning and control that has grown out of political nationalism, the nationalization of natural resources, inequities in world economics, and revolutionary pressure on these governments from below. Manuel Tavares Justo was, in the early 1960s, a young Dominican nationalist and leftist who admired Castro and was no ideologue but a charismatic leader; he was killed in guerrilla warfare in 1963, but in a real sense, his cause triumphed ten years later when the Arabs clamped on the oil boycott.

According to Gunnar Myrdal, the idea of economic planning came to South Asia first from the Soviet Union, then from the West. This order was reversed in the Caribbean. When, after 1932, President Franklin D. Roosevelt overturned the old order and launched a program of massive government intervention, his reforms echoed in the Caribbean—the ferment of the New Deal would have greatly influenced domestic policy on those countries even without the Good Neighbor policy; for the United States, by its sheer gigantic mass, exerts an almost planetary pull on the Caribbean. President Kennedy's Alliance for Progress carried forward Roosevelt's program and encouraged Caribbean governments to restructure their societies, but gradually, through "peaceful revolution." What we are witnessing now may be a revolt against gradualism. The whole area—from Panama to Guyana, from Puerto Rico to Venezuela—is lurching left. We may have definitively reached the end of the Muñoz-Alliance period. Private enterprise has failed to soak up unemployment. Gradual reforms have failed to produce social justice. We may now be entering a new period when the state will own natural resources, run industry, and turn to radical social reform. Such states may find it easier to trade with the communist states, with the Third World, and even with the socialist governments of Western Europe than with the United States. Russian and Chinese, especially Chinese, influence is likely to increase. At the same time, the Third World seems to make the Soviets a trifle nervous, as it does us. On some issues, such as the Law of the Sea, Third World pressures may force the United States and the Soviet Union together.

The Caribbean countries can finance their enterprises in part through such multilateral agencies as the World Bank and the IADB. But the lack of trained manpower has plagued every Caribbean leader—including Castro—whenever he has tried to take over industry. The Jamaican ambassador in Washington has said, "We need fifty trained people—not fifty million dollars." In Trujillo's time, the government undertook to build and operate tourist hotels; the results were disastrous. At Port-of-Spain, the Holiday Inn is partly owned and the Hilton wholly owned by the Trinidad-Tobago government, and they are abominations, and one wonders whether political pressures put incompetents on the payroll.

Finally, these countries seem to be heading toward one-party government. For all practical purposes, Guyana and Trinidad-Tobago already have reached that goal. These Caribbean leaders tend to emulate such African countries as Tanzania and the one-party government of Nyerere. Some see parallels between the racial politics of Guyana (and several other Caribbean countries) and the racism of Amin of Uganda. Many middle-class people in the Caribbean fear the future—a future, they foresee, of socialism, racism, and one-party government that will become increasingly repressive, especially if its economic policies fail.

All this makes us nervous. Secretary Kissinger has said, "The radicalization of the Third World and its consolidation into an antagonistic bloc is neither in our political nor our economic interest. A world of hostile blocs is a world of tension and disorder."

Bauxite and Other Commodities. Historically, the rich countries—the Western industrialized nations—have based their development on access to and control over cheap food, raw materials, and minerals. The major European powers were heavily dependent on foreign sources, mainly their colonies, for commodities. Their colonies' economies were geared to producing and exporting two or three commodities needed by the mother country. The United States was fortunate in possessing vast resources within its own borders and thus throughout the nineteenth and part of the twentieth centuries was largely able to avoid such relationships. Today, we find ourselves increasingly dependent on Third World commodities.

Theoretically, the dependence of poor countries on a few export commodities in a free market may be either good or bad: good if specialization allows a country to produce goods for which it enjoys a competitive advantage while importing goods that can be produced more cheaply elsewhere, or bad if a country's inability to produce more than one or two commodities puts it at the mercy of a world market over which it has no control. The Caribbean countries are in the latter situation. The economic power and technological superiority of the rich countries have given them a kind of domination over the poor countries. When, in 1973, OPEC turned the tables on the rich nations, it showed that commodity producers also might be able to exercise economic power. It was a time of shortages or fears of shortages; many commodity prices reached all-time peaks; and for the first time, we in the United States doubted our ability to remain in control and feared that real power had shifted to the Third World. A war to win raw materials was suddenly thinkable.

For generations, the Caribbean countries have based their economies on sugar, coffee, and bananas; sugar in the Caribbean islands, and coffee and bananas in Central America. In recent years, the region's mineral resources also have become important: oil in Trinidad and Venezuela, iron ore in Venezuela, and bauxite in Jamaica and Guyana (and, to some extent, Haiti and the Dominican Republic). When OPEC showed the Third World the way in 1973, other poor countries tried to cartelize their own commodities.

Sugar is a special case. Sugar can be produced in virtually every country in the world and in the past has been sold profitably almost exclusively in controlled markets at subsidy prices. About three-fourths of world sugar production is sold in the countries that produce it; of the rest, until 1974, slightly more than half was traded under special arrangements—the British Commonwealth Sugar

Agreement, the bilateral arrangements among Cuba and Russia and its satellites, and the U.S. Sugar Act. Political, not economic, considerations usually decided which countries benefited from access to those premium-price markets. In 1974, the British and U.S. measures expired, and since then most sugar has been traded freely on world markets, except that controlled by such special arrangements as that of Cuba and the Soviet Union. Early in Castro's regime, he tried to break Cuba out of its one-crop economic straitjacket. He failed and fell back on sugar. Although the Soviet Union agreed to buy Cuban sugar at 6¢ per pound, which was well above the world market price at the time, the overall terms of Cuban-Soviet sugar trade appear to favor the Soviet Union.[10] In recent years, Castro has been trying to reduce Cuba's dependence on the Soviet Union, and in the past three years, sugar exports from Cuba to the Soviet Union have averaged only 30 percent of Cuba's total shipments.

Traditional U.S. sugar policy has had three objectives: (1) to ensure the American people an adequate quantity of sugar each year; (2) to preserve and protect within the United States a sugar industry of our own; (3) to stabilize prices and production of both our domestic and foreign sugar (much foreign sugar is produced by U.S. corporations). In 1934, when the U.S. Sugar Act took effect, both our domestic sugar industry and Cuban sugar (largely controlled by U.S. interests) were suffering acute distress. The act provided that, each year, the secretary of agriculture would determine how much sugar we would need in the coming year, that we would prop up the domestic price above the world price, and that a statutory quota would be established for all domestic producers and each foreign producer. After amendment in 1936, the act allocated about 55.5 percent of our market to our domestic producers and gave foreign countries quotas as follows: 28.6 percent to Cuba, 15.4 percent to the Philippines, and 0.4 percent to other foreign countries. In the 1950s, we imported about 45 percent of our sugar and got about 70 percent of our imports from Cuba. After Castro came to power, we banned Cuba's sugar and parceled out its quota among other nations. In 1959, we had imported only 148,600 metric tons from Caribbean countries other than Cuba; in 1969, we imported 603,300 metric tons from them; by 1973, we were importing 1,155,700 metric tons from the non-Cuban Caribbean.[11]

Coffee is the second most important commodity in world trade, ranking behind only oil. It has long been a boom-and-bust commodity, suffering like other tree crops from the lag between planting and initial production. After maturing, the tree bears fruit for many years; high prices encourage growers to plant excessively, and the additional trees persist in bearing and so drive prices down. The cycles of boom and bust tend to be longer and more devastating in tree crops than in other commodities.

Many attempts have been made to stabilize world coffee prices. By 1962, fifty-four nations had signed a worldwide International Coffee Agreement negotiated under UN auspices. Seeking to adjust production to demand, it used export controls to ensure that prices would not decline below the 1962 levels. By late 1970, the agreement was in trouble, and the nations party to it decided to drop the price-control mechanisms and adopted a new agreement providing for little more than study and data collection. Since then, the signatories have made several efforts to strengthen the market by establishing joint marketing policies. Few of these efforts have amounted to much. As a major consumer nation, ideologically opposed to any interference with the free market, the United States had traditionally opposed such international agreements, but toward the end of the Eisenhower administration, we changed our mind and encouraged such a move. Our decision to sign the agreement, during the Kennedy administration, was a political decision, coordinated with the policy orientation of the Alliance for Progress. It artificially propped up an industry plagued by overcapacity and inefficiency in order to maintain Latin American coffee export earnings. In 1975, a new agreement was negotiated in London; we participated, but it initially contained no economic provisions.

Bananas are grown in a worldwide belt lying 30° north and 30° south of the equator. Costa Rica, Guatemala, Honduras, Panama, Jamaica, and the Windward Islands (and Colombia) produce bananas for export. Over the years, the banana-exporting countries have tried to negotiate, if not a full-fledged international banana agreement, at least cooperative policies in marketing and taxation that would strengthen their hands against the giant American companies, mainly United Fruit (now United Brands), Standard Fruit, and Del Monte. In 1974, following the OPEC oil boycott, seven Latin American nations met to create an organization that would control exports and impose an export tax on bananas, originally set unrealistically high at $1 a box. But Ecuador refused to join; Colombia and Guatemala refused to impose the tax; and Costa Rica, Panama, and Honduras were left to negotiate a tax with the banana companies. Honduras initially imposed a tax of 50 cents a box, Costa Rica 25 cents, and Panama 35 cents. The disclosure that United Brands had bribed the Honduran chief of state to lower the tax reopened the whole question. It remains doubtful that any international banana agreement can be negotiated; bananas are perishable and cannot be stockpiled, and the interests of the low-cost Central American producer diverge from those of the islands, with higher costs but closer access to markets.

Bauxite is different from all those commodities. The United States is at present critically dependent on foreign bauxite for its aluminum industry. Aluminum oxide, the main ingredient of bauxite and the basic source of aluminum, is scattered all over the earth in virtually everything. One could, theoretically, make aluminum out of clay, but at present, it can be made profitably only out of bauxite. Bauxite is an ore that may be found in three generally recognized forms: Jamaican, Surinamian, and European. Each requires its own method of processing. Except in Europe, bauxite mining generally is open-pit, and since bauxite is soft, mining it does not require heavy capital investment. The intermediate step in aluminum production—the production of alumina—requires an estimated investment of $600 to $800 per ton of capacity (as of 1974), more than double the investment required for mining. Producing alumina near the bauxite mines saves transportation costs. The final stage of producing aluminum is the electrolysis of alumina. This process uses a great deal of electricity and requires an investment of $1,500 to $1,800 per ton of capacity.

The bauxite, alumina, and aluminum industries are highly concentrated. In 1973, six corporations—the Aluminum Company of Canada (Alcan); the Aluminum Company of America, Reynolds Metals, and Kaiser, all of the United States; and a French company and a Swiss company (plus their subsidiaries)—produced no less than 57 percent of the Western world's capacity in bauxite, 69 percent of its alumina, and 63 percent of its aluminum. Each of these corporations is fully integrated, performing every step of the process from bauxite mining to manufacturing finished aluminum products.

The Caribbean seems to be a huge bauxite bowl. Jamaica for years was the world's largest source of bauxite and now is second only to Australia. Alumina production is largely concentrated in the industrialized countries and aluminum even more so. The Caribbean (except for Surinam) produces no aluminum. In 1973, U.S. corporate investment in bauxite mining and alumina production in the Caribbean amounted to $745 million.[12] The price of aluminum ingots has risen from 25 cents per pound in 1973 to 39 cents today, an increase of nearly 60 percent. But energy costs have risen so high that even at 39 cents aluminum production may not be profitable enough to generate the investment needed for expansion. In 1973, observing the success of OPEC, Jamaica took the lead in trying to cartelize bauxite, and at Conakry, Guinea, in March 1974, Jamaica joined Australia, Guyana, Guinea, Surinam, Sierra Leone, and Yugoslavia in forming the International Bauxite Association (IBA). Ghana, Haiti, and the Dominican Republic joined later. These countries account for about 70 percent of world production.

The idea had been germinating in the minds of Jamaican leaders, especially Sir Egerton Richardson, for several years. Jamaica persuaded the other countries to band together, just as Venezuela persuaded the oil countries. By the time IBA was actually formed, the Jamaicans had done excellent staff work, and during the negotiations that each country subsequently undertook with the companies, Jamaican experts waited in the wings, offering advice. The purpose of IBA is to secure for its members what they consider fair and reasonable returns for their bauxite and to protect them against the multinational corporations. Ultimately, in all probability, IBA will try to move toward a uniform world price, an extremely complicated task because of the differences in grades and kinds of bauxite (although crude oil, too, comes in varying grades and kinds).

Even before taking power in Jamaica, the Manley government had planned to increase its revenues from bauxite, to regain ownership of its bauxite, and to gain participation in the industry. Jamaica might have moved slowly, seeking to act in concert with its IBA partners; but the OPEC price rise drove it to desperation. In March 1974, with the support of IBA, it imposed a production tax that raised its revenue from about $1.35 per ton of bauxite to approximately $11.60. Shortly thereafter, it negotiated the repurchase of its lands from the North American companies and acquired equity participation in their operations. Other bauxite countries have followed Jamaica's lead.

The outlook for IBA is uncertain. One key to its future is Australia, whose participation is less than enthusiastic and whose production costs are low. For the short term, those companies geared to using Caribbean bauxite have no real alternative—a company whose plant is geared to Jamaican bauxite cannot readily use bauxite from somewhere else. Over the longer term, however, a number of countries, including Australia, Guinea, and Brazil, appear anxious to expand production, and these countries can produce bauxite and alumina below the present price. Moreover, in periods of slack demand, the members of IBA will encounter the major problem faced by all cartels: how to allocate production cutbacks among themselves. The aluminum companies are intensifying their research on alternatives to bauxite. In short, IBA's price raising is limited by the ability of the members to maintain solidarity in adversity and by the cost to companies of switching sources.

In the fall and winter of 1973, the United States feared an apparently inevitable massive transfer of resources to the oil nations and the prospect that the sources of other commodities would form similar cartels. Today, oil prices remain high, but signs of conflict have appeared within OPEC, and the worldwide recession sharply cut the demand for oil and forced down production. (More recently, demand and production have again increased.) Our fears of 1973 regarding other commodities appear unrealistic today, although the success of OPEC has raised the question of collective bargaining in other commodities.

The Terms of Trade. When the American colonies revolted against the mother country, Great Britain was practicing mercantilism—buying raw materials from its colonies cheaply and selling them its manufactured goods dearly. The colonials objected to these "terms of trade"—as do the nations of the Third World today. As foreign aid and foreign investment decline, the Caribbean nations see trade as their only hope. Trade policy has become crucial in the hemisphere. As Sir Egerton Richardson observes:

> For years and years, there was talk of the terms of trade. But the talk was always in forums dominated by the industrialized nations. And so the talks always centered on: how much *aid* they would give us. All the talk in UNIDO and UNCTAD and

the General Assembly and ECOSOC during the vaunted Development Decade, proclaimed by the UN, amounted to talk of grants or loans. We keep saying: "We want trade, not aid." But the great powers were not listening. In October of 1972, our Prime Minister [Manley] went to the UN to make the Jamaican speech. He said: "Trade, Not Aid—you have got to change the terms of trade. You must pay us more for the raw materials we sell you." That has become the theme of all developing countries. So we formed the IBA.

Formerly, Richardson says, the cost of bauxite was 7 percent of the cost of aluminum. IBA wants to increase it to, say, 25 percent: "The aluminum companies and consumers will have to be content with 75 percent, not 93 percent." He says that after Jamaica increased its tax on bauxite, the price of aluminum in the United States rose 14 cents a pound but that the new Jamaica tax represented only 3 cents of this increase; the other 11 cents, he maintains, went to the big aluminum companies. The companies argue that they need the rest to pay for energy and to expand. Richardson also says that only 15 percent of the total price increase in oil represented what the producing nations received; the rest went to the big oil companies. (Some experts would question this figure.) "They are getting rich," he says, although the U.S. government and the press say otherwise. "It's almost a conspiracy. Why doesn't someone investigate the companies?" Richardson also speaks of the desire of the poor countries to process their raw materials themselves.

The big question is—how much do we do this *with* the big companies? Jamaica says partnership. Guyana was taking a different line [outright expropriation]. We say let's work together. We are trying to increase the Third World participation without excluding the companies. The companies don't all understand this. Edgar Kaiser does—he is working with us. Far different from Alcoa. We want your technology and we want to pay for it. But your big companies only want to give it as a part of equity. We need to regain control of our own resources. Years ago we made you buy the land. Now we need to buy it back. In the future we intend to have a majority share in plants for processing it in Jamaica—in all phases of production.

And we'll *buy* that share.

Prime Minister Manley argues that as long as the aluminum and other extractive industries remain exclusively in the hands of foreign multinational corporations, the independence of poor nations will be in jeopardy. But he concedes that the corporations have made large investments and provided technology and access to markets. The solution, Manley believes, must lie in joint ownership. "Indeed," he says, "the future of the world" may depend on the ability of the Third World to pursue joint ownership with calm and skill and on the ability of the rich countries to understand Third World aspirations and to cooperate with them. As he sees it, "the fundamental problem of the world today" is not conflicting ideologies but the economic relationship between the rich and poor countries. Throughout the world, the poor must work in concert, he says: "The Caribbean must be as concerned about the fate of Ghana's cocoa as Ghana should be concerned about the fate of Caribbean sugar."

During the 1960s, the gap between the rich and the poor nations continued to widen. Today, every Third World leader declares in his every speech his determination to bring about a "new world economic order." But even the most committed Third World advocates sense that the ability of the poor countries to obtain a fair share of the world's wealth and to bring about a more equitable distribution of wealth at home may be limited.

Richardson says, "We are determined to go as far as we can." A Venezuelan lawyer predicts that the nations of the Third World will run into market realities. He explains that, in the event of a depression, OPEC and IBA will confront a declining demand for raw materials in the industrialized nations; the OPEC and IBA countries, seeing their revenues sinking, will start cutting prices, and their joint arrangements will collapse. Richardson observes, "The price-cutting must be orderly. That will be the true test." In the last couple of years, Third World nations and international bodies have watched the U.S. economy anxiously, for they believe that a major U.S. depression would hurt the rest of the world far more than the depression of the 1930s—the nations of the world have become more interdependent and the United States more powerful now than then. How far the poor countries can push the rich will depend on such matters as the rich nations' stand, the amount of sovereignty each poor nation is willing to relinquish, and domestic policies inside each poor country. If in time of recession the poor countries hold back production in order to maintain high prices for their raw materials, they may find unemployment increasing among their own people and may be obliged to persuade their unemployed to bear the cost of maintaining the international cartel. It will not be politically easy.

As for the ability of individual countries to redistribute their rising wealth more equitably among their own people, a Caribbean diplomat says, "It's not a question of can we do it. We must. If we don't redistribute wealth democratically, there will be socialism here followed by military dictatorship."

The U.S. Response. Late in 1974 and throughout 1975, as a result of the worldwide recession, high commodity prices began to drop precipitously. At the same time, oil prices went up again. These shifts squeezed the poor countries cruelly, and they mounted an aggressive campaign to improve and stabilize commodity prices by forming producer cartels, negotiating with the rich nations, and even withholding their commodities from the rich nations. At a special session of the UN General Assembly in April 1974, the Third World nations made what the U.S. under secretary of state for economic affairs, Charles W. Robinson, later called "increasingly strident and unrealistic demands," threatening to divide the world across a North-South line. The assembly adopted a declaration and a program of action on the establishment of a new international economic order. The rich nations began to consider the advisability of some sort of modus vivendi with the poor in order to discourage the development of new producer cartels. The rich countries entertained the notion of joining the poor in some sort of joint producer-consumer arrangements. An unprecedented flurry of international meetings ensued.

In February 1975, at Dakar, 110 nations met and established a commission to develop price guidelines for a wide range of commodities and to prepare to present them as demands to the rich countries. In Geneva, a meeting of the UNCTAD Committee on Commodities proposed to establish, under international control, and with a fund of about $11 billion, buffer stocks of nineteen commodities, including sugar, coffee, bauxite, alumina, and iron ore. In Lomé, Togo, the European Common Market countries met with representatives of forty-six African, Pacific, and Caribbean nations and agreed to put up nearly $4 billion to finance export stabilization guarantees covering several tropical products. Early in May, at a meeting of commonwealth nations in Jamaica, Prime Minister Wilson announced that his government "fully accepts" that the balance between rich and poor nations "is wrong and must be remedied" and that "the wealth of the world must be redistributed in favor of the poverty-stricken and the starving." Wilson addressed at length the question of indexation, which the poor countries have been demanding—a scheme to link the prices of their commodities to the prices of manufactured goods they import—and did not reject the approach out of hand, although he pointed out its difficulties. For example, the index price might be set at the existing price, the peak price, or a fixed number of percentage points below it. Not all commodities peak at the same time. Sugar producers might favor a date late in 1974, when sugar was at its peak; during the same period, however, the price of Zambian copper was down, and that date would be unacceptable to President Kaunda of Zambia. Wilson argued that indexation would not be equally beneficial to every country and not at all beneficial to some. (Wilson did not say so, but rich nations oppose indexation not only because it is difficult to devise and administer but also because it costs them money, interferes with basic trade and free market policy, and may, in some circumstances although not all, "recycle" inflation, that is, if inflation drove up the price of, say, American automobiles, the price of the raw materials the United States imports would automatically rise equally, and such price increases would force automobile producers to raise their prices again, and so on, endlessly.) Instead of indexation, Wilson proposed that rich and poor nations recognize their interdependence and the need for agreed, equitable arrangements that would guarantee adequate supplies of raw materials to rich nations and fair material prices to poor nations. To promote these goals, he then proposed a six-point program: (1) to establish better exchanges of information on supply and demand; (2) to elaborate specific rules to define the circumstances under which import and export restrictions may be applied to commodities; (3) to encourage the development of producer/consumer associations for individual commodities; (4) to give fresh impetus to rich-poor efforts to "conclude commodity agreements designed to facilitate the orderly conduct and development of trade" (first, perhaps, by identifying commodities appropriate for such agreements; second, by analyzing each commodity to determine the appropriate mechanism to regulate trade, including international buffer stocks, coordination of nationally held stocks, production controls, and export quotas; and, third, by examining how any financial burden imposed by these mechanisms should be financed); (5) to agree that the regulatory mechanisms would be "directed towards the maintenance of market prices within a range negotiated in accordance with the principles already proposed"; and (6) to establish "the framework of a scheme for the stabilization of export earnings from commodities."

Scarcely had Wilson ceased speaking when Prime Minister Burnham of Guyana arose. He scornfully rejected Wilson's proposals as wholly inadequate and as designed to protect the rich. He did not spell out a procedure to bring about the new world economic order he demanded, but he called for more "producer associations" (he thought *cartel* pejorative), such as OPEC and IBA, indexation, and the appointment of commonwealth experts to draw up plans.

Traditionally, the United States has favored the concept of free trade worldwide. It has admitted imports of raw materials duty free, but it has levied duties on manufactured and semimanufactured goods, and it has opposed most commodity agreements on the ground that they interfere unduly with the free market. While favoring free trade in theory, the United States has frequently erected tariff and other barriers to protect American industry. Moreover, when American farmers got in trouble, the U.S. government set up a system of price supports, and when American and American-owned Cuban sugar mills got in trouble, it passed the Sugar Act of 1934. Although a few countries do favor relatively free trade and open markets, in recent years the rich countries, especially the EEC countries, have moved toward commodity agreements, as in the Lomé Convention. Thus, the United States may be isolating itself in its somewhat stubborn opposition to international cooperation in commodities and may run an increasing risk of being blamed for all commodity price disasters.

In April 1975, a year after the General Assembly called for a new economic order, the United States, together with the European Economic Community and Japan, met in Paris with seven poor nations in a preparatory conference for what the State Department called "the producer-consumer dialogue." (The seven were Saudi

Arabia, Algeria, Iran, Venezuela, Brazil, India, and Zaire.) We went into the meeting expecting to discuss only energy. Instead, the seven poor countries united in demanding that the discussion be broadened to include raw materials and all the world's financial and monetary problems. After eleven days of bitter debate, the meeting broke down and all went home. Under Secretary Robinson said the meeting was not a failure, but perhaps "the most important single international meeting of this decade," for "it made all of us aware of the broad, deep gulf that separated the industrialized and developing world. It forced us to sit down and reassess our position."

Starting the following month, in May, Secretary Kissinger made a series of speeches on economic issues that indicated if not a reversal of traditional U.S. policy, at least a reconsideration and possible realignment of it. On May 13, 1975, in a speech at Kansas City, Kissinger said that while we were convinced that the present economic system had "generally served the world well," nevertheless we would propose that trade negotiations then under way in Geneva develop new rules and procedures on such questions as freer access to supplies and markets and the promotion of processing industries; we would propose that the World Bank explore new ways of financing raw material investment in producing countries; and we "are prepared to discuss new arrangements in individual commodities on a case-by-case basis as circumstances warrant." Kissinger probably would have preferred to go much further and set forth imaginative proposals such as mechanisms to reduce price fluctuations, assured access to raw materials for consumers, financing for buffer stocks and new resource investment, infusion of better technology and management, closer cooperation with other rich countries, comprehensive negotiations with the poor countries, and more. But the secretary of the treasury, William E. Simon, was a true believer in the free market and opposed any new policies that might interfere with it. And in the Ford White House, there was no machinery to resolve such interdepartmental disputes. So Kissinger moved cautiously. Two weeks later, he went to Paris and told the OECD that "misused economic power" (he had OPEC's policies in mind) could hurt everyone and that "confrontation and cooperation cannot be carried on simultaneously," but he went on to repeat what he had said at Kansas City, including the statement that we were prepared to discuss with rich and poor countries "new

arrangements for individual commodities on a case-by-case basis,"
and he added that we were now prepared to consider mechanisms for
stabilizing the export earnings of poor countries, especially IMF
mechanisms to protect poor countries "against excessive fluctuations
in their export income."

U.S. diplomats in the Caribbean and Caribbean diplomats themselves feared all this might be mere rhetoric and might therefore raise
and then disappoint hopes, making matters worse than ever. They
knew, too, that both the Treasury Department and the Department
of Agriculture would oppose commodity market intervention. Some
members of Congress, such as Congressman Fascell, favored giving
Caribbean nations trade advantages, for example, by eliminating the
duty on alcoholic beverages based on sugar (rum), but the diplomats
knew that Treasury would oppose such measures. Moreover, many
other members of Congress tended to view commodity agreements as
raids on the American housewife's pocketbook.

The 1974-1975 drive of the Third World came to a climax on
September 1, 1975, when a special session of the UN General
Assembly was convened at its demand. Ordinarily, at the UN,
economic matters were buried in obscure committees, but this time,
the Third World had forced its demands into the open political arena
of the General Assembly, where it could command a majority. The
Third World's mood was incendiary and might have blown the UN
apart, if Kissinger had not clearly indicated that the United States—
at least the State Department—intended to revise its foreign
economic policies. Perhaps deliberately, instead of going to New
York to deliver his speech in person, Kissinger had the U.S.
ambassador to the UN, Daniel Patrick Moynihan, read it. It was not
the first time Kissinger had absented himself from a Latin American
or Third World forum. (He did so this time ostensibly because Israel
and Egypt were on the verge of an agreement regarding the Sinai
peninsula, and he feared it would fail if he absented himself from the
negotiations.) But the speech itself advanced more than a score of
proposals for discussion:

1. To create a new $10 billion arm of the IMF to help poor
countries stabilize their export earnings. It would give loans of up to
$2.5 billion in a single year to sustain development projects when
commodity price drops reduce export earnings. Under certain
conditions, the poorest countries would be allowed to convert their

loans into grants. The grants would be financed by selling IMF gold channeled through the proposed $2 billion trust fund under negotiation. Eligible countries could draw most or, under some conditions, all of their IMF quotas in addition to their normal drawing rights, and much of these funds could be drawn in a single year if necessary. This program would provide "unprecedented protection" against commodity price swings, and it would reinforce traditional aid, which was often canceled by price swings. For rich countries, it would mean a steadier export market; for poor countries, it would mean assurance that development could be pursued without disruption.

2. To expand the World Bank's International Finance Corporation from $100 million to "at least" $400 million.

3. To create an international investment trust under the World Bank's International Finance Corporation in order to mobilize portfolio capital for investment in local enterprises: public, private, and mixed.

4. To contribute actively to the IMF–World Bank effort to find ways to help poor countries borrow directly in the capital market.

5. To join with other nations in increasing bilateral support for training and technical assistance to help poor countries find new sources of energy.

6. To help poor nations in various ways with technology for industrialization.

7. To help the world community deal with the problems, "real and perceived," of multinational corporations. Kissinger undertook to propose guidelines. The responsibilities of multinational corporations, he said, were to obey local law; not to intervene in host countries' domestic affairs; to employ and if necessary train qualified local personnel; and to take into account local public policy, national development priorities, and customs. The responsibilities of host governments were to treat the corporations "equitably" and in accordance with international law, and to make clear their development priorities and standards of behavior and to maintain them consistently. Governments and corporations must respect their contractual obligations and settle disputes through fact-finding and arbitration. Principles established for multinational corporations should, where applicable, also be applied to domestic enterprises, including state-owned and mixed enterprises. Governments should "harmonize" their tax treatment of corporations.

8. To negotiate further trade preferences beyond those that would go into effect January 1, 1976, under the U.S. Trade Act of 1974.

9. To adapt nontariff trade barriers to the situations of the poor countries.

10. To work for "early agreement" on tariffs for tropical products.

11. To negotiate changes in the system of protection in the rich nations, a system that favors the import of raw materials over manufactured and semimanufactured goods. "Nothing," Kissinger said, "could be better calculated to discourage and limit the growth of processing industries in developing countries. The United States will give high priority in the Geneva negotiations to reducing these barriers."

12. To create a producer-consumer forum for every key commodity and to discuss methods of promoting the efficiency, growth, and stability of its market, especially in the case of grains and copper.

13. To sign the new international agreement on tin, subject to ratification by the U.S. Senate. (That agreement emphasizes buffer stocks, avoids direct price-fixing, and employs last-ditch export controls.)

14. To continue to participate actively in the negotiations on coffee.

15. To join in the forthcoming negotiations on cocoa and sugar.

16. To support liberalization of the IMF's financing of buffer stocks.

17. To launch a major new international effort to expand raw material production in poor countries.

18. To create an IMF trust fund of $10 billion for emergency balance-of-payments relief in the poorest countries due to global recessions and commodity price swings.

19. To give the poorest nations preferential access to concessionary financial aid.

20. To substantially replenish the International Development Association of the World Bank, which makes soft loans to the poorest countries, provided that Congress approves and that the oil countries also make "a significant" contribution.

21. To ask Congress to double our bilateral food aid to poor countries to $582 million this year.

22. To create a new international fund for agricultural develop-

ment to help poor countries grow more of their own food. For this purpose, Kissinger said, the Ford administration would ask Congress for a direct contribution of $200 million.

Kissinger's program lacked the scope and soaring rhetoric of Kennedy's Alliance for Progress. As he introduced it, he said, "We can deal in rhetoric or we can deal in reality. . . . So let us get down to business." Offering concrete, though limited, proposals, his program was in keeping with the United States' chastened mood and modest aims following Vietnam and Watergate. And it was the first real initiative the Nixon-Ford administration had undertaken affecting the Caribbean. The reaction at the UN was, on the whole, favorable. Even the Algerian representative, often a leader of extremist Third World actions, said that the speech contained "many positive things" that required study.

When, in January 1976, the IMF met in Jamaica to consider fundamental reforms in the world's monetary system, it faced strong demands for reform from the poor countries. U.S. Secretary of the Treasury Simon led the rich nations' resistance. At one point, the poor nations threatened to wreck the conference. But the ministers succeeded in reaching a compromise that gave the poor countries something, though far less than they had demanded. They agreed to abolish the official price of gold, to sell 25 million ounces of IMF gold, and to put the profit into a trust fund to aid poor nations; they agreed to increase from 25 percent to 75 percent the amount of their IMF contributions poor countries can borrow from the IMF in the first credit *tranche* to help them meet their balance-of-payment deficits.[13]

Those two IMF measures were among Kissinger's proposals. On the whole, the Kissinger program, if fully implemented, would have gone some distance toward meeting Third World demands. Unlike the proposals of previous Republican administrations, it did not stress too greatly the role of private enterprise, and it did not cling stubbornly to such economic dogmas as the sanctity of the free market. It continued the U.S. trend away from bilateral aid and toward multilateral aid. Of course, new arrangements along the lines Kissinger had proposed could not be worked out quickly. And of course, the U.S. Congress would have to agree to some of the proposals. But if the United States showed signs of backtracking on its own program, an explosion would almost surely occur. Indeed, if anything, the poor nations seemed likely to demand that the rich go a good deal farther than Kissinger proposed.

Meanwhile, a new and pressing issue emerged: debt. The loans the poor countries took in the 1960s began to fall due, and they found their debt burden crushing. Some even talked of abandoning their indexation demand if they could get their loans forgiven or rescheduled. Buried in this large issue lay a narrower one, potentially explosive and dangerous to the United States: many of the poor countries are heavily in debt to private American banks.

At meetings in 1975 and 1976, the poor countries continued to press their demands, and the United States, its policy whipsawed between State and Treasury, continued to fight a rearguard action, resisting indexation and various other interventions in commodities prices, offering instead new multilateral schemes to "develop"—or, as the poor countries read the term, "exploit"—natural resources. As the months wore on, it became increasingly clear that the discussions were sharpening the issues and bringing pressure to bear on the most tender point of our international economic relations—the point at which the domestic free enterprise interests of the United States collide with its foreign policy interests as a world power.

Conservative economists argue that the United States should continue to oppose artificial price-fixing of basic commodities by means of international agreements. They argue that removing the price mechanism and eliminating competition through artificial allocation of market shares distorts the economic system and that governmental intervention in one sector of the economy creates problems that can be solved only through further intervention. They point out that commodity markets have proved difficult to regulate in the past and are likely to remain so. They maintain that government lacks the wisdom to determine the "right" price for a commodity and cannot resist political pressures. Furthermore, they say, rigid price and production controls and indexation are actually against the best interests of the poor nations themselves. The price of an item, they hold, should be related to its cost of production rather than to the cost of something else. They insist that if the price of a commodity is too high, consumers will use substitutes and keep on using them. Thus, if the IBA pushes the price of bauxite so high that the aluminum companies find it cheaper to shift to, say, a by-product of shale oil, once they have made the technological change they will never go back to bauxite. They predict the OPEC's stunning success will not be duplicated in many, if any, other commodities;[14] they note that neither producer cartels nor international commodity agreements have a good track record of permanent accomplishment. At bottom, conservative economists simply believe that the free market will do a better job of balancing supply and demand than commodity agreements. Their faith in the free market is almost religious. And some officials of the Ford administration applied this faith directly to policy.

Several months after Kissinger publicly stated that we would participate in negotiation of an international cocoa agreement, such an agreement was reached. Gerald L. Parsky, an assistant secretary of the treasury, then announced that the United States would refuse to sign it, and he went on to describe the horror with which Secretary Simon viewed commodity agreements.

In the past, the United States has stubbornly refused tariff preferences to the Third World, opposed commodity agreements, and reduced its foreign aid. These measures contributed to the radicalization of the Third World—and to our own isolation. Sooner or later the United States must face today's realities. Given the world's political climate and the very real financial problems of the poor nations, the United States may have to modify its economic tenets for political reasons. We cannot isolate ourselves in the world economy. Nor can we hope to have prosperity ourselves in a chaotic world economy. The time has come to recognize the elements of justice in the Third World's demands and to readjust policy.

Some thoughtful people believe that the issues we confront today are wholly different from those we have faced before.[15] These contemporary issues are technical and complicated; cannot be resolved by spending money; involve the interests of the widest variety of groups; deal with economic resources that are shrinking; and require us to make sacrifices by reducing our consumption instead of merely bestowing gifts upon others as we did during the periods of the New Deal, the New Frontier, and the Great Society. The three leading new issues are food, raw materials, and energy. The issue of energy is linked to those of inflation, recession, unemployment, the Middle East, transportation, the balance of payments, housing, taxes, cities, economic concentration and antitrust, regional differences within the United States, arms sales abroad, the environment, architecture, our relations with our

European allies and Japan, and the relations among the rich and poor countries. In our efforts to reconcile so many conflicting interests, we have become paralyzed and wholly unable to adopt an energy policy. But the rest of the world will not forever allow us, with 6 percent of the world's population, to use up 30 percent of its dwindling oil. These new issues will force increased government intervention. The poor people of the poor countries simply will not permit us to prosper while they get steadily poorer.

To build their new order, the poor countries want: (1) improved access to markets for both agricultural and industrial products; (2) a chance to process their own raw materials for sale on the world market so that they can retain for themselves the value added; (3) more control over production and marketing of their resources; and (4) indexation.

The United States wants (1) an assured supply of raw materials at reasonable prices; (2) security for U.S. foreign private investment; (3) no producer cartels but, grudgingly, case-by-case study of negotiated producer-consumer commodity agreements; (4) no indexation of commodity prices; and (5) sufficient domestic production capacity (where possible) to reduce our strategic vulnerability.

As the largest or one of the largest markets in the world, we are in a position to exert considerable influence on any international economic arrangement. Until recently, it was assumed that only the poor countries needed or benefited from commodity stabilization agreements. But OPEC's oil embargo and the ensuing worldwide rise in commodity prices awakened us to the enormous economic importance of our own agricultural and raw material exports. We have begun to consider that even we may benefit from price stabilization in certain commodities. Some years ago, apparently reasoning that any commodity that affects sixty countries is politically too important to ignore, we quietly abandoned our rigid opposition to international commodity agreements in the case of coffee. We may come to more such political judgments. We need not accept all Third World demands, for some are unrealistic and some are unfair. But in our own long-run interest as well as in that of the Third World, we do need to adjust our policies.

1. We should, as Kissinger proposed, negotiate agreements on coffee, tin, and cocoa and examine other commodities case by case. (Once we have normalized relations with Cuba, we should join

an international effort to rationalize the world sugar market.)

2. We should, as Kissinger proposed, adopt special measures at the IMF and other international financial institutions to cushion the effect of wide commodity price swings on poor nations and try to develop other mechanisms for the same purpose.

3. We should implement fully the Trade Act of 1974, amend its cartel provision and go beyond it, as Kissinger proposed (see below).

4. We should reduce or eliminate our tariffs on processed raw materials, such as cocoa butter, reduce or eliminate our tariffs on Caribbean manufactured products, such as alcoholic beverages based on sugar, and pay subsidies to damaged U.S. industries for a time, as necessary. Surely a great nation would not suffer from importing a few textiles or some cocoa butter.

5. We should reconsider our traditional policy of preferring globalism to regionalism in trade arrangements. We should give special preferences to the Caribbean (a question to be discussed more fully later).

6. We should support, as Kissinger proposed, increased financial assistance from the World Bank and the IADB for the development of natural resources. (Formerly we opposed such programs on the grounds that they competed with private enterprise.)

7. To satisfy the poor nations' desire for more control over their raw materials and to protect U.S. investors, we should encourage more joint ventures; in some developments, such as building alumina capacity, which require sizable initial investments, we should encourage the International Finance Corporation to participate in equity financing.

These measures do not represent permanent solutions to the economic problems of the poor countries. But they will buy a few years' time. The poor countries may use that time to bring about real changes in the structures of their economies. If, as is more likely, they simply relax because their problems have been temporarily alleviated, then nothing will come of the program. But we should try.

Some economists see the Caribbean's drift to the Third World as transitory because the Caribbean can never develop important trading relationships with Africa and Asia. But today's political realities say otherwise. Indeed, the problems subsumed under the heading "Third World drift" now dominate our government's thinking about the Caribbean. The Panama Canal and Cuba are, of course, the issues that get the headlines, but underlying these very issues is Third Worldism. In the spring of 1975, the United States was in accord with the conciliatory attitude of Prime Minister Harold Wilson at the Commonwealth Conference in Kingston. But Forbes Burnham of Guyana was not to be conciliated. He replied, in effect, "The trouble is, Mr. Wilson, that you are a gradualist and I am a revolutionary." A while back, Fidel Castro said, "We and the United States are neighbors but we belong to different worlds." That is indeed the problem, and not only with respect to Cuba. A UN official from the Caribbean has commented:

> Eisenhower and Nixon thought private enterprise could solve Latin America's problems. It can't. The United States should act with greatness toward the small. Open markets is only part of it. It pains me to see Latin America looking to Asia and Africa for demagogic reasons. We are a part of Western civilization. Intellectuals in the United States and the Caribbean should play a part in the dialogue. They aren't.

Other thoughtful people in the Caribbean have accused the United States of supporting the Dominican Republic, Haiti, and Central America more generously than the rest of the Caribbean precisely because those nations are far less deeply into the Third World orbit than the rest of the Caribbean. As a professor at the University of the West Indies in Trinidad said, "In Kennedy's time, you were sympathetic with the plight of the peoples, you were a friend of democracy, you cared. What are the chances of going back to that?" Far more is involved here than commodity prices, the governor-general of Trinidad-Tobago points out:

> One has to be in a group somewhere at the UN, and the Third World is where we belong. People can't find Angola and Mozambique on the map, but they have to be told that we are supporting the freedom fighters. The political leaders capitalize on this. A place in the sun. The ordinary man here is not anxious to give money to Bangladesh, if he really had to choose between giving up carnival [the traditional Trinidad celebration] or helping the starving people of Africa, he would ask them to starve a little longer. But he will raise his clenched fist

and shout the slogans.

A U.S. diplomat says, "Venezuela and Panama are shooting for Third World leadership, and on Third World issues we'd better try to line up with them or all the Third World attacks will be targeted on us." He thinks we should formulate a new development program in the Caribbean countries, initially concentrating on agriculture (but avoiding the impression that we intend to force the Caribbean to remain predominantly agricultural).

Not least among the problems posed by Third Worldism in the Caribbean is the nationalization of American private enterprises. On the whole, the State Department under Nixon-Ford handled such situations well, and so, to a considerable extent, have the American enterprises themselves. "We have no differences with Venezuela over its takeover of equity," Assistant Secretary Rogers has said, "as long as the compensation is prompt and fair. And it is." Certain American businessmen complained that they were getting no support from State, but it is hard to see what support State could usefully provide. The nations that wish to take over U.S.-owned enterprises can do so regardless of opposition from the U.S. government, and we may fare better by agreeing at the outset than by interposing obstacles, dragging out negotiations, causing bitterness, and in the end, doing with ill grace what we could have done cheerfully at the outset—as the U.S. government has done all too often.

The increasing tendency of Caribbean governments to acquire all or a majority share of control of foreign enterprises raises questions about the future of private American investment in these statist societies. With a few exceptions, U.S. investment in extractive mineral enterprises and plantation agriculture is a thing of the past. The U.S. ambassador to Guyana said, "I see no role for private U.S. investment in Guyana in the future." Sir Egerton Richardson of Jamaica believes that U.S. investors should be willing to participate in some ventures on a minority basis. He observes, "you can't afford to dominate any more." We could, he thinks, invest most usefully in high technology manufacturing, which requires skilled labor that we would have to train. He opposes U.S. investment in land, banking, and public utilities.

Venezuela says it encourages foreign investment—on a minority basis. But American investors are, understandably, reluctant to accept only a minority interest in an enterprise; they fear they cannot safeguard their investment against inefficient management caused by local political pressures.

Enterprises mixed in curious ways have evolved. Reynolds Metals proposed an aluminum operation owned 50-50 by Reynolds and the Venezuelan government; a Japanese group proposed an operation of which it would own a majority and the Venezuelan government a minority. Venezuela said no to both and worked out an arrangement whereby Venezuela will own 80 percent and the Japanese 20 percent; Reynolds will design the project, oversee its construction, operate it for five years, and help market its production. Reynolds, which considers the arrangement "very satisfactory," had encouraged President Pérez to work with the Japanese group if only to ensure a Japanese market for its aluminum, pointing out that if the big U.S. companies shift to clay from bauxite, his expensive plant would be obsolete.

Sears Roebuck, facing divestiture in Caracas, watched the Reynolds negotiation with interest and explored its own possible role as a service contractor after the government took control. Such formulas can be adopted elsewhere. Venezuelan farmers have turned to the Kraft cheese company for technical assistance in quality control, administration, and marketing—and were willing to pay $2 million for it. Venezuela, which will be short of technology and trained personnel in many fields for many years, has commenced a foreign manpower recruiting program, thus opening opportunities to foreign companies in service contracts. Some Venezuelans expect the American colony there actually to expand. Trinidad-Tobago appears to offer fewer opportunities to U.S. investors.

The Honduran government has been planning a lumber company (it or private Honduran citizens would own 51 percent) and has been searching actively for an American or European company to provide minority capital and manage the project. Similar developments are afoot in other Central American countries.

The whole situation is so new that no one really knows how it will work out. The U.S. economy and the Caribbean economies are mixed in different ways. The trend toward statism in the Caribbean does not mean total state control of everything, as in the Soviet Union. It means government control of land and raw materials and ultimately probably local government or local private control of nearly all enterprises. Assistant Secretary Rogers is optimistic:

> U.S. enterprise is always composed of several parts—capital, technology, markets. In this new era, the world belongs to people who are ready to break that package out. U.S. industry will be willing to sell technology without equity, competitively with Japan and Europe. The steel companies that were nationalized in Venezuela are very pleased, almost smirking— they've made a deal for technology and marketing. The Caribbean needs U.S. know-how and markets. We have to adjust to this new reality. We will—the U.S. and the Caribbean need each other.

The Trade Act of 1974. The United States traditionally has admitted imports of raw materials duty-free while levying duties on manufactured and semimanufactured products; and the Third World countries have complained for many years that this policy prevents them from processing their own raw materials and thereby industrializing and developing—that it keeps them in perpetual colonial status. Bauxite and alumina, for example, come in to the United States free, but unwrought aluminum is dutied at 1¢ per pound, unwrought aluminum coils at 1.2¢ per pound, and wrought aluminum products at 2¢ per pound. This system is a result of joint labor and business political pressures on the U.S. Congress. Transferring American workers out of such labor-intensive industries as textile and shoe manufacturing would help deal with the problem but has never been done. Although many Third World countries cannot undertake sophisticated manufacturing, they could operate such labor-intensive industries if given a chance. But tariffs and other devices deny them our market. Absurdities result—our U.S. textile industry feels threatened by a few textiles from Haiti.[16] Such fears raise questions: do we really want to help these countries? And at what price? Solutions could be devised: for example, the U.S. government could open its market to Haitian textiles and pay a subsidy to the U.S. textile industry for a period of years while American workers and plants were moved out of textiles. But that involves a high degree of central economic planning, which creates political issues, and it would of course be opposed by the lobbies of textile manufacturers and textile workers' unions. No one would lobby for the State

Department view. Before beginning such planning, we would need a national consensus on its desirability, and American tradition runs against such central planning. Arguments, however, exist for it—our moral duty to our neighbors aside, helping them is in our own interest, for in the long run if they develop their economies, they will become a larger market for us. Moreover, it is not in our political interest to keep these countries poor and, therefore, in turmoil; they would then never attain enough political stability to work with us in international forums. But who is to make these arguments? Once again, textile workers and their bosses vote: the State Department and Haiti do not. Although central planning to the degree suggested may be impossible, and even undesirable, a case-by-case approach, falling short of heavy central planning but going farther than the existing "adjustment assistance" program, might be possible.

Perhaps we should decide that we will give special treatment to the Caribbean only. This would violate our traditional policy of global, not regional, trade arrangements. Some Western European nations have such special regional arrangements; for example, France allows its former African colonies' products in duty-free. We have opposed such regionalism. But perhaps we should make an exception of the Caribbean. If we can persuade the world (and ourselves) to go to free trade through some such mechanism as GATT, we would not need to devise a Caribbean exception. But since we probably cannot so persuade the world, perhaps we should consider special treatment for the Caribbean. Technically, we could do it under the Trade Act of 1974. The Caribbean nations are our nearest neighbors. We have interests there that we have virtually nowhere else. The Congress might be more willing to help the Caribbean that to help such remote places as Bangladesh. On the other hand, giving special treatment to the Caribbean would be hard to justify to the world since UNCTAD believes all poor countries should be given special treatment, and in the United Nations we might make enemies of fifty nations in the course of making friends of ten.

The Caribbean and other poor countries of the world in UNCTAD have often asked the United States (and other rich countries) to give a Generalized System of Preferences (GSP) to the poor nations. Although, early in his administration, President Nixon promised to work for GSP and also promised to urge Western Europe to consider it, Congress delayed—trade legislation is always slow owing to the multiplicity of interests and intense lobbying—and the administration did not push. Western Europe did give poor countries GSP, but years passed before, in the closing hours of Congress in December 1974, Congress enacted the first major U.S. trade legislation since the Trade Expansion Act of 1962. The new Trade Act of 1974 did include GSP—but it contained a provision that forbade the president to give GSP treatment to any member of OPEC or any member of any other cartel that fixed raw materials at unreasonably high prices or withheld raw materials from the United States. Pandemonium broke out in the Caribbean. Venezuela (and Ecuador) were clearly excluded from GSP; Jamaica and other bauxite nations might be excluded because of IBA; and various Caribbean nations that were trying to form other cartellike producer associations might also be courting exclusion. As the Caribbean nations saw it, after years of pleading and diplomatic maneuvering, they had finally been given what they wanted—and then had had it, in essence, taken away.

The State Department claims that it tried to warn Congress about the probable Latin American reaction to the OPEC proviso. But members of Congress and their staffs say the State Department did little or nothing to warn them, and that when it did it was too late. Most Latin American ambassadors in Washington were taken completely by surprise. The Trade Act, stalled in committee for two years, moved to passage with surprising speed. The OPEC proviso was added in committee at the last minute and because the bill moved so fast at the end, Congress probably spent little if any time considering the proviso's effects on Latin America. Congress thought it was denying GSP to the Arabs and other malefactors at the time when both protectionism and economic nationalism were rising. However, it is by no means certain that Congress would have dropped the OPEC proviso even had it been warned.

Venezuela took the lead in raising an outcry of protest. At every opportunity, President Pérez and his ministers denounced publicly and shrilly this latest piece of U.S. perfidy and imperialism. Privately, he sought the support of other Caribbean nations—for example, he urged President Somoza of Nicaragua to make a declaration against the United States. Brazilians thought he was trying to focus the anger of poor countries on the United States, thereby deflecting it from Venezuela and its OPEC allies. Pérez would win either way; if his pressure persuaded Congress to eliminate the cartel proviso, he could claim a victory; if it did not, he would still have the issue, which he was using to assert Venezuelan Caribbean leadership. Country after country in the Caribbean joined Venezuela's cry for justice, even though the proviso would not hurt them and the rest of the bill would help them. Even Honduras supported Venezuela against the United States. The issue became the focal point of the Caribbean economic confrontation with the United States. The OAS declared "its deep concern" over the "deterioration of inter-American solidarity" caused by the Trade Act. Thus it was that the hemisphere foreign ministers gathered in Washington in May 1975 in a charged atmosphere, expecting a confrontation with the United States over both the Trade Act and the Panama Canal issue. (The Cuban issue was also boiling at that time.) But the issues were defused when Assistant Secretary Rogers launched a counterattack, meeting with Latin American ambassadors to explain matters, and when Secretary Kissinger let it be known that he would ask Congress to exempt Venezuela and Ecuador from the proviso (a move that might backfire if he was unable to persuade Congress, which tends to react badly to foreign pressures). The ministers went home mollified because we were able to say that we agreed that the hemisphere should be exempted from the Trade Act proviso and that we and Panama were near final agreement.

By this time, too, sober analysis had led many experts to believe that of the Latin American countries, only Brazil, Mexico, and Argentina manufactured enough products to benefit greatly from GSP. Moreover, the administration determined that the IBA was not a cartel within the meaning of the proviso, thus making Jamaica and other bauxite producers eligible for GSP.

In retrospect, it appears that the proviso really did not seriously damage the Caribbean. Venezuela does not need GSP, and Jamaica will get it. What really angered them was that the proviso was obnoxious, and that we were the last of the rich nations to adopt GSP—and a less generous GSP than the Europeans adopted. Once again, United States policy aimed at another part of the world had unexpectedly affected the Caribbean; Congress, aiming at the Arabs, had clumsily swatted the Caribbean—indicating how little we considered their concerns. On the night Congress passed the Trade Bill, the Jamaican ambassador to Washington, said sadly, "We are not an important country—decisions are taken that affect us and we're not told. If only someone had asked us."

The Third World at the UN. When the UN began, the General Assembly had fifty-one members, and the Western and Latin American nations constituted a two-thirds majority that could be counted on. As the UN grew, in order to maintain that majority, we were obliged to add more and more African and Asian states. As early as 1955, we needed 35 percent of the Afro-Asian bloc. In the 1960s, the UN entered a period of "swirling majorities"—the African and Asian states sometimes voted with the United States and sometimes with the USSR. Today, the UN has 144 members, and sometimes, especially on racial or economic issues, the black Africans, the Arabs, the Iranians, the South Asians, most of the Southeast Asians, and a good part of Latin America as well as all the communist countries—are almost solidly lined up against the United States. They constitute an overwhelming majority in the General Assembly.

The assembly, of course, can only pass resolutions. But the Security Council wields real power, including armed force. During the UN's first twenty-five years, the United States refused to use its veto while the Soviet Union was forced to veto often. This, of course, resulted from politics, not principle—at that time, the Security Council had only eleven members (five permanent—the United States, the Soviet Union, France, Britain, Nationalist China—and six rotating members) and its decisions required a constitutional majority of seven. Thus, any five members could block action by merely abstaining. Since Britain, France, and Nationalist China were then our firm allies, we had only to persuade a single one of the six rotating members to abstain to have the effect of a veto. But in 1966, the council was enlarged to fifteen, which meant seven votes for abstention had to be found. Assembling seven votes in the council on racial issues became difficult, if not impossible, because by then Gaullist France was no longer dependable and the Latin Americans were swinging into the Afro-Asian neutralist orbit. We cast our first veto in 1970 (on a proposal to apply sanctions to Rhodesia). Moreover, although our policy has been to keep hemisphere matters out of the UN and in the OAS, where the Soviet Union has no vote, we can seemingly no longer continue to sequester hemisphere questions when the Latin American nations are themselves using the UN and the OAS is in disarray. (Panama, as we have seen, took its dispute with us to the UN Security Council, and successfully.) Moreover, as noted, the Third World first developed its demands for a new order at a UN body, UNCTAD. And in the last two UN sessions, some or all of the Caribbean states voted against us on such issues as seating the PRC, seating the Sihanouk delegation from Cambodia, inviting the leader of the Palestine Liberation Organization to address the Assembly, suspending South Africa from the UN, adopting the Charter of Economic Rights and Duties heavily weighted in favor of the Third World, various resolutions calling for a new world economic order, various resolutions on racial issues in Africa, and various resolutions condemning Israel and supporting the Arabs, including one in 1975 equating Zionism with racism. But the Caribbean states are by no means unanimous on all these issues, Guyana probably votes more consistently with the Algeria-Tanzania group than any other Caribbean state; the Dominican Republic and most of Central America seldom do. On the resolution equating Zionism with racism, for example, *Grenada, Guyana, Mexico,* and *Cuba* voted with Algeria, Uganda, Tanzania, and the Soviet bloc majority; the *Bahamas, Barbados, Costa Rica, the Dominican Republic, El Salvador, Haiti, Honduras, Nicaragua,* and *Panama* stayed with us in voting against the resolution; and *Guatemala, Jamaica, Trinidad-Tobago,* and *Venezuela* abstained. Guyana was a sponsor of a Security Council resolution condemning Israel for air raids on Palestinian targets in Lebanon (Cameroon, Iraq, Mauritania, and Tanzania were cosponsors), which the United States vetoed. Early in 1976 *Guyana* and *Panama* joined Pakistan, Benin (formerly Dahomey), Rumania, and Tanzania in sponsoring a Mideast peace resolution weighted in favor of the Arabs; we stood alone in vetoing it.

The reasons that the Caribbean votes with the Afro-Asian Third World bloc against the United States vary. Those that voted to condemn Zionism did so to maintain Third World solidarity and because of anti-Americanism and anti-Zionism, effective lobbying by the Palestinians, and the persuasive influence of OPEC, which may have promised them preferential treatment on oil and investment capital in return for their votes. Burnham of Guyana has always sided against the United States and with the Third World in opposing America's war in Vietnam and in favoring Peking's admission, total Israeli withdrawal from "all Arab territories," and the cause of the Palestine Liberation Organization. A Jamaican diplomat has said,

"We don't want to break with the United States but to maintain our credibility we can't be an Uncle Tom to the United States—and on South Africa we feel strongly." Honduras usually votes with the United States—but not on Panama. The Bahamas is less closely tied to the Third World than its neighbors. The Trinidad-Tobago ambassador to Washington has said, "America can put pressure on us on Chinese representation, but they can't ask us not to condemn apartheid." Sir Egerton Richardson says, his usually cool voice charged with emotion, "We have duties. We've quarreled with the UK over Rhodesia, but our strongest feelings are about Southwest Africa—because it was a UN mandate and never should have been handed over to the racists there. Formerly we were a rank-and-file member of the nonaligned group. Under Manley we have moved up to the front bench."

When the Caribbean countries, with the support of much of the Third World, were pressing their own economic demands on the UN, their position was sound and unexceptional, whether or not one agreed with everything they said. But when they moved from purely economic issues that affected them directly to such purely political issues as "anti-Zionism," they found themselves supporting resolutions that were often irresponsible, unfair, extremist, and sometimes absurd.

What is the reaction to this in the United States? At the end of 1974, our ambassador to the UN, John Scali, called the General Assembly's increasing tendency to pass one-sided resolutions it knew could not be implemented "deeply disturbing," and he warned that support for the UN was eroding in the United States and that the UN was in danger of becoming "irrelevant." Although his successor, Ambassador Daniel Patrick Moynihan called the special session in 1975 (at which Kissinger made his important economic policy speech) a success, another U.S. delegate made it clear that the United States "cannot and does not accept" the idea that the world has now embarked upon a "new international economic order." Ambassador Moynihan took an increasingly hard line with the Third World; when the Assembly adopted its resolution equating Zionism with racism, he said, "The United States rises to declare . . . before the world, that it does not acknowledge, it will not abide by, it will never acquiesce in, this infamous act. . . . The proposition . . . is a lie." A little later when an Assembly committee found that the United States was maintaining bases in the Virgin Islands as a threat against Caribbean nations, Moynihan called the UN "a theater of the absurd" and said "the world's increasing contempt [for the UN] is increasingly deserved." Moynihan's strong campaign against the Third World and flamboyant tactics aroused opposition in the United States State Department and among our closest allies, including the British. In February 1976, Moynihan resigned (and soon was elected senator).

By that time, Congress was angered by such resolutions as the one on Zionism-racism. Some members thought the United States should withdraw from the UN, others spoke of cutting off its funds, and both houses unanimously adopted resolutions condemning the Zionist-racism resolution and calling for a reassessment of our relationship to the UN. Others spoke of cutting off aid to Third World nations that consistently opposed the United States in the UN. President Ford deplored the Zionist-racism resolution. Subsequently, the House Foreign Affairs Committee asked President Ford to provide a report within ninety days that would justify aid to countries that had voted for the resolution, but the Senate Foreign Relations Committee disagreed and urged that aid be insulated from politics. By January, nevertheless, the State Department was cutting off aid to certain nations, including a development aid program in Guyana. We also made representations to other governments. Before the resolutions on South Africa, the Sihanouk delegation, and the PLO came to a vote, Kissinger had approached Manley of Jamaica and other Caribbean leaders, and an ARA diplomat told the Jamaican ambassador that anti-UN sentiment in the United States was growing, especially in the Midwest, where people were saying, "Here we give those countries all that money and they spit in our eye." In theory, the United States could, by financial and other means, establish a position of such influence that it could all but force the Caribbean to support us. But that would require congressional and administration consensus, and no such consensus exists. (Whether we should use financial aid for such political purposes is, of course, a different question.)

Cuba Again

Secretary Kissinger's speech in Houston on March 1, 1975, revealed the change that had taken place in United States policy toward Cuba in the eleven years almost to the day since Secretary Rusk had delineated the "two fundamental nonnegotiable points"; Cuba's military connection with Moscow and its export of revolution. Kissinger said our main concern was still the military connection with Moscow, but he said, "We are prepared to move in a new direction if Cuba will." Kissinger's speech signaled a move to reverse U.S. policy toward Cuba.

Pressures to change that policy have been mounting since about 1969, when Castro indicated a willingness to cooperate with us in dealing with airplane hijackers. The sources of pressure are many—the abatement of the Cold War, the change in American relations with Peking, the desire of American businessmen to do business with Cuba, the apparent end, after Ché Guevara's death in Bolivia, of Castro's policy of exporting his revolution throughout the hemisphere, the eagerness of other hemisphere—especially Caribbean—states to normalize their bilateral relations with Cuba, and the growing Third World kinship among Caribbean countries. But the president and the State Department dragged their feet. Chester Bowles and others have observed that getting a policy established at the State Department was a good deal like trying single-handedly to carry a double-bed mattress up a narrow spiral staircase to the attic—and that, once you got it up there, the only way to move it again was to throw it out the window. Policy reversal comes slowly. In 1971, Senators Fulbright and Church introduced a resolution declaring it the sense of the Senate that the president should review our policy toward Cuba. Fulbright had thought he was being helpful; the Senate could make it easier for State to change policy at a time when the Nixon administration seemed to want to relax tensions. To Fulbright's annoyance, State even disapproved of sending the Senate Foreign Relations Committee's staff expert on Latin America, Pat M. Holt, to study Cuba. After President Nixon went to Peking, more and more people on Capitol Hill asked, as Senator McGee put it, "If the President can go to Peking and Moscow why can he not go to Havana?" At hearings in 1973, McGee pointed out that Chile, Peru, Mexico, Jamaica, Barbados, Trinidad-Tobago, and Guyana now had relations with Cuba and that even Venezuela was moving in that direction. "So," McGee said, "the next question is, who is being isolated in the hemisphere, Cuba or the United States?" The State Department continued to maintain its position. Later that year, immediately after

Kissinger became secretary, Fulbright renewed his request that State validate Pat Holt's passport for travel to Cuba, and Kissinger did so, reluctantly.

Holt was in Cuba from June 29 to July 8, 1974. He concluded that the Cubans are right when they say that our policy of isolating Cuba has been a failure. He said that with massive help from the Soviet Union, the Cubans were on the verge of making their system work. They claimed a per capita GNP of $1,587, a figure perhaps inflated by socialist accounting practices but which, even if cut in half, was still impressive. Cubans were proud of what they had accomplished, particularly in education and health and in the redistribution of wealth. Shortages and rationing existed. Slums and poverty also existed, but far less of it than elsewhere in Latin America. Cubans felt that the worst was past, that times were good and would get better, that Cuba's place in the hemisphere and the world was steadily improving. Trade with Latin America, Europe, and Japan was increasing. But our boycott hurt: it denied Cuba equipment replacements and spare parts and piqued Cuban pride. Thus, lifting the boycott was an essential prelude to normalization of relations. Cuba's export of revolution to the rest of the Caribbean, Holt thought, had been "minimal" for several years. He had "the clear impression" that while Cubans would welcome better relations with us, the initiative would have to come from us. Therefore, he recommended that Congress reexamine the laws affecting third countries trading with Cuba and that State consider relaxing travel restrictions on Americans who wanted to go to Cuba and on the movement of Cuban diplomats at the UN, who are presently confined to New York City.

As part of the reexamination, two members of the Senate Foreign Relations Committee, Jacob K. Javits and Claiborne Pell (D.-R.I.), visited Cuba from September 27 to 30, 1974. (Later Senator George McGovern [D.-S.D.] went.) Javits and Pell told Castro that a normalization of relations would depend on several matters of concern to us: "the security implications of the Soviet military presence in Cuba"; Cuba's export of revolution in the hemisphere; humanitarian issues, including the plight of political prisoners in Cuba, the separation of Cuban families, and political repression; and compensation for seized American property. The Cubans gave them the strong impression that they had wanted normalization; they even released four American prisoners, "an important gesture of goodwill," the senators thought. As a result, Javits and Pell suggested that the U.S. government relax travel restrictions "somewhat" and that it signal its interest in normalizing relations to the OAS foreign ministers' meeting the following month in Quito. The reaction of the U.S. press to the Javits-Pell trip was by and large favorable. Some American diplomats, however, complained privately that their trip had undercut State's bargaining position with Castro. They felt that such visits allowed Castro to give an impression of friendliness and reasonableness without in any way actually altering his own position on relations with the U.S. government. In this view, Castro considers the absence of relations with the United States a bulwark of his regime and the best guarantor of what freedom of action the Soviet Union permits him.

In any case, it was in this atmosphere that the United States approached the OAS foreign ministers' meeting at Quito in November 1974. The meeting, which was to consider lifting OAS sanctions against Cuba, had been called at the urging of Venezuela, Colombia, and Costa Rica and its foreign minister, Gonzalo Facio. At the time, Cuba was the most urgent issue in Latin America. Latin American ambassadors in Washington, who besieged ARA trying to discover what our position would be, were told that at present the U.S. position was one of complete neutrality. The Venezuelan and Costa Rican foreign ministers thought they had the two-thirds vote, fourteen, required under the Rio Treaty, but they miscalculated and got only twelve votes. Only Chile, Uruguay, and Paraguay voted against lifting sanctions, but six abstained—Bolivia, Brazil, Nicaragua, Guatemala, Haiti, and the United States. Facio of Costa Rica and the Venezuelan foreign minister complained bitterly that the United States had rounded up the abstentions—which we denied. (The foreign ministers were offended, too, because Secretary Kissinger himself did not attend the meeting—events in the Middle East kept him away.) Some American diplomats viewed this with a certain wry humor: Latin Americans complain whenever the United States throws its weight around in the OAS, but now they were complaining because we did not. Why did we abstain? Probably, quite simply, because Secretary Kissinger was not yet ready to decide his Cuban policy. He was preoccupied with the Middle East and the Soviet Union, and until he was ready, he was unwilling to let Gonzalo Facio make United States foreign policy. This does not imply disdain for Facio or his nation; it simply says that Cuban policy is relatively easy for a small country like Costa Rica. It is a problem of entirely different scale for a large nation with power relationships all over the world—including those with the Soviet Union. Kissinger, a great-power secretary, instinctively viewed Cuba as unimportant in itself but important in world geopolitical terms. The trouble was, of course, that Kissinger lacked the time to consider Cuban issues carefully, one price of his brand of personal diplomacy.

After Quito, several countries announced they intended to resume relations with Cuba anyway. Since a resumption of relations would seriously weaken the Rio Treaty under which the sanctions had been voted, in July 1975 the OAS Permanent Council met in San José, Costa Rica, and amended the Rio Treaty to provide that sanctions could be lifted by a simple majority. The foreign ministers immediately constituted themselves a Meeting of Consultation of Foreign Ministers and lifted the sanctions against Cuba. Only Chile, Paraguay, and Uruguay voted against it; Brazil and Nicaragua abstained. Thus, after eleven years the OAS ended its effort to isolate Cuba, an action that Assistant Secretary Rogers viewed with satisfaction.

Cuba is quintessentially a Caribbean state. It has far more in common with the rest of the Caribbean than it has with, say, Argentina or Chile—or, for that matter, with Eastern Europe and the Soviet Union. Cuba was discovered and developed at the same time and in the same way as the rest of the Caribbean, and the Soviet Union cannot erase three hundred years of history in a couple of decades. Castro's actions, except in Angola, seem to indicate that he realizes that in the long run, if Cuba is to play a role in world affairs, it will have to play it in the Caribbean. He has been improving the missions he sends to other Caribbean states; he has also probably stopped training guerrillas from other Caribbean nations, although Caribbean revolutionaries still visit Cuba to raise their own spirits. Indeed, the romantic era of Ché Guevara is over. (Or at least so it seemed until the Angola adventure.) Castro appears to believe that other Caribbean nations will have to make their own revolutions, to believe that Cuba cannot do it for them. He can police the Caribbean no more than we can police Southeast Asia. He has a Nixon Doctrine of his own.

Like Venezuela and Mexico, Cuba may see its future as the preeminent power in the Caribbean. It seems unlikely that Castro will reenter the OAS; rather he appears to think that history is going his way, that in time it will be not Cuba but the United States that is isolated, and that his interest lies in promoting a new organization of Latin American states that excludes the United States, a political extension of SELA, the new economic grouping launched by Venezuela and Mexico. Castro has received trade and diplomatic missions from all over the Caribbean. In 1975 he received Echeverría of Mexico, Torrijos of Panama, Burnham of Guyana, Williams of Trinidad-Tobago, Manley of Jamaica, and others. The first meeting of the Caribbean Development and Cooperation Committee of the UN's ECLA was held in November 1975 in Havana. By 1976, ships waited to unload in Havana's harbor, and Havana's international airport was busy with flights to and from Mexico, Peru, Jamaica, Barbados, Panama, Trinidad-Tobago, and Guyana as well as Europe. Jamaica has shown a downright eagerness to strengthen its Cuban ties, for Manley feels he can learn much from Cuba about how to improve education and health. Early in 1976, Cuban construction workers arrived to build a school equipment factory as well as an agricultural school, and Cubans were reported training the Jamaican police. (Jamaica denied it.) Cuban troops were reported in Guyana, Cubans were helping Guyana modernize its fishing industry, and the Cuban Ballet Troupe visited Santo Domingo. Prime Minister Williams of Trinidad-Tobago calls Castro's literacy campaign his "key achievement." Castro sent 300,000 people to teach the populace and quickly reduced the illiteracy rate to 4 percent; but "most important of all, unemployment has been eliminated." Williams adds, however, that the other side of the coin is totalitarianism, and he is wary of Cuban domination of the Caribbean sugar industry. Cuba was the first to send humanitarian relief to Honduras when it was flattened by a hurricane, but it also sent propaganda. In fact, Haiti appears to be almost the only Caribbean island country where Cubans are clearly not welcome.

The big question is whether Cuba will normalize its relations with the United States. Most specialists believe Castro wants to; but some, including the thoughtful Philip Bonsal, believe Castro will do so only on terms humiliating to the United States, terms that would recognize his claim to infallibility. (His agitation in the Puerto Rican matter and his adventure in Angola, Bonsal believes, have postponed the day when, in the interest of his own people, he will need seriously to consider resuming relations with us on a basis of reciprocal concessions; Castro believes, in Bonsal's view, that what remains of the mystique of his personal regime would suffer if an appreciable movement of people, goods, and services were resumed between Cuba and the United States.) Those who think Castro would welcome normalization point out that he needs spare parts and replacements for worn-out machinery—these he can get more easily and cheaply from the United States than from Europe and the Soviet Union. To some, resuming relations would be a victory for Castro. It would diminish his economic dependence on the Soviet Union, and it might get him a better price for sugar—the Soviet Union allows him to index his commodity prices and the index base could be changed. He has to some extent de-radicalized his revolution: he has "liberated" prices, skewed the ration system, substituted financial incentives to workers for moral incentives, and denounced egalitarianism and his own idealistic errors made when the revolution was young. Another possible indication of Castro's desire for normalization appeared in an interview in which he praised Kissinger; in another, he praised Ford. He may feel that as other Caribbean countries gain new power, as Venezuela has done with oil, Cuba is in danger of being left behind; normalizing relations with the United States would help put Cuba back in the mainstream.

In the United States, although a major roadblock disappeared when President Nixon resigned, normalizing relations between us and Cuba is extremely complicated. Numerous interests are involved. Castro, of course, wants us to unconditionally lift our boycott as a precondition to negotiations. But we should end the boycott only after getting substantial concessions from Castro. Subjects for discussion include: something over $3 billion of claims, reduced to about $2 billion by the Foreign Claims Commission, for personal and industrial property that Castro confiscated; a number of American and other political prisoners held by Castro as agents of the CIA; the rights of thousands of Cuban families that have been surrendered when some people fled to the United States and left relatives behind. Various political questions would also arise: Castro could be expected to demand that we get out of Guantánamo and pledge not to intervene in Cuba's internal affairs; we could be expected to raise questions about the Cienfuegos base for Soviet submarines, and indeed the entire Cuban-Soviet relationship, Castro's intervention in Angola and other Afro-Asian countries as well as in the hemisphere, and his violations of the human rights of his own people. Nearly every one of these issues is complex; negotiating a settlement would take time, but does not seem impossible. Cuba today is the only nation on earth with both Soviet and U. S. military bases; perhaps we would be willing to give up Guantánamo in exchange for Cienfuegos, all other Soviet-used facilities, and the removal of Soviet troops now in Cuba. Castro has declared he will never pay our claims, but he has paid others. And a mutual nonintervention pledge might be possible. Probably the most difficult issues would be the human issues—prisoners, refugees, human rights of Cubans—and the international political issues, mainly Cuba's relationship to the Soviet Union. Finally, we should consider the effects of negotiating an agreement with Castro on other Caribbean states and on world commodity markets. If we normalize relations with Cuba, some American tourists will probably desert Puerto Rico for Havana, which is closer, less crowded, and more interesting. Cuban sugar might erode or destroy the U. S. market for Dominican, Trinidadian, and other Caribbean sugar. Cuban rum and cigars might resume a dominant position, hurting Puerto Rico, Honduras, and Nicaragua. Surely we shall have to compensate countries that stood with us when we stood against Castro if they are injured by our resumption of relations with him.

Some ask, "What's in it for us?" Politically, normalizing relations with Cuba would do us more good in the hemisphere than almost anything else except ratifying a new Panama Canal treaty. For more than fifteen years, the Cuban-American confrontation has poisoned everything in the hemisphere. Ending the confrontation would be a great boon. Moreover, as Senator Pell has pointed out, both countries would enjoy considerable trade benefits from normalization—cigars and commodities would come into the United States, Cuba would buy equipment and consumer goods from us. American business-men seem to agree. A growing number of U.S. corporations, including Dow Chemical, Union Carbide, RCA, Burroughs, and Ford, have started looking at Cuba as an important new market. In fact, more than one hundred American firms have recently asked State about Cuban trade, and the Nixon administration approved the sale to Cuba of certain American products made in Argentina and Canada. Castro, too, has made gestures. He welcomed the U.S. trade move as a "positive gesture," returned $2 million of ransom money confiscated from an airplane hijacker, and announced that the removal of our embargo on medicine and food would constitute evidence of U.S. willingness to negotiate, which seems to modify his previous insistence on a complete lifting of the embargo. Castro also quietly invited a representative of the Chase Manhattan Bank to Cuba and made quiet overtures to a U.S. mining company.

Nobody expects that if we normalize relations, American tourists will overrun Havana and Varadero as they did before Castro's time, using Cuba as a sort of super saloon, bordello, and casino. Nor does anyone think Castro will hand Cuba's production plant over to U.S. private investment as his predecessors did. No one, indeed, wants any of this to happen. Some U.S. companies, however, hope to find a role to play.

Opposition to normalizing relations with Cuba does exist on Capitol Hill, but it is probably weaker than opposition to a new Canal treaty. Shortly after Kissinger made his Houston speech ("We are prepared to move in a new direction if Cuba will"), Senator Richard Stone and others introduced a resolution opposing the normalization of relations. But Senator Kennedy (D.-Mass.) introduced a bill to lift legislative prohibitions on Cuban trade, Senators Javits and Pell introduced a sense-of-the-Senate resolution calling for normalization, and a high State Department official said those moves were not unwelcome. The Senate clearly would support normalization; opposition in the House may be somewhat stronger. The State Department should obtain Congress's advice and consent in advance.

In recent years, the Cuban issue has risen in virtually every congressional hearing on Latin America. Assistant Secretary Rogers feels we have overemphasized the Cuban question to the point where, in 1974, it overshadowed and obscured everything else—a distortion of the Cold War. Thus, at the very juncture in Caribbean affairs where economic and social issues were rising and political and strategic issues were receding, the question of Cuba—an anachronistic issue, a relic of the Cold War, just as the Panama Canal is an anachronistic issue, a relic of gunboat diplomacy—came to a head. Indeed, in 1975-1976, Cuba and the Canal, together with the Trade Act of 1974, were the hottest issues in the Caribbean. Interestingly enough, the importance of all three was largely symbolic.

In 1975-1976, just as movement on the Cuba question began, we learned that Castro was sending about one-eighth of his standing army to lead the victorious faction of Angolan nationalists supported by the Soviet Union and opposed by us. It was a novel initiative, and world capitals did not know what to make of it. Secretary Kissinger called it a "geopolitical event of considerable significance." Whether this initiative was taken by Castro or forced on him by the Kremlin was not clear. Nor was it clear whether, as C. L. Sulzberger of the *New York Times* put it, the Cuban troops in Angola were helots or zealots—ideological mercenaries at Russia's beck and call or dedicated activists of Castro's international revolution. If the latter, they might be expected to turn up in, say, the Canal Zone or Puerto Rico. (It was possible, of course, that Castro, unable to find employment for the fiery young men he trained and indoctrinated in his days of "continental mission," was glad to find somewhere in Africa to sent them.) It was not clear why Castro would stop exporting revolution to the Caribbean but begin exporting it to Africa.[17]

At about the same time that Castro's troops were involved in Angola, Cuba and its Third World friends in Asia and Africa repeatedly raised in the UN the question of what they called the American "colony," Puerto Rico.[18] Kissinger said on November 11, 1975, "We were making progress earlier this year in improving relations with Cuba. But [the Puerto Rico and Angola issues] . . . have given us some pause." On December 19, the Senate, fearing another Vietnam, cut off U.S. funds to support two rival Angolan nationalist factions, and the next day President Ford said at an impromptu news conference, "The action of the Cuban Government in sending combat forces into Angola destroys any opportunity for improvement of relations with the United States." The *Washington Post* was not alone in thinking President Ford was "grossly overreacting" and indulging in a "fit of bad temper." Soon, however, it became clear that this was no mere fit of temper. President Ford and Secretary Kissinger repeatedly declared that, as Kissinger put it on March 22, "The United States will not accept further Cuban military interventions abroad," even against white minority regimes in Africa that we do not support. Neither he nor Ford said what the United States would do if Cuba did interfere again, but Kissinger refused to rule out any move—including a military invasion of Cuba. The Third World countries of the Caribbean publicly disagreed with the United States; in the same week that President Ford called Castro "an international outlaw," the foreign minister of Jamaica called him "one of the greatest men in our lifetime," and Prime Minister Manley said, "We regard the assistance that Cuba gave [in Angola] as honorable and in the best interest of all those who care for African freedom and, above all, freedom from white supremacy rule." Of course, Ford's and Kissinger's denunciation of Cuba may have had less to do with high-level policy than with the contest between Ford and Reagan for the Cuban vote in the Florida presidential primary election—yet another example of how domestic politics affects our foreign policy. Nonetheless, the Puerto Rico and Angola issues, taken together, seem likely to delay any movement toward normalization.[19] Yet, in the long run, Cuba's future inevitably lies with the United States, not with the Soviet Union. And in our own interest, we should solve the problem because it is difficult for us to do anything at all in the Caribbean as long as the Castro issue (and the Canal issue) remain. We should normalize relations—but only on a basis of reciprocal concessions.

Puerto Rico Today

In 1953, after Puerto Rico voted itself commonwealth status, the United States informed the United Nations that it would no longer supply it with information on Puerto Rico—its new status removed it from the category of non-self-governing territories. The General Assembly concurred. Thus it conferred international legitimacy on Puerto Rico's self-governing status. (Puerto Rico is officially the *"asociado libre"* state of Puerto Rico—that is, the *free* state of Puerto Rico associated with the United States. This has been loosely translated as "commonwealth." (For further discussion of its status, see chapter 4, section 5.) Thereafter, the United States has regarded any attempt by the UN to deal with Puerto Rico as interference in the internal affairs of the United States. In recent years, however, Cuba and its communist and Third World friends have accused the United States of holding Puerto Rico in colonial thralldom. In 1973, the Cuban ambassador, speaking before the UN Committee on Decolonization, urged the withdrawal of U.S. military forces from Puerto Rico and asked that Puerto Rico be added to the committee list of non-self-governing territories. In addition, the president of the Puerto Rican Independence Party and the secretary-general of the Puerto Rican Socialist Party appeared before the committee. The committee adopted a resolution sponsored by Congo, Iraq, Mali, and Syria that (1) reaffirmed Puerto Rico's right to self-determination and independence; (2) requested the United States "to refrain from taking any measures which might obstruct" those rights; (3) requested the committee's rapporteur to compile information on Puerto Rico; and (4) decided to keep the question under continuous review.[20] The United States viewed the action of the committee as "blatant interference" in our internal affairs. In the summer of 1975, a leader of the Puerto Rican independence movement told the committee that U.S. and Puerto Rican secret police were persecuting Puerto Ricans who favored independence, and he accused the United States of "imperialistic exploitation" of Puerto Rico. But the United States put heavy pressure on the committee's members, telling them that another vote for an independence resolution would be considered an "unfriendly act," thus indicating that the United States might withhold or withdraw U.S. aid; as a result, the committee voted to postpone consideration indefinitely. U.S. diplomats considered it a "great success."

When the General Assembly met in the fall of 1975, the Cuban delegate reiterated support for Puerto Rican independence. Early one morning a few weeks later, bombs exploded almost simultaneously at government buildings, corporation offices, and banks in New York, Chicago, and Washington, and a terrorist group calling itself the Fuerzas Armadas de Liberación Nacional Puertorriqueña claimed credit. At the same time, nearly 20,000 people attended a rally in Madison Square Garden for Puerto Rican independence. A few days later, independence leaders told the UN Committee that "North American imperialists," embarked on a "plan of genocide" in Puerto Rico, had sterilized 200,000 Puerto Rican women.

Senator Rubén Berrios of the Puerto Rican Senate, president of the Puerto Rican Independence Party, has said that the same issue will be taken to the UN every year. He says that the Arab nations help the cause, that Jamaica, Trinidad-Tobago, and Guyana support it, and that "in five or six years the whole Caribbean" will support it. Assistant Secretary Rogers has described Cuba's involvement as "an effort to substitute the will of Havana for the free choice of the people of Puerto Rico." Secretary Kissinger has said that a U.S. policy of conciliation toward Castro "will not survive Cuban meddling in Puerto Rico or Cuban armed interventions in [Angola]." Numerous other bombings have occurred in Puerto Rico and New York. Some experts blamed leftist extremists in the independence movement, some blamed rightist anti-Castro refugees from Cuba, and Berrios said he would not be surprised to learn that the CIA did it.

The Puerto Rico Independence Party has a long history. In 1952, it was the second strongest party in Puerto Rico, but it went into a steady decline through the 1950s and 60s. In 1970, the party members asked themselves, "Independence for what?" Under the leadership of Senator Berrios, they answered, "For socialism." Ever since, Berrios claims, the party has grown. When Berrios ran for the Senate in 1968, he received only 25,000 votes; in 1972, he received 94,000. Berrios, an impressive, intelligent young leader, educated at Yale and Oxford, formerly a professor of law, describes himself as a "pro-Puerto Rican socialist democrat" and says:

> We're a new breed of people in the Caribbean. We want to visit China and the United States and the Soviet Union. We want an adequate distribution of wealth. I studied economics at Oxford, and the textbooks defined the terms of trade as the ability of the industrialized nations to sell high and buy cheap— why didn't everyone realize that that had to change? OPEC was inevitable. Something similar must start in the Caribbean. The Caribbean wants to be independent, it wants to be socialist. Socialism was inevitable in Venezuela. It is the defense of small nations against large. It preserves civil liberties and democracy. If Venezuela wants its own iron ore and oil, and if Puerto Rico wants to put its supermarkets into co-ops, why not? Why not for Puerto Rico a policy of independence plus political and commercial and cultural relations with the United States—on the basis of absolute respect? I think the world is going that way. The general orientation of Jamaica, Trinidad-Tobago, Guyana will be left nationalist. Neither Soviet ideological influence nor United States imperialism likes these develop-ments—though I must say I don't know what U.S. policy is toward the black Caribbean. We are in a new world, a different world. The time of Muñoz is past.

Berrios thinks that the great success and long rule of the Muñoz party was a result of Puerto Rico's postwar bourgeoisie; it was a period of labor–management peace because management paid high wages:

> Everything was roses, everybody was happy, why have a labor union? Capitalism came to us all of a sudden, complete with welfare payments that the American labor movement had won over many many years. That's why the Muñoz party was in power so long. It worked no miracles. It simply rode the crest of a wave that included the postwar boom and 150 years of labor's gains. Socialism made no sense then. But it does today.

In 1968, with inflation and unemployment high, Muñoz's party split and lost to the statehood party, which, in office, proved incompetent. In 1972, Muñoz's party regained power, but Puerto Rico's economy continued to slump badly, about a third of the working force was unemployed, prices skyrocketed, the Muñoz-Moscoso development program was called into question, and so was the whole Puerto Rico–U.S. relationship. Some maintain that industrialization has tied Puerto Rico as closely to the mainland economic cycle as New York or Chicago but has not given it the same advantages. Berrios sees his Independence party's opportunity in these problems. "Nine percent of the people receive 40 percent of the national income," he says. "Sixty-five percent of the arable land is out of cultivation. A whole new proletariat has risen—in government, service industries, and factories—young people born after 1940—and they have forgotten the old slogan about Muñoz." Berrios considers giant U.S. companies and the Pentagon the obstacles to Puerto Rico's proper development. Young leftist Puerto Ricans see Moscoso as the agent of American big business and imperialism. In the election of 1976, the statehood party won narrowly over Muñoz's party, and the Independence party ran a poor third. The election turned on economic issues, not on the status issue.

Muñoz was always aware of the hidden strength of the independence movement and believed that many people who favored commonwealth would, if forced to choose, choose independence. For that reason, he never said that commonwealth was a permanent solution; he always left the future in doubt. President Ford's curious declaration for Puerto Rican statehood shortly before he left office embarrassed the Puerto Rican statehood leaders, angered the commonwealth leaders, and may, in the long run, unless allowed to die, strengthen the independence leaders. A mischievous declaration, though probably not so intended, Ford's statement tended to polarize Puerto Rican opinion into statehood/independence and to cut the ground from under commonwealth.

Some Puerto Ricans wish Puerto Rico had its own foreign policy. Puerto Rico has applied for membership in the new Caribbean Development Bank—then changed its mind. In 1973, the foreign minister of Venezuela paid an official visit to Puerto Rico; a Puerto Rican delegation attended the inauguration of President Pérez. Foreign Minister Facio of Costa Rica and the Puerto Rican secretary of state, Víctor Pons, exchanged visits, recalling the days when Figueres and Muñoz led the democratic left Caribbean, and when Puerto Rico, with U.S. consent, worked out a trade agreement with Costa Rica. Under the commonwealth arrangement, the United States remains responsible for Puerto Rico's foreign relations.

Although a new leader of the caliber of Muñoz has yet to appear, the new generation of Puerto Rican leaders and politicians contains impressive men. Puerto Rico is blessed with able, educated middle-level executives and administrators in both business and government, and it is also more fortunate than other Caribbean areas in its political stability. Henry Wells, an authority on Puerto Rican political affairs, attributes Puerto Rico's stability to several factors—its security under the U.S. defense system, which has the added advantage of leaving Puerto Rico with no military of its own that might make or break governments; the safety valve of freedom of emigration to the United States, which gives the discontented an alternative to aggression; the small number of divisive issues in Puerto Rican politics; the tendency of voters to group themselves behind strong leaders in two solid political parties; and the cohesion (until 1968) of Muñoz's party. American tutelage and example also play a part. But it remains to be seen whether Puerto Rican democracy can withstand the severe strain of world recession, shortages of food and fuel and fertilizer, and the stagnation of Operation Bootstrap.

In 1973, President Nixon and Governor Hernández Colón once again established a joint committee to study Puerto Rico's status, especially the automatic application of U.S. laws to Puerto Rico and Puerto Rico's ill-defined representation in Washington. Puerto Rican affairs are handled by the Committees on Interior and Insular Affairs of the House and Senate. Although Puerto Rico cannot deal with the State Department officially, as do sovereign nations, its

tion plots, it may have missed a different issue, one far more dangerous to American democracy: the suggestion that the CIA has sometimes ordered its agents to establish a "cover" abroad by posing as
employees of large U.S. corporations. It is hard to imagine anything
more dangerous than a link between big business and a secret
intelligence agency that sometimes acts as a quasi-military force.

Although almost everyone agrees that the United States needs an
intelligence-gathering agency, some would argue that it ought not
conduct secret operations as well. But in the jungle of Caribbean
politics, both intelligence gathering and covert operations seem
necessary. There are, however, two questions to consider: where
should covert operations stop and who will oversee and control
them? The first question is the harder to answer. The Dominican
Republic was a shattered society after Trujillo's death, and it was a
society in which power lay within the grasp of almost anyone.
Moscow and Havana were secretly training and supplying money to
communist and other leftist extremist parties; therefore, it seemed
necessary for the CIA secretly to provide money to the democratic
parties. At that time, probably few Americans would have had
objections. A little later the CIA provided both money and arms to
Haitians bent on overthrowing Duvalier. The attempt failed, but if it
had succeeded, and if Duvalier had been killed in the process, would
Americans have condoned the CIA's role? Probably not, odious as
Duvalier's tyranny was. So a line must be drawn somewhere between
supplying money to democratic political parties and supplying guns
to would-be assassins. And such a line probably cannot be drawn by
statute or rigid rule, since circumstances vary so widely and since
contingencies are quite unforeseeable. At this point the second
question arises: who should control the CIA? Of late, numerous
proposals have been made, including more searching congressional
oversight, and they will probably be translated into laws and
regulations. But congressional oversight is awkward, it may raise
questions about the separation of powers, and it may cause security
leaks. An alternative—or supplement—is available: the ambassadors.
President Kennedy made it clear that each of his ambassadors was
responsible for everything the U.S. government did in his country.
An ambassador could, if he wished, give the CIA station chief
freedom to do whatever he wished so long as the ambassador was not
informed. But he could also tell the station chief to inform him in

advance about every important operation, and he could continuously review the cable traffic between the station chief and Washington CIA headquarters.[21] If the ambassador and station chief disagreed, they could appeal to the White House, and the White House would decide. This arrangement creates a firm line of responsibility reaching straight to—in major matters—the president. Though some feel that no such power should be handed to political cronies and campaign contributors who are appointed ambassador, it is still true that a president, knowing that his ambassador—and thus ultimately he himself—would be held responsible for the CIA's doings, might hesitate to appoint a crony or a campaign contributor. This would be a clear gain for the national interest.

Multinational Corporations

Throughout the Caribbean, especially in the dominant political left, the phrase *multinational corporations* has almost replaced *imperialism* as the leading pejorative. The multinationals are hated and feared as the instruments of exploitative Yankee imperialism. The ambassadors of Caribbean countries are likely to claim that their poor little countries are no match for these corporate giants, and no doubt it is often true. But surely the tough, sophisticated Venezuelan petroleum economists and the tough, sophisticated Jamaican bauxite economists are at least a match for the multinationals.

Since about 1950 the multinationals have grown rapidly because of the common markets, such as the EEC, which increased restrictions of imports from the United States, and because of the lower costs (in the 1960s) of production abroad as compared with costs in the United States. In the 1970s, however, the growth of U.S. investment abroad slowed as production costs abroad rose, international currency exchange rates were adjusted, and, in the Caribbean, poor nations became determined to regain control of their own natural resources and to industrialize for export themselves.[22]

Poor nations have long complained about the unfair practices of the multinationals. The latter can, for example, manipulate transfer prices between the parent company and its overseas subsidiaries in order to minimize the parent's tax liability; shift profits from jurisdictions with high tax rates to those with low tax rates; borrow where interest rates are low and put the money to work where rates are high. The poor countries complain that the multinationals charge their Caribbean affiliates exorbitant prices in order to shift profits back to the United States. (On the other hand, the U.S. Internal Revenue Service argues that the companies undercharge their affiliates.)

The U.S. government no longer views the national interest and a corporation's interest as identical. When in 1975, during the Ford administration, United Brands got in trouble in Honduras, the State Department made it clear that United Brands was on its own. Following the suicide of United Brands' chairman, the Securities and Exchange Commission discovered that United Brands had paid a bribe of $1.25 million to a high Honduran government official, possibly to General López, the chief of state, in order to get the tax on bananas halved. When the SEC stepped in, United Brands' lawyers asked the State Department to help it prevent the SEC from disclosing the bribe. Assistant Secretary Rogers of ARA refused. He told United Brands' lawyers that the behavior of multinational corporations had come under increasing scrutiny in Latin America; that the U.S. government agreed with the poor nations that multinational corporations must respect the laws of the nations where they operated, consistent with international law; and that they should refrain from improper interference in the internal affairs of other nations. Rogers declared that the U.S. government could not and would not countenance illegal corporate activities and went on to say that the behavior attributed to United Brands in Honduras would, if it had indeed occurred, clearly fall within the definition of impermissible activity—to be strongly condemned.

Because Rogers took this position, the "Bananagate" affair, as it quickly came to be called, had no adverse effect on U.S.-Honduran relations. It did, however, have other far-reaching effects: General López was overthrown, and demands for nationalization of the fruit companies and of natural resources increased; the affair reawakened memories of fruit company domination and cost the companies heavily. Moreover, it threatened to break the Honduran economy— if the fruit companies pulled out or were thrown out, the results would be catastrophic. Worst of all from the standpoint of U.S. government policy, Bananagate seemed to prove all the accusations of U.S. imperialism made by the extreme left in the Caribbean. And Bananagate was followed by revelations of other U.S. corporations' bribes to other foreign government officials, especially in the airplane, defense, and oil industries. Unfortunately, United Brands was not an exception or a rarity in corporate activity. The corporations tried to defend themselves by saying bribes, or exorbitant fees or commissions to foreign middlemen, were a normal part of the cost of doing business in various parts of the world; but bribery is bribery, corruption is corruption, and corporate executive stupidity is corporate executive stupidity.

As a result of the public outcry, several corporations began discussing a "code of ethics." The OECD even drew up a voluntary code, but many business leaders thought such codes little more than publicity stunts. Secretary Kissinger, who was both deploring "improper financial relationships" of multinationals yet saying they could be "powerful engines for good," said that although a multinational treaty establishing binding rules for multinational enterprises did not seem possible in the near future, the United States was prepared to explore an agreed statement of basic principles, and in fact, was discussing guidelines for one and would support "the relevant work of" the UN Commission on Transnational Corporations. He had already suggested his own guidelines. It was a weak approach.

Honduras and Guatemala

Honduras, the poorest, most backward, and perhaps the most attractive and picturesque country in Central America, has had a long history of warfare with its neighbors, violent internal politics, and domination by the U.S. fruit companies. For a good part of its political life, the Conservative party ruled, often in authoritarian fashion, in alliance with the army and the banana companies. The Liberal president, Villeda Morales, however, cooperated with the Alliance for Progress enthusiastically; he undertook measures to increase private investment, encourage democratic trade unions, build schools, roads, hospitals, and a hydroelectric system; and he established complete press and individual freedom. United Fruit and Standard Fruit opposed certain of his reforms, including agrarian reform and the labor code, and he did modify them somewhat; but the Kennedy administration diluted the companies' influence.

In the 1963 election, the Conservative party was split in two, which all but assured the election of Luis Modesto Rodas Alvarado, the candidate of Villeda Morales's Liberal party. Villeda had skillfully avoided both authoritarian measures and soft policies that might have alarmed the military, but his candidate, Rodas, unwisely campaigned for civilian control over the military. As the election, to be supervised by the OAS, approached, rumors spread that the army would perpetrate a coup to prevent the election of Rodas. The American ambassador sought to dissuade the armed forces chief, Colonel Oswaldo López Arellano, but López overthrew Villeda bloodily. Central Americans view the Villeda coup in Honduras much as they view the Arbenz coup in Guatemala—as the basic turning point where liberal, homegrown democracy was strangled in its crib. The coup came only a few days after the overthrow of President Bosch in the Dominican Republic. Senator Gruening of Alaska said, "If we don't do everything we can against military takeovers we might as well kiss the Alliance [for Progress] good-bye." The president of Costa Rica said, "If President Kennedy was able to stop the Russian ships carrying weapons to Cuba, I do not see why he cannot stop the colonels who have made themselves the masters of Latin American politics." López promised to hold elections, and we recognized his government. The promise of elections here, as in the Dominican Republic, was little more than a face-saving device for the administration after its policy of non-recognition had failed. Honduras held its election in 1965; the conservatives won. Adolf Berle, an official observer, wrote in his diary, "It was a beautiful exercise in how to steal an election."

The new government of Honduras was not, at least at the outset, repressive. Nor was it ideological. The political parties were by and large conservative, but the parties did not have real power. Power lay in the labor unions, in the peasant leagues, and, above all, in the military.

The velocity of history varies greatly in the Caribbean. Central America, especially Honduras, seemed in the 1970s to be still engrossed with issues of the 1930s and 1940s; the English-speaking black Caribbean islands were light years ahead of Central America.

The Honduras-Salvador "soccer war" of 1969-1970 was regarded elsewhere as something of a joke but not in Honduras, where it was viewed as only an acute symptom of a chronic ailment: Salvador is so overpopulated that its people tend to spill over the border into Honduras. The OAS quickly stifled the conflict, but it disrupted the Central American Common Market (CACM) and still has not been

The Nixon-Ford Years

221

resolved. U.S. diplomats in the area have pressed Washington for help with the conflict, but in the years of the Nixon-Ford low profile Washington has refused. ARA annually prepared a Country Action Strategy Paper for each Latin American nation; our diplomats in Central America have urged a regional paper as well. A Honduran businessman, asked how U.S. policy looked to Honduras, said, "There is no policy toward Honduras. You maintain a presence here only because if you don't, someone else will fill the vacuum."

In the last fifteen years or so, Central America has changed less than the rest of the Caribbean, and the United States still has considerable influence there. Guatemala is a permanent political problem, somewhat like the post-Trujillo Dominican Republic. Since the 1960s, Guatemala has been periodically wracked by widespread terror, including the murder of an American ambassador.

Guatemala had been sorely troubled ever since the Arbenz coup. President Ydígoras Fuentes, a crafty and redoubtable opportunist, foe of communism, and friend of John Foster Dulles, had ruled since 1958. It was a corrupt scandalous regime with rigged elections and widespread bribery and violence. Ydígoras, with an eye on the Pentagon and CIA and the Guatemalan armed forces, denounced all opponents as communists. Opposition to him mounted; so did violence. In 1963, as Ydígoras's term was coming to an end, Arévalo, the liberal leftist who had preceded Arbenz and whom many Guatemalans regarded as the only hope for peaceful revolution, announced from exile in Mexico that he would return to run for president. Ydígoras announced that he had proof that Arévalo was a Communist party member and therefore could not return to Guatemala. The Guatemalan supreme court disagreed. Arévalo denied he was a communist and said he would return before the end of the month. Disturbances mounted throughout the country, general rioting began, and, with the capital streets a battleground for riflemen and tanks, Ydígoras imposed a state of siege. The army regained control of the city.

Arévalo returned secretly, but news of his presence in Guatemala spread and the army rose, overthrew Ydígoras, and sent him off to Nicaragua. Arévalo returned to Mexico—and Ydígoras's minister of defense, Colonel Enrique Peralta Azurbia, took power.

Guatemalans, prepared ever since the Arbenz coup to believe that all Guatemalan political decisions are really made by the CIA, were sure that the CIA had engineered Peralta's coup. American correspondents reported that the coup had at least tacit U.S. support. Reaction to the coup in Washington was mixed, but the new Guatemalan military regime gave a vague promise to hold elections, and we recognized it. After that elections became rare and so rigged that they were essentially meaningless. Leftist violence was matched by rightist violence. No victims complained about the violation of human rights, since dissenters were killed, not jailed. Such parties as existed were rightist; even the Christian Democrats were rather conservative, for Guatemala since the Arévalo-Arbenz affair has been a conservative country. In the 1974 election, all three candidates came out of the military.

Some thoughtful Guatemalans feel they could have democracy if the United States supported it, but the United States has shown few signs of doing so. Officially, the press is free—there is no official government prior censorship—but in practice, the press censors itself, never criticizing the president.

The United States pays relatively little heed to Guatemala except in time of great disaster, such as the 1976 earthquake. But our attention may be drawn there by a new issue: Belize. Belize, also called British Honduras, a small territory on the Caribbean northeast of Guatemala, is a self-governing British dependency claimed by Guatemala. If it becomes independent and the British garrison leaves, Guatemala may try to seize it. Some years ago Guatemala asked the United States to mediate its claim to Belize, but that effort came to nothing. And now Guatemalans accuse Mexico of sending settlers into Belize, preparing to take it if the British leave, and some Guatemalans even suggest that war could erupt between Guatemala and Mexico.

Costa Rica, Vesco, and Democracy

In recent years, the reputation of that shining hope of the 1960s, Costa Rica, has become tarnished. By 1970, Pepe Figueres had retired from government to operate his *finca* and family enterprises, but his enterprises were not prospering. Figueres, seeking power, ran for president again and won. In 1972, Figueres and his friend, Foreign Minister Gonzalo Facio, allowed the American fugitive financier, Robert L. Vesco, to enter Costa Rica. Figueres received some $2.5 million from a Vesco associate to resuscitate his private ranching and industrial enterprises. Vesco began investing in key segments of Costa Rican society and the press and political parties; Figueres sponsored a revision of the extradition law. When the United States tried to extradite Vesco, the extradition failed. Many Costa Ricans are convinced that the Nixon administration really wanted to protect Vesco and therefore deliberately drew a faulty extradition application. In 1974, Figueres, unable to succeed himself, supported Daniel Oduber for president. Oduber won, but with less than a majority of the votes. At the time of his inauguration, Oduber declared that Vesco could stay in Costa Rica. After a while, his government became increasingly unpopular, and Costa Rica's economy was running downhill along with those of the rest of the world. Figueres began to appear in public wearing a Mao jacket, muttering about a coup d'etat or a constitutional amendment to permit him to run yet again for president. He said that democracy had not worked in either Costa Rica or the United States, that the government was ineffective, that what Costa Rica needed was a dictator and a system patterned on that of Rumania. Perhaps we misjudged him in the 1960s. His early allies were not what one would normally expect of a social democratic leader. They were the middle class, the upper-middle class, and the small landowners who feared communism; they were not the university people, labor, the lower-middle class. Figueres had always said he was a businessman first and a politician second. The labor unions were weak when Figueres came to power and they are still weak. Costa Rica has long been conservative and racist. Traditionally, the Costa Rican press and television have been free, but today they are threatened by Vesco and the government, which blames the press for criticizing Vesco and thus damaging Costa Rica's reputation and reducing its tourist trade. The government has said that our Securities and Exchange Commission (which uncovered United Brands' bribery in Honduras and has interested itself in Vesco) is nothing but another CIA, an agency used to overthrow governments. Figueres's apologists say that Vesco's money is as good as anyone else's and that he is investing it in Costa Rican development. (His critics wonder if one should welcome investment from any source whatsoever.)

In the late 1950s, Costa Rica had adopted Figueres's policy of giving retired Americans living on pensions inducements, such as certain tax and duty exemptions, to settle permanently in Costa

Rica, where it was hoped they would spend their money as well as their retirement years. Between 2,000 and 2,500 *pensionados* have done so. At first the system was widely applauded; more recently it has been criticized. Some *pensionados* illegally work in Costa Rica, some sell the automobiles they brought in duty-free at big profits. Some buy beach property (now forbidden) and cattle lands, thus driving real estate prices up, and in a country as small as Costa Rica, so many Americans seem overwhelming. Anti-Americanism is increased by the controversies surrounding Vesco, the big banana landholdings of United Brands, and the bauxite exploration of Alcoa. A Costa Rican editor has said, "I have never read so many anti-American editorials as in the last five years." It is all rather sad.

Somoza's Nicaragua

In the nineteenth century in Nicaragua, the Liberal party stronghold was at León and the Conservative party stronghold at Granada. Following the U.S. military occupation, Nicaragua moved straight from that ancient city-state system to the Somoza system. Somoza's party is called the Liberal party. The Conservative party has degenerated into a catch-all of anti-Somoza movements including Marxists, Social Christians, and everything else.

Somoza, who succeeded his father and brother as president of Nicaragua, is a big, intelligent, articulate man. A graduate of West Point, he speaks good English and married an American. He has sent one of his sons to Harvard and one to West Point. In foreign policy, he adheres to one straightforward principle: the closer to the United States, the better. He views with disfavor or suspicion the rise of Venezuela and Mexico in the Caribbean. He has little use for the Third World, although he sometimes reflects sadly that the United States treats nations that blackmail it better than it treats its true friends. He applauded the Alliance for Progress because it created a "community feeling of closer relations with the U.S." Asked if the Caribbean still looks to Washington for leadership, he quoted Trudeau: "'If you live next to an elephant and sleep with him, you have to watch out when he rolls over.'" Asked how he would identify America's interests in the Caribbean if he were our secretary of state, he replied:

To have friendly nations in the Caribbean. By hook or crook. And friendly people. Help the poor people. Pour money in.

Encourage diversity. Don't try to make them all like the U.S. This is all central because you have no southern DEW (a distant early warning system to warn of missile attack). A hostile Cuba was only an incident. But four or five or six hostile Caribbean countries could be serious.

Somoza maintains that he stays in power by having the best-organized political machine in Latin America and compares it with that of Mayor Richard J. Daley in Chicago. He points out that he has 20,000 government jobs to use for political patronage, a lot in a small country, and declares his party is strong in every one of the country's 1,500 precincts. He has reached an understanding with the Conservative party that gives it a voice in the legislature (though not in the executive branch); he wants to maintain the two-party system and to prevent the rise of a hypothetical third party. The United States, he says, has encouraged parties to proliferate elsewhere in the Caribbean and the result has been, first, "cannibalism and chaos," and then, of necessity, repressive military government. He also maintains himself in power, he says, by anticipating change and staying one step ahead of its advocates. In recent years, he has launched an agrarian reform program and increased the income tax. He imposed a 10 percent export tax that he estimates cost him personally $4 million. He has launched a rural electrification program and knows its smallest details. He considers that American-style two-party democracy cannot succeed in the Caribbean: "The problem is that the price paid by the defeated party is too great. They get killed." He maintains that he has no population controls or checkpoints as his father had. "In the past they used rather primitive methods. Now we have other methods of surveilling those who plot to overthrow us." He is aware of his reputation abroad: "Some in the States denounce us as dictators. We mind our own affairs. We don't denounce you for killing all the niggers who are going communist." He also says, "If you haven't got the guts to kill people when it has to be done, it won't work."

Liberals throughout the hemisphere consider Somoza the epitome of Caribbean military dictatorship, and they denounce the United States for, as they see it, supporting him. But opinion is not unanimous on this. A State Department specialist has said, "Somoza is the most misunderstood man in Latin America. He's not a vicious military dictator in the classic sense. He's much more of a political boss—he'd be like Daley if Daley had 40 percent of all the money in Chicago plus his political machine." A U.S. ambassador close to Somoza maintains that "nothing bad would happen to" a Nicaraguan who opposed Somoza, although nothing good would happen to him either. He denies that Somoza has infringed human rights and adds, "The liberals want me to spit in Somoza's face. Why should I do that?" Another U.S. diplomat maintains that Somoza shows a certain respect for individual freedom although he is always ready to suspend freedom when he thinks it necessary. He did so in 1975. After a raid by a band of terrorists calling themselves Sandinistas in honor of the Nicaraguan guerillas of the 1920s who fought the U.S. occupation, Somoza launched a nationwide manhunt and suspended press and other freedoms. In ordinary times, Somoza cares little what the newspapers print because few people read them anyway; he maintains tight censorship on radio because nearly everyone has a transistor radio. A well-informed diplomat considers Somoza and his government somewhere near the center of the spectrum of Latin American governments: not so authoritarian as some, not so liberal as others, and certainly less repressive that the first Somoza's government. He says the Nicaraguan opposition objects not to repression but to forty years of one-family rule. The Somoza family has amassed an enormous fortune. It includes controlling interest in nearly every sector of the Nicaraguan economy and an outright monopoly in some.

Even the most visible leader of the opposition to Somoza concedes that Nicaragua's present chief of state differs considerably from both Trujillo and the original Somoza, who were products of the U.S. military occupations and came to power through the military. The present Somoza, he says, sometimes permits freedom of the press for long periods of time, as Trujillo never did; he buys off and corrupts dissenters, whereas Trujillo had them killed; and he wields his power coolly and in a reasoned way usually designed to increase his fortune, whereas Trujillo's tyranny sometimes seemed capricious and half-mad. This opposition leader also accepts the comparison of Somoza with Daley, although he reports that Somoza uses spies, informers, wiretaps, and other totalitarian methods. The most impressive proof that Somoza is something other than a bloodthirsty tyrant is that this opposition leader, who was caught participating in at least two attempts to overthrow the regime, is still alive. Of course, he is useful to Somoza, who can point to him as living proof of Nicaraguan political freedom, as a sort of tame revolutionary.

A previous U.S. ambassador sought to persuade Somoza to retire, ascend as a statesman, and receive the world's applause. He refused—"They wouldn't believe I'd really let go. And they'd be right." He seems to be training his sons to succeed him.

Democracy

Nearly sixty years ago, Americans heeded Woodrow Wilson's call to "make the world safe for democracy," imagining that they would carry free government everywhere.[23] But the latest count shows only twenty-nine representative democracies in the whole world. We are a dwindling band. Increasingly, under the pressures of racial conflict, poverty and downright hunger, economic hardship and uncertainty, political instability and breakdown, the world's masses seem to be turning to authoritarianism, usually home-grown. The collapse of democracy in India—now apparently reversed—and the anti-Zionist resolution at the UN are only symptoms of a trend. The belief that poor nations would turn to democracy as they developed has turned out to be an illusion. Establishing elections, constitutions, and parliaments guarantees nothing. Neither does economic development. Neither does foreign aid. It behooves what few democracies remain to collaborate more closely than ever before.

Democracy, we believe, goes hand in hand with political liberty, individual freedom, free speech and free press, and respect for human rights. But Gunnar Myrdal has concluded that never in history has a severely underdeveloped country established a lasting and effective political democracy. In the rich Western countries, people fought for democracy for many decades; in the poor countries, democracy was handed down from above, and the masses were hardly involved at all. Myrdal believes that democracy is not essential to development. Leaders of poor states are far more likely to talk about their peoples' nobility than about their political immaturity. When they criticize orthodox democracy, they tend to fall back on some romantic concept of "village democracy," as Sukarno did and as Torrijos of Panama appears to be doing. Some devise various systems of "guided" democracy with limited suffrage.

How does democracy fare in the Caribbean today?

In the English-speaking Caribbean, Jamaicans, who assert that they have a deep working commitment to democracy and will not give it up, cannot understand why we sometimes seem more friendly to undemocratic states than to them. They feel their democracy is secure because of its long tradition; their relative wealth, which enables them to afford democracy; and their educated and sophisticated leadership. Manley's opponents, however, profess fear that he is taking Jamaica down a leftist, statist road, and indeed democracy is difficult to sustain with a bankrupt treasury and large numbers of unemployed young people. Barbados has a working two-party system. Guyana, on the other hand, seems to be turning to one-party rule, and Trinidad-Tobago may be heading in the same direction, though more slowly.

In the Spanish-speaking Caribbean, Venezuela is a functioning democracy with full press freedom and no repression; it is, however, moving left toward economic statism. Puerto Rico has a working two-party system and full freedom. The Dominican Republic has no effective two-party system, the press is free but to some extent censors itself, and political repression is probably somewhat less severe than formerly. Haiti is still governed by a dictatorship, but the lunacy of Duvalier I is gone. Cuba, of course, is a totalitarian state: in a certain limited sense, Castro is the last Trujillo. In Central America, democracy scarcely exists except in Costa Rica, and of late it has seemed a bit shaky even there.

To the man at the bottom, does it make any difference whether he lives under a democratic or an authoritarian regime? At first glance, one would think that he merely wants change, and it matters little how change is brought about. And certainly to the man who is still living on the land, it matters not at all—government is remote and hardly effective. But it makes a big difference to the man who is moving to the city—and millions are—for in the city he will feel the weight of government and politics.

Does it make any difference to the United States whether democracy flourishes or fails in the Caribbean? Again, on the face of it, it is none of our business how those countries choose to organize their governments and their societies. We cannot, in any case, determine their political affairs, and we ought not try, though we might hope those governments will not kill too many of their own people. On the other hand, if one returns to the point made earlier— that the few remaining democracies should forge closer links for survival—then perhaps it does behoove us to encourage democracy on our Caribbean doorstep. U.S. power is limited; and it is probably even in decline. We learned that we could not save or, rather, construct democracy in Vietnam. We know now we simply lack the power to do everything everywhere. But this does not mean that we cannot or ought not exert political influence in areas where our interests are clear and our traditional influence considerable. The Caribbean is such a place. Although we now have far less influence there than in the past, our interests are no less important. We take our commitment to individual liberty, political freedom, and human rights seriously. The power of a great nation rests not only on its arms but on its prestige, and nations acquire prestige in many ways, including by remaining true to their own professed ideals. We will earn little respect in the Caribbean by shutting our eyes to repression. It may well be that we cannot and even should not impose our brand of democracy on reluctant or indifferent people. A truly popular government can take forms quite different from ours. We should make it absolutely clear by our words, but even more by our diplomatic deeds, that we prefer popular government to totalitarianism, that we prefer freedom to repression, and that we cherish human rights. A political program without economic content means little; so does an economic program without a beating political heart.

The Mini-States

In the eastern end (and in the south-central area) of the Caribbean lie small islands that, until recently, were colonies. All but those owned by the French are or soon will be independent states. (Martinique, Guadeloupe, and French Guiana are overseas departments of France.) Some have been troubled by political or racial riots or both; others will be. In 1953, the UN approved the status of Puerto Rico as a U.S. associated state; in 1954, the Netherlands established two Dutch associated states; and beginning in 1966, the United Kingdom established what are today five British associated states. It is beyond the scope of this book to treat these mini-states in detail. But mention should be made of them.

Since the 1950s, when we supported the British-imposed Caribbean Federation, the United States has favored federation of these territories. But Jamaica pulled out of the federation, thereby wrecking it, and, along with the other larger territories of Trinidad-Tobago, Guyana, Barbados, and the Bahamas, went the route of independence. A similar process is now at work among the smaller islands. We still favor federation. And some of the leaders of the Caribbean mini-states agree that they are too small and too poor to make it alone. Many of them have no natural resources except a climate and geographical location suitable for tourism. At various times, individual small islands have tried to organize federations, usually unsuccessfully. Federation would appear essential for such a place as Monserrat, which, with only 12,000 people and only thirty-two square miles, is no market at all and therefore offers no internal opportunity for development. Most of these small islands have joined the Caribbean Common Market (CARICOM).

Grenada, although a member of CARICOM, has turned away from federation and gone the route of full independence, despite its stormy recent history. This insistence on independence has created problems at the OAS and the UN, some of whose members wonder whether a country with only 133 square miles of territory and only 95,000 people should have the same single vote that, say, vast China has in the UN and Brazil has in the OAS. Grenada alone makes little difference, of course, but if all these countries choose independence, each will have its own vote. The Commonwealth of the Bahamas also has chosen to go it alone and, since it gained independence in 1973, has even remained outside CARICOM. Heeding the old adage, "If life gives you nothing but lemons, make lemonade," the Bahamas, blessed with no resources except climate and location, has sought to build its economy through tourism, banking—a banking system not unlike the Swiss secret numbered accounts that have made Switzerland an international banking center—and gambling. The Bahamas has attracted gamblers' money from Las Vegas and the U.S. Mafia, fugitives from justice with large bank accounts, U.S. banks that want to escape Federal Reserve scrutiny, real estate speculators, "hot" money of all sorts, narcotics dealers, and such celebrities as Robert Vesco and Howard Hughes. It is hard for any government, even that of the United States, to control its citizens overseas; it is hard for small, poor countries to resist their blandishments. The Bahamas has tried to deport or keep out American gangsters and now maintains that its gambling operation is, in the words of its ambassador to Washington, "as clean as such a thing can be, as Las Vegas is." The Bahamas government has also tried to diversify into light industry, salt mines, and agriculture. But it still imports 80 percent of what its people consume, and 50 percent of its GNP and 75 percent of its foreign exchange still come from tourism (1,400,000 tourists in 1974). Thus, it remains extremely vulnerable to U.S. economic recession and to heightened racial tensions among its people. Its prosperity is artificial and fragile, for a government cannot base sound and self-sustaining economic growth, or even self-respect, on tax havens, free ports, flags of convenience, numbered bank accounts, gambling, unregulated towns, and sales of the land itself to unscrupulous foreign investors.

The British and the Dutch want to leave the Caribbean (Dutch Guiana became independent Surinam in 1976). They have hoped that we would retain our interest in their former dependencies and give them aid. Canada, too, maintains an interest and lends its assistance. We are by no means alone in the Caribbean. But the European metropolitan powers recognize that our interests in the Caribbean transcend theirs. And they have hoped that we would, in large part, pick up the burden they lay down. But we have shown little enthusiasm and have pursued no clearcut policy at all beyond vague support, largely verbal, for the concept of federation. The United States is not a member of the Caribbean Development Bank, although we have made a few relatively small, soft loans to it. At one time, ARA hoped to couple the Bank with a parallel organization to give technical assistance to these small countries; nothing came of the idea. Our embassy at Barbados has only a half dozen officers to cover the entire vast area of the eastern Caribbean (minus Trinidad-Tobago and Guyana). Our indifference, coupled with the withdrawal of the European powers, may spawn a vast slum in our backyard. By 1980, a dozen or more mini-states may have achieved a dubious independence. If we spend no money and exert no influence there after the British and Dutch depart, someone or something else will move in to fill the vacuum. Assistant Secretary Rogers has said:

I suppose in the past we have ignored them because they were so small and because of the British and Dutch there. But their problems are serious and hard to solve. They are uneconomic—there will be lots of poverty. And lots of self-appointed dictators. Should we say: OK, let it happen, let them ruin themselves? Or should we do something? If we decide to ignore them, we should take that decision consciously.

We could probably devise an AID program that would offer the mini-states financial incentives to federate. Or we could offer AID programs designed to encourage them to become individually independent. We could even offer them associate statehood along Puerto Rican lines; they would simply transfer their "association" from the UK or the Netherlands to us. This arrangement would solve the problem of votes in the OAS and UN. We might try to persuade the OAS to establish a trusteeship over them for the time being. Not one of these proposals is easy to carry out. And the mini-states would probably resist any of them, especially if they came from us. The earlier Federation of the West Indies failed in part because Caribbean leaders felt that it was nothing more than a British ruse to escape responsibility. All Third World political pressures push them toward full individual independence, but they are painfully conscious of the economic pressures that push them toward federation.

Despite Third World rhetoric regarding the imperialistic tendencies of the United States, these small Caribbean islands with their manifold problems have little that recommends them as objects of policy interest—other than the fact that their problems will eventually be ours anyway. If we are to be in on the crash landing, we may do well to be in on the takeoff as well.

What is needed is a decision at the White House that a slum in the Caribbean is more important to us than a slum in Bangladesh. But strong White House leadership in dealing with the Caribbean has not been forthcoming in recent years. When in 1974 the White House announced that President Ford would meet with the president of France at Martinique, ARA proposed that he stop at Trinidad-Tobago and meet for a few hours with black Caribbean leaders; he did not do so, and it is doubtful that the proposal ever actually reached Ford.

Some Social Issues

Terrorism. The rural guerrilla movements of the 1960s failed because the conditions for a successful violent revolution on a national scale did not exist, despite Ché Guevara's conviction that they did; because central governments, some with American advice and aid, firmly, and sometimes violently, suppressed them; and because Cuba, the Soviet Union, and China all decided to stop supporting guerrilla warfare in the Caribbean at about the same time the Nixon administration decided to lower our own profile. In the 1970s, guerrilla movements came to the cities to engage in terrorism, kidnapping, and robbery. Some of their actions were political; some were simply criminal involving, in a number of cases, narcotics. So widespread did the urban guerrilla movements become that the OAS held a special meeting in 1971 to draft an international convention on terrorism and kidnapping. (Little came of it.) Spectacular as the urban crimes have been, they seem less likely to spark revolution than the deeds of earlier guerrillas on the hills; the proletariat of Caribbean cities is not inherently revolutionary, and the police can lay hands on outlaws more easily in the cities than in the hills. History appears to afford no case where urban insurgency without rural support succeeded in making a revolution. The best United States response, if any at all is proper, would appear to be cooperation with international police agencies in combating organized crime.

Education. In the Caribbean, everything, in the long run, depends on education. The United States has tried to help improve education, especially in primary and secondary schools; we should continue to do so and should expand our role in vocational education. We have found it hard to do much at Caribbean universities; the best thing we can do there is to expand exchange programs between American and Caribbean universities, perhaps with private foundation help.

In recent years, universities in the Caribbean, like those in the United States, have been mushrooming. Even the student body of the University of Nicaragua has increased by 16 percent every year for the last ten. One result is that the intellectual class is expanding more rapidly than the job market. This phenomenon is, according to many theorists, a symptom of revolution to come. When students receive academic degrees and then are unable to find jobs, they become alienated as well as idle, they become convinced the social and government systems are wrong, and they are easy prey for demagogues. Virtually every country in the Caribbean has trained far too many lawyers and philosophers. Some students, realizing they will find no jobs, delay graduation; bored, they become on-campus political agitators, deflecting the universities from their purpose as institutions of learning. Caribbean students have always been in the vanguard of demonstrations and agitation. And given the Latin American traditions of university autonomy and student control, governments can do little to restrain students' political activities. All this has happened at a time when U.S. campuses seemed to be quieting down.

Urbanization. Probably the most visible and most alarming phenomenon in the Caribbean in recent years is the explosion of the urban slums. Millions of people have left the land and gone to the city; there they are producing little but more millions of people. It has been estimated that the population of the cities in the region doubles every ten years. Slums are engulfing whole metropolitan areas. The living conditions in these slums are simply unbelievable—no sanitation, no water or lights, no privacy, no pavements, no jobs, shacks and hovels, little to eat. This "urbanization of poverty," as one student has called it, may well have explosive force in the future. Poverty in a strange city can be far more cruel than poverty on the land of one's own fathers; it can make men desperate. In the long run, it may radicalize the urban proletariat. In the past, development efforts have been aimed not at slicing up the economic pie differently but at baking a bigger pie so all will have more—no man would get less money, but many would get more. In the future, governments may be forced to divide up the existing pie differently, even at the cost of development.

Agriculture. With the best climate and some of the richest soil on earth, the Caribbean islands are, nevertheless, big food importers. They even import fish. Jamaica, although blessed with rich farmlands, imports such staples as meat, corn, and wheat. Venezuela, a huge country with much good farmland, wastes much of the foreign exchange earned by its oil on food imports. Throughout the Caribbean, agriculture is vital to the economy. In Honduras, some 67 percent of the labor force works in agriculture, some 57 percent in Guatemala, some 20 percent even in urbanized Venezuela—compared to 5 percent in the United States. Food exports, such as bananas and sugar and coffee, earn more than half the foreign exchange many Caribbean countries receive. If governments such as that of Venezuela shifted their emphasis from industrialization to agricultural development, they could simultaneously improve the nutrition of their people, save foreign exchange, enlarge opportunities for young people trained as agricultural technicians, reduce rural unemployment and misery, and perhaps even arrest the awful stream of people to the cities. But in recent years, agricultural production has increased barely enough to keep pace with the population increase.

A laudable trend toward increasing the use of fertilizer was slowed in 1973 by an increase in world fertilizer prices. The Caribbean nations have made little use of the "green revolution"—new varieties of wheat, corn, and rice that have tripled and quadrupled crop yields per acre elsewhere. It is not enough to give a farmer a piece of land or to perform research on crop yields. It is necessary to bring new knowledge and techniques to the individual farmer. Doing so requires agricultural specialists, and they, in turn, require secondary agricultural schools.

As for agrarian reform, unfortunately, our experience under the Alliance for Progress shows that reform to make land tenure systems equitable almost inevitably results in at least a temporary drop in production. At present, most Caribbean countries urgently need to increase production; they should train specialists, teach farmers, improve techniques, and only later, when conditions are right, move on to agrarian reform aimed at bringing about social justice.

In the agricultural sector, if in no other, the United States may have a role to play in the Caribbean. Our own agriculture is the most advanced and productive on earth. If we can teach others anything, we can teach them to grow food. The United States can offer agricultural development assistance to the Caribbean at little cost to ourselves, in a sector where Caribbean governments badly need help and would welcome it. In a time of growing world food shortages, help can come none too soon.

Immigration. One of the most troublesome of all issues between the United States and the Caribbean countries is immigration. People in the Caribbean tend to see the United States as the land of opportunity, and they resent it when we keep them out. People in the United States tend to see immigrants from the Caribbean as cheap laborers and undesirable aliens—and black aliens at that. Immigration is a social, political, and economic issue. To the people and governments of the Caribbean, emigration offers both a safety valve to relieve the pressures of overcrowding and unemployment, and access to political freedom, dignity, and economic opportunity. Nothing damages the reputation of the United States more than the sight of long lines of people besieging the U.S. consulates in such places as Santo Domingo and Kingston, begging and cajoling, trying to get visas. After the fall of Trujillo, our consulate was torn up almost daily by visa riots; we moved it out to the edge of town, brought in extra staff, and established security guards only after the ambassador brought the problem to the attention of Secretary Rusk himself.

In 1972, more than 64,000 of a total of 385,000 legal immigrants to the United States came from the Caribbean islands (not counting Puerto Rico). About a million and a half Puerto Ricans live on the mainland (and only three million in Puerto Rico itself). They are concentrated in New York, New Jersey, Florida, Connecticut, and Chicago. Paterson, New Jersey, is almost half Spanish-speaking, and the Bronx is one-third Puerto Rican. About 100,000 Dominicans live in New York. About 10 percent of Trinidad-Tobago's population has migrated to the United States. About half of Trinidad-Tobago's nurses have gone to the United States and Canada. Out of two million Jamaicans, 500,000 live in the United States—400,000 in New York City alone. Jamaican officials complain of the Jamaican brain drain. New York has so many Latinos that its ballots and some of its street signs are printed in Spanish as well as English. It has been estimated that the United States contains between two and five million people who entered from the Caribbean illegally. These people come to the United States for many reasons, but the one that overshadows all is jobs.

Probably the worst thing we could do would be to shut the door. In the long run, the real solution lies in developing the Caribbean economies to a point where unemployment, and hence the impetus to migrate, is reduced; in developing Caribbean education so that the skills of Caribbean immigrants will be more acceptable in the United States than they are now; and in reducing the Caribbean birthrate. But we cannot count on the long run—in the short run, we should liberalize our immigration laws and regulations. No doubt, it is politically impossible to remove all restrictions on immigration into the United States, especially with nearly 8 percent of our own labor force unemployed. The recent recession brought complaints from American labor unions about illegal immigrants—and raids by the Immigration Service to catch them. (These events illustrate the inescapable link between foreign policy and domestic politics.) And even if unrestricted immigration were politically possible, it probably would not be in the best interests of Caribbean countries, for it would almost surely convert the brain drain into a hemorrhage.

The thoughtful governor-general of Trinidad-Tobago, Sir Ellis

Clarke, wonders whether it would not be cheaper and better for the United States to liberalize immigration than to inject large amounts of capital into the Trinidad-Tobago economy in an effort to produce development and reduce unemployment. He thinks that the West Indian black starts out ahead of the American black and is easily assimilated in U.S. society. An infusion of West Indian blacks, he suggests, might leaven and improve the American social climate. The cost of such a program would be minimal to the United States, he argues, but a tremendous relief to the Caribbean states. Black unemployed West Indians in the Caribbean, instead of trumpeting Black Power slogans against the United States, might go to the United States, find work, and come home to show how well they had done there. He emphasizes that in this area, the United States has an opportunity to formulate an exclusively Caribbean policy.

Two International Issues

Law of the Sea. In 1945, President Truman unilaterally proclaimed that the United States owned the mineral resources—he was thinking primarily of offshore oil—of its continental shelf. He was careful to reaffirm that, in our view, existing international law set a three-mile limit to our sovereignty over the territory of the sea off our coast, and that we did not intend to impede freedom of navigation on the high seas above the continental shelf outside the three-mile limit. Nonetheless, Peru and Chile, later joined by Ecuador, took umbrage and claimed sovereignty and national jurisdiction over the sea to a distance of 200 nautical miles offshore. Subsequently, El Salvador, Nicaragua, Argentina, Panama, Uruguay, and Brazil made the same claim. It was another early hint of growing Latin American nationalism. Because the United States, confronted with this claim, requested international consideration, the First UN Law of the Sea Conference was held in Geneva in February-April 1958. It broke down on the one crucial issue: over how much territory off its coasts was a state entitled to exercise sovereign jurisdiction? The conference split into two camps—the traditional maritime powers, headed by the United States and Great Britain, who upheld the traditional narrow three-mile limit; and a cluster of new nations, later called the Third World, supported by the Soviet Union, who demanded sovereignty over a 200-mile territory. The United States reluctantly accepted a compromise extending the three-mile limit to six with a further six-mile zone in which the coastal state would have exclusive fishing rights. But when that proposal failed to achieve the needed two-thirds majority, the United States announced it would return to its historic three-mile limit.

The Second UN Conference on the Law of the Sea, held in Geneva in 1960, devoted itself entirely to issues of the breadth of the territorial sea and national fishing zones. The same rich-poor voting pattern developed; the United States offered the same compromise— a six-mile territorial sea and a further six-mile exclusive fishing zone—but the conference could not resolve the issue. (We would go no farther territorially mainly because the Defense Department felt that to do so would hamper our navy's operations near neutral states and would offer too many hiding places for the Soviet Union's submarines.)

When the Third UN Conference met at Caracas fourteen years later, the whole issue had become infinitely more complex.

While Ecuador worried about big new U.S. and Japanese tuna boats off its coast, fishermen in New England and the Pacific Northwest worried about greatly expanded Soviet and Japanese fishing fleets. President Johnson signed a bill in 1966 extending the exclusive U.S. fishing zone from three to twelve miles. The United States engaged in fishing disputes with Brazil, Peru, Ecuador, and others; and Iceland and Great Britain nearly came to hostilities. But what really transformed the whole question was a speech at the UN General Assembly in 1967 by Arvid Pardo, the ambassador of Malta. Pardo called attention to the mammoth, unexplored natural resources that lay on the seabed of the world's oceans beyond the limits of national jurisdiction, he discussed the issues connected with mining those riches, and he called for an international agency to govern their exploitation to ensure that they were shared by all nations and put to the service of all mankind. The assembly established a permanent Seabed Committee and requested nations and private corporations to refrain from all activities on the seabed pending the outcome of the committee's work.

The lines were shifting; the United States and the Soviet Union were moving toward each other. President Johnson's unilateral twelve-mile fishing zone brought us closer to the Soviet Union, which had already claimed a twelve-mile limit. In April 1970, the United States and the Soviet Union launched a joint attack on the

200-mile proposal: we submitted a draft treaty to ban nuclear weapons from the seabed within twelve miles of shore to the UN Disarmament Conference. The 200-milers, all Latin Americans, promptly adopted a Declaration of Principles including the right to explore and exploit the natural resources of the sea and seabed off their coasts up to 200 miles. Other Third World nations joined them.

The United States was adjusting its policy. President Nixon said that we were prepared to agree to a twelve-mile territorial limit if freedom of transit through and over international straits was guaranteed. Such a guarantee is critical in the Caribbean; many of its islands are so close together that an extended limit would create overlap and conflict among islands. The United States had now moved from a three-mile territorial limit to a six-mile limit to a twelve-mile limit; but it was still a long way from the Third World's 200-mile demand. The confrontation between the Third World and the American-Soviet bloc came at the 1970 UN General Assembly on a procedural question. The poor nations won, and a Latin American diplomat exclaimed, "We've now got Africa and Asia behind us, it's no longer the 'extreme' Latin American [200-mile] position. It's the developing countries against the big powers."

On June 2, 1971, the U.S. State Department said that the Brazilian 200-mile territorial limit was not in accord with international law and told U.S. fishing boats not to buy Brazilian licenses but to continue fishing; and a few days later, the U.S. House of Representatives held up the international coffee agreement, vital to Brazil. Brazil promptly denounced this as "intolerable economic pressure on a matter concerning the sovereignty of the Brazilian state," and its foreign minister toured Central America, where he discussed coffee. He also toured the Caribbean, including Guyana, where he discussed a trans-Amazonian highway linking Georgetown with Brazil—inferentially supporting Guyana against Venezuela's territorial claims. Thus does the Law of the Sea become entangled with nearly every other imaginable issue. Senator Muskie (D.-Maine) sponsored a bill claiming U.S. jurisdiction over lobsters on our continental shelf, and Maine lobster fishermen rejoiced. The Bahamas retaliated with a law claiming jurisdiction over lobsters on *its* continental shelf, and Florida lobstermen cried out in anguish—what Maine lobstermen won, Florida lobstermen lost, $6 million a year. Such controversies stir up great turmoil in Congress.

In 1971, Venezuela invited the nations bordering the Caribbean to a conference in Caracas to discuss the forthcoming UN Conference on the Law of the Sea. It was the first time that an attempt was made to formulate a common "Caribbean position" on this or anything else. Subsequently, the Caribbean nations signed a new compromise: they supported a sovereign territorial limit of twelve miles but "patrimonial waters" of up to 200 miles. In "patrimonial waters," coastal states would have full sovereignty over natural resources in the sea and on the seabed, but they would have no jurisdiction over navigational rights beyond the twelve-mile limit.

By this time, the discussion was turning more and more toward mineral riches beyond territorial limits. Some proposed that these riches be exploited by some international agency (the United States wanted private exploitation) and the proceeds turned over to the United Nations for use in developing poor nations—it would be a pool of money much greater than could ever be obtained from any other source and one unencumbered by politics. But others objected that the UN was incapable of such an undertaking and, furthermore, that neither the United States nor any other nation was prepared to "give away" what is regarded as "its" patrimony, including strategic materials, particularly at a time when raw materials shortages loomed. From here the discussion moved to "the abyssal ocean floor," truly deep water beyond the continental shelf. "Abyssal" ocean floor development, a technology that was only now emerging, appeared more likely to involve harvesting manganese nodules than producing petroleum. Such undertakings were huge; probably no more than a dozen expeditions would be undertaken, and each would cost hundreds of millions of dollars. Cost and technical difficulties aside, political questions arose: Poor nations that depend heavily on producing manganese, copper, cobalt, and nickel from their soil would surely try to limit production from the seabed in order to prop up the prices of their land-produced commodities; but the interests of the rich consumer nations were diametrically opposed. Thus, Third World countries without mineral resources would probably heartily favor getting all the money possible for the UN out of the deep sea minerals, Third World countries with mineral resources would oppose, and the consumer countries would oppose both.

The stakes were high: rights of passage on and above the high seas and through some 100 threatened straits, an estimated 1,500 billion barrels of oil under the sea floor, an endangered fish stock that yields about $18 billion worth of high-protein food annually, an estimated $3 trillion worth of manganese and other minerals, the right of free scientific research in the oceans, and the right to control pollution that threatens to destroy all life. The 70 percent of the earth's surface that is covered by water may prove to be far richer than the 30 percent that is dry land.

At long last—June 20, 1974—the Third UN Conference convened at—where else?—Caracas. More than 5,000 delegates and observers from 148 nations attended; it was the biggest international conference in history and lasted more than two months. They worked under fatal handicaps. The agenda was unmanageable; such diverse matters as military navigation, commercial navigation, pollution, fisheries, petroleum, manganese, and much more cannot be handled at a single conference. And 5,000 delegates are equally unmanageable. Moreover, nearly every interest imaginable was involved. And the geography, ideology, development level, and needs of so many varied nations are nearly impossible to reconcile—landlocked states had special problems, so did states bordering on international straits and such archipelagoes as the Philippines and the Bahamas.

The United States proposed a modified "patrimonial" scheme providing for three economic zones: the first zone would include the continental shelf and would be entirely under control of the coastal state, the second would be a wider trusteeeship zone where the coastal state would control exploitation but would share royalties with an international agency, and the third would be a deeper zone whose manganese and other riches would be under full international control. (It was emphasizing the seabed, in part, because of pressure from U.S. mining companies with a technical lead in seabed mining.) But the U.S. scheme was doomed by the 1973 OPEC oil boycott— oil-buying coastal countries refused to share any of their areas that might contain oil or gas. The Caracas Conference adjourned without reaching an agreement. A second session in 1975 produced an "informal negotiation treaty" and seemed to be moving toward consensus on a twelve-mile territorial limit and a 200-mile "patrimonial" zone with freedom of navigation and overflight guaranteed. The deep sea problem remained in dispute.

The third negotiating session of the UN Conference opened at the UN in New York on March 15, 1976. By this time, strong pressure was building up from U.S. mining interests eager to get at the seabed. (Probably no one else in the world possesses the technical capability of mining two miles down, and the companies were eager to begin while they still held a technological lead.) When after several weeks the conference seemed to be making little progress, Secretary Kissinger, in a speech to a different group, sought to prod it. He warned:

> If the deep seabeds are not subject to international agreement, the United States can and will proceed to explore and mine on its own. [This would lead eventually, he thought, to economic warfare and military confrontation.] Our country cannot delay in its efforts to develop an assured supply of critical resources through our deep seabed mining projects. We strongly prefer an international agreement to provide a stable legal environment before such development begins, one that insures that all resources are managed for the good of the global community and that all can participate. But if agreement is not reached this year, it will be increasingly difficult to resist pressure to proceed unilaterally.

He offered other U.S. views, including the view that the United States could not agree to give an international authority exclusive right to seabed minerals and that even if an international authority were so limited, it should be governed by weighted voting, not one-nation one-vote. Acting unilaterally, the U.S. Congress passed a bill extending U.S. control of fishing from twelve to 200 miles off our coast. Appearing to feel that further delay might invite domestic political meddling and possibly turn the Senate against any treaty, Kissinger pressed the conference to move expeditiously, and although it adjourned May 7 with basic disputes still unsettled, it did agree, over Third World objections, to reconvene August 2, 1976.

Cuba may be expected to play a role in future Law of the Sea developments in the Caribbean. Prime Minister Williams of Trinidad-Tobago enlisted Castro's support in the fight by Trinidad and other Caribbean islands to maintain their rights to their territorial waters and the seabed that, they feared, might be threatened by Venezuelan imperialism; if the 200-mile limit were adopted, Williams has argued, Venezuela, with nearly 1,100 miles of Caribbean coastline, would control nearly one-tenth of the Caribbean's total economic resources. Williams seemed to be suggesting a special arrangement under which all Caribbean states would obtain equal rights to the Caribbean Sea except for the twelve-mile territorial limit of each. (The United States, of course, with the longest usable coastline in the world, would gain more territory—2.2 million square miles—than any other nation under a 200-mile zone.)

A Law of the Sea is so complex, so new and unexplored, and so entangled with other issues that laying down a detailed U.S. policy is impossible at this time. Broadly speaking, however, certain approaches appear possible.

Observing the extraordinary difficulties encountered by the Caracas Conference and its unmanageable agenda, one is struck by a certain analogy to the difficulties attending the establishment of the United Nations itself at the end of World War II. Furthermore, one recalls that at the end of World War II, certain leaders believed that the world was not yet ready for a worldwide United Nations and that a better approach would be to begin with a series of regional organizations that would lead to the emergence of a true world organization only in the future. Just possibly it would be in our interest to work for a special sea arrangement in the Caribbean. Despite their variety, Caribbean nations do have things in common. A Law of the Sea takes on special meaning in the Caribbean when one considers the narrow passages that separate Trinidad-Tobago from Venezuela, or the 760-mile Bahaman archipelago, or the mere ninety miles or less between Cuba and the United States, between Cuba and Mexico, between Cuba and Jamaica, and between Cuba and Haiti— not to mention the stepping-stone arc of the Leewards and Windwards. Moreover, the Caribbean, with its great deeps—more than 28,000 feet in the Puerto Rico Trench—and its vast shallow shelves, banks, and ridges off the Bahamas, Central America, Mexico, and Florida, with its known oil and other resources, is a small sample of the oceans and seas of the world. If regionalism could solve its problems, the solutions might be adapted elsewhere. Finally, the Caribbean should be more manageable than the world at large. Perhaps we should, as part of a larger effort to develop a special relationship with the Caribbean, encourage the Caribbean nations to seek a special arrangement among themselves—and with us. They might resist such a proposal because it came from us, but they would have to take it into consideration, since their offshore limits at certain points would conflict with ours and since they would need technology if they were to mine the seabed. They might work through their own CARICOM; they might channel portions of their sea and seabed revenues through their Caribbean Development Bank to the poorer lands among them. We could offer technical help. At the same time, we should continue to search for a UN Law of the Sea along the lines of our previous three-zone proposals.

Restructuring the OAS. In 1964, when CECLA, the autonomous Latin American forum on tariff and trade, was established, its proponents hoped to make it Latin America's coordinated voice on foreign economic policy, with a mandate to negotiate with the United States and the EEC. In 1971, President Nixon introduced a 10 percent surcharge on U.S. imports of manufactured goods with no exception for Latin America. Responding swiftly and sharply, IA-ECOSOC adopted a resolution containing five economic demands; the United States voted against one and abstained on the rest. A respected Colombian economist resigned his chairmanship of an inter-American body, saying that the time had come for a reshaping of inter-American relations, including cooperation with Europe and perhaps with the Soviet Union and its satellites.

When IA-ECOSOC met in 1973, the Latin American delegates adopted a resolution denouncing multinational corporations, announced their intention to deal with the United States jointly, and made various economic demands, for their countries were on the verge of bankruptcy, and massive foreign debt repudiations seemed to lie ahead. Assistant Secretary Meyer cast a lone vote against the Latin Americans' demands. Harsh words and bitter confrontations ensued, with all the hemisphere arrayed against us. (A year later, a different assistant secretary, Jack Kubisch, said that this meeting "marked the low point" in our relations with the Latin Americans, and that Nixon's successors would have to live with the political upheavals that would probably accompany debt repudiation.) A month later our lone veto at the UN Security Council meeting in Panama made matters worse. The Cuban deputy premier called for the expulsion of the United States and the European nations from ECLA so that it would be purely Latin American. The Peruvian foreign minister proposed radical reform of the OAS and relocation of its headquarters from Washington to Panama. President Echeverría of Mexico called for the "reincorporation of Cuba" into the OAS, implying that he was suggesting an OAS without the United States. By its intransigence and neglect, the Nixon administration had united Latin America against us as almost never before. Latin America seemed ready to break away from the United States and go it alone. The OAS was clearly approaching a crisis, and when it met in Washington in 1973, it adopted a resolution that referred to "general dissatisfaction" with the OAS and the need for "restructuring or general reform" and established a special committee to study all aspects of the organization and "propose its restructuring."

For a number of years, the OAS had acted as a virtual rubber stamp for U.S. policies. As recently as 1965, it had cloaked with legitimacy President Johnson's unilateral military intervention in the Dominican Republic. But since then, although the United States still controlled enough votes to get key decisions out of the OAS General Assembly and still had veto power over IADB soft loans, the OAS had become a sounding board for Latin American complaints about the United States, and our representatives did not always take criticism well. At about the time of the 1973 OAS meeting in Washington, William D. Rogers, then a private attorney, but soon to become assistant secretary for ARA, published a piece in the *Washington Post* entitled "Adios, OAS: A U.S. Pullout Would Help." The piece pointed to "new realities," deep divisions, pronounced nationalism, and increasing diversity in the hemisphere, and to Latin America's "vivid feeling of differentiation—from the United States." Noting that Washington had never viewed the OAS with enthusiasm, Rogers said that in the past, the OAS had served as an alternative to the UN, which was dominated by the Cold War; but now, détente with Russia and renewed relations with China had made the OAS less essential. He described the organization's shift from cooperation to confrontation. Increasingly, he reported, OAS meetings consisted of two stages: first, the Latin Americans met among themselves; then they called in the United States and announced what decisions they had reached. "In short, the OAS in fact is already virtually a Latin American organization." The United States was not blameless, Rogers observed; we had used the OAS "irresponsibly, and at times shamelessly." But in any case, the time had come, he thought, for us to withdraw formally "to some associated role." The OAS could then concentrate on legitimate regional issues, he thought. Our withdrawal would make it harder to accuse the United States of dominating Latin America and would "say something" to the Soviets about East Europe; it also would permit us to give up our "painful and often ludicrous" efforts to maintain a low profile. He warned that the move must be executed carefully to avoid the impression that we were turning our back on Latin America altogether. Thus, he said, we should pledge continuing hospitality and financial support to the OAS, reaffirm our support for the IADB, strengthen our bilateral relations with such major countries as Brazil and Mexico, and make it clear that we were by no means retreating from our commitments— expressed in the OAS Charter—to development, nonintervention, human rights, and peaceful settlement of disputes.

By the time the special committee on restructuring the OAS met, the idea of a Latin American organization without the United States had firmly taken root. Peru, Chile, and Argentina seemed strongly in favor of it, and several other nations, including Panama, Venezuela, Ecuador, Costa Rica, Jamaica, Barbados, and Trinidad-Tobago, were greatly interested. Some favored readmitting Cuba and expelling the United States. A Cuban argued for a Latin American union, saying, "We believe that the shark should stay in the fish tank and the sardines in theirs." But he met resistance. Foreign countries, mainly the United States, control 40 percent of Latin America's GNP; a majority of Latin American exports go to the United States; and most loans to Latin America come from the United States. Many Latin Americans feared that, as one observer wrote, if they threw out the shark, he might take all the water with him. The committee gradually achieved consensus in favor of a new structure that would enhance the Latin Americans' role and diminish that of the United States. In the end, the committee proposed four charter reforms: to allow ideological pluralism; to define "aggression," under the Rio Treaty, as including "economic aggression" (the most controversial proposal); to establish a convention on "economic security" (a murky proposal); and to establish a convention on development that would end the paternalistic concept of foreign aid. The United States proposed that the recommendations be thrown out and that a "joint reassessment" be made. The purpose of the next OAS meeting was to amend the Rio Treaty so that only a simple majority, not two-thirds, would be required to lift sanctions; the participants also amended the treaty to affirm the right of states to choose their own forms of political, economic, and social organization (thus overturning the principle on which Cuba had been suspended).

Meanwhile, CECLA met to develop a joint approach to the new round of GATT negotiations in Tokyo. Latin America sent a strong delegation to the fourth nonaligned conference held in Algiers. Venezuela proposed a purely Latin American summit. It collapsed. When the OAS meeting at Quito failed to lift sanctions against Cuba, the OAS was perceived as indecisive and ineffective. Pérez of Venezuela instructed his foreign minister to meet with the foreign ministers of the Caribbean islands to prepare an agenda for a Caribbean island summit in 1975. He also requested a special OAS meeting in Washington to discuss the odious U.S. Trade Act of 1974; the meeting was held scarcely a month after the Act passed. At the same time, early in 1975, Venezuelan and Mexican cabinet ministers were traveling around South America and the Caribbean trying to round support for a new economic organization, the Latin American Economic System (SELA), which would not include the United States, and which had been proposed by President Echeverría of Mexico. He and Pérez, together with Cuba, had discarded their first alternative, a political OAS without the United States, simply because of Pérez's success in using the OAS to attack the U.S. Trade Act. On August 2, 1975, twenty-five countries meeting in Panama voted SELA into being. The aims of the new organization would be: to market raw materials jointly and maintain their prices, to establish multinational Latin American companies, to unite in opposing decisions by rich countries or multinational corporations deemed harmful by SELA members, to finance national development schemes that could use local labor or raw materials, and to support development programs that might otherwise exhaust their capital. The treaty itself was signed at an October ministerial meeting in Panama by twenty-three nations: Argentina, Bolivia, Brazil, Colombia, *Costa Rica, Cuba,* Chile, Ecuador, El Salvador, *Honduras, Guatemala, Guyana, Haiti,* Mexico, *Jamaica,* Paraguay, *Nicaragua, Dominican Republic, Panama,* Peru, *Trinidad-Tobago,* Uruguay, and *Venezuela. Barbados* and *Granada* were expected to sign later. The Political Council of SELA—potentially a political OAS without the United States—held its first meeting on October 17 and agreed to coordinate Latin American policy for the fourth UNCTAD to be held in May 1976 in Nairobi.

While Venezuela and Mexico were promoting SELA, however, Brazil and Argentina were trying to postpone and limit it because they feared the uncertainties of the new association between Venezuela and Mexico, both oil states, and because they thought SELA might provoke confrontation with the rich nations, which alone can furnish the capital, technology, and markets essential to poor country development. Although SELA's member countries are deeply divided ideologically, SELA's basic aims—to reduce economic dependence on the United States and to reduce chronic trade deficits with the United States, perhaps by turning to Western Europe and Japan—are shared by most Latin American nations.[24] At the first SELA meeting in Caracas in January 1976, ministers of the black English-speaking Caribbean expressed concern that the Spanish-speaking countries were dominating SELA. The meeting condemned "any form of economic coercion" against the poor countries and once more called for "a new world economic order." The ministers would carry this position to a meeting of poor countries in Manila as well as to UNCTAD at Nairobi. The meeting paid little attention to a principal aim of SELA, to found Latin American multinational companies. A few weeks later, making his long delayed journey to Latin America, Secretary Kissinger promised cooperation with SELA but made it clear that he wanted SELA to concentrate on such matters as the transfer of technology and a code for multinationals and that he hoped SELA would not become another forum for confrontation with the United States, which, of course, is precisely the purpose for which it was founded. He may have chosen to mention the areas of technology and multinationals rather than commodity supplies, prices, and markets because the State Department and the Treasury Department still disagreed on those issues.

A Long View of the Nixon-Ford Years

Nixon has been so thoroughly discredited that it is hard to take seriously the notion that he had a Latin American policy. But the fact remains that he *was* president for more than five years and, therefore, *did* exert great influence on policy, including Latin American policy. Because of his excessive secrecy and Secretary Kissinger's personal diplomacy, and because Nixon memoir-writers have flocked to publishers only to rehash Watergate, many of Nixon's high policy moves remained veiled. We still are not completely informed about the "arrangement" with the Soviet Union about the submarine base at Cienfuegos in Cuba. Nonetheless, we know enough to attempt to put the Nixon administration in perspective.

In many ways, the Republican 1970s resembled the Republican 1920s. At that time, World War I had ended, and therefore the urgency of our strategic interests in the Caribbean had diminished. Policy, however, absentmindedly continued to go in the same general direction it had gone under Theodore Roosevelt, Taft, and Wilson; but it was policy without content. In the same way, in the 1970s, with the Cold War against communism declared ended, the urgency of our strategic interests in the Caribbean again diminished, but policy continued to speak in the idiom of the Alliance for Progress. Again, it was policy without content. There was, however, a big difference between the 1920s and the 1970s: in the 1920s we were not going anywhere and neither was the Caribbean; in the 1970s, we were not, but the Caribbean *was*—it was drifting toward the Third World. In perspective, it appears that President Kennedy capped a long, long period (stretching back to the last century) of American hegemony and of Latin American supplications by responding to those supplications with the Alliance for Progress. It was a climactic hour in hemisphere history. But Kennedy was murdered, the Alliance died, and Nixon buried it. And perhaps buried with it forever was the long, long period of supplication and hegemony. The climactic hour passed; the opportunity is gone; we awake in a different world.

In the 1920s, exhausted after great exertion, we did not actually withdraw, we subsided. Just so, when Nixon came to power at the end of the 1960s after the country had passed through a period of great exertion and considerable peril—the Cuban missile crisis, the confrontation at Berlin, the Dominican intervention, Vietnam, the assassination of the Kennedy brothers and other leaders, the black revolution and the white backlash, the youth revolt, the urban crisis—again, we subsided. Nixon saw that after the uproar of the 1960s, in the 1970s the people did not want to be bothered. For a president, that way lay popularity. Hence, he set out to, as he would have put it, "cool it." He made much of "bringing us together," he announced that in foreign affairs we would "lower our profile," and he proclaimed "the Nixon Doctrine." This worked out in Asia to

"Vietnamization" of the war (let somebody else fight our war). In Latin America it worked out to simple neglect.

Every administration policy-maker who went up to Capitol Hill testified that we were "forging a more mature partnership" with the Latin Americans. They all emphasized that Latin Americans must help themselves, and they stressed trade, not aid (without in any way acknowledging what the true trade issues were). Everyone said we were quitting our role as policeman and tutor; everyone said we must deal with governments as we found them. And all this was reinforced by Congress's own mounting disenchantment, for other reasons, with all forms—political, military, or developmental—of aid.

Aid declined; the Peace Corps sent fewer and different people to Latin America; Nixon instructed U.S. representatives at the IADB and World Bank to oppose loans to countries that expropriated American property without compensation. Nixon had learned that isolationism was unacceptable and so cloaked his doctrine in the rhetoric of international cooperation while jettisoning its substance. Nixon perceived that it was unacceptable to tell Latin Americans they were on their own, so he disguised his empty policies with the rhetoric of the Alliance for Progress. Time after time, Secretary Kissinger promised "a new dialogue" with Latin America, but by the time he at long last made a short trip to South America, he was reduced to defining our opposition to Cuba's Angola policy. It was all a fraud. Kissinger did bring in William D. Rogers as assistant secretary for ARA; he did set Ellsworth Bunker to work on the Panama Canal question; he did indicate concessions on the terms of trade; he did vote to lift the OAS's Cuban sanctions (after it was clear that would happen whatever we did).[25]

It is unclear whether the Nixon-Ford administration deliberately embarked on the policy of the lowered profile in the belief that it was best for us and the Latin Americans or whether it used that policy as an excuse to do other things—cut foreign aid, pursue our own economic nationalism through private enterprise, and leave the Latin Americans to shift for themselves while the "free market" operates and the devil takes the hindmost. In any case, the Nixon-Ford policy was basically a policy of neglect.

In the Caribbean, when the United States abandons leadership, other forces take over. When the Third World took over in the 1970s, the Caribbean ceased to look to us for leadership. Instead, politically, it looked to itself and to the Third World; economically, it defied us. Richard Nixon said in his inaugural address, "After a period of confrontation, we are entering an era of negotiation." But in the Caribbean, after a long period of cooperation, confrontation came for the first time under Nixon. President Ford, in his 1976 State of the Union Address, referred to "our traditional friendships in Latin America" and to "a serious and hopeful dialogue." But our "traditional friendships" in the Caribbean have crumbled. And the nations of the Caribbean are indeed conducting a "new dialogue"— but not with us.

ROADS TO RICHES

Strategies of Development

Assistant Secretary Rogers of ARA asserted in 1975, as others had before him, that the heart of our long-term relationship with Latin America is not such issues of the moment as the Panama Canal or Cuba, but rather, development—the process of change that will alter those nations and enable them both to meet the demands of their peoples and to play a larger role in world affairs.

As "underdeveloped" nations, the Caribbean countries share a number of characteristics. They are poor—per capita GNP is highest in Venezuela at about $1,410 per year and lowest in Haiti at $145 a year.[1] Income distribution is highly skewed, owing to the extremely uneven ownership of productive assets, principally land. These nations depend on the export of a limited number of agricultural or mineral products for foreign exchange and for highly significant portions of both GNP and government revenues, and often foreigners have controlled those agricultural or mineral products. Their manufacturing and service sectors are so limited that, in most of them, upwards of 60 percent of their people work in agriculture.[2] Their populations are growing rapidly—regionally, the fastest on earth—and nearly 50 percent of the population of some countries is under fifteen, which means nonproductive mouths to feed and minds to educate and bodies—many diseased or undernourished—to treat.[3]

Moreover, all these countries lack the financial institutions, the interconnected industries (from parts to assembly line), and the organizational and entrepreneurial skills needed to take advantage of the available national market. Their societies do not function as units; people cannot move quickly and freely about in a well-coordinated and dynamic system, owing to inadequate transport and communications as well as to the poverty of human resources. All these countries suffer from low productivity of the masses, owing to lack of education, skills, health and horizons; low productivity is the principal impediment to development. Finally, all these countries, except for Venezuela, are small. Because they are small in area, their resources are quite limited, and they must rely heavily on foreign trade; because they are small in population, they must produce for export as well as the small domestic market—and thus must rely on foreign trade.

Since World War II, because of such phenomena as the rise of socialism in Europe, the Keynesian revolution, the Marshall Plan, and the independence of former colonies, rapid economic development has come to seem both a realistic possibility and a government responsibility. Rich countries have loaned or given billions of dollars to poor countries for development, and additional billions have come from such international agencies as the World Bank, regional development banks, and the UN.

In 1973, the total net flow of government and private money from the seventeen countries accounted rich[4] to the 142 poor countries and territories amounted to about $24.43 billion (in 1963, the total had been only $8.57 billion). Although it is a lot of money, since the poor countries had a combined population of about 1.84 billion, the largess came to only about $13.30 per capita. It is hard to believe that $13 per person per year will radically alter anyone's life.

For the United States, foreign aid began in April 1948 with the Marshall Plan for Europe. Following that triumph, and at the time of the fall of the Kuomintang in China and the Korean War, we poured aid into Asia—at the peak in 1954-1955, some 75 percent of our worldwide commitment. It was during this period of U.S. globalism that lending in the Caribbean began on a small scale.[5] The Bandung Conference of 1955—a precursor of later Third World meetings—encouraged the USSR to expand its own aid program. Castro's rise and Nixon's rebuff in Caracas awakened us—and awakened other rich countries. Between 1956 and 1961, the annual flow of net official resources to poor countries and multilateral agencies rose from $3.28 to $6.05 billion, an annual rate of increase of 13 percent. Between those same years, U.S. contributions grew from $2.01 to $3.45 billion. Therefore, U.S. aid grew much more slowly, reaching only $3.53 billion in 1968. Since then, it has actually declined—in 1973 to $3.44 billion, about the 1961 figure. Under Kennedy-Johnson, our aid to Latin America, which averaged only 6.8 percent of our global total, increased rapidly: the 1962-1965 average jumped to 23.4 percent, and the 1968 figure was 25.9 percent. In 1973, however, it dropped to 20.4 percent of a declining total. Outright grants formed 61 percent of aid to Latin America in 1953-1961, 23 percent in 1962-1965, and then 68 percent in 1973.

The United States has disbursed more than $150 billion in worldwide aid since 1946. We have justified such expenditures by saying that the United States cannot survive as a rich island in a sea of poverty, that economic development is essential to a peaceful and stable world, and that in any case assistance to the poor countries is for us a moral imperative. At the outset, we thought we could quickly solve development problems by sending money and technicians. But today, development seems to be as far away as ever, and the problems remain despite all the money and energy expended. Rich and poor countries alike have become disillusioned and discouraged, for although some countries have made a certain amount of progress, others have actually slipped back. Usually, progress depends on skilled local manpower and local politics, and development requires radical change that requires sacrifice. In some countries, the people are unwilling to sacrifice and leaders unready to lead. In the Caribbean, the English-speaking countries have done better with fewer resources than the Central American countries because England, unlike Spain, left a comparatively educated populace with traditions conducive to development—and people are the key.

Traditionally, and as recently as the 1950s, the United States believed that Latin America could get along with private investment, commercial and Export-Import Bank credits, and technical assistance. But it became apparent that these instruments would have to be supplemented by public funds; the poor countries, including the Caribbean, lacked the basic infrastructure necessary if private capital were to succeed. Increasingly, the poor countries called on the World

Bank and the IADB for loans for highways, railroads, port equipment, electric power generation, and communications equipment. And the United States began its bilateral aid programs, which culminated in the Alliance for Progress.

Our foreign aid has nearly always had humanitarian, developmental, and political purposes. The basic political purpose of the Marshall Plan was to strengthen Western Europe sufficiently to enable it to resist Soviet expansion. Throughout the Cold War, this basic political purpose was maintained, especially in the Caribbean. Under the Alliance for Progress, for example, President Kennedy tried to use AID in the Dominican Republic to build "a democratic showcase next door to Castro's Cuba." We have used AID not merely to oppose communism but also to help governments we favor (and we withheld it to punish regimes we do not favor, such as Duvalier's).

But propping up a weak government is almost certain to weaken it further; it learns to rely on us instead of on itself. Far from winning friends, this practice is almost certain to create resentment. Yet there are times when such actions seem absolutely essential. It does little good to establish an elaborate long-range educational program if the government that wants it falls to a dictatorship that does not. The questions are not easy. And in Latin America (and in Asia), the goals of AID were far less clear than they were in Europe with the Marshall Plan—there it had only been a question of rebuilding, not of building.

We do not really know how to achieve development. In the early postwar years, the poor nations, observing the machines and factories that were the visible evidence of wealth in the rich countries, viewed development as essentially an economic problem, as little more than industrialization. They associated agriculture with backwardness and poverty; they argued that agriculture, no matter how much improved, was by itself incapable of producing per capita income growth in the face of population growth. Thus was born the idea, promoted heavily by the Economic Commission for Latin America (ECLA) and Raúl Prebisch, that the answer to development lay in import-substitution manufacturing. But too often these new industries merely added new demands for imported capital goods, parts, and raw materials; too often they were merely assembly plants given excessive tax and tariff benefits, which caused foreign exchange problems and reduced government revenues from customs duties; too often they were inefficient producers shielded artificially so that the consumer was obliged to purchase high-cost, low-quality goods. Economists came to realize that import substitution was not a complete answer. At the outset, too, Caribbean leaders had thought that industrialization would help lower unemployment. They looked to the United States and Puerto Rico as models, but U.S. and Puerto Rican industry has been developed for U.S. and Puerto Rican conditions, which prevail nowhere else in the Caribbean. Moreover, automated machinery does not help unemployment, as Puerto Rico discovered. (Perhaps they should have looked to Japan for their model; its industry is labor-intensive.) Even our own AID people tended to model programs in the Caribbean after U.S. programs and seemed reluctant to build on what local people were doing or wanted to do; indeed, they often insisted on leaping from the wooden plow to the most advanced technology. Such factors as skilled labor, entrepreneurship, and management, not to mention agriculture, were ignored. But development involves far more than building industry; it involves nothing less than a structural transformation of society—essentially the changes sought by the Alliance. But such changes inside each country can be made in only two ways: either violently, through revolution and dictatorship of the left or right, or peaceably, through democracy with strong local support from below and strong local leadership from above. Development is not the result of studies and statistics produced by economists; what is needed is intuition and imagination.

What we know about development is often contradictory. We say that only industrial countries prosper; yet such agricultural countries as Denmark and New Zealand have high standards of living. We say that small countries lack natural resources and so remain poor; yet Japan, a world power, has only meager resources, and Switzerland, with one of the highest per capita incomes in the world, started with little more than scenery. Nations need to develop naturally, out of what they have. To develop further, the Caribbean countries must manufacture for export. Probably they should base their manufacturing on their own resources, including minerals and food, and on cheap labor. The U.S. Congress could help the Caribbean by relaxing its restrictions on the import of processed food that would compete with U.S. products, canned fruit and vegetables and shrimp, textiles, shoes, clothing, and the like. But U.S. shrimp-packers vote in U.S. elections; would-be Caribbean shrimp-packers do not, and the restrictions remain.

Perhaps the greatest obstacle to further industrialization in most of the Caribbean is the shortage of skilled labor and experienced management. Large-scale technical education and training are necessary; foreign skills brought in by contractual arrangements would help, as would foreign investment. Foreign enterprises should be made to carry out on-the-job training programs; cottage industries and small-scale manufacturing must be developed. Industries should not be protected by high tariff walls, and agriculture must be developed.[6] Financial institutions should be expanded to mobilize domestic savings and relieve the pressure to borrow abroad. Local manufacturers should concentrate on mass consumption articles rather than capital-intensive consumer durables. Incentives that discourage the substitution of labor for capital should be phased out, and licensing and other controls that tend to discriminate against small industrialists should be discontinued. Maximum use of existing plants through double-shift or triple-shift production should be encouraged. (Even so innocent a step as instituting a midnight shift in a factory in the Caribbean suggests the depths of the cultural revolution required.)

Given the related problems of unemployment, urbanization, and population growth, the service sector is of special importance. But it would not be easy to expand it by forced draft. Tourism would help, but tourism is a mixed blessing.[7] Certain countries have special advantages—Venezuela's oil wealth may allow it to become a major financial center of the Latin American Free Trade Association (LAFTA); Jamaica aspires to become the headquarters of worldwide activities expected under the Law of the Sea; Panama's geographic location plus its use of the U.S. dollar permit it to expand both financial and commercial operations. But major expansion of the service sector in most countries must await increasing industrialization.

Proponents of aid say that, because poor countries produce little and immediately consume most of what they do produce, little is available for development. Aid, by supplementing domestic savings and speeding up growth, promotes development. At some point, the country's economy will reach a new level of growth high enough to make growth self-sustaining. At that point, aid will not be necessary, and indeed foreign debts could be amortized. The number of years this takes will vary from country to country. Not all economists, of course, agree on this theory of the value of aid.

Critics of foreign aid ask: what if savings do not increase and, instead, governments use up their foreign aid as they receive it and refuse to impose unpopular taxes to increase their own public savings? Some critics argue that aid, by displacing both private and public savings, perpetuates the poor countries' dependence. Others argue that aid concentrates the benefits of development in the hands of the rich, who bank it abroad, whereas savings mobilized through taxation of these same rich people, which would be unavoidable if there were no aid, would move resources to productive use. There is a certain truth in these criticisms. But on balance, the volume of aid is not big enough to enable governments to continue to ignore with impunity the mounting demands of their peoples. And while some governments have wasted foreign aid on spectacular showcase projects, on the other hand many essential endeavors with slow rates of return, such as education and health and electric power, will never be undertaken at all unless governments undertake them—and that requires foreign aid.

The terms of U.S. aid hardened during the 1960s but now appear to be softening. In 1973, grants were equal to 68 percent of our global aid (49 percent to the Caribbean countries). The rest were loans. Average loan maturity was 40.1 years; average grace period was 10.7 years; and interest averaged 2.6 percent.[8] But loans must be repaid, and all the development lending in the past twenty-odd years has piled up huge debts in Latin America. In the Caribbean area, the debt burden is continuing to grow, and the grace periods granted during the Alliance are beginning to expire. In these circumstances, any collapse in commodity prices could be disastrous, and so could the tendency for imports of essential intermediary goods to increase faster than exports. The Caribbean situation is precarious.

The poor countries say that our tying aid to purchases of U.S. goods has imposed additional costs (as much as 20 percent) on them. Since 1971, the United States has moved toward untying its aid. Poor countries complain too of delay in negotiating a loan—it often takes a year and a half or more—and in the costs and delay of feasibility studies. Meeting that objection would mean loosening the reins on the use of aid and relying more on the poor countries' own ability to plan and execute projects, a possible move given the experience poor countries have gained in recent years. It would help, too, if IMF compensatory financing could be softened and made more flexible.[9] IMF loans at present are short-term and quite hard; moreover, the IMF often requires a country to reform its budget and otherwise put its house in order before it will make a loan. This often forces countries to adopt restrictive policies and thus, by worsening unemployment and business conditions, generates powerful political reactions that in turn jeopardize long-run economic stability—a truly vicious circle.

In the 1960s, the United States, weary of its burdens, began to propose sharing the burden with other rich countries, especially those Western European nations that had so greatly benefited from the Marshall Plan. This attempt to "globalize" aid disrupted the one-to-one relationship between donor and poor. The rich countries began consulting among themselves and trying to establish worldwide norms; as a result, their attention was diverted from the particular needs of each poor country—and such needs vary widely. The rich countries began presenting their programs as a group to poor countries, which came to feel that they were having development plans almost forced on them by outsiders and that they were thereby losing whatever chance they had had to shape their own programs. They tried to appeal to the United Nations, but they found that the UN was largely nonoperational. In 1964, they held the first UN Conference on Trade and Development (UNCTAD). UNCTAD's purpose was to create a world forum to discuss such problems faced by poor countries as commodity prices, access to rich nations' markets, and the terms of trade. The poor countries devoted this first UNCTAD largely to denouncing the United States and other rich nations. It was there, however, that other Third World nations joined Latin America's demands for improving the terms of trade. Proud Caribbean nationalists spurned aid, declaring they wanted fairer terms of trade—simple justice, not charity. The U.S. Congress, confronted with denunciations and rising nationalism in the poor countries, preoccupied with the black revolution and other social crises at home as well as with Vietnam, disappointed and frustrated at AID's failures, began to view foreign aid first with skepticism then with hostility. At a hearing in 1972, Senator Fulbright observed that

Mexico, which had never become dependent and had accepted little aid from us, had far better relations with us than any other Latin American nation has had.

Although at one point it appeared that Congress might actually end foreign aid altogether, about 1970 it began shifting from bilateral to multilateral aid, which would be nonpolitical and purely developmental. Fulbright had said in 1969, when Rockefeller submitted his report, "I do not like the continuation of this bilateral intervention, whether it be military or economic. After watching these bilateral operations I am very strongly committed to the multilateral administration of international assistance." At a Senate hearing in 1970, Secretary of the Treasury David M. Kennedy urged the advantages of multilateralism: other nations would share our burden, lending judgments would more likely be made on purely economic grounds than on political grounds, and "economic discipline" could more readily be applied on borrowing countries by collective action. The under secretary of the treasury added in 1971 that multi-lateralism took advantage of international expertise, promoted fair treatment of foreign investment, encouraged self-help, and provided a "shielding device" for the United States. President Nixon's messages emphasized multilateralism. But some authorities remained skeptical. In 1971, for example, Congressman Fascell called multilateral assistance "the cliché of the 1970s," since it "has something for everyone," and pointed out that international banks, which were obliged to make a profit, might pursue leading policies that were socially destructive; he also noted that making aid multilateral may not have de-politicized it but merely raised political problems to a new and higher level (as indeed seemed to be happening in 1977).

As U.S. aid has declined, bilateral programs have grown in such rich countries as Canada, the Netherlands, Japan, Norway, and Sweden (indeed, Sweden has come closer to meeting the UN goal of using 1 percent of its GNP for foreign aid than any other nation). And the World Bank, IADB, and other international institutions have grown in importance, and it is at the banks that the poor countries of the Caribbean increasingly seek to wield influence.

Bilateral aid should not wholly replace multilateral aid; each has a role to play. Bilateral lenders can more readily give soft terms than international banks; they have flexibility in providing emergency relief and in rescheduling or even canceling past debts in cases of extreme hardship; they can more precisely tailor their programs to fit each country's need instead of trying for global programs; and they can use their aid to advance their own interests. Aid can never be made completely nonpolitical; if we end bilateral aid, we will almost inevitably further politicize the international banks, presenting them with responsibilities they are not equipped to assume. Finally, we should not repeat the mistake of trying to sell foreign aid to the American people by calling it charity or humanitarianism; we should explain that it is an instrument of our foreign policy intended to advance our own interests.

Because Congress has recently shown increased interest in aiming aid at the poorest of the poor, AID has shifted its emphasis away from infrastructure and toward helping the rural poor. The best way of helping the poorest people in the poorest countries is not clear. For example, building a jet airport at Port-au-Prince to attract tourists really might, in the long run, do more for Haiti's rural poor than, say, nutrition programs. The World Bank, working on the theory that most of the absolute poor live in rural areas and that the only cure for poverty is to help the poor become more productive, has outlined a strategy in Nairobi designed to reduce poverty—a whole cluster of projects. In a 1975 speech, McNamara of the World Bank said that the consequences of worldwide inflation, the sudden rise in the cost of oil, the deterioration of the terms of trade, and the prolonged recession in rich nations has combined to endanger the economic future of the poor countries. "And it is the very poorest countries, countries that collectively contain a billion human beings, which face the bleakest prospects."

Population growth impedes development by skewing the distribution of income, for when large numbers of people are entering the labor force to compete for jobs, wages tend to drop, while at the same time the earnings of owners of capital and land tend to rise. But controlling population is not easy. Throughout the 1950s, the United States was most reluctant to become involved officially in a matter so personal and so laden with moral and religious overtones. But by the early 1960s, this view was eroded as we realized the serious, even critical, damage that population growth was doing to development. By 1965, the Johnson administration announced that the U.S. government would "seek new ways to use our knowledge to help deal with the explosion in world population and the growing scarcity in world resources." The Foreign Assistance Act of 1968 contained explicit support for "programs relating to population growth." In 1969, President Nixon sent to Congress the first White House message on population. He also asked the secretary of state and the administrator of AID to give population and family planning priority. Congress concurred: U.S. AID commitments to population programs grew from $2.1 million in fiscal year 1965 to a proposed $201.5 million in fiscal year 1976. Other nations and the UN also became involved; so did the World Bank, which estimates that if fertility is halved in a generation, by the end of that period per capita income can be 20 to 40 percent higher than if fertility remains constant. The poor countries have responded; in the Caribbean, the Dominican Republic (which has a Vatican Concordat), Jamaica, Barbados, and Trinidad-Tobago have official government policies or programs for family planning. All the Central American governments now support "responsible parenthood" and offer services within their national health programs. In Venezuela, family planning is virtually a nationwide program carried out by the Venezuelan Family Planning Association. Nevertheless, cultural and religious objections still abound, and so does the Marxist notion that population control is a neo-colonialist plot designed by the United States to "kill guerrillas in the womb."

Education is also central to development. In the past, governments have all too often relied on investments in machines and buildings to bring about development and have paid too little heed to education and vocational training. Since education and training require large-scale investment and are slow to pay off, they constitute an area where foreign aid can be particularly useful. Rapidly and effectively imparting knowledge and skills to masses of people in the poor countries is perhaps the greatest challenge educators have ever faced and is an area where the United States can help. Traditional methods may be unable to solve the problem. New methods, especially television, are being tried.

Of late, three other factors have hindered Caribbean development: recession in the rich countries, high oil prices, and worldwide inflation. Rises in the prices of bauxite and coffee, and a temporary rise in sugar, only partly offset the inflated price rises of manufactured exports from the rich countries. At the same time, the recession in the rich countries has severely curtailed the demand for goods produced by the poor countries. Moreover, skyrocketing oil prices nearly ruined some Caribbean countries. Finally, the Caribbean countries suffered from their own inflation—by mid-1974 only Venezuela had maintained an inflation rate below 10 percent, and inflation in Trinidad-Tobago, Jamaica, and Barbados exceeded 20 percent per year.[10]

The likely swing leftward toward statism in much of the Caribbean carries with it the danger that politicians may allow doctrine to distort natural development. There is nothing sacred about a free market, nor does a pristine free market exist even in the United States. The market, however, does perform functions not easy for politicians and all-out state planners to improve on, especially if they are inexperienced, as the guerillas in Cuba learned once they came to power. Development, often involving radical cultural change, will probably be painful to some, and politicians, seeking to alleviate the pain in order to avoid confrontations with angry voters, may lose track of development itself. Change for the sake of change has no merit, for the rate or direction of change may be harmful. The Caribbean countries have often modeled their industrial development on that of the United States, and they have also adopted social legislation appropriate to a mature industrial society, but the legislation places unsupportable financial burdens on immature poor countries. Failure to develop has not been anybody's fault; it is nothing other than the failures of the country itself—not the wickedness of multinational corporations or other foreign devils. But neither local politicians nor officials of rich countries dare say so.

In spite of all the difficulties and disappointments, the Caribbean countries have made progress. They increased their GNP by 112 percent (not per capita) in the period from 1960 to 1973. While it is not utopia, neither is it stagnation or backsliding.

Islands in the Sun: Tourism

Many Caribbean countries seeking development have turned to tourism. For some, like the Bahamas, sun and sand are virtually their only resources. For others, tourism is an overlooked asset. International travel increased during the 1950s, though tourism in the Caribbean was concentrated in a few countries—Cuba, Mexico, and the Bahamas. In the 1960s, with the rise of Castro in Cuba and the consequent shift of U.S. tourists to Puerto Rico and the Bahamas, increasing affluence and leisure in the United States, the coming of the jet airplane, declining sugar prices and stagnating agriculture, and other conditions contributing to a need for new sources of foreign exchange, emphasis on tourism grew. Like the sugar industry, tourism could be organized along traditional lines. It could be built with foreign capital and technology; it was labor-intensive and would alleviate unemployment; and it would benefit local land-owners and other powerful figures important to politicians. Since 1960, tourism to the Caribbean countries has grown at an annual rate of about 12 percent.[11] In some countries, it has been the fastest-growing sector of the economy. In recent years, there has been a slowdown of tourism in the former British colonies, a rapid increase in Central America, Haiti, the Dominican Republic, and Venezuela. Unfortunately, the slowdown in some islands has coincided with a rapid increase in tourist accommodations. Hotel occupancy rates fell to only 45 percent in Jamaica in 1972—the break-even point is considered 60 percent—but the Jamaican government continued to build more rooms.

Tourism requires sizable initial capital investment—several million dollars for a moderate-sized hotel. Governments have offered free land, customs exemptions, and other incentives to foreign investors. Most early tourist development capital in the Caribbean was private. Later, governments became directly involved and obtained loans from the World Bank and IADB.[12] Tourism creates jobs, though how many is hard to say. A study for the World Bank estimated that one person was employed directly per hotel room. An IADB study suggests that one local job is created for every ten tourists. But tourism is seasonal, and hence, so is employment. Tourism requires heavy outlays for infrastructure—airports, roads, electric power links, water supply, sewage disposal—and it can create serious problems in land use, planning, and ecology.

At the outset, nearly every country welcomed every investment in tourism and every tourist, but some countries have had second thoughts. The profits from tourism are not dependable; many factors beyond the control of the country affect tourism, such as international air fares and recessions in rich countries. Leakage—the portion of the tourist dollar that is lost to the local economy—has turned out to be greater than expected. Construction material, hotel kitchen equipment, lobby furniture, chandeliers, beds, even foods and beverages must be imported, thus leaking money away to the rich countries. Advertising must be placed in the rich countries. And foreign hotel owners send profits back to the rich countries. The meager data available suggest that leakage ranges from one-third to one-half of gross receipts and that the profits from tourism benefit chiefly the multinational corporations that own the hotels and supply the goods needed to run them. Moreover, tourists are notoriously fickle. Both countries and individual resorts enjoy periods of great popularity, but today's "in" place may be forgotten tomorrow. Political upheaval, demonstrations and riots, police retaliation, guerrilla warfare, and urban terrorism frighten tourists off. And if black natives murder a white tourist, to the accompaniment of heavy newspaper publicity, tourists vanish. Worst of all, tourism may unwittingly sharpen racial conflict: poor black servants resent hotel guests who are rich and white. Black Power may be waning, but it has brought to the surface ancient black-white hostilities, which are not likely to disappear, and may even be exacerbated by tourism. A Belize official said, "We won't put everything into an effort to build a nation to produce a crop of waiters, guides, and drink-mixers for rich tourists." Tourism may very well create more jobs per million dollars invested than any other industry, but they are not the jobs wanted, and they present a serious political problem. A dinner check for four at a tourist hotel in the Caribbean will exceed a week's wages and tips for the waiter (and more than a year's wages for his cousin in the interior). Moreover, a decision that all the Bunnies in the Playboy Club in Jamaica must be Jamaican could only create resentment—and so would a decision the other way. Tourism, like U.S. television, also corrupts by setting up false values and unrealistic hopes. When an official publication of the government of Trinidad-Tobago says that tourism may "put in jeopardy the social fabric of the country," it is voicing a widespread unease. Many Caribbean leaders believe that tourism can demoralize and ruin a country, that it smacks of colonialism, even of slavery. They encourage it only reluctantly and only because they are too poor to be proud.

Since American tourists are not ambassadors of goodwill, it would appear unwise for the U.S. government to encourage the undue growth of the tourist industry. Just so, Caribbean governments would be wise not to regard tourism as the mainstay of their economies—except perhaps where they have no choice, as in the Bahamas—but to control its growth as carefully as they can and to use the foreign exchange it earns to develop other sectors of the economy.

Regional Economic Integration

In their quest for development, the Caribbean nations (and the rest of Latin America) have attempted regional economic integration in various forms—as have, since World War II, beginning with the European Economic Community, nearly all nations. The Caribbean nations, trying to industrialize, realized that large-scale enterprises, to be economic, must reach high levels of production and that high production requires mass consumer markets. But since each Caribbean nation was by itself too small and too poor, they must export. Because the United States denied some of their products access to its huge market, the solution seemed to be the formation of a regional trading bloc that would create a mass market. Moreover, a regional grouping could trade with the United States on a more nearly equal basis than could any single small nation, and such a group could exert more influence on international councils than could individual nations. Furthermore, reducing the barriers to free movements of labor and capital within the region could result in mutual benefits to all members by eliminating inefficient production in some countries and expanding efficient production in others. (Of course, a high external common tariff, set to protect infant industries within these countries, could become an artificial shield for inefficient producers and penalize consumers.) In the 1950s, Raúl Prebisch and others at the Economic Commission for Latin America (ECLA) and Caribbean leaders themselves began discussing economic integration. In 1960, Latin American nations took the first steps: they formed the Central American Common Market (CACM) and the Latin American Free Trade Association (LAFTA). LAFTA need not concern us here—it involved Mexico and South America and excluded Central America and the Caribbean countries (save Venezuela); in any case, its performance has been uneven and disappointing, in large part because it is attempting to integrate economies as disparate as those of Bolivia and Brazil, Ecuador and Argentina. But the Central American Common Market, which embraces the nations of Central America and was, at least at the outset, hugely successful, does concern us.

Central America proved fertile soil for economic integration, in part because these five countries[13] had joined together completely, early in their independent history, as the Central American Republic, in part because their economies are basically similar—all were small (each possessed an internal market no bigger than a medium-sized U.S. city), poor, and at roughly the same stage of development. CACM's basic goals were gradually to eliminate intraregional trade barriers, to move toward a common external tariff, and to establish a zonal central bank payments system and "integration industries" (industries requiring large plants with heavy capital investment, such as a paper pulp mill or an automobile tire factory, which were arbitrarily allocated to different countries because all five countries taken together could support only one plant). This program quickly became controversial both within the CACM and in the United States. All the countries wanted the same industries. The United States opposed the whole idea on the ground that it created monopolies, froze out other private investors, and—an ideological argument—interfered with the free market. The United States refused to lend money for "integration industries" and even blocked loans to them at the World Bank and IADB. No such industry was established until the mid-1960s, when the U.S. attitude softened and the CACM resolved internal differences.

Nevertheless, even at the outset, the CACM was highly successful. Exports of member countries to their CACM partners rose from only 7 percent of their total foreign trade in 1960 to 25 percent in 1968, a compound annual growth rate of more than 28 percent. Of the total expansion, moreover, nearly 75 percent was in manufactured or semimanufactured goods and only about a fourth in food or minerals. By 1968, CACM took 17.1 percent of Nicaragua's total exports, 17.5 percent of Honduras's, 22.2 percent of Costa Rica's, 34.9 percent of Guatemala's, and 39.8 percent of El Salvador's. And all five countries came to depend on the CACM for a large share of their imports: Guatemala for 19.8 percent, Costa Rica for 22.8 percent, Nicaragua for 24.9 percent, Honduras for 26.3 percent, and El Salvador for 30.4 percent. Yet this huge increase in intraregional trade did not seriously affect trade between the CACM and the United States— the share of CACM imports from the U.S. declined only slightly, from 49.8 percent in 1963 to 46.3 percent in 1969.[14] Economic integration strongly attracted foreign private investment; the flow of outside capital to the countries more than tripled between 1960 and 1968, the annual rate going from $20 million to more than $60 million. This investment capital was supplemented by lending from the new Central American Bank for Economic Integration, which by 1968 had approved loans totaling $120 million, about half to the private sector for industrial projects and half to the government sector for transportation, communications, and power development. The United States has made ten loans to the Central American Bank totaling $182.5 million. As a result of trade liberalization, increased investment, and an export boom, income grew rapidly.

But by 1969, the CACM was encountering serious problems. Rates of growth, both in trade and GNP, slowed drastically; they had reached a plateau. Regional industrial policies had stagnated, protection of infant industries was too high and encouraged inefficient producers, policies regarding agricultural products conflicted, and the members disagreed on "rules of origin"—how to determine the percentage of local content in manufactures. Moreover, Guatemala and El Salvador enjoyed a trade surplus at the expense of deficits for Costa Rica, Nicaragua, and Honduras. Negotiations to reform the CACM began. In July 1969, in the midst of negotiations, armed conflict broke out between Honduras and El Salvador. The OAS restored military peace but not economic peace; when the CACM sought to establish a special fund to help Nicaragua and Honduras in the Central American Bank, El Salvador blocked it and prevented CACM reorganization until Honduras opened the Inter-American Highway to traffic from El Salvador. In retaliation, late in 1970, Honduras, again faced with a rising trade deficit, imposed duties on CACM imports and demanded a thorough restructuring of the CACM before resuming participation. Two separate four-country markets began to form, with the three neutrals joining El Salvador in one market and Honduras in the other.

Despite all these problems, the overall volume of intraregional trade continues to grow. Imports reached a record $525 million in 1974, an increase of nearly 1500 percent from the $33 million at the start of CACM in 1960. The CACM has been crucial to Central America's growth. Within the four-country market including El

Salvador, more than 93 percent of all items in the intercountry tariff schedules are exempt from duty. Progress toward a common external tariff has been even greater—it now covers about 99 percent of all items in the schedule. The Central American Bank has grown, and by June 1973, it had approved 385 loans for $406 million, of which 61 percent went for infrastructure, 28 percent for industry, and 11 percent for housing. Nearly everyone agrees that although the CACM faces serious problems, it has increased trade within Central America without unduly disturbing Central America's trade relations with the United States; it has created employment and expanded industrial output; and it has successfully promoted economic growth.

The Caribbean Community and Caribbean Common Market (CARICOM) includes "the big four" of the black English-speaking Caribbean—Barbados, Guyana, Jamaica, and Trinidad-Tobago—plus smaller black English-speaking places—Belize and the seven Leeward and Windward Islands. (These last seven have also formed the Eastern Caribbean Common Market, a subregional group within CARICOM.) Although its forebears go back to the late 1950s, CARICOM did not come into being until August 1973. Guyana, Jamaica, and Trinidad-Tobago achieved a virtually complete common external tariff by August 1973; Barbados was given until August 1976, and Belize and the small islands longer. The Caribbean Development Bank, set up primarily to help develop the smaller and poorer Caribbean countries, began operations in 1970. Its members include, besides the members of CARICOM, the Bahamas and the smaller commonwealth territories of the British Virgin Islands, the Cayman Islands, and the Turks and Caicos Islands, the United Kingdom, and Canada. Colombia and Venezuela joined as non-borrowing members. The United States, while not a member, has made it three soft loans totaling $32.2 million; Canada and the United Kingdom have also made loans. As of December 31, 1974, the Caribbean Development Bank had approved loans of $86.4 million, mostly for infrastructure in the poorer states. Disbursements have been slow. The leaders of smaller member nations, including Antigua and Grenada, have complained that the bank is slow and unreliable in making loans. The bank, however, feels that the blame lies with the borrowing countries themselves.

CARICOM has not enjoyed the spectacular early successes of

the CACM. Caribbean intraregional trade still constitutes only a small fraction of total trade. In 1969, the imports of CARICOM (then called CARIFTA) member countries from other member countries were 3.9 percent of total imports, in 1974, 6.4 percent. The "big four" continue to dominate intraregional trade both in volume (81 percent of intraregional imports in 1968, 96 percent in 1972) and rate of growth (77 percent in 1968-1970 compared to 35 percent for the smaller members).

One of CARICOM's purposes is to coordinate the foreign policies of the members, who feel that, acting together, they can increase their bargaining power with the outside world, that is, with the United States, the EEC, and the multinational corporations. Member nations established a Standing Committee of Ministers responsible for foreign affairs, whose recommendations must be unanimous, but are not binding on any member. At UN conferences on the Law of the Sea, the CARICOM members—nearly all islands—try to present a single position. They also hoped to present common positions at other international meetings.

Although Venezuela, in economic integration as in everything else, looks to the Caribbean, it keeps an anchor to the south: it is simultaneously a member of the Caribbean Development Bank and the Latin American Free Trade Association (LAFTA), and, more importantly, of the Andean Group. The Andean Subregional Integration Agreement was signed in 1969 by Colombia, Ecuador, Peru, Bolivia, and Chile; Venezuela joined later. The Andean Group was formed because of disappointment in LAFTA. The Andean countries felt they were more homogeneous than the unwieldy South American-Mexican LAFTA and could integrate subregionally more easily, leaving continent-wide integration until later. The Andean Group took three basic approaches to integration: (1) joint planning of industrial development and harmonization of economic and social policies, (2) increased intrazonal trade through tariff reductions, and (3) preferential treatment for Bolivia and Ecuador, the poorest of the group. The four largest powers are to eliminate trade barriers among the group and to adopt a common external tariff by the end of 1980; Bolivia and Ecuador are to do this by 1985. The group provides an arrangement similar to that of the "integration industries" of the CACM. It establishes an Andean Foreign Investment Code that will by 1986 (1993 for Bolivia and Ecuador) reduce foreign ownership in most enterprises to no more than 49 percent equity, will forbid foreign investment in areas already covered by local investors, and will forbid foreign purchase of local companies. (Caribbean businessmen frequently complain that the monetary power of the U.S. multinationals virtually forces them to sell out.) Other restrictions apply to foreign banks, insurance companies, radio, television, and newspaper publishing.

Trade among the Andean countries increased only moderately from 1969 to 1973, the year of OPEC. The next year, however, seemed not only to increase the dollar value of the oil trade but of other products as well. Preliminary 1974 data indicated that trade among the Andean countries was nearly 380 percent over 1969, exports among the nations was $170 million in 1969 and $817 million in 1974, including oil. Even without oil, the figures were $104 million in 1969 and $411 million in 1974. And trade with the United States does not appear to have suffered. On the whole, economic progress has been somewhat slow. Nonetheless, the Andean Group is the most dynamic integration movement on the South American continent. It has acquired a certain political importance—if Pérez of Venezuela wants to become the leader of Latin America, he can hardly neglect regional economic integration.

The U.S. attitude toward economic integration is complex. Integration was listed as one of the original goals of the Alliance for Progress in 1961. In 1964, integration was one of the few conclusions reached by UNCTAD that the United States felt it could support. In 1965, President Johnson, citing the success of widened markets in Europe, said, "We must try to draw the economies of Latin America much closer together," and in 1967, he signed a declaration calling for the creation of a Latin American common market no later than 1985. (It is still a vague dream.) In 1969, President Nixon declared that the United States "stands ready to help" Latin American integration. In 1973, in Lima, Peru, Secretary of State Rogers told members of the Andean Group that the United States supported all such economic integration movements. From time to time, the United States has made loans to the Andean Development Corporation, the Central American Bank for Economic Integration, and the Caribbean Development Bank.

Nevertheless, since economic integration requires a large amount of state economic planning, the United States feels intuitively and ideologically uncomfortable with it. The relationship between the United States and Latin America had traditionally been based on bilateral political relations and support of U.S. private investment in Latin America. In the early 1960s, American businessmen, suspecting that Latin American integration would hurt them, persuaded the U.S. government to fight proposals for "integration industries." After a time, however, the failure of the Alliance to spur rapid growth and the increasing reluctance of Congress to appropriate money for aid led the United States to a reassessment. As a result, the United States began to lean toward the view that integration did offer the best hope of stimulating the stagnant Latin American economies. Economic integration did not appear to damage U.S. trade; in fact, it seemed to create trade, not divert it, as had been feared. Even U.S. businessmen began to invest in developing Central America. In 1976, as CARICOM moved to a common external tariff, the *Wall Street Journal* reported that U.S. firms expected to benefit, since the new tariff would remove the British Commonwealth advantage.

The future of Caribbean (and Latin American) integration is uncertain. It faces problems not encountered by Europeans in their successful efforts. Western European economies were highly diversified and exported manufactured goods; Caribbean economies are simple and export primary commodities. Intraregional trade had always been highly important in Europe, which possessed well-integrated transportation and communications systems. The Caribbean had neither the trade nor the systems. Europe possessed a huge pool of highly skilled workers and a thick layer of highly educated and experienced managers and bureaucrats; the Caribbean did not. In other words, European success by no means guarantees Caribbean success; many uncertainties lie ahead.

Economic adversity—and American refusal to open up its own markets—could push the integrated economies to look inward and erect high protective tariff walls around inefficient producers. It could push them toward policies that would divert, not create, trade.

Intense Caribbean political nationalism may subvert economic integration—although, significantly, many young leftists appear to favor it. The relationship between CARICOM and the Spanish, French, and Dutch Caribbean is uncertain. Some Caribbean leaders believe Puerto Rico, Haiti, and the Dominican Republic should join CARICOM, and moves are afoot to bring Cuba into CARICOM, an important decision. A few leftist nationalists—but only a few—envision a full-fledged "Caribbean state," integrated economically and politically, independent and aligned with neither the United States nor the Soviet Union nor Venezuela and, in fifty years, playing an increasingly important role midway between the United States and Brazil, which they see as a future world power.

The United States could take a number of different positions on economic integration. First, we could reverse course and oppose integration. The only obvious reason for doing so would be the fear that an integrated Caribbean would close us out, deny its market to us. This is unlikely—the United States can supply many products better and more efficiently than the Caribbean, and U.S. companies are well-established there and unlikely to be eliminated even though they lose their majority position. United States trade with the Caribbean will alter as the Caribbean industrializes; it is unlikely to disappear.

Second, we could continue our present policy, which is, essentially, to provide verbal and moral support for integration without really doing much beyond occasional modest loans.

Third, we could actively and tangibly support integration. We could do so in several ways. The United States could lend more money to the Caribbean and Central American integration movements. We could open our own vast market to some of their manufactured products, especially products that are labor-intensive and low-technology. We could learn how to move our own labor out of low-skill, labor-intensive industries, such as textiles, clothing, and shoes, and into high-technology, capital-intensive industries. To do so, we would no doubt need to pay subsidies to U.S. labor-intensive industries as they phase themselves out.[15] The United States could help establish a Caribbean-wide school, or cluster of schools, to train Caribbean engineers, managers, and skilled labor. Caribbean educators have accumulated experience in regionwide education through the University of the West Indies; indeed, it was established long before CARICOM. Moreover, the United States could channel a high percentage of aid to regional, rather than national, purposes— to such projects as international highway links, integration industries, telecommunications networks, technical research, and electric power development serving more than one country (Honduras, for example, is undertaking a hydroelectric plant financed by the Central American Bank and capable of generating more electricity than Honduras alone needs). In doing so, the United States would extend a policy it already pursues on a small scale: that of giving aid to Central America regionally rather than country by country.

The United States should give additional and tangible support for integration only if the Caribbean nations want us to. We should not exert either political or economic pressure to force these countries into integration. Rather, we should offer assistance that they are entirely free to accept or reject. And we should take care not to dominate or appear to dominate. Political gain at the United Nations and elsewhere might be a result, but we should not exact it as the price of our assistance. This third alternative—additional and tangible support for integration—seems the policy most consistent with our professed ideals and our tradition of assistance to poor nations. The continued development—and friendship—of the Caribbean countries is assuredly in our long-term interest.

8
SUMMARY AND POLICY
RECOMMENDATIONS

The United States is linked to the Caribbean by history, by tradition, and, above all, by geography. When Jefferson looked south, he looked not to South America but to the Caribbean. The United States may differ with certain Caribbean nations on ideology or on economic issues, but neither we nor they can escape geography. In all the world only two other places occupy the same geographical position relative to us—Canada and Mexico—and the Caribbean needs our friendly attention, our understanding, and our assistance more than they. Tourists view the Caribbean as islands in the sun, politicians see the Panama Canal as an issue in our domestic politics, the press pays attention only during such crises as our military interventions. Only when the president takes the Caribbean seriously does our policy take it seriously.

It is the underlying thesis of this book that the United States has vitally important economic, political, and strategic interests in the Caribbean; that we have neglected the Caribbean for at least a decade; that during that time much of the Caribbean has been transforming itself radically; that it has been detaching itself from us politically and making economic demands on us, some of them legitimate, to which we have responded inadequately; and that it is now time to adopt a whole new set of Caribbean policies. Although we have had no policy toward the Caribbean, we have not yet "lost" it entirely—if indeed it was ever ours to lose.

Our major interests in the Caribbean are strategic, political, and economic.

Our Strategic Interests. In the age of jet bombers and nuclear missiles, the Caribbean may be less vital to our defense than in Admiral Mahan's day. Nevertheless, it remains of great importance. If it came under the rule or pervading influence of a foreign power hostile to us, it could be used as a base from which to launch offensive operations against our mainland. Furthermore, only by crossing the Caribbean can we obtain such raw materials as bauxite and oil, vital to us in peace or war. The Caribbean is an important seaborne logistic route as well as a vital link in world trade routes, and through it and the Panama Canal we resupply our own West Coast and the west coast of South America. (We can and should agree to a new treaty with Panama on the Canal, but any such treaty must guarantee us unrestricted passage through it.) In time of high world tensions or conventional warfare, control of the Caribbean would be vital. In case of nuclear war, most strategists think the Caribbean would be of little importance; but despite the best efforts of contingency planners, the shape of future wars is never certain. It is only prudent to regard a friendly Caribbean as extremely important strategically—at least as important as a friendly Canada or Mexico.

Our Political Interests. We have always considered it our primary political purpose in the Caribbean to prevent the encroachment there of an inimical European power. Theodore Roosevelt resisted Germany; Eisenhower, Kennedy, and Johnson resisted Russia. Thus our primary political purpose has been based at bottom on strategic considerations. This remains an important political interest of ours. In addition, from time to time, we have tried to encourage the growth of freedom and representative democracy in the Caribbean, in part to strengthen our ties for strategic reasons but also out of higher motives: to extend what we like to think of as the blessings of freedom and democracy to what we like to think of as our family of neighbors. Today, as many Caribbean countries move increasingly toward statism and even authoritarianism, this purpose seems nearly hopeless. Yet it retains an interest for us. And we have a third and a highly important political interest: to behave in the Caribbean in such a way as to enhance our prestige around the world. Any great power is judged in part by the opinion its closest neighbors hold of it. Of late the Caribbean countries have been voting against us in the OAS, UN, and other international forums. Such a course, if unchecked, may seriously undermine our worldwide prestige. We could take two steps now to enhance our political position in the Caribbean: normalize our relations with Cuba and conclude a new Canal treaty with Panama. Neither would in any way compromise our strategic interests. Both would shore up our declining prestige. Our stubborn refusal to negotiate a new and equitable Canal treaty has seriously damaged our prestige in the Caribbean, South America, and around the world. Cuba, having resumed relations with Caribbean countries, aspires to their leadership and is making headway, which is hardly in our political interest.

Our Economic Interests. In recent years, U.S. private direct investment in the Caribbean has been declining precipitously as one after another Caribbean nation has nationalized or taken a controlling interest in such large U.S. enterprises as bauxite mining and oil production. Nevertheless, the remaining U.S. investment is still large and remains an important interest of ours. Moreover, it appears likely that U.S. corporations will increasingly sell their technology, managerial experience, access to markets, and other expertise to Caribbean governments unable to manage the complex industries they have taken over. This trend has already begun and, if carried further, will create a new economic interest of ours. And it seems unlikely that U.S. merchandisers will abandon or be shut out of the Caribbean market. Nor is it probable that a more distant nation will soon if ever replace us as the Caribbean's foremost trading partner. So the stake of U.S. private investment in the Caribbean will not be inconsiderable. Aside from that, we have a vital interest in obtaining Caribbean raw materials—oil, bauxite, other minerals, and certain primary agricultural products. In a time of nascent economic nationalism, raw materials become increasingly important.

So much for our interests. What do the Caribbean nations want from us?

They want us to pay attention to them. But they want us to stop interfering in their internal politics. They want to be free of us politically and economically. Politically, they want to make common cause with the rest of the Third World. They insist that we allow them to develop their economic and political systems as they wish; they cannot see why it is our business if they choose to manage their economies centrally rather than through the free market. Economically—and this is the heart of their demands—they want us to reform and make more equitable the terms of trade. True, they want to break what they consider the stranglehold of the multinational corporations, they want to nationalize their natural resources and the industries based on them, they want our private investment on a minority equity basis in joint ventures, they want to diversify and develop their economies, they want multilateral, not bilateral, aid and loans, they want regional economic integration, they want a voice in reform of the international monetary system, they want to redistribute their internal wealth more equitably among their people. But above all they demand that we improve the terms of trade.

At bottom, that means two things: give them free access to our markets for their manufactured and semimanufactured goods; change the system that forces them to sell raw materials to us cheaply while paying dearly for our manufactured goods. If we do this, they say, we will narrow the gap between rich and poor nations and bring about a new world economic order. All this is proceeding under great difficulty. For, with a few notable exceptions, the Caribbean nations seem to be heading, in desperation, toward an ungainly one-party statism. Partly because the development policies of the Alliance for Progress did not meet their expectations, with the result that unemployment remains chronic and high while wealth remains inequitably distributed; partly because of the inherent weakness of raw-material economies (they are shackled to a few commodities with fluctuating world prices); partly because they are ever propelled by pride and nationalism; and for a host of other reasons, most of these countries seem to be in a state of political demoralization, with little but instability ahead. If some seem to be taking Cuba, not Puerto Rico, for their model, it is less out of considered political judgment than out of desperation, out of a sense of not knowing where to turn next before the deluge. This makes them doubly difficult to deal with.

The Caribbean peoples are puzzled and embittered to find that their lot has not been much changed by the independence their leaders so eloquently assert. Just as their leaders formerly blamed their plight on colonialism, now they blame it on imperialism, neo-colonialism, world capitalism, and exploitation of the poor by the rich. The bogey of a foreign foe may help keep down domestic turmoil and give the leaders time for maneuver, but it will hardly stimulate serious consideration of the following central question: regardless of what economic system they adopt, and considering the human and natural resources available, what can soberly and realistically be expected for these unhappy and underendowed lands? The great leap forward to utopia exists only in politicians' speeches. The most that can probably be achieved is steady upward movement under stable conditions. If we are to play a part in this, it will have to be in an atmosphere of mutual trust, if not goodwill. Demagogic denunciations of the Yankee predator by Caribbean leaders are of no more help than moralistic lectures on free enterprise by our own leaders.

Can our interests and those of the Caribbean states be resolved?

Any accommodation must be based on mutual self-interest. We share certain common ground with the Caribbean countries. We do not want them to fall under the domination of an extra-hemisphere power but want them to maintain their independence. They agree. We want to defend them militarily against outside aggression (in order to defend ourselves). With some reservations, they agree. We want to buy their raw materials and sell them our manufactures, want to remain their natural and foremost trading partner. They agree (though on their terms, not ours; "the terms" is the principal issue between us). We want them to develop and to improve their people's lot, since we believe that development in all its aspects leads to stability, and that without stability the peace is in danger. They agree. We want to expand private U.S. investment in the Caribbean countries. They agree (but only on a minority equity basis—whether this will work remains to be seen). We want them to integrate their economies regionally. They agree. We have benefited in the past from cultural and educational exchange with the Caribbean countries. So have they. We and they share certain traditions and the intangible but undeniable heritage of belonging to the New World. Despite transitory difficulties, we are old friends. Finally, and forever, we and they occupy the same part of the globe, and if proximity sometimes breeds conflict, so does it also command accommodation. We need the Caribbean, and the Caribbean needs us.

All this is a considerable mass of material to build on. Surely our prospects of reaching mutual understanding and solid cooperation with the Caribbean are better than with, say, Southeast Asia. More than forty years ago, Franklin Roosevelt reversed decades of Latin American resentment with his Good Neighbor policy. Aside from nonintervention, that policy included the Exim Bank and Reciprocal Trade Agreements. By making extensive use of them, Latin America prospered. Today they demand something similar in the name of justice and for the purpose of development. In our own long-range interest, we must respond. We must alter the terms of trade and adopt other economic measures to meet the legitimate economic demands of the Caribbean countries. It will not be easy. Some of their economic demands are wrongheaded, some are unrealistic. Central economic planning may not succeed if a complex economic infrastructure is lacking. (The Jamaican government found it easy to take over supermarkets, far harder to establish a distribution system that would stock them; the Venezuelan government may find it easy to double or triple steel production, hard to move steel to market without heavy trucks or even roads that will carry heavy trucks.) Some states simply lack the size and the resources necessary to full economic development; nobody really knows what the mini-states can do. Even larger countries will make serious mistakes—and they have little margin for error. Their and our objectives are not entirely clear. They know what they *don't* want—outside domination, economic underdevelopment and poverty—and we know what we don't want for them—roughly the same things. But neither of us knows with equal precision what we *do* want or how to get it. Helping them realize their legitimate aspirations will cost us money, how much is hard to say. It may cause us difficulties with South American countries; we shall have to adjust policies there. It may make trouble for the administration in the Congress and in domestic politics; only presidential leadership can deal with that. It will require all the courage and magnanimity and long-range vision one expects of a great nation. If we do it, we may find that the Caribbean countries will welcome a revival of our interest in them and will close the gulfs that separate us on other issues and that, in the long run, our relationship with them will be healthier than in the past.

*   *   *

It is far harder to devise policies for the Caribbean today than at the height of the Cold War. Nor can their expense be justified to the American people today on the ground of anticommunism. We can, of course, continue to follow the Nixon-Ford policy of neglect. It seems safe to predict that the ultimate result will be bitterness and anti-Americanism. We would not be comfortable, we might not even be safe, with a Caribbean filled with poverty-stricken, resentful, and hostile people. We had best heed such men of much experience and wisdom as Teodoro Moscoso when they say, as Moscoso did recently, "The Latin Americans resent us now as never before in my lifetime."

No set of policies is ever wholly new. Some of the following proposals are adapted from policies of the past, especially from the Alliance for Progress. Others break new ground. The United States government, in its executive and congressional branches, should now consider the following.

1. *We should develop a truly special relationship with the Caribbean, a relationship separate and distinct even from our relationship with the rest of Latin America.*[1] We should take a national decision that the development of our neighbors in the Caribbean toward peaceful and progressive societies in which their citizens can look forward to a better life is in the vital interest of the United States. We should place that interest high up on our list of priorities, perhaps in fourth or fifth place or right after the survival of Israel. We should determine as a nation that we will devote the resources and the energy necessary to make our own backyard secure and an example to the world of what a great power can do to help its neighbors. To these ends we should develop a truly special relationship—and it should be as close a relationship as the Caribbean states wish. This is the fundamental recommendation of this book. From it flows nearly every other recommendation. We should undertake it only after careful and close consultation with the Caribbean countries themselves. It will require a presidential decision. In making it, the president should consult Congress. Once

he has made it, he should support State against Treasury, Agriculture, Commerce, and other executive departments that may oppose it. This special relationship should entail close and continuing co-operation with the Caribbean states on political, economic, strategic, and social issues of mutual concern. It should be aimed at maintaining our mutual security; at concerting our positions in world and regional forums; at promoting the Caribbean countries' development through special aid from us, through helping them process their own raw materials, and through opening our trade market to them on a preferential basis; at ensuring our access to their raw materials at fair and stabilized prices and ultimately at enlarging their markets for our goods; at helping attack poverty, misery, and injustice in the Caribbean and asking in return nothing more than friendship. This special relationship must take into account our global policies and interests but should attempt as far as possible to insulate the Caribbean from them. Our aim should not be hegemony. Rather, it should be to respond to their needs and ours—the true, sovereign, and dignified interdependence of good neighbors.[2]

2. *Without fanfare, the president should appoint, with rank of ambassador, a special deputy assistant secretary of state for the Caribbean.* (If, as President Nixon and others have proposed, Congress should decide to elevate the assistant secretary for ARA to undersecretary rank, an assistant secretary for the Caribbean should serve under him. But this change seems both unlikely and unwise.)

3. *The assistant secretary for ARA should quietly detach a group of experienced, thoughtful officers from the handling of day-to-day affairs, constitute them a policy planning staff for ARA, and charge them with responsibility for studying and planning future policies.* They should address themselves urgently to developing a policy toward the associated states and other emerging mini-states in the Caribbean [see pp. 229ff], as well as toward Guyana, Surinam, and French Guiana, the inflammable former three Guianas.[3] (Too often problems take us by surprise, for we have been so preoccupied with the pressures of today that we have neglected to look to tomorrow, and often we are slow to react, with the result that we end up after bitter confrontation doing grudgingly what we could have done gracefully at the outset.) To avoid being insulated from day-to-day realities, the planners should visit the Caribbean often and should there consult not only our ambassadors and CIA station chiefs but also their senior staff members and, in addition, local people of every sort—not merely government officials and opposition politicians but also labor leaders,

businessmen, farmers, editors and publishers, intellectuals, military men, and others. To make the planners' papers operational, the deputy assistant secretary should feed them for consideration into the action line running through the ambassadors, desk officers, area officers, and the assistant secretary.

4. *The State Department and the president, in consultation with Congress, must control our Caribbean policy* to the exclusion or subordination of other governmental agencies and outside interests.

5. *The State Department should improve its relations with the Congress.* To that end, the secretary should appoint in each geographic bureau (including ARA) a substantive man with ambassadorial rank, preferably not a bureaucrat but a man with political experience and even with some political base of his own, to keep the key members of the Senate and House informed of approaching crises and of State Department policy and its rationale. When important steps are to be taken, such as normalizing relations with Cuba, he should not only inform but also consult members of Congress informally well in advance. He should constantly encourage members to visit the Caribbean; nothing promotes understanding more than on-the-spot observation. The president should send key members of both houses of Congress and of both political parties as part of our delegations to important hemisphere conferences. The White House and the Congress should make staff studies of a proposal by Benjamin V. Cohen to institutionalize the State-Congress flow of information—a commission of eight (two from the House, two from the Senate, four from the executive branch) empowered to exchange information and views on foreign policy [pp. 122ff].

6. *We should learn to live with socialist or statist societies in the Caribbean,* setting up new governmental machinery to trade with them if necessary.

7. *We should dispose of the three currently cutting issues in the Caribbean*— a new Panama Canal treaty, normalization of relations with Cuba, and the OPEC proviso of the Trade Act of 1974. These three issues are largely symbolic, and the first two are anachronistic. But until we clear the decks of them, our Caribbean policies cannot succeed. Accordingly, as soon as possible, *we should*: (a) *sign and ratify a new Canal treaty* negotiated under the guidelines already agreed to [pp. 146ff], (b) *initiate movement toward normalizing our relations with Cuba*, recognizing that the process will take time and that many important issues must be resolved, perhaps along such lines as these: fair compensation for nationalized U.S. property, resolution of human

rights issues (including broken families and political prisoners), agreement to end all foreign (both Soviet and American) bases, troops, and military installations on Cuban soil, an exchange of pledges of nonintervention (we will not invade Cuba, Cuba will not export revolution within or outside the hemisphere, including Africa), resumed trade [pp. 205ff], and (c) *Congress should remove the OPEC proviso from the Trade Act of 1974 or exempt the Caribbean from its application* [pp. 193ff].

8. *We should recognize the considerable elements of justice in the Caribbean's Third World complaint about the terms of trade.* We should go somewhat further than the Kissinger proposals of September 1, 1975 [pp. 182ff], and press for producer-consumer agreements on those commodities that lend themselves to such agreements, establishing machinery to stabilize the prices the Caribbean countries receive and obtaining from them agreement to guarantee our access to their commodities at fair prices. (Negotiating "fair prices" would not be easy, considering the pressures of U.S. consumers and Caribbean producers; but with mutual goodwill and trust, it should not prove impossible.) With respect to the more developed Caribbean countries, we should encourage trade by helping them process their raw materials and by eliminating or at least reducing as far as possible tariffs (and other barriers) on their manufactured and semi-manufactured products, paying subsidies where necessary to injured domestic producers in lieu of giving foreign aid; with respect to the less-developed and poorer Caribbean countries, we should increase our aid. (For detailed recommendations, see pp. 188ff.) If we do not improve the terms of trade and promote and participate in producer-consumer commodity agreements, we risk social storms that would wreck stability and might even endanger the peace.

9. *We should not choose between bilateral and multilateral aid, nor between aid and trade, but should use all four*—concessional bilateral aid for humanitarian and political purposes (short-term budget support to such foundering countries as Jamaica, large-scale development assistance in certain cases); multilateral aid for development projects; in general, aid for the less-developed and poorer countries, trade for the advanced [pp. 260ff]. We should untie aid. We should limit grants to repairing natural disasters and dealing with such special political situations as the Dominican Republic after the fall of Trujillo.

10. *Our aid should in most places emphasize agriculture, education, energy, and technology.* But it should respond to those countries' needs, not to our views. We should help them to increase agricultural production now. We should leave it to each country to decide whether to postpone structural agrarian reform—more equitable land tenure systems—until later. Each country should undertake such reform only to the extent it wishes [pp. 234ff], though we should encourage and assist in reform if it wishes. In concert with them, we should establish areawide schools to train managers, administrators, and policy-makers for work in government, in government-owned industries, and in private industries; we should also work with them to establish vocational schools, including training for employment in industry, government service, and especially agriculture [pp. 159ff, 263ff].

11. *We should strengthen our encouragement and help of Caribbean regional economic integration,* offering technical assistance and loaning money to the Caribbean Development Bank and similar institutions, but only if they want it and can demonstrate a need for it and an ability to use it wisely [pp. 267ff]. (We might, however, offer help toward federation that the associated mini-states could not refuse.)

12. *We should promote the transfer of technology to the Caribbean through both private industry and AID.* This should include solar power and other energy sources. One would think that if solar energy is feasible anywhere on earth, it would be feasible in the year-round sun-drenched Caribbean.

13. *We should continue to encourage responsible and constructive private American capital to invest in the Caribbean—on terms satisfactory to the Caribbean.* But the Caribbean countries' sovereign right to own their own natural resources must override our interest in protecting private enterprise, provided compensation is fair and prompt. Nationalized U.S. companies—and not the U.S. government—should negotiate their settlements with the Caribbean states. We should encourage private U.S. industry to sell technology to the Caribbean without equity [pp. 191ff]. We should resist economic nationalism and protectionism in the United States. We should not overpromote tourism and should recognize its dangers [pp. 264ff].

14. *We should get our multinational corporations under control.* This is a two-way street: multinationals should obey our laws and those of the countries they operate in; those countries should treat them fairly

and consistently. We may well want to join other nations at the UN, both rich and poor, in developing a code of ethics for multinational–poor country relations. But we should recognize that such a code is not enforceable and could become meaningless. Therefore, the Congress should make it a crime in the United States to bribe a foreign official—a crime punishable by imprisonment. (The language of such a law would have to be carefully drawn to avoid circumvention through such devices as the payment of exorbitant "commissions" or "fees," and it should make companies' highest executives liable.) In keeping an eye on corporate behavior [pp. 217ff], State might work more closely with the Attorney General and and the Securities and Exchange Commission than it has.

15. *We should stay in the OAS and try to strengthen it.* It is sometimes said we should not remain in an organization where we are constantly criticized. Instead of leaving, we should change the policies that are criticized when complaints are just—of late, the Canal Treaty, Cuba, and the Trade Act [pp. 244ff]. We should seek to cooperate with SELA [pp. 246ff].

16. *At the UN, we should try to persuade the Caribbean nations to consider resolutions on their merits,* from the point of view of the Caribbean nations' own intersts, and not automatically to vote with either us or Algeria. Our ambassadors in each Caribbean country should push the same line in their capitals [pp. 197ff].

17. *We should work with them to develop common positions on global issues* that directly affect them and us, such as the Law of the Sea [pp. 237ff].

18. *We should encourage Venezuela and Mexico to assert themselves as Caribbean powers.* They could be a counterweight to Cuba and Brazil—and indeed to us: they could take up part of our burdens [pp. 154ff, 246ff].

19. *We should single out certain key countries in the Caribbean*—perhaps Venezuela, Mexico, Jamaica, and Panama—and strengthen our bilateral relations with them, though more quietly than Kissinger attempted with Brazil.

20. *The president and secretary should send no ambassador to a Caribbean country who is not qualified for the job.* Those countries are too important to us to entrust to campaign contributors and political cronies.

21. *The CIA.* Congress appears bent, at this writing, on getting the CIA's covert activities under control through legislation,

probably providing closer congressional oversight. The president and secretary of state could help by making it clear that everything we do in another country, including the CIA's covert activities, shall be done only with the approval of our ambassador. This makes the ambassador—and hence ultimately the man he represents, the president—responsible for the CIA's covert activities. In case of disagreement between an ambassador and the CIA station chief, the White House should decide [pp. 215ff]. The CIA should sever all connections with overseas U.S. corporations.

22. *We should cooperate, if requested to do so, in birth control programs* [pp. 262ff].

23. To the extent politically possible, *we should liberalize our immigration laws and regulations* [pp. 235ff]. Perhaps more important, we should recognize that the illegal immigrants already among us constitute a frightened, furtive, unstable population; *we should confer legality upon them.*

24. *We should relinquish military bases in the Caribbean if we must—before they become overwhelmingly damaging to us politically,* as they already are in Panama but are not in Puerto Rico; *and, if we need them, we should seek alternative bases* (e.g., in the Dominican Republic to replace Guantánamo [pp. 139ff].

25. *We should maintain our strong naval presence in the Caribbean.* We should continue or resume military training, intelligence gathering, and sales (and in a few cases aid) [pp. 140ff].

26. *The State Department should increase its efforts to educate the American people—and the Congress—on the importance and wisdom of our Caribbean policies.* They cannot forever be justified as necessary to the Cold War. They should be justified on their merits—that they advance our national interests.

27. *We should take a number of other steps*—pay our arrearage at the IADB; modify the nearly complete application of U.S. laws to Puerto Rico in order to give Puerto Ricans a further incentive to remain an associated state with us ("commonwealth status"); help quietly and perhaps indirectly to resolve disputes between El Salvador and Honduras, between Guatemala and Belize, and between Guyana and Venezuela and Guyana and Surinam; extradite Robert Vesco and others like him; cooperate with international and Caribbean police agencies in combatting the narcotics trade and the influence of U.S. organized crime on Caribbean gambling; reconstitute the Peace

Corps as it was originally established; increase cultural and educational exchange; and undertake jointly with the Caribbean nations marine research.

28. *Human Rights. We should make clear in every way possible our preference for governments that respect their citizens' human rights.* Our emphasis should be on rights rather than on representative democracy, though of course we like democracy. We can make our preference clear by such symbolic but important acts as inviting the representatives of such countries as Venezuela—but not the representatives of dictators—to White House receptions and by sending high-level officials to those countries, such as the vice-president, senators, and congressmen. We can make our preference clear more tangibly by giving those representatives access to the high levels of the State Department. And we can make it clear still more tangibly by dealing promptly and sympathetically with whatever specific problems they wish to take up with us, including their loan applications and the terms of their trade. We should also, of course, strongly support such agencies as the Inter-American Commission on Human Rights.

29. *Intervention.* Philip Bonsal has perhaps put most cogently the arguments against intervention.[4] He has said that our *influence* on other countries is a force that flows from our own achievements at home. When we have been fumbling in our approach to racial, educational, or other social problems at home, or when we have adventured abroad, as in Vietnam or the Dominican Republic, our influence diminishes. It was never so high in Latin America, Bonsal thinks, as during FDR's first two terms, when the hemisphere could plainly see our leaders coming to grips with fundamental problems, some of which were common to other nations in the hemisphere— when we were not talking about but showing "what the American people live for and . . . what they have proved willing to die for." *Influence,* Bonsal has said, can perhaps best be regarded as a lubricant that serves to smooth the asperities and reduce the frictions between countries of unequal power. It depends upon a well-founded belief by the weak in the benevolence and justice of the strong. It is difficult to achieve so long as so many small nations are pursuing the will-of-the-wisp of absolute sovereignty to do what they please when they please, however reckless they may be. Good international relations require give-and-take. *Intervention,* on the other hand, in Bonsal's view,

is the use of, or the threat to use, our power—whether military, economic, or political—in another country to secure a result that the latter, if left alone, would not have willed. The Bay of Pigs, certain actions in the Dominican intervention, such threatening devices as the Hickenlooper Amendment, overzealous protection of U.S. private interests from sovereign foreign governments, refusing to recognize or working to overthrow governments of which we do not approve, working to bolster those we do approve—all these and more are interventions, in Bonsal's view, and he considers them as dead as colonialism. Intervention, Bonsal holds, is justified only when the survival of the intervening power or the lives or any appreciable number of its citizens appear to be threatened by the actions or by the impotence of the country in which the intervention occurs. Aside from such circumstances, Bonsal wrote, our influence will grow to the extent that we turn away from war in Southeast Asia to solving the problems of our own society, as we adapt our foreign policy to our capacities, and as we seek to create conditions that will "affirm the responsibility of the governments and the people of the Latin American countries for their own destinies."

All this is true. But it leaves lingering doubts. Some years ago, while Pérez Jiménez was still dictator of Venezuela, a group of Venezuelans opposed to him approached a foreign service officer in our embassy and asked whether the United States would recognize their government if they overthrew Pérez. The officer replied that he was not speaking officially and that he was only a first secretary in the embassy, but in his opinion Washington would be out of its mind if it refused recognition. Pérez Jiménez fell. Had we intervened to overthrow him? In a certain sense, even foreign aid is intervention. Indeed, in a certain sense, we intervene constantly in the Caribbean by merely existing. Some experts have concluded that we may as well intervene politically—we will be blamed for it in any case. Talleyrand is said to have remarked, "Nonintervention is a political and metaphysical term and means about the same as intervention." Intervention is risky. No one can with certainty predict the outcome. It is also often, though not always, unwelcome. It always carries heavy responsibility. But it might be healthier all round if, instead of neglecting the Caribbean for years and then suddenly sending in troops, we intervened continuously, pursuing an activist policy as a politician does—through discussions, compromises, painstaking arrangements, symbolic gestures, giving a bit of aid quickly here, withholding it for a time there. A wise politician not only distributes Christmas baskets to the poor; he also sees to it that a poor man who is sick gets into the county hospital, that a stop sign is erected at a dangerous intersection, that a dead tree on the parkway is cut down before it falls on a child. He never resorts to force or economic power except in the most dangerous emergencies and only after all else has failed. He sees to it above all that his own interests are advanced— and not necessarily at the expense of others.

In a perfect world, no doubt we should refrain entirely from intervention in other countries' affairs; no doubt, we would be able to refrain. But the world is imperfect. And in a part of the world so close to home and so important to us, although in most times and at most places we should not intervene, it would appear inevitable that rare occasions will arise when we believe that intervention of some sort is essential—though one would hope that we would never again feel the need to intervene militarily in the Caribbean. Perhaps if we adopt a wise and truly special Caribbean policy, we will not.

APPENDIXES

APPENDIX A

Costa Rica's GDP increased 6.2 percent in real terms in 1973, a slower pace than the 7.5 percent annual average for 1970-1972 but still comparable to the rate during the 1960s and slightly more per capita since the annual population increase declined from 3.6 percent in 1963 to 2.7 percent in 1973. Preliminary estimates for 1974 indicated a much slower rate of increase, about 4.7 percent, because of the rise in oil prices, world inflation, and a drop in European demand for Costa Rican exports. Over the years, Costa Rica's government has resorted frequently to exchange and import controls; as a result, its international credit rating has deteriorated.

The Dominican Republic's GDP rose by 11.2 percent at constant prices in 1973, continuing the economic expansion begun in 1969. This growth was accompanied by social progress and by an acceleration of inflation. In 1973, per capita GDP at 1962 prices was 397 pesos ($1 = 1 peso), with an annual increase of 8.8 percent in real terms during 1969-1973. The expansion of recent years was the result of a 1966 government decision to expand the economic and social infrastructure before undertaking major social reforms and a fiscal policy of reducing the overall deficit in relation in GDP. It was also a result of a response by the private sector to opportunities created by an expansionist credit policy. Early 1974 data indicated continued rapid growth despite higher oil prices and inflation in the rich countries, both of which were partly offset by better prices for Dominican sugar, cacao, and ferro-nickel. Private investment fueled by economic expansion increased. So did foreign credits. More recently, the government has launched social programs in education, water supply, housing, electric power, rural development, and unemployment. In 1973, manufacturing generated 17.4 percent of GDP at 1962 prices. It expanded by 13 percent over 1972 and exceeded the average 11.8 percent growth of 1970-1972. The evolution of this sector, however, tended to show that the easy stage of import-substitution is reaching an end.

Guatemala's real growth rate has been increasing since 1970. In 1973, GDP grew 7.6 percent compared to 7.3 percent in 1972 and to an annual average of 6.5 percent between 1970 and 1972. Expansion resulted from a sharp rise in the value of exports and a real increase of 27 percent in capital investment. The GDP per capita has risen more slowly because of 3 percent per year population growth. The main economic worry was inflation—the consumer price index rose by 13.8 percent in 1973, and by a further 5.6 percent in the first five months of 1974. This compares sharply with a total rise of only 6.6 percent for the five years from 1967 to 1972. The government adopted a policy of domestic controls whose results are as yet unknown, including export licenses in basic goods considered necessary to meet internal demands, price controls on basic commodities, subsidies for petroleum products used in industry, and frozen rents. The long-term economic effects of the 1976 earthquake cannot yet be measured either. Value added in manufacturing was 16 percent of GDP in 1973; the best-performing industries were foods, beverages, tobacco, footwear, garments, and chemical products. The tax structure continues to rest on indirect taxes, especially those on foreign trade, alcohol, petroleum derivatives, and stamp taxes. Such taxes are easy to collect but are more likely to introduce distortions into the economy than direct taxes. In the absence of well-developed savings institutions, the concentration of wealth in Guatemala has provided capital for investment. The climate and scenery have attracted a substantial tourist industry.

Haiti's economy has improved somewhat since the late 1960s. Real GDP grew at an annual rate of 5.3 percent from 1970 to 1973, compared to an average of less than 1 percent from 1963 to 1967. Investment expenditure was the single most important factor in recent growth, increasing at an annual average of 28 percent between 1970 and 1973. The private sector provided the bulk of total investment to finance expansion. Manufacturing has been growing at an annual average of 18 percent since 1970, notably in cement output, sugar refining, and small-scale manufacturing. Private industry is divided into two parts: assembly operations in about 200 plants producing sporting goods, electric parts, and clothing for export to the United States; and several small plants turning out such basic necessities as vegetable oils, footwear, and textiles for the domestic market. Tourism has been increasing—the number of visitors to Haiti rose from about 65,000 in 1970 to 168,000 in 1973. Further expansion is hampered by inadequate facilities and a limited transport network. Haiti's attractiveness to tourists—its exotic culture, spectacular scenery, and highly original art—is perhaps its greatest asset. Nevertheless, with 4.5 million largely illiterate people living on 10,700 square miles of mountainous eroded land, Haiti's future looks grim.

Honduras's economy expanded at an average annual rate of 4.6 percent from 1970 to 1973. Population growth of 3.5 percent, however, reduced growth of per capita GDP to 1.1 percent. In 1973, per capita GDP was only $315, one of the lowest in Latin America. Foreign exchange reserves seemed sure to decline because of high oil prices and trouble in the banana industry. At the same time, inflation was running at 18 percent, upsetting Honduras's traditional price stability. The industrial sector contributes approximately 14 percent of GDP and gives employment to 9 percent of the labor force. Dislocation of regional trade arising out of the 1969 conflict with El Salvador resulted in a decline in industrial growth to 4 percent in 1973. In recent years, the government has given highest priority to roads and development of agriculture and timber resources, since 73 percent of the population is rural. Though Honduras's situation is by no means as hopeless as Haiti's, nevertheless, because of its mountainous terrain, poor soils, and illiterate people, it seems likely to remain one of the poorest countries in Latin America.

Jamaica's economy depends, to a large extent, on the performance of mining, tourism, and manufacturing. During 1973, the economy was subjected to great strains: lagging output in agriculture and manufacturing; severe shortages of food and raw materials ac-companied by unprecedented inflation (more than 20 percent per year); sustained pressure for wage increases; a continuing fiscal deficit; a serious deterioration in the balance of payments; and the worsening of unemployment—all in a climate of increasing political turmoil. Consequently, real GDP increased only slightly in 1973, and despite the relatively high per capita product of $799, its distribution is extremely uneven. Unemployment remains Jamaica's most pressing socioeconomic problem. Although the number of workers gainfully employed increased slightly in 1973, new entrants to the labor force offset the gains, and the jobless rate remained at around 22 percent. This situation persists despite family planning, a slow rate of population growth (1.5 percent), and emigration to the United States and Canada. Economic growth has not concentrated on the sectors absorbing the most labor but, rather, on the capital-intensive mining sector. Agricultural development is hampered by the tradition of estate agriculture dependent on subsidy, the primitive subsistence nature of the smaller farms, and the absence of good agricultural research. Nevertheless, agriculture, together with tourism, offers the best opportunity for improvement.

Belize's working population is primarily—over 50 percent—engaged in farming, and almost 75 percent of foreign exchange earnings come from agricultural exports, primarily sugar. Of the record 1974 sugar crop, 20,500 long tons were sold to the United Kingdom under the Commonwealth Sugar Agreement and an additional 8,600 long tons to the United Kingdom at the world market price. The United States purchased 54,900 long tons. Belize exports citrus fruits and bananas and encourages the production of meat, poultry, rice, corn, and beans for domestic consumption. The tourist industry, which welcomes but controls foreign investment, is developing. Some 58,000 tourists visited Belize in 1973, a 15 percent increase over 1972. Airlines serving Belize from North America and Central America have recently expanded their schedules. To attract foreign capital, Belize makes many tax and other concessions. But it intends to keep landownership local. In 1974, Belize became a member of the Caribbean Common Market.

Trinidad-Tobago's economy is characterized by a relatively high-wage petroleum industry and a large service sector. Since independence, economic expansion has reflected the cyclical nature of petroleum production and the government's fiscal measures to stabilize these patterns. Per capita GDP, strongly influenced by the predominantly foreign-owned oil industry, stood at approximately $1,100 in 1973. High oil prices and production resulted in real GDP growth for 1974 considerably in excess of the 1970-1972 average of 3.9 percent. The highly visible middle class, together with a large system of social welfare, suggests that the distribution of income is more equitable in Trinidad than in most Caribbean countries. Until 1970, the population of Trinidad grew at an annual rate of only 0.6 percent due to emigration and declining birthrates. Since 1971, the birthrate has increased slightly, and emigration has declined. Partly in consequence, unemployment is rising. Petroleum production and refining make up the backbone of Trinidad's economy. Manufacturing, construction, tourism, and public administration have also been increasing their share of GDP, while agriculture, though still important as the employer of 21.3 percent of the labor force, had fallen to only 4.6 percent of GDP in 1972.

Nicaragua's real GDP increased by 3.2 percent in 1973, compared to 5.1 percent the previous year, despite an earthquake that destroyed much of the capital and the worst drought in almost half a century. Important contributors to the 1973 growth rate were increases in construction, public expenditures, and agricultural output. The rate of inflation in 1973 was roughly 20 percent, a sharp increase over the 4 percent annual rate in the previous three years. Prices continued to rise in 1974 because of agricultural shortages, a rapid expansion in the money supply, and bottlenecks in supplies after the earthquake. The Central Bank has adopted new deflationary policies, which include increasing minimum bank reserve requirements, restricting commercial and industrial lending, and increasing interest rates. The earthquake badly disrupted the manufacturing sector, which, as a result, accounted for only 18.8 percent of GDP in 1973, a decline of 2.6 percent from the previous year. Manufactured exports comprised almost 16 percent of total exports. The government, which, as part of its plan to diversify exports, encourages production of rice, tobacco, and beef, hopes to improve the rural infrastructure, encourage new land settlements, bring about modernization of farm techniques, and improve marketing efficiency and credit facilities. The government continues to encourage foreign investment by allowing foreign companies to repatriate registered capital, earnings, profits, and interest; to reexport goods imported for investment; and to enjoy the benefits of all guarantees and exemptions enjoyed by local capital.

Nicaragua has substantial potential for development—good soils, a rather wide climatic range, mineral resources, and the largest area of land in Central America suitable for mechanized agriculture.

Panama's real GDP grew at an annual rate of 7.1 percent between 1969 and 1973. The country's dollar currency, favorable banking legislation, and geographical position attracted foreign banks and deposits. Construction was stimulated by a substantial public investment program as well as by the private sector's construction of new office and residential buildings in Panama City. The growth rates of agriculture and manufacturing output have, in contrast, slackened compared with the 1960s. In agriculture, the government has sought social goals rather than increasing output; among manufacturers, changes in government policies have caused uncertainties. Banana production, which is efficient and, in fact, represented about half of all exports in 1972 and 1973, utilizes only about 10 percent of Panama's farmland. Livestock production is inefficient and could be improved and expanded so that Panama could take advantage of its excellent international transport network to export beef. Since 1968, the growth rate of the industrial sector has been falling, owing to uncertainty. Projected annual industrial growth up to the 1980s is 7 percent, and a higher rate would be difficult, though manufacturing for export could expand because of transport and commercial advantages. There is no Panamanian central bank; the United States dollar is legal tender, and, accordingly, there are no exchange controls. Investment and the transfer of funds are unrestricted; income on foreign loans and investment is tax-free. As a result, Panama has become a major offshore fund area. Foreign liabilities of private banks, which rose from $76 million in 1968 to $226 million at the end of 1970 and to $2,023 million at the end of 1973, are primarily responsible for the increase in the total deposits of the banking system. Most of the foreign deposits are re-lent abroad; overseas loans from private banks rose from $77 million in 1968 to $287 million in 1970 and to $2,155 million at the end of 1973. The contribution of the Canal Zone to the Panamanian economy, though still important, has been declining in relative terms. Net income originating in the Zone in 1973 represented 12.5 percent of GDP at current prices compared to 15.4 percent in 1970 and substantially more a decade earlier. Over half of the 1973 income (55 percent) originating in the Zone was from salaries and wages paid to Panamanian workers, 44 percent was purchases of goods and services by Zone residents, and the rest was from the annual fee paid by the United States for use of the canal.

Venezuela's real growth rate during 1973-1974 increased within a fiscal setting dominated by the extraordinary rise in the price of petroleum. Government accounts and the balance of payments registered important surpluses, while the strong expansion of monetary liquidity brought about an acceleration of inflation after many years of relative stability. Sudden oil wealth led the government to revise its development strategy, undertake long-range institutional reforms, strive to make the economy better able to absorb the new riches, and channel part of its funds abroad. In 1973, real GDP increased 5.9 percent as compared to an average of 4.7 percent during 1970-1972. During 1970-1973, real GDP per capita grew at a yearly rate of 1.6 percent to U.S. $1,169 at 1970 prices. Gross fixed investment in real terms increased 15.5 percent in 1973, double the rate during 1970-1972, and accounted for 28 percent of GDP. Public investment grew faster than private investment, and, as a share of the total, it rose from 16 to 26 percent between 1970 and 1973. Venezuela's population reached 11.3 million in 1973 and was growing at 3.4 percent a year, one of the highest rates in Latin America. According to the 1971 census, the Caracas metropolitan area contains about one-fifth of the total population (14 percent in 1950) of Venezuela. The labor force is less than one-third of the total population. Between 1950 and 1971, illiteracy declined from 49 to 23 percent of the population ten years of age or older. The manufacturing subsector has been growing at a rate approaching 8 percent; the most dynamic are the paper industry and its by-products, beverages, furniture, textiles, and metal products. Venezuelan agriculture, however, is characterized by extensive cultivation, limited technology, and low productivity. During 1970-1973, the area of cultivated farmland declined 14 percent, while real gross investment remained at about 1970 levels. The result was insufficient domestic output, which had to be supplemented by imports; on the average, imports accounted for 24 percent of the total supply of farm products. Agriculture's share in real GDP also declined slightly—to 6.7 percent—but accounted for 22 percent of the employed population. Corn, beans, and potatoes, staples of the Venezuelan diet, continued to decline in the past several years due to bad weather and government pricing policies. From 1970 to 1973, corn, bean, and potato output fell 43 percent, 26 percent, and 14 percent, respectively, and the area sown was cut back considerably; as a result, the government increased prices in 1973. From January to December 1974, monetary liquidity rose 30.5 percent over the same period of 1973. This sharp expansion, together with poor crops and increases in the price of imported goods, resulted in an acceleration of the inflation rate to approximately 13 percent. In 1974, the Organic Act of the National Treasury was amended to allocate to the new Venezuelan Investment Fund 50 percent of the government's revenue from taxes on the petroleum industry as well as the tax on income derived from that sector (see p. 156). The fund's objectives include financing the expansion and diversification of the economy, making profitable placements abroad, and promoting programs of international cooperation to help enhance the nation's financial and economic stability.

Over the years, oil has made Venezuela one of the most fortunate of the underdeveloped countries in the world. Oil revenues have enabled the government to build much of the basic infrastructure essential to development, to encourage and subsidize both agriculture and industry where necessary, and to make significant progress in education and training. With the enormous increase in oil revenues since 1973, one might imagine that few problems would remain. Nevertheless, some clouds are beginning to appear on the horizon:

1. Because of falling world demand for oil at present prices, Venezuelan production is down from about 3.4 million barrels per day in 1973 to 1.9 million barrels per day in March 1976—a huge drop, which has offset, to a degree, the effect of the quadrupling of oil prices. As a result of this precipitous decline in production, and because the government budget has shown alarming propensities to expand, the Investment Fund will receive substantially reduced funds in 1975 and probably no new funds at all in 1976. It received $3.02 billion in 1974, $2.23 billion in 1975. Venezuela had a balance-of-payments surplus of $6.1 billion in 1974, but only $3.1 billion in 1975, and indications were for a very small surplus in 1976 and even a possible significant deficit in 1977.

2. Since nationalization, Venezuela has been obliged to depend on technical assistance from the big international companies in order to administer the industry successfully.

3. Despite the efforts of the government, through the Investment Fund and other devices, to insulate the economy from the shock of sudden oil riches, the rate of inflation increased sharply and shows signs of further rises in the year ahead.

4. Venezuela and the other OPEC countries are in danger of losing the almost unanimous support they have thus far enjoyed in international forums from the rest of the Third World. There are now mounting signs that many of these poor countries are beginning to realize that high oil prices are largely responsible for a massive downturn in their economies. World Bank figures show that increases in oil prices added $8.5 billion to the import bill of the poor countries in 1974, nearly paralyzing some economies.

5. Venezuela has long been too dependent on oil. This has resulted in high-cost industry and agriculture, which is not competitive in world markets and which is, in fact, highly dependent on government protection.

Cuba, a special case. One student of Cuba under Castro, Carmelo Mesa-Lago, identifies five stages in the evolution of Cuban society since 1959. In the first stage, between the fall of Batista and early 1961, the guerrillas in power systematically liquidated or gained control of the prerevolutionary power centers: the army, political parties, unions, and farmers' and professional associations. For them it substituted the rebel army, the militia, and Committees for the Defense of the Revolution. The government tried to collectivize the means of production, but, lacking a clear economic program and experienced government officials, was unable to do effective central planning. Widespread economic disorganization resulted.

After the declaration of socialism in 1961, the government entered a second stage, in which it tried systematically to apply the Soviet Union's own system of politico-economic organization to Cuba. Intending to substitute centralized planning (performed with Soviet technical assistance) for free-market mechanisms, it began training managers, transmitting orders through the unions, and curtailing consumption to increase investment in the hope of accelerating industrialization and economic growth. But what worked well in the USSR did not work at all in Cuba, and much of the central planning and development strategy failed.

During the third stage, two schools of revolutionary thought developed. Ché Guevara, the leader of one faction, proposed radical (and romantic) solutions—total elimination of the market through full collectivization of the means of production; a highly centralized, computerized planning system; central financing of all state enterprises through budgetary appropriations; and the gradual elimination of money and material incentives. To succeed, the system required the creation of a self-sacrificing, frugal, socialized, and egalitarian human being, "the new man." Guevara planned to create this "new man" by raising mass consciousness through education, propaganda, mobilization, unpaid voluntary labor, and moral incentives. This system would, ultimately, promote capital accumulation and economic development. Guevara criticized the institutionalization of the Soviet Union and instead favored permanent revolution.

He was opposed by a moderate, pragmatist pro-Soviet group drawn from the old Cuban Communist party and led by an economist, Carlos Rafael Rodríguez. The Rodríguez group advocated computerized central planning but would permit some autonomy to enterprises and make partial use of market mechanisms. It opposed budgetary appropriations and would require about one-third of the state enterprises to finance themselves through interest-bearing loans from the central bank and permit them to retain a good part of their profits for reinvestment and expansions. The Rodríguez group favored economic institutionalization, an efficient bureaucracy, and high labor productivity through the Soviet system of work quotas and material incentives. It favored a strong Communist party, Soviet-style unions, close links with the USSR, and flexibility in Cuba's relations with Latin America.

For four years, Castro held himself aloof from the controversy; finally, he sent the two protagonists abroad. His path cleared of potential opponents, he opened the fourth stage of the revolution (mid-1966 to mid-1970) by endorsing Mao-Guevarism, embellished by Castroism.

In this stage, the important economic decisions were made by Castro and his inner circle. Castro placed even more emphasis than Guevara on egalitarianism, moral incentives, mobilization, capital accumulation, and the abolition of money. He set grandiose production targets for coming years, including the famous ten-million-ton sugar harvest of 1970. He increased the army's influence greatly and allowed the party to stagnate.

But Guevara's death in Bolivia and the failure to achieve the goals of the sugar harvest in 1970, together with a sharp decline in production in other sectors and severe economic dislocation—both caused by the all-out effort in sugar—destroyed the Mao-Guevarist system and even eroded Castro's own position.

As a result, since 1970 the Soviet (and the Rodríguez group's) influence has increased. Institutionalization has become pervasive, and certain of Castro's powers have been diffused. The regime has strengthened the central planning apparatus, channeled manpower and capital rigidly to increase productivity, expanded material incentives, drastically reduced labor mobilization, and set realistic output targets.

Socialist accounting being what it is, results are hard to quantify. But Barclay's Bank and *The Economist* have recently published suggestive reports. In 1974, postrevolutionary Cuba enjoyed its first significant trade surplus ($500 million) thanks to a sugar harvest of 5.9 million tons and high sugar prices under revised long-term contracts with the Soviet Union. Cuba still depends on sugar for 85 percent of its foreign exchange earnings, and Comecon, the East European trading bloc, still represents over half of Cuba's export market. Since Cuba joined Comecon in 1972, its exports to Eastern Europe and the Soviet Union have more than tripled, to $1.5 billion in 1974. Exports to Japan and Western Europe have risen rapidly from $218 million in 1970 to $860 million in 1974. Imports from Japan and the West have risen from $362 million to $846 million. The recent lifting of OAS sanctions will no doubt result in expanded trade between Cuba and Latin America. Argentina, Mexico, and Canada had already established significant trade relations with Cuba, and no doubt Cuba will seek to substitute at least some Venezuelan for Soviet oil—if the price is right. Cuba apparently is interested in U.S. technology in sugar harvesting, nickel mining, and cattle raising if U.S.-Cuban relations are normalized.

APPENDIX B

The tables in Appendix B were prepared by J. Phillip Rourk and updated by Elsa Marisa Loza. The reader may find it useful to divide them into five categories:

1. Tables B1–B3, data on intraregional trade relations.
2. Tables B4–B14, material on trade relations of individual nations with the United States.
3. Tables B15–B27, data on the economic situation of each country and B28, important internal statistics for each country in the group.
4. Tables B29–B40, basic facts that help throw light on national living conditions.
5. Tables B41–B51, data on foreign aid given the Caribbean nations over the last two decades.

A perusal of the tables will reveal that underdeveloped countries are not the best or easiest subjects for statistical analysis. Information for certain years is missing in many categories. A country undergoing dramatic governmental and social upheavals does not always have the financial means to count newspaper readers or physicians; moreover, the outside organizations that might wish to do such work often find conditions difficult and basic information unavailable. The information in these tables, however, is a useful addition to our understanding of the Caribbean.

LIST OF ABBREVIATIONS

AID - Agency for International Development

CARICOM - Caribbean Community and Caribbean Common Market

CARIFTA - Caribbean Free Trade Association

FAA - Foreign Assistance Act

GDP - Gross domestic product

GNP - Gross national product

IBRD - International Bank for Reconstruction and Development

IDA - International Development Association

IDB - Inter-American Development Bank

IFC - International Finance Corporation

IFS - International Financial Statistics

IMF - International Monetary Fund

MAP - Military Assistance Program

MSA - Mutual Security Act

OECD - Organization for Economic Cooperation and Development

PL 480 - Public Law 480, U.S. Congress

SIECA - Central American Common Market (Secretaria de Integracion Economica de Centro América)

UNESCO - United Nations Educational, Scientific, and Cultural Organization

USDA - United States Department of Agriculture

USDC - United States Department of Commerce

World Bank Group - The IBRD, IDA, and IFC

TABLE B-1

Central American Common Market,

Total and Intrazonal Imports 1960-74[a]

Year	Total Imports (Mil. U.S. $)	A: Intra-zonal Imports (Mil. U.S. $)	A as % of Total Imports	B: U.S. Exports to: (Mil. U.S. $)	B as % of Total Imports	U.S. Imports from: (Mil. U.S $)
1960	514.1	32.7	6.4	250	48.6	211
61	495.8	36.8	7.4	230	46.4	228
62	552.1	50.8	9.2	254	46.0	241
63	652.6	72.1	11.0	289	44.3	252
64	770.5	106.2	13.8	335	43.5	236
65	889.3	135.5	15.2	364	40.9	283
66	937.0	174.7	18.6	385	41.1	293
67	1030.4	214.0	20.8	400	38.8	312
68	1057.4	258.8	24.5	366	34.6	343
69	1065.6	249.0	23.4	353	33.1	368
1970	1249.7	299.4	24.0	425	34.0	416
71	1313.6	275.6	21.0	408	31.0	447
72	1379.5	304.7	22.1	439	31.8	485
73	1855.3	388.5	20.9	621	33.5	686
74	2922.0	525.0	18.0	1033	35.3	788

Sources: SIECA, IMF, and USDC.

[a]Member Countries: Costa Rica, El Salvador, Guatemala, Honduras, Nicaragua

TABLE B-2

Andean Pact,

Total and Intrazonal Imports 1969-74[a]

Year	Total Imports (Mil. U.S. $)	A: Intra-zonal Imports (Mil. U.S. $)	A as % of Total Imports	B: U.S. Exports to: (Mil. U.S. $)	B as % of Total Imports	U.S. Imports from: (Mil. U.S. $)
1969	4161	170	4.1	1651	39.7	1748
1970	4566	174	3.8	1841	40.3	1982
71	5111	225	4.4	1815	35.5	1933
72	5641	231	4.1	1899	33.7	2149
73	6945	352	5.1	2349	33.8	2896
74	10123	817	8.1	3957	39.1	6690

Sources: Unofficial estimates of Andean Pact Junta, IDB, and USDC.

[a]Member Countries: Bolivia, Chile, Colombia, Ecuador, Peru, Venezuela

TABLE B-3

CARIFTA – CARICOM,

Total and Intrazonal Imports 1968–74 [a]

Year	Total Imports (Mil. U.S. $)	A: Intrazonal Imports (Mil. U.S. $)	A as % of Total Imports	B: U.S. Exports to: (Mil. U.S. $)	B as % of Total Imports	U.S. Imports from: (Mil. U.S. $)
1968	1051.4	54.4	5.2	274	26.1	402
69	1199.6	67.9	6.1	306	25.5	433
1970	1442.0	83.6	5.9	392	27.2	484
71	1622.0	92.1	5.6	413	25.5	452
72	1913.0	142.1	7.4	435	22.7	499
73	1891.0	--	--	519	27.4	667
74	--	--	--	686	--	1678

Sources: USDC and IMF.

[a] CARICOM Member Countries: Barbados, Belize, Guyana, Jamaica, Leeward and Windward Islands, and Trinidad-Tobago

311

TABLE B-4

BARBADOS

Year	U.S. Imports from (Mil. U.S. $)	U.S. Exports to (Mil. U.S. $)	U.S. Investment (Mil. U.S. $ Book Value)	U.S. Agri- cultural Exports to (Mil. U.S. $)
1958	1.1	3.8	--	--
59	0.9	3.9	--	--
1960	0.8	5.8	--	--
61	1.2	6.0	--	--
62	1.5	6.3	--	--
63	2.5	6.5	--	--
64	3.5	8.5	--	--
65	4.5	8.8	--	--
66	3.5	11.0	--	--
67	7.0	13.0	--	--
68	6.0	14.0	--	--
69	8.0	18.0	--	3.3
1970	9.0	22.0	--	4.0
71	7.0	20.0	--	3.9
72	8.0	25.0	--	5.0
73	12.0	34.0	--	6.5
74	32.0	38.0	69.0	7.5
75	33.8	42.1	--	

Sources: Columns 2 and 3, USDC and UN Monthly Bulletin of Statistics (August 1977); column 4, AID; column 5, USDA.

TABLE B-5

COSTA RICA

Year	U.S. Imports from (Mil. U.S. $)	U.S. Exports to: (Mil. U.S. $)	% Share of Exports to U.S.	% Share of Imports from U.S.	U.S. Investment (Mil. U.S. $ Book Value)	U.S. Agricultural Exports to: (Mil. U.S. $)	Index of Per Capita Food Production[a]
1958	36.0	42.5	--	--	--	--	--
59	32.8	41.4	--	--	--	--	--
1960	34.9	44.6	--	--	62.5	--	--
61	40.1	42.8	--	--	--	--	--
62	39.9	50.1	--	--	--	--	--
63	41.6	54.2	--	--	--	--	--
64	54.0	61.1	--	--	--	--	--
65	57.0	61.0	--	--	--	--	101
66	59.9	62.2	46	39	--	--	106
67	70.0	64.0	48	39	--	--	107
68	88.0	74.0	47	38	--	--	107
69	101.0	77.0	47	35	130.0	7.0	115
1970	117.0	94.0	42	35	--	9.8	127
71	109.0	103.0	41	33	--	11.6	120
72	130.0	110.0	40	33	--	11.2	127
73	142.0	150.0	33	35	--	20.3	131
74	170.0	232.0	--	--	--	28.7	116
75	199.9	241.6	--	--	--	--	--

Sources: Columns 2, 3, 4, 5, USDC and UN Monthly Bulletin of Statistics (August 1977); column 6, AID; columns 7 and 8, USDA.
[a]The food production index is based on 1961-65 = 100.

TABLE B-6

DOMINICAN REPUBLIC

Year	U.S. Imports from: (Mil. U.S. $)	U.S. Exports to: (Mil. U.S. $)	% Share of Exports to U.S.	% Share of Imports from U.S.	U.S. Investment (Mil. U.S. $ Book Value)	U.S. Agricultural Exports to: (Mil. U.S. $)	Index of Per Capita Food Production[a]
1958	71.7	79.5	--	--	--	--	--
59	75.2	61.1	--	--	--	--	--
1960	110.5	41.9	--	--	--	--	--
61	89.6	29.6	--	--	--	--	--
62	153.4	72.4	--	--	--	--	--
63	140.2	93.6	--	--	--	--	--
64	127.7	115.6	--	--	--	--	--
65	110.6	76.2	--	--	--	--	--
66	128.3	88.1	88	49	--	--	87
67	134.0	97.0	87	55	--	--	91
68	156.0	115.0	89	52	--	--	89
69	165.0	124.0	89	50	--	--	83
1970	184.0	143.0	84	45	--	24.8	99
71	175.0	164.0	74	52	--	31.7	100
72	232.0	183.0	63	50	--	41.1	105
73	308.0	229.0	--	--	--	45.8	103
74	471.0	410.0	--	--	200.0	63.4	102
75	585.6	453.1	--	--	--	117.3	100

Sources: Columns 2, 3, 4, 5, USDC and UN Monthly Bulletin of Statistics (August 1977); column 6, AID; columns 7 and 8, USDA.
[a]The food production index is based on 1961-65 = 100.

TABLE B-7

GUATEMALA

Year	U.S. Imports from: (Mil. U.S. $)	U.S. Exports to: (Mil. U.S. $)	% Share of Exports to U.S.	% Share of Imports from U.S.	U.S. Investment (Mil. U.S. $ Book Value)	U.S. Agricultural Exports to: (Mil. U.S. $)	Index of Per Capita Food Production[a]
1958	66.0	79.9	--	--	--	--	--
59	65.1	65.4	--	--	--	--	--
1960	58.7	63.8	--	--	151.0	--	--
61	63.1	61.8	--	--	--	--	--
62	62.6	62.7	--	--	--	--	--
63	69.8	76.6	--	--	--	--	--
64	62.7	85.4	--	--	--	--	--
65	66.7	96.5	--	--	--	--	103
66	82.0	90.5	31	42	--	--	105
67	65.0	91.0	31	41	--	--	110
68	71.0	93.0	28	41	--	--	116
69	76.0	84.0	28	34	179.0	10.4	117
1970	87.0	100.0	28	35	--	14.9	119
71	95.0	98.0	31	32	--	16.7	128
72	108.0	102.0	29	32	--	17.5	127
73	168.0	148.0	33	32	--	23.5	129
74	211.0	240.0	--	--	193.0	40.7	131
75	419.5	499.5	--	--	--	--	--

Sources: Columns 2, 3, 4, 5, USDC and UN Monthly Bulletin of Statistics (August 1977); column 6, AID; columns 7 and 8, USDA.
[a]The food production index is based on 1961-65 = 100.

TABLE B-8

HAITI

Year	U.S. Imports from: (Mil. U.S. $)	U.S. Exports to: (Mil. U.S. $)	U.S. Investment (Mil. U.S. $ Book Value)	U.S. Agricultural Exports to: (Mil. U.S. $)	Index of Per Capita Food Production [a]
1958	22.6	25.2	--	--	--
59	16.2	24.0	--	--	--
1960	18.2	25.4	--	--	--
61	19.0	26.3	--	--	--
62	24.4	24.4	--	--	--
63	25.5	21.3	--	--	--
64	24.1	23.6	--	--	--
65	20.5	21.4	--	--	91
66	18.7	21.6	--	--	91
67	21.0	22.0	--	--	84
68	26.0	24.0	--	--	80
69	29.0	24.0	--	6.3	80
1970	32.0	34.0	--	8.3	82
71	40.0	37.0	--	9.0	83
72	51.0	53.0	--	9.8	84
73	64.0	77.0	--	15.5	81
74	112.0	125.0	30.0	27.5	80
75	131.1	223.6	--	--	--

Sources: Columns 2 and 3, USDC and UN Monthly Bulletin of Statistics (August 1977); column 4, AID; columns 5 and 6, USDA.
[a]The food production index is based on 1961-65 = 100.

TABLE B-9

HONDURAS

Year	U.S. Imports from: (Mil. U.S. $)	U.S. Exports to: (Mil. U.S. $)	% Share of Exports to U.S.	% Share of Imports from U.S.	U.S. Investment (Mil. U.S. $ Book Value)	U.S. Agricultural Exports to: (Mil. U.S. $)	Index of Per Capita Food Production[a]
1958	27.8	36.2	--	--	--	--	--
59	24.6	32.8	--	--	--	--	--
1960	33.6	34.8	--	--	100.0	--	--
61	32.8	37.0	--	--	--	--	--
62	32.4	44.2	--	--	--	--	--
63	31.5	44.6	--	--	--	--	--
64	41.5	49.7	--	--	--	--	--
65	71.6	53.9	--	--	--	--	105
66	85.4	67.8	56	50	--	--	111
67	72.0	71.0	44	48	--	--	109
68	89.0	75.0	45	46	--	--	112
69	95.0	75.0	48	43	190.0	5.5	104
1970	102.0	89.0	55	41	--	8.1	100
71	121.0	84.0	64	47	--	9.6	111
72	116.0	79.0	56	44	--	9.4	98
73	150.0	103.0	--	--	--	11.0	98
74	150.0	159.0	--	--	230.0	21.0	91
75	145.3	165.6	--	--	--	--	--

Sources: Columns 2, 3, 4, 5, USDC and UN Monthly Bulletin of Statistics (August 1977); column 6, AID; columns 7 and 8, USDA.
[a]The food production index is based on 1961-65 = 100.

317

TABLE B-10

JAMAICA

Year	U.S. Imports from: (Mil. U.S. $)	U.S. Exports to: (Mil. U.S. $)	% Share of Exports to U.S.	% Share of Imports from U.S.	U.S. Investment (Mil. U.S. $ Book Value)	U.S. Agricultural Exports to: (Mil. U.S. $)	Index of Per Capita Food Production[a]
1958	52.8	32.3	--	--	--	--	--
59	46.9	36.0	--	--	--	--	--
1960	54.2	48.1	--	--	--	--	--
61	73.3	48.5	--	--	--	--	--
62	99.3	54.5	--	--	--	--	--
63	103.1	63.2	--	--	--	--	--
64	115.7	80.1	--	--	--	--	--
65	125.0	87.1	--	--	--	--	104
66	133.2	115.1	38	36	--	--	103
67	144.0	126.0	40	39	--	--	94
68	138.0	147.0	39	39	--	--	88
69	151.0	175.0	38	42	--	--	80
1970	187.0	218.0	48	43	--	29.5	76
71	170.0	216.0	45	40	--	35.0	77
72	181.0	221.0	44	37	--	39.1	78
73	176.0	268.0	41	39	--	41.3	72
74	233.0	337.0	--	--	850.0	63.1	74
75	298.9	422.6	--	--	--	83.5	--

Sources: Columns 2, 3, 4, 5, USDC and UN Monthly Bulletin of Statistics (August 1977); column 6, AID; columns 7 and 8, USDA.
[a]The food production index is based on 1961-65 = 100.

TABLE B-11

NICARAGUA

Year	U.S. Imports from: (Mil. U.S. $)	U.S. Exports to: (Mil. U.S. $)	% Share of Exports to U.S.	% Share of Imports from U.S.	U.S. Investment (Mil. U.S. $ Book Value)	U.S. Agricultural Exports to: (Mil. U.S. $)	Index of Per Capita Food Production[a]
1958	21.1	37.4	--	--	--	--	--
59	15.4	28.2	--	--	--	--	--
1960	20.8	30.1	--	--	12.0	--	--
61	25.3	33.0	--	--	--	--	--
62	27.6	47.0	--	--	--	--	--
63	35.1	46.8	--	--	--	--	--
64	33.6	58.6	--	--	--	--	--
65	36.0	68.9	--	--	--	--	103
66	31.2	70.8	23	46	--	--	105
67	42.0	70.0	28	43	--	--	107
68	50.0	62.0	29	38	--	--	107
69	56.0	59.0	32	38	61.0	5.5	107
1970	61.0	77.0	33	36	--	5.8	106
71	70.0	63.0	35	33	--	7.6	115
72	82.0	75.0	34	32	--	8.0	102
73	109.0	109.0	33	34	--	16.9	109
74	97.0	200.0	--	--	75.0	18.3	104
75	114.9	166.5	--	--	--	--	--

Sources: Columns 2, 3, 4, 5, USDC and UN Monthly Bulletin of Statistics (August 1977); column 6, AID; columns 7 and 8, USDA
aThe food production index is based on 1961-65 = 100.

TABLE B-12

PANAMA

Year	U.S. Imports from: (Mil. U.S. $)	U.S. Exports to: (Mil. U.S. $)	% Share of Exports to U.S.	% Share of Imports from U.S.	U.S. Investment (Mil. U.S. $ Book Value)	U.S. Agri-cultural Exports to: (Mil. U.S. $)	Index of Per Capita Food Production[a]
1958	23.9	97.3	--	--	--	--	--
59	24.9	91.6	--	--	--	--	--
1960	24.1	89.8	--	--	--	--	--
61	22.6	108.9	--	--	--	--	--
62	22.9	105.9	--	--	--	--	--
63	31.9	111.1	--	--	--	--	--
64	40.1	113.3	--	--	--	--	--
65	59.6	124.7	--	--	--	--	--
66	68.1	137.7	68	41	--	--	112
67	76.0	139.0	77	40	--	--	110
68	78.0	136.0	79	39	--	--	111
69	75.0	164.0	66	36	--	15.6	126
1970	76.0	208.0	63	39	--	20.1	131
71	66.0	209.0	49	36	--	32.1	121
72	55.0	216.0	44	34	187.5	25.0	123
73	67.0	286.0	43	35	--	30.4	122
74	108.0	364.0	--	--	--	56.7	107
75	214.8	494.3	--	--	--	--	95

Sources: Columns 2, 3, 4, 5, USDC and UN Monthly Bulletin of Statistics (August 1977); column 6, AID; columns 7 and 8, USDA.
[a]The food production index is based on 1961-65 = 100.

TABLE B-13

TRINIDAD

Year	U.S. Imports from: (Mil. U.S. $)	U.S. Exports to: (Mil. U.S. $)	% Share of Exports to U.S.	% Share of Imports from U.S.	U.S. Investment (Mil. U.S. $ Book Value)	U.S. Agricultural Exports to: (Mil. U.S. $)	Index of Per Capita Food Production[a]
1958	46.5	30.0	--	--	--	--	--
59	44.1	30.7	--	--	--	--	--
1960	55.2	35.5	--	--	--	--	--
61	85.9	35.9	--	--	--	--	--
62	85.2	41.6	--	--	--	--	--
63	110.9	55.0	--	--	--	--	--
64	113.3	54.7	--	--	--	--	--
65	142.3	74.6	--	--	--	--	101
66	163.2	59.2	36	14	--	--	94
67	184.0	60.0	43	15	--	--	91
68	216.0	62.0	47	15	--	--	101
69	232.0	61.0	52	15	--	13.3	107
1970	232.0	84.0	51	16	--	14.9	90
71	215.0	117.0	45	18	--	16.8	86
72	251.0	122.0	47	19	--	20.6	93
73	410.0	133.0	56	16	--	33.6	77
74	1273.0	192.0	--	--	650.0	50.0	78
75	1342.6	615.9	--	--	--	--	--

Sources: Columns 2, 3, 4, 5, USDC and UN Monthly Bulletin of Statistics (August 1977); column 6, AID; columns 7 and 8, USDA.
aThe food production index is based on 1961-65 = 100.

TABLE B-14

VENEZUELA

Year	U.S. Imports from: (Mil. U.S. $)	U.S. Exports to: (Mil. U.S. $)	% Share of Exports to U.S.	% Share of Imports from U.S.	U.S. Investment (Mil. U.S. $ Book Value)	U.S. Agri-cultural Exports to: (Mil. U.S. $)	Index of Per Capita Food Production[a]
1958	888.8	831.0	--	--	2658.0	--	--
59	889.8	758.3	--	--	2690.0	--	--
1960	947.7	566.6	--	--	2659.0	--	--
61	898.0	529.1	--	--	--	--	--
62	975.8	480.0	--	--	2826.0	--	--
63	935.8	522.0	--	--	2808.0	--	--
64	956.4	618.6	--	--	--	--	--
65	1018.0	625.6	--	--	2715.0	--	--
66	1002.4	598.0	31	50	--	--	108
67	980.0	587.0	34	51	--	--	109
68	950.0	655.0	33	51	--	--	113
69	940.0	708.0	34	50	2700.0	--	113
1970	1082.0	759.0	35	46	--	--	112
71	1216.0	787.0	40	44	--	90.9	112
72	1298.0	924.0	41	44	2684.0	98.1	116
73	1787.0	1033.0	--	42	--	108.6	117
74	4679.0	1768.0	--	--	--	137.1	111
75	3624.0	2243.0	--	--	--	159.7	108
						323.3	112

Sources: Columns 2, 3, 4, 5, USDC and UN Monthly Bulletin of Statistics (August 1977); column 6, AID; columns 7 and 8, USDA.
aThe food production index is based on 1961-65 = 100.

322

TABLE B-15

BARBADOS

Year	Exports (Mil. U.S. $)	Imports (Mil. U.S. $)	Exports Less Imports	Industry as % of GDP	Agriculture as % of GDP	Petroleum Imports (Mil. U.S. $)
1958	23	43	-20	--	--	--
59	28	44	-16	--	--	--
1960	24	49	-25	14.0	28.0	--
61	25	47	-22	16.0	26.0	--
62	29	52	-23	16.0	25.0	--
63	41	58	-17	15.0	30.0	--
64	35	64	-29	16.0	26.0	--
65	37	67	-30	16.0	26.0	--
66	41	76	-35	16.0	26.0	--
67	41	76	-35	18.0	25.0	--
68	40	84	-44	18.0	19.0	--
69	37	97	-60	18.0	16.0	--
1970	39	117	-78	18.0	15.0	--
71	40	121	-81	18.0	13.0	--
72	44	142	-98	--	12.4	7.2
73	54	168	-114	--	--	10.7
74	84	203	-119	--	--	25.5

Sources: Columns 2 and 3, IMF; columns 5 and 6, UN Yearbook of National Accounts Statistics; column 7, IDB.

TABLE B-16

BELIZE

Year	Exports (Mil. U.S. $)	Imports (Mil. U.S. $)	Exports Less Imports	Manufacture as % of GDP	Agriculture as % of GDP
1958	--	--	--	--	--
59	--	--	--	--	--
1960	8	13	-5	--	--
61	--	--	--	--	--
62	--	--	--	30.0	33.5
63	--	--	--	34.0	30.3
64	--	--	--	28.0	37.0
65	12	24	-12	--	--
66	13	27	-14	--	--
67	15	25	-10	--	--
68	15	26	-11	--	--
69	17	30	-13	--	--
1970	19	33	-14	15.0	14.0
71	20	35	-15	--	--
72	18	32	-24	--	--
73	22	39	-17	--	--
74	--	--	--	--	--

Sources: Columns 2 and 3, IDB; columns 5 and 6, UN Monthly Bulletin of Statistics

TABLE B-17

COSTA RICA

Year	Exports (Mil. U.S. $)	Imports (Mil. U.S. $)	Exports Less Imports	Manu-facture as % of GDP	Agri-culture as % of GDP	Petro-leum Imports (Mil. U.S. $)
1958	92	99	-7	--	--	--
59	77	103	-26	--	--	--
1960	86	110	-24	18.0	24.0	--
61	84	107	-23	17.0	26.0	--
62	93	113	-20	18.0	25.0	--
63	95	124	-29	19.0	25.0	--
64	113	139	-26	19.0	24.0	--
65	112	178	-66	19.0	25.0	--
66	136	178	-42	20.0	23.0	--
67	144	191	-47	21.0	24.0	--
68	171	214	-43	21.0	24.0	--
69	190	245	-55	21.0	25.0	--
1970	231	329	-98	21.0	22.0	--
71	225	349	-124	21.0	20.2	--
72	281	373	-92	--	19.5	14.6
73	344	455	-111	--	20.1	20.1
74	395	653	-258	--	--	52.2

Sources: Columns 2 and 3, IMF; columns 5, 6, 7, UN Monthly Bulletin of Statistics

TABLE B-18

DOMINICAN REPUBLIC

Year	Exports (Mil. U.S. $)	Imports (Mil. U.S. $)	Exports Less Imports	Manu- facture as % of GDP	Agri- culture as % of GDP	Petro- leum Imports (Mil. U.S. $)	Index for GDP (In 1970 Prices) GDP	GDP p.c.
1958	128	149	-21	--	--	--	--	--
59	130	135	-5	--	--	--	--	--
1960	174	100	74	17.1	27.4	--	60	81
61	143	80	63	16.2	27.2	--	59	76
62	172	148	24	16.2	27.7	--	69	87
63	174	184	-10	16.4	25.8	--	74	90
64	179	221	-42	15.3	25.5	--	78	93
65	123	100	23	14.3	27.2	--	69	79
66	137	185	-48	16.7	25.6	--	78	87
67	156	201	-45	17.7	23.9	--	80	88
68	164	226	-62	16.3	23.1	--	81	86
69	183	250	-67	17.3	24.2	--	91	93
1970	214	307	-93	18.5	23.2	--	100	100
71	243	358	-115	18.4	22.2	--	110	106
72	347	388	-41	17.5	20.6	48.3	--	--
73	442	485	-43	17.9	20.9	48.1	--	--
74	637	774	-137	--	--	144.0	--	--

Sources: Columns 2 and 3, IMF; columns 5 and 6, IBRD; column 7, IDB; columns 8 and 9, UN Yearbook of National Accounts Statistics.

TABLE B-19

GUATEMALA

Year	Exports (Mil. U.S. $)	Imports (Mil. U.S. $)	Exports Less Imports	Petroleum Imports (Mil. U.S. $)	Index for GDP (In 1970 Prices) GDP	GDP p.c.
1958	108	150	-42	--	--	--
59	108	134	-26	--	--	--
1960	117	138	-21	--	59	80
61	113	134	-21	--	61	81
62	118	136	-18	--	63	81
63	154	171	-17	--	69	86
64	158	202	-44	--	72	87
65	187	229	-42	--	76	88
66	228	207	21	--	80	91
67	198	247	-49	--	83	91
68	231	249	-18	--	90	96
69	259	250	9	--	95	98
1970	298	284	14	--	100	100
71	290	303	-13	--	106	103
72	338	324	14	25.2	112	108
73	445	431	14	33.2	--	--
74	586	700	-114	102.1	--	--

Sources: Columns 2 and 3, IMF; column 5, IDB; columns 6 and 7, UN Yearbook of National Accounts Statistics.

TABLE B-20

GUYANA

Year	Exports (Mil. U.S. $)	Imports (Mil. U.S. $)	Exports Less Imports	Manu- facture as % of GDP	Agri- culture as % of GDP	Mining as % of GDP
1958	57	68	-11	--	--	--
59	60	65	-5	--	--	--
1960	74	86	-12	10.4	26.2	11.1
61	86	86	0	10.9	26.4	13.0
62	96	74	22	11.7	25.7	16.4
63	102	69	33	14.5	27.0	13.0
64	95	87	8	12.3	24.4	17.8
65	98	105	-7	13.1	24.0	16.6
66	108	118	-10	12.4	21.7	17.2
67	113	129	-16	12.4	21.4	17.7
68	108	110	-2	12.1	19.7	19.6
69	121	118	3	12.0	20.4	19.6
1970	133	134	-1	12.2	19.3	20.4
71	149	134	15	12.2	20.3	19.1
72	150	145	5	12.2	19.8	18.4
73	136	164	-28	9.7	16.5	12.5
74	--	--	--	--	--	--

Sources: Columns 2 and 3, IMF; columns 5 and 6, 1960-72: IBRD, 1973: UN Monthly Bulletin of Statistics.

TABLE B-21

HAITI

Year	Exports (Mil. U.S. $)	Imports (Mil. U.S. $)	Exports Less Imports	Manufacture as % of GDP	Agriculture as % of GDP	Petroleum Imports (Mil. U.S. $)	Index for GDP (In 1970 Prices) GDP	GDP p.c.
1958	39	43	-4	--	--	--	--	--
59	28	30	-2	--	--	--	--	--
1960	33	36	-3	10.1	49.9	--	90	110
61	32	42	-10	--	--	--	--	--
62	42	46	-4	--	--	--	--	--
63	41	39	2	--	--	--	93	107
64	40	41	-1	--	--	--	--	--
65	36	34	2	10.3	50.8	--	--	--
66	36	38	-2	--	--	--	--	--
67	34	36	-2	--	--	--	--	--
68	36	38	-2	9.9	51.9	--	96	100
69	37	39	-2	9.8	51.7	--	100	102
1970	40	53	-13	10.1	50.7	--	100	100
71	46	59	-13	10.0	49.9	--	106	104
72	43	64	-21	10.3	48.9	3.9	110	106
73	52	74	-22	10.9	46.9	6.6	--	--
74	72	--	--	--	--	12.2	--	--

Sources: Columns 2 and 3, IMF; columns 5 and 6, IBRD; column 7, IDB; columns 8 and 9, UN Yearbook of National Accounts Statistics.

TABLE B-22

HONDURAS

Year	Exports (Mil. U.S. $)	Imports (Mil. U.S. $)	Exports Less Imports	Manu- facture as % of GDP	Agri- culture as % of GDP	Petro- leum Imports (Mil. U.S. $)	Index for GDP (In 1970 Prices) GDP	Index for GDP (In 1970 Prices) GDP p.c.
1958	70	76	-6	--	--	--	--	--
59	69	71	-2	--	--	--	--	--
1960	63	72	-9	10.0	38.0	--	63	87
61	73	72	1	10.0	39.0	--	66	89
62	81	80	1	10.0	39.0	--	69	91
63	83	95	-12	10.0	38.0	--	71	90
64	95	102	-7	11.0	38.0	--	75	91
65	127	122	5	11.0	38.0	--	79	93
66	143	149	-6	11.0	38.0	--	83	95
67	154	164	-10	11.0	38.0	--	88	97
68	178	185	-7	12.0	37.0	--	93	100
69	169	184	-15	12.0	35.0	--	96	99
1970	176	222	-46	13.0	33.0	--	100	100
71	192	193	-1	13.1	31.3	--	105	104
72	206	193	13	13.3	31.6	11.3	109	105
73	237	262	-25	13.5	30.9	17.4	--	--
74	258	382	-124	--	--	50.0	--	--

Sources: Columns 2 and 3, IMF; columns 5 and 6, UN Monthly Bulletin of Statistics; column 7, IDB; columns 8 and 9, UN Yearbook of National Accounts Statistics.

TABLE B-23

JAMAICA

Year	Exports (Mil. U.S. $)	Imports (Mil. U.S. $)	Exports Less Imports	Manufacture as % of GDP	Agriculture as % of GDP	Mining as % of GDP	Petroleum Imports (Mil. U.S. $)	Index for GDP (In 1970 Prices) GDP	GDP p.c.
1958	133	181	-49	12.5	13.5	8.8	--	--	--
59	129	192	-63	13.2	13.3	7.9	--	--	--
1960	159	217	-58	13.4	12.3	8.7	--	61	70
61	172	211	-39	13.3	12.7	8.6	--	63	71
62	182	223	-41	13.3	12.5	8.8	--	64	72
63	202	226	-24	15.4	13.4	8.9	--	66	73
64	218	289	-71	15.4	12.5	9.5	--	71	76
65	214	289	-75	15.0	11.6	9.7	--	77	82
66	228	327	-99	14.5	11.0	14.4	--	80	84
67	225	348	-123	14.3	10.8	14.2	--	82	86
68	220	384	-164	14.7	9.9	12.7	--	86	89
69	254	436	-182	14.0	8.9	14.3	--	92	93
1970	342	525	-183	13.6	8.1	15.2	--	100	100
71	342	556	-214	14.0	9.3	13.6	--	102	100
72	392	642	-250	14.3	9.1	12.2	46.2	--	--
73	392	664	-272	12.9	8.1	10.5	62.5	--	--
74	649	936	-287	--	--	--	174.5	--	--

Sources: Columns 2 and 3, IMF; columns 5, 6, 7, IBRD; column 8, IDB; columns 9 and 10, UN Yearbook of National Accounts Statistics.

TABLE B-24

NICARAGUA

Year	Exports (Mil. U.S. $)	Imports (Mil. U.S. $)	Exports Less Imports	Manufacture as % of GDP	Agriculture as % of GDP	Petroleum Imports (Mil. U.S. $)	Index of GDP (In 1970 Prices) GDP	GDP p.c.
1958	64	78	-14	17.2	27.2	--	--	--
59	65	67	-2	18.1	28.0	--	--	--
1960	56	72	-16	17.6	26.2	--	50	70
61	61	74	-13	18.1	26.1	--	54	73
62	82	97	-15	23.9	33.9	--	60	79
63	100	110	-10	29.0	38.6	--	66	85
64	118	136	-18	20.5	28.0	--	74	92
65	144	160	-16	20.8	28.1	--	81	97
66	142	182	-40	22.9	25.5	--	84	97
67	151	202	-51	23.0	25.5	--	90	100
68	162	185	-23	23.8	24.9	--	91	97
69	158	177	-19	24.5	25.0	--	97	100
1970	178	199	-21	25.2	24.5	--	100	100
71	187	210	-23	25.2	25.7	--	106	102
72	249	218	31	25.6	23.8	11.7	110	103
73	276	327	-51	--	--	17.9	--	--
74	382	563	-181	--	--	48.9	--	--

Sources: Columns 2 and 3, IMF; columns 5 and 6, IBRD; column 7, IDB; columns 8 and 9, UN Yearbook of National Accounts Statistics.

TABLE B-25

PANAMA

Year	Exports (Mil. U.S. $)	Imports (Mil. U.S. $)	Exports Less Imports	Manu-facture as % of GDP	Agri-culture as % of GDP	Petro-leum Imports (Mil. U.S. $)	Index for GDP (In 1970 prices) GDP	GDP p.c.
1958	33	110	-77	--	--	--	--	--
59	35	115	-80	--	--	--	--	--
1960	27	128	-101	12.0	23.0	--	47	63
61	30	146	-116	12.0	24.0	--	52	67
62	48	171	-123	13.0	23.0	--	56	71
63	59	192	-133	14.0	22.0	--	61	74
64	71	195	-124	14.0	23.0	--	63	75
65	78	224	-146	14.0	24.0	--	69	80
66	89	253	-164	14.0	23.0	--	74	84
67	94	271	-177	14.0	22.0	--	81	88
68	100	266	-166	15.0	23.0	--	86	91
69	113	305	-192	--	--	--	94	96
1970	111	357	-246	15.9	19.2	--	100	100
71	117	396	-279	16.0	18.2	--	109	105
72	122	440	-318	16.0	17.5	48.0	116	109
73	143	488	-345	--	--	73.9	--	--
74	205	800	-595	--	--	260.2	--	--

Sources: Columns 1 and 2, IMF; columns 4 and 5, UN Monthly Bulletin of Statistics; column 7, IDB; columns 8 and 9, UN Yearbook of National Accounts Statistics.

TABLE B-26

TRINIDAD-TOBAGO

Year	Exports (Mil. U.S. $)	Imports (Mil. U.S. $)	Exports Less Imports	Manu-facture as % of GDP	Agri-culture as % of GDP	Petro-leum as % of GDP	Petro-leum Exports (Mil. U.S. $)
1958	248	240	8	12.7	13.2	32.4	--
59	262	261	1	12.9	11.9	32.7	--
1960	287	294	-7	12.5	11.9	30.4	--
61	346	341	5	12.5	11.3	30.0	--
62	345	353	-8	13.1	10.3	28.9	--
63	373	377	-4	--	--	--	--
64	405	426	-21	--	--	--	--
65	403	477	-74	--	--	--	--
66	432	457	-25	8.7	4.8	23.3	--
67	440	416	24	9.6	4.8	23.3	--
68	473	428	45	9.7	5.0	24.9	--
69	475	484	-9	11.6	5.0	20.2	--
1970	482	543	-61	11.7	5.2	17.7	--
71	521	675	-154	11.6	4.6	15.3	--
72	556	767	-211	12.3	4.6	14.5	66.3
73	702	796	-94	--	--	--	230.1
74	2038	1848	190	--	--	--	587.5

Sources: Columns 2 and 3, IMF; columns 5, 6, 7, IBRD; column 8, IDB.

TABLE B-27

VENEZUELA

Year	Exports (Mil. U.S. $)	Imports (Mil. U.S. $)	Exports Less Imports	Manufacture as % of GDP	Agriculture as % of GDP	Mining as % of GDP	Petroleum Exports (Mil. U.S. $)	Index for GDP (In 1970 Prices) GDP	GDP p.c.
1958	2321	1599	722	--	--	--	--	--	--
59	2369	1577	792	--	--	--	--	--	--
1960	2432	1188	1244	--	27.0	6.0	--	47	81
61	2413	1092	1321	--	29.0	6.0	--	60	82
62	2594	1096	1498	--	31.0	6.0	--	66	87
63	2629	950	1679	--	31.0	7.0	--	70	90
64	2742	1269	1473	--	28.0	7.0	--	77	95
65	2783	1454	1329	--	27.0	7.0	--	82	97
66	2346	1331	1015	--	25.0	7.0	--	84	96
67	2479	1464	1015	--	25.0	7.0	--	87	97
68	2549	1636	913	16.0	23.0	8.0	--	92	98
69	2519	1693	826	16.0	22.0	8.0	--	95	98
1970	2663	1851	812	17.0	20.0	7.0	--	100	100
71	3221	2117	1104	16.6	19.3	6.5	--	104	101
72	3151	2431	720	17.2	18.8	6.2	2924	110	104
73	4761	2834	1927	18.6	22.6	6.1	4458	--	--
74	10769	4200	6569	--	--	--	10700	--	--

Sources: Columns 2 and 3, IMF; columns 5, 6, 7, UN Monthly Bulletin of Statistics; column 8, IDB; columns 9 and 10, UN Yearbook of National Accounts Statistics.

TABLE B-28

Country	1974 Population (Thousands)	1960–74 Population Growth Rate (%)	1960 Urban Population (%)	1974 Urban Population (%)	Growth in Real GNP 1958–73 (%)	Growth in Real GNP Per Capita (%)
BARBADOS	240	0.2	40.3	45.1	3.7	3.5
BELIZE	--	--	--	--	--	--
COSTA RICA	1934	3.1	32.7	41.2	5.9	2.7
DOMINICAN REP.	4555	2.9	30.1	44.6	5.8	2.7
GUATEMALA	5356	2.8	33.6	33.6	5.4	2.9
GUYANA	800	3.1	--	--	--	--
HAITI	4516	1.7	15.9	21.7	1.2[a]	--
HONDURAS	2645	2.1	22.8	31.0	4.5	1.1
JAMAICA	1984	1.5	23.7	50.1	5.4[b]	3.8
NICARAGUA	2085	2.8	38.4	50.8	5.9	2.9
PANAMA	1618	3.0	41.5	49.5	7.8	4.6
TRINIDAD–TOBAGO	1076	2.1	39.2	54.1	--	--
VENEZUELA	11709	3.4	66.7	80.6	6.0	2.6

Sources: Columns 1 through 4, IDB; columns 5 and 6, AID.
[a] Data for Haiti based on 1960–1972.
[b] Data for Jamaica based on 1960–1973.

TABLE B-29

COSTA RICA

Year	Balance of Payments Goods & Services (Mil. U.S. $)	Population (Millions)	% Increase	Death Rate per 1,000	Population per Physician	Real GNP (Millions 1972 U.S. $)	% Increase	Real Per Capita GNP (1972 U.S. $)	% Increase	Newspaper Circulation per 1,000
1958	-1.6	1.07	--	--	2820	--	--	--	--	--
59	-4.6	1.12	4.7	9.0	--	--	--	--	--	101
1960	-3.6	1.17	4.5	8.6	--	581	--	463	--	92
61	-3.0	1.22	4.3	7.9	--	592	2.0	455	-1.7	94
62	-3.3	1.27	4.1	8.5	--	629	6.2	468	2.8	--
63	-4.9	1.34	5.5	8.5	2600	670	4.9	482	3.0	--
64	-4.4	1.38	3.0	8.8	--	663	-1.0	461	-4.3	--
65	-10.7	1.49	8.0	8.5	--	727	9.6	489	6.1	--
66	-7.9	1.54	3.4	7.4	--	774	6.5	504	3.1	--
67	-8.3	1.59	3.2	6.9	--	837	8.3	528	4.8	--
68	-51.5	1.63	2.5	6.5	1970	911	8.8	557	5.5	--
69	-60.1	1.69	3.7	6.9	--	964	5.8	572	2.7	--
1970	-80.0	1.73	2.4	6.6	--	1022	6.0	589	3.0	101
71	-121.8	1.80	4.0	5.9	--	1060	3.7	594	0.8	101
72	-106.6	1.84	2.2	5.9	2663	1144	7.9	623	4.9	93
73	-116.1	1.87	1.6	5.1	--	1231	7.6	653	4.8	--
74	--	1.92	2.7	--	--	--	--	--	--	--
75	--	1.97	3.0	--	--	1790	45.4	910	39.3	--

Sources: Column 2, IMF/IFS; columns 3, 4, 5, UN Monthly Bulletin of Statistics and Demographic Yearbook World Bank Atlas, 1976; column 6, UN Statistical Yearbook (for given year); columns 7 and 9, AID; column 11, UNESCO.

TABLE B-30

CUBA

Year	Population (Millions)	% Increase	Death Rate per 1,000	Population per Physician	Real GNP (Millions 1972 U.S. $)	Real Per Capita GNP (1972 U.S. $)	Newspaper Circulation per 1,000
1958	6.55	--	--	1020	--	--	--
59	--	--	--	--	--	--	--
1960	6.82	--	--	--	--	--	--
61	6.94	1.7	--	--	--	--	88
62	7.07	1.9	--	--	--	--	--
63	7.23	2.3	--	1200	--	--	--
64	7.43	2.8	8.5	--	--	--	--
65	7.72	3.9	--	--	--	--	--
66	7.90	2.3	6.5	--	--	--	--
67	8.05	1.9	6.4	--	--	--	--
68	8.20	1.9	--	1153	--	--	--
69	8.34	1.7	7.5	--	--	--	--
1970	8.47	1.6	--	--	--	--	--
71	8.60	1.5	6.0	--	--	--	94
72	8.77	2.0	--	--	3970	450	95
73	8.92	1.7	--	--	--	--	--
74	9.09	1.9	--	--	--	--	--
75	9.33	3.0	--	--	7430	800	--

Sources: Columns 2, 3, 4, UN Monthly Bulletin of Statistics and Demographic Yearbook World Bank Atlas, 1976; column 5, UN Statistical Yearbook (for given year); columns 6 and 7, IBRD; column 8, UNESCO.

TABLE B-31

DOMINICAN REPUBLIC

Year	Balance of Payments Goods & Services (Mil. U.S. $)	Population (Millions)	% Increase	Death Rate per 1,000	Population per Physician	Real GNP (Millions 1972 U.S. $)	% Increase	Real Per Capita GNP (1972 U.S. $)	% Increase	Newspaper Circulation per 1,000
1958	-22.1	2.80	--	8.4	5150	884	6.4	295	3.1	--
59	1.6	2.90	3.6	10.4	--	885	0.1	287	-2.7	25
1960	45.6	2.99	3.1	9.0	--	943	6.5	298	4.2	27
61	35.0	3.11	4.0	8.4	--	907	-3.8	278	-6.7	--
62	-16.3	3.22	3.5	--	--	1064	17.3	317	14.0	--
63	-48.6	3.33	3.4	--	5680	1154	8.4	334	5.4	--
64	-80.4	3.45	3.6	--	--	1198	3.8	337	0.9	--
65	-32.8	3.51	1.7	--	--	1074	-10.3	293	-13.1	27
66	-74.1	3.62	3.1	7.1	--	1204	12.1	320	9.2	--
67	-69.9	3.72	2.8	7.6	--	1246	3.5	322	0.6	--
68	-85.2	3.83	2.9	--	1680	1258	0.9	315	-2.2	27
69	-93.0	3.95	3.1	14.7	--	1410	12.1	344	9.2	--
1970	-134.5	4.06	2.8	14.7	--	1553	10.1	367	6.7	32
71	-144.0	4.18	2.9	6.0	2044	1705	9.8	390	6.3	36
72	-75.0	4.30	2.9	--	--	1925	12.9	426	9.2	38
73	-128.6	4.43	3.0	6.5	--	2059	7.0	441	3.5	--
74	--	4.56	2.9	--	--	--	--	--	--	--
75	--	4.70	3.0	--	--	3380	--	720	--	--

Sources: Column 2, IMF/IFS; columns 3, 4, 5, UN Monthly Bulletin of Statistics and Demographic Yearbook World Bank Atlas, 1976; column 6, UN Statistical Yearbook (for given year); columns 7 and 9, AID; column 11, UNESCO.

TABLE B-32

GUATEMALA

Year	Balance of Payments Goods & Services (Mil. U.S. $)	Population (Millions)	% Increase	Death Rate per 1,000	Population per Physician	Real GNP (Millions 1972 U.S. $)	% Increase	Real Per Capita GNP (1972 U.S. $)	% Increase	Newspaper Circulation per 1,000
1958	-50.0	3.54	--	--	6530	1040	4.5	266	1.9	--
59	-40.2	3.65	3.1	17.3	--	1091	4.9	273	2.6	22
1960	-25.6	3.76	3.0	17.5	--	1117	2.4	274	-0.4	--
61	-24.2	3.88	3.2	16.3	--	1163	4.1	279	1.8	23
62	-23.0	4.02	3.6	17.3	--	1205	3.7	282	1.1	--
63	-20.8	4.14	3.0	17.2	3600	1319	9.5	302	7.1	--
64	-56.6	4.30	3.9	19.0	--	1378	4.5	308	2.0	--
65	-41.8	4.44	3.2	--	--	1440	4.5	315	2.3	--
66	-23.3	4.56	2.7	16.6	--	1506	4.6	321	1.9	--
67	-79.8	4.70	3.1	--	--	1567	4.0	327	1.9	--
68	-61.4	4.84	3.0	--	--	1700	8.5	346	5.8	--
69	-32.4	4.97	2.7	17.0	--	1778	4.6	353	2.0	--
1970	-25.4	5.10	2.6	14.9	3617	1884	6.0	364	3.1	--
71	-74.5	5.24	2.7	14.4	--	1985	5.4	374	2.7	45
72	-48.6	5.39	2.9	13.3	--	2113	6.4	387	3.5	39
73	-7.7	5.54	2.8	15.4	--	2275	7.7	406	4.9	--
74	-124.5	--	--	--	--	--	--	--	--	--
75	--	6.08	10.0	--	--	3530	55.1	650	60.0	--

Sources: Column 2, IMF/IFS; columns 3, 4, 5, UN Monthly Bulletin of Statistics and Demographic Yearbook World Bank Atlas, 1976; column 6, UN Statistical Yearbook (for given year); columns 7 and 9, AID; column 11, UNESCO.

TABLE B-33

GUYANA

Year	Balance of Payments Goods & Services (Mil. U.S. $)	Population (Millions)	% Increase	Death Rate per 1,000	Population per Physician	Real GNP (Millions 1972 U.S. $)	Real Per Capita GNP (1972 U.S. $)	Newspaper Circulation per 1,000
1958	--	0.53	--	10.2	4045	--	--	--
59	--	0.55	3.8	10.0	--	--	--	71
1960	--	0.56	1.8	9.5	--	--	--	67
61	--	0.58	3.6	9.1	--	--	--	79
62	--	0.60	3.4	8.0	--	--	--	--
63	13.5	--	--	--	2600	136	--	--
64	-9.8	--	--	9.5	--	150	--	--
65	-20.5	0.66	--	--	--	162	245	--
66	-29.8	0.68	3.0	8.3	--	171	--	--
67	-31.8	0.70	2.9	--	--	187	--	--
68	-16.1	0.72	2.8	7.7	4410	203	--	--
69	-13.8	0.74	2.8	6.6	--	218	--	54
1970	-20.6	0.71	--	--	--	233	360	58
71	-6.6	0.73	--	--	4328	252	330	--
72	-11.3	0.74	--	--	--	300	360	54
73	-53.7	0.76	2.7	--	--	--	--	--
74	--	0.77	1.3	--	--	--	--	--
75	--	0.77	0	--	--	450	560	--

Sources: Column 2, IMF/IFS; columns 3, 4, 5, UN Monthly Bulletin of Statistics and Demographic Yearbook World Bank Atlas, 1976; column 6, UN Statistical Yearbook (for given year); columns 7 and 8, IBRD, AID; column 9, UNESCO.

TABLE B-34

HAITI

Year	Balance of Payments Goods & Services (Mil. U.S. $)	Population (Millions)	% Increase	Death Rate per 1,000	Population per Physician	Real GNP (Millions 1972 U.S. $)	Real Per Capita GNP (1972 U.S. $)	Newspaper Circulation per 1,000
1958	-9.3	--	--	--	--	--	--	--
59	--	--	--	--	--	--	--	10
1960	-7.8	--	--	--	--	--	--	11
61	-22.5	--	--	--	10600	--	--	--
62	-14.3	--	--	--	--	--	--	--
63	-7.1	--	--	21.6	--	--	--	--
64	-14.2	--	--	--	--	--	--	--
65	-22.5	3.91	--	22.0	--	--	--	11
66	-21.9	3.97	1.5	--	--	--	--	--
67	-16.9	4.03	1.5	--	--	--	--	--
68	-10.5	4.10	1.7	--	13420	--	--	5
69	-15.3	4.16	1.5	19.7	13213	--	--	--
1970	-20.2	4.24	1.9	19.7	--	--	110	5
71	-18.2	4.31	1.6	--	--	440	90	16
72	-28.0	4.37	1.4	--	--	560	113	16
73	-36.5	4.44	1.6	--	--	--	--	--
74	--	4.51	1.6	--	--	--	--	--
75	--	4.58	2.0	--	--	810	180	--

Sources: Column 2, IMF/IFS; columns 3, 4, 5, UN Monthly Bulletin of Statistics and Demographic Yearbook World Bank Atlas, 1976; column 6, UN Statistical Yearbook (for given year); columns 7 and 8, IBRD, AID; column 9, UNESCO.

TABLE B-35

HONDURAS

Year	Balance of Payments Goods & Services (Mil. U.S. $)	Population (Millions)	% Increase	Death Rate per 1,000	Population per Physician	Real GNP (Millions 1972 U.S. $)	% Increase	Real Per Capita GNP (1972 U.S. $)	% Increase	Newspaper Circulation per 1,000
1958	-9.2	1.72	--	11.7	4710	421	1.2	231	-2.1	--
59	--	1.78	3.5	10.0	--	443	5.2	236	2.2	24
1960	3.1	1.84	3.4	9.8	--	467	5.4	241	2.1	--
61	0.5	1.89	2.7	9.5	--	470	0.6	235	-2.5	--
62	-2.7	1.96	3.7	9.6	--	487	3.6	236	0.4	--
63	-16.8	2.02	3.1	--	--	501	2.9	235	-0.4	--
64	-15.2	2.09	3.5	16.0	--	507	1.2	230	-2.1	--
65	-3.3	2.18	4.3	--	--	547	7.9	240	4.3	--
66	-10.2	2.26	3.7	9.0	--	592	8.2	251	4.6	--
67	-23.2	2.33	3.1	--	--	619	4.6	253	0.8	--
68	-30.8	2.41	3.4	--	3700	674	8.9	267	5.5	--
69	-37.8	2.49	3.3	17.1	--	694	3.0	266	-0.4	--
1970	-70.4	2.51	0.8	--	--	714	2.9	264	-0.7	--
71	-27.4	2.60	3.6	--	--	746	4.5	267	1.1	42
72	-15.4	2.65	1.9	7.9	3449	783	5.0	271	1.5	--
73	-21.0	2.78	4.9	--	--	815	4.1	273	0.7	--
74	--	2.93	5.4	--	--	--	--	--	--	--
75	--	3.04	4.0	--	--	1010	24.0	350	28.2	--

Sources: Column 2, IMF/IFS; columns 3, 4, 5, UN Monthly Bulletin of Statistics and Demographic Yearbook World Bank Atlas, 1976; column 6, UN Statistical Yearbook (for given year); columns 7 and 9, AID; column 11, UNESCO.

TABLE B-36

JAMAICA

Year	Balance of Payments Goods & Services (Mil. U.S. $)	Population (Millions)	% Increase	Death Rate per 1,000	Population per Physician	Real GNP (Millions 1972 U.S. $)	Real Per Capita GNP (1972 U.S. $)	Newspaper Circulation per 1,000
1958	--	1.54	--	--	3740	--	--	--
59	--	1.58	2.6	10.4	--	--	--	54
1960	--	1.61	1.9	8.9	--	--	--	63
61	--	1.63	1.2	8.8	--	--	--	63
62	--	1.66	1.6	9.0	--	--	--	--
63	--	1.69	2.2	9.1	2200	--	--	--
64	--	1.73	2.4	7.8	--	--	--	--
65	--	1.76	2.3	8.5	--	--	--	69
66	--	1.78	1.1	7.8	--	--	--	--
67	--	1.81	1.7	7.0	--	822	454	--
68	-116.1	1.83	1.1	7.6	--	871	476	--
69	-137.9	1.84	0.5	7.6	--	945	513	66
1970	-174.7	1.87	1.6	7.3	2817	1046	590	--
71	-193.1	1.91	2.1	7.6	--	1178	592	114
72	-224.6	1.94	1.6	7.2	--	1560	683	100
73	-274.2	1.98	2.1	7.2	--	--	--	--
74	-309.1	2.00	1.0	--	--	--	--	--
75	--	2.04	2.0	--	--	2630	1290	--

Sources: Column 2, IMF/IFS; columns 3, 4, 5, UN Monthly Bulletin of Statistics and Demographic Yearbook World Bank Atlas, 1976; column 6, UN Statistical Yearbook (for given year); columns 7 and 8, IBRD, AID; column 9, UNESCO.

TABLE B-37

NICARAGUA

Year	Balance of Payments Goods & Services (Mil. U.S. $)	Population (Millions)	% Increase	Death Rate per 1,000	Population per Physician	Real GNP (Millions 1972 U.S. $)	% Increase	Real Per Capita GNP (1972 U.S. $)	% Increase	Newspaper Circulation per 1,000
1958	-13.4	1.33	--	9.5	2860	411	-0.5	300	-3.2	--
59	4.6	1.37	3.0	8.6	--	419	1.9	298	-0.7	66
1960	-11.3	1.41	2.9	8.6	2800	426	1.7	295	-1.0	--
61	-7.7	1.45	2.8	8.0	--	458	7.5	309	4.7	--
62	-13.3	1.49	2.7	7.5	--	508	10.9	333	7.8	--
63	-9.0	1.54	3.3	7.1	--	556	9.4	355	6.6	--
64	-14.6	1.60	3.9	--	--	631	13.5	392	10.4	--
65	-29.7	1.62	1.3	--	--	675	7.0	407	3.8	49
66	-56.3	1.66	2.5	7.2	--	688	1.9	403	-1.0	--
67	-69.9	1.70	2.4	8.0	--	749	8.8	426	5.7	--
68	-46.1	1.74	2.4	--	1970	743	-0.8	410	-3.7	51
69	-42.8	1.79	2.9	16.5	--	806	8.5	432	5.4	--
1970	-45.3	1.83	2.2	--	2060	864	7.2	448	3.7	--
71	-49.4	1.89	3.3	7.1	--	915	5.9	461	2.9	28
72	-13.6	1.95	3.2	--	--	950	3.8	463	0.4	27
73	-94.5	2.01	3.1	6.6	--	975	2.6	461	-0.4	--
74	--	2.08	3.5	--	--	--	--	--	--	--
75	--	2.16	3.8	--	--	1510	55.0	720	56.1	--

Sources: Column 2, IMF/IFS; columns 3, 4, 5, UN Monthly Bulletin of Statistics and Demographic Yearbook; columns 7 and 9, AID; column 11, UNESCO. World Bank Atlas, 1976; column 6, UN Statistical Yearbook (for given year).

345

TABLE B-38

PANAMA

Year	Balance of Payments Goods & Services (Mil. U.S. $)	Population (Millions)	% Increase	Death Rate per 1,000	Population per Physician	Real GNP (Millions 1972 U.S. $)	% Increase	Real Per Capita GNP (1972 U.S. $)	% Increase	Newspaper Circulation per 1,000
1958	-33.5	1.01	--	--	3530	441	1.6	440	-1.3	--
59	--	1.03	2.0	9.1	--	475	7.7	461	4.8	104
1960	-32.4	1.06	2.9	8.3	--	510	7.4	481	4.3	--
61	-28.2	1.11	4.7	8.0	--	569	11.6	521	8.3	--
62	-18.7	1.14	2.7	7.2	--	619	8.8	550	5.5	--
63	-25.6	1.17	2.6	8.0	--	673	8.7	580	5.4	--
64	-16.0	1.21	3.4	7.5	3100	708	5.2	592	2.1	--
65	-19.7	1.23	1.6	--	--	760	7.3	614	3.7	81
66	-42.1	1.27	3.2	7.1	--	819	7.8	645	5.0	--
67	-33.3	1.31	3.1	6.7	--	883	7.8	674	4.5	--
68	-15.2	1.35	3.0	7.2	1970	943	6.8	699	3.7	--
69	-37.8	1.39	2.9	8.8	--	1025	8.7	737	5.4	--
1970	-64.9	1.43	2.9	--	--	1097	7.0	765	3.8	92
71	-76.2	1.48	3.5	6.7	--	1190 *	8.5	809	5.7	--
72	-97.8	1.52	2.7	6.0	1421	1277	7.3	839	3.7	78
73	-128.1	1.57	3.3	--	--	1360	6.5	867	4.5	--
74	--	1.63	3.8	--	--	--	--	--	--	--
75	--	1.67	2.4	--	--	1770	30.1	1060	22.2	--

Sources: Column 2, IMF/IFS; columns 3, 4, 5, UN Monthly Bulletin of Statistics and Demographic Yearbook World Bank Atlas, 1976; column 6, UN Statistical Yearbook (for given year); columns 7 and 9, AID; column 11, UNESCO.

TABLE B-39

TRINIDAD-TOBAGO

Year	Balance of Payments Goods & Services (Mil. U.S. $)	Population (Millions)	% Increase	Death Rate per 1,000	Population per Physician	Real GNP (Millions 1972 U.S. $)	Real Per Capita GNP (1972 U.S. $)	Newspaper Circulation per 1,000
1958	--	0.79	--	--	3000	*	--	--
59	--	0.81	2.5	9.1	--	--	--	81
1960	--	0.84	3.7	7.9	--	--	--	84
61	--	0.87	3.6	8.1	--	--	--	70
62	-54.9	0.89	2.3	7.2	2600	--	--	--
63	-58.3	0.92	3.4	7.1	--	--	--	--
64	-50.0	0.95	3.3	6.2	--	--	--	--
65	-80.3	0.97	2.1	8.0	--	--	--	102
66	-26.5	0.99	2.1	7.1	--	591	597	--
67	-19.2	1.01	2.0	--	--	641	635	--
68	17.1	1.02	1.0	--	2313	746	731	--
69	-17.9	1.03	1.0	6.9	--	764	742	119
1970	-68.4	1.03	0	6.8	--	800	776	148
71	-124.1	1.03	0	6.8	--	964	918	134
72	-157.6	1.05	1.9	7.0	--	1020	1060	--
73	-89.8	1.06	0.9	6.9	--	--	--	--
74	--	--	--	--	--	--	--	--
75	--	1.08	2.0	--	--	2050	1900	--

Sources: Column 2, IMF/IFS; columns 3, 4, 5, UN Monthly Bulletin of Statistics and Demographic Yearbook World Bank Atlas, 1976; column 6, UN Statistical Yearbook (for given year); columns 7 and 8, IBRD, AID; column 9, UNESCO.

TABLE B-40

VENEZUELA

Year	Balance of Payments Goods & Services (Mil. U.S. $)	Population (Millions)	% Increase	Death Rate per 1,000	Population per Physician	Real GNP (Millions 1972 U.S. $)	% Increase	Real Per Capita GNP (1972 U.S. $)	% Increase	Newspaper Circulation per 1,000
1958	-46.0	6.88	--	8.7	1865	6000	7.1	819	3.8	--
59	-77.0	7.12	3.5	8.0	--	6530	8.8	863	5.4	97
1960	482.0	7.36	3.4	7.5	--	6750	3.4	868	0.6	96
61	466.0	7.61	3.4	7.1	--	7050	4.4	873	0.6	83
62	462.0	7.87	3.4	6.7	--	7640	8.4	916	4.9	--
63	555.0	8.14	3.4	--	1300	8180	7.1	950	3.7	--
64	276.0	8.43	3.6	9.5	--	9230	12.8	1037	9.1	--
65	62.0	8.71	3.3	--	--	9760	5.7	1062	2.4	70
66	44.0	9.01	3.4	6.8	--	10020	2.7	1056	-0.6	--
67	73.0	9.31	3.3	6.6	--	10480	4.6	1069	1.2	--
68	-126.0	9.62	3.3	--	1120	11020	5.2	1089	1.9	73
69	-121.0	9.94	3.3	7.8	--	11400	3.4	1091	0.2	71
1970	-44.0	10.28	3.4	--	--	12330	8.1	1143	4.7	--
71	110.0	10.61	3.2	6.5	1057	12730	3.2	1144	0.1	93
72	-30.0	10.94	3.1	6.6	--	13410	5.3	1166	1.9	--
73	547.0	11.28	3.1	--	--	14330	6.9	1206	3.4	--
74	5422.0	11.63	3.1	--	--	--	--	--	--	--
75	--	11.99	3.0	--	--	26670	86.1	2220	84.0	--

Sources: Column 2, IMF/IFS; columns 3, 4, 5, UN Monthly Bulletin of Statistics and Demographic Yearbook World Bank Atlas, 1976; column 6, UN Statistical Yearbook (for given year); columns 7 and 9, AID; column 11, UNESCO.

TABLE B-41

COSTA RICA[a]

Year	AID Loans	AID Grants	PL 480 II	Peace Corps	MAP Grants	Ex.-Im. Bank	Other[b] U.S. Govt.	IBRD[c]	IDA	IDB	UN	Total All Sources	Debt Service	As % of Exp. Rev.
1953-61 MSA	10.9	9.2	1.0	--	0.1	19.4	31.0	17.3	--	--	1.5	90.4	--	--
1962-65 FAA	25.0	8.2	4.5	1.7	1.4	4.5	12.0	30.7	4.6	11.7	2.8	107.1	14.1	--
66	0.5	2.0	0.8	1.1	0.2	10.1	0.3	0.3	--	10.7	0.5	26.5	19.6	10.3
67	5.0	1.9	0.5	0.8	--	--	6.8	--	--	1.8	1.6	18.4	20.7	12.0
68	3.5	1.6	0.6	0.9	--	--	4.9	3.0	--	--	0.4	14.9	25.1	12.0
69	12.2	1.7	1.0	0.5	--	--	3.1	--	--	7.5	0.3	26.3	24.4	11.9
1970	17.4	2.1	0.5	0.6	--	0.2	0.1	34.2	--	8.0	0.2	63.3	27.6	10.6
71	4.2	2.2	0.8	0.7	0.1	0.5	--	--	--	10.1	0.6	19.2	28.2	9.7
72	--	1.7	1.1	0.7	--	0.1	0.3	33.0	--	9.6	1.4	47.9	--	9.9
73	--	1.3	0.8	0.5	--	0.9	--	7.6	--	1.5	1.2	13.8	--	10.0
74	7.9	1.0	0.5	1.2	--	3.5	--	23.5	--	16.0	0.4	54.0	--	--
Total 1953-74	86.6	32.9	12.1	8.7	1.8	39.2	58.5	149.6	4.6	76.9	10.9	481.8	--	--

Sources: Columns 2 through 13, AID; columns 14 and 15, IBRD.

[a] All figures in millions of U.S. $.
[b] Includes $49.3 million for inter-American highways.
[c] Includes IFC: 0.3 (million U.S. $) in 1962-65; 0.3 (million U.S. $) in 1966.

TABLE B-42

DOMINICAN REPUBLIC[a]

Year		AID Loans	AID Grants	PL 480 I	PL 480 II	Peace Corps	MAP Grants	Ex.-Im. Bank	Other U.S. Govt.	IBRD	IDA	IDB	UN	Total All Sources	Debt Service	As % of Exp. Rev.
1953-61	MSA	--	2.1	--	--	--	6.7	--	--	--	--	--	0.6	9.4	--	--
1962-65	FAA	42.6	66.3	12.9	23.9	3.8	8.5	15.1	8.4	--	--	11.0	4.3	196.8	27.5	--
66		39.5	54.8	--	5.4	0.9	3.0	8.1	--	--	--	0.2	0.7	112.6	20.1	12.7
67		47.1	6.6	--	4.3	0.8	2.7	--	--	--	--	3.0	1.4	65.9	13.6	7.3
68		37.8	5.7	10.1	4.1	1.0	2.5	5.8	--	--	--	24.8	1.5	93.3	15.4	7.7
69		8.0	4.3	6.4	6.8	0.8	2.5	2.2	--	--	--	7.4	1.6	40.0	19.6	8.6
1970		1.8	3.4	7.8	6.2	0.6	2.0	--	--	25.0	--	--	0.5	47.3	13.1	5.1
71		10.9	2.6	5.7	7.1	0.5	1.0	--	1.5	--	9.0	7.6	1.9	47.8	19.5	6.7
72		5.1	1.8	12.5	6.5	0.5	2.0	2.9	0.5	--	--	0.1	2.6	34.5	--	4.1
73		--	1.0	9.7	4.5	0.5	2.1	8.8	5.7	7.4[b]	13.0	28.3	2.3	75.9	--	--
74		12.0	0.6	--	4.2	0.5	0.8	30.7	3.9	--	--	37.4	0.9	98.4	--	--
Total 1953-74		204.8	149.2	65.1	73.0	9.9	33.8	73.6	20.0	32.4	22.0	119.8	18.3	821.9	--	--

Sources: Columns 2 through 12, U.S. Overseas Loans and Grants Assistance from International Organizations, AID; columns 13 and 14, World debt tables, IBRD.

[a]All figures in millions of U.S. $.
[b]1974 figure for IFC, not IBRD.

TABLE B–43

GUATEMALA[a]

Year	AID Loans	AID Grants	PL 480 II	Peace Corps	MAP Loans	MAP Grants	Ex.- Im. Bank	Other[b] U.S. Govt.	IBRD	IFC	IDB	UN	Total All Sources	Debt Ser- vice	As % of Exp. Rev.
1953–61 MSA	16.4	73.6	5.1	--	0.1	1.4	13.4	26.2	18.2	0.2	0.1	3.1	157.8	--	--
1962–65 FAA	8.4	12.6	5.8	2.3	--	9.3	4.3	16.3	--	--	8.2	5.0	72.2	11.8	--
66	1.6	2.5	0.9	0.4	--	1.4	--	3.6	--	--	--	0.6	11.0	14.8	5.7
67	8.0	3.5	1.9	0.7	--	2.1	1.8	--	15.0	--	15.1	0.8	48.9	17.3	7.4
68	8.6	2.6	1.9	0.7	--	1.0	--	3.7	7.0	--	6.0	0.7	32.2	20.9	7.8
69	2.6	3.5	2.2	0.6	0.4	1.9	70.0	0.2	6.3	--	9.1	2.3	99.1	24.1	8.0
1970	25.1	4.0	2.5	0.6	--	1.3	--	--	--	--	15.5	1.8	50.8	27.0	7.7
71	9.5	4.7	2.0	0.5	4.0	2.1	2.9	--	4.0	--	6.6	0.7	37.0	27.7	8.2
72	8.4	4.1	3.4	0.7	--	1.8	--	--	16.0	--	2.6	0.4	37.4	--	10.5
73	5.8	3.7	1.7	0.7	2.6	0.9	13.5	0.6	--	--	10.0	0.6	40.1	--	--
74	--	2.5	1.2	1.0	--	1.4	0.6	0.9	--	15.0	31.8	1.2	55.6	--	--
Total 1953–74	94.4	117.3	28.6	8.2	7.1	24.6	106.5	51.5	66.5	15.2	105.0	17.2	642.1	--	--

Sources: Columns 2 through 14, AID; columns 15 and 16, IBRD.

[a]All figures in millions of U.S. $.
[b]Includes $41.3 million for inter-American highways.

TABLE B-44

GUYANA[a]

Year	AID Loans	AID Grants	PL 480 I	PL 480 II	Peace Corps	Ex.-Im. Bank	Other U.S. Govt.	IBRD	IDA	UN	Total All Sources	Debt Service	As % of Exp. Rev.
1953-61 MSA	--	1.7	--	0.6	--	--	--	0.9	--	1.3	4.5	--	--
1962-65 FAA	5.5	9.2	--	0.9	--	--	--	--	--	1.4	17.0	4.8	--
66	4.0	2.2	--	1.2	0.1	--	--	--	--	3.5	11.0	4.9	5.9
67	8.1	1.3	--	0.1	0.2	--	--	--	--	0.3	10.0	5.1	5.2
68	7.2	1.1	--	0.1	0.2	--	--	--	--	0.2	8.8	6.3	6.0
69	15.4	1.3	0.3	0.3	0.3	--	--	7.9	2.9	0.3	28.7	5.1	3.5
1970	--	1.3	--	--	0.3	--	--	--	--	0.3	1.9	5.8	3.9
71	--	1.2	0.3	0.4	0.1	--	--	5.4	2.2	0.4	10.0	4.3	2.8
72	14.3	1.3	0.3	0.8	--	1.1	--	--	4.4	1.2	23.4	--	4.9
73	--	0.7	--	0.2	--	2.4	0.1	6.0	--	2.0	11.4	--	--
74	--	0.1	--	0.1	--	3.6	--	12.9	--	0.7	17.4	--	--
Total 1953-74	54.5	21.4	0.9	4.7	1.2	7.1	0.1	33.1	9.5	11.6	144.1	--	--

Sources: Columns 2 through 12, AID; columns 13 and 14, IBRD.

[a] All figures in millions of U.S. $.

TABLE B-45

HAITI[a]

Year	AID Loans	AID Grants	PL 480 II	MAP Grants	Ex.-Im. Bank	Other U.S. Govt.	IBRD	IDA	IDB	UN	Total All Sources
1953-61 MSA	7.9	44.2	8.9	3.4	11.0	--	2.6	--	2.9	2.9	83.8
1962-65 FAA	3.2	12.1	4.5	0.7	--	--	--	0.4	2.4	5.0	28.3
66	0.2	2.4	0.7	--	3.0	--	--	--	--	0.5	6.8
67	0.2	1.8	0.7	--	--	--	--	--	1.3	1.0	5.0
68	0.1	2.0	1.3	--	--	--	--	--	--	0.4	3.8
69	0.1	1.9	1.3	--	--	--	--	--	--	0.5	3.8
1970	--	1.6	2.1	--	0.1	--	--	--	5.1	0.4	9.3
71	--	2.8	1.5	--	--	--	--	--	--	3.4	7.7
72	--	3.2	1.7	--	--	0.4	--	--	1.8	0.7	7.8
73	3.7	2.6	1.2	--	--	--	--	--	10.0	0.8	18.3
74	6.0	2.7	2.0	--	--	0.7	--	10.0	22.2	2.0	45.6
Total 1953-74	21.4	77.3	25.9	4.1	14.1	1.1	2.6	10.4	45.7	17.6	220.2

Sources: Columns 2 through 12, AID.

[a]All figures in millions of U.S. $.

TABLE B-46

HONDURAS[a]

Year	AID Loans	AID Grants	PL 480 II	Peace Corps	MAP Grants	Ex.-Im. Bank	Other[b] U.S. Govt.	IBRD[c]	IDA	IDB	UN	Total All Sources	Debt Service	As % of Exp. Rev.
1953–61 MSA	12.8	15.0	2.8	--	1.1	2.7	4.6	19.9	8.4	2.2	2.0	71.5	--	--
1962–65 FAA	11.5	9.9	1.6	2.0	3.3	0.4	7.6	6.4	3.5	17.4	2.1	65.7	3.3	--
66	9.9	2.1	1.0	1.0	1.1	--	--	--	--	2.7	0.4	18.2	3.4	2.4
67	7.0	2.1	0.6	0.6	0.8	--	--	13.2	--	9.2	0.4	33.9	3.5	2.1
68	11.0	2.1	0.4	0.7	0.9	--	0.1	7.5	4.0	5.3	2.0	34.0	3.4	2.0
69	0.5	2.2	0.8	0.8	0.7	--	--	--	--	10.5	1.1	16.6	4.3	1.8
1970	2.7	2.8	0.9	0.8	0.4	1.0	--	5.5	8.1	--	0.4	22.6	5.6	2.3
71	2.0	3.2	1.2	0.8	0.7	0.2	--	6.0	--	13.8	1.7	29.6	7.0	2.9
72	--	3.6	1.2	0.8	0.6	1.6	0.1	12.3	--	7.6	1.5	29.3	--	3.3
73	2.0	3.6	0.9	0.7	0.5	7.3	--	18.8	--	10.4	1.0	45.2	--	3.4
74	22.1	2.5	1.2	1.0	0.6	3.2	0.2	3.0	9.6	8.4	0.1	51.9	--	--
Total 1953–74	81.5	49.1	12.6	9.2	10.7	16.4	12.6	92.6	33.6	87.5	12.7	418.5	--	--

Sources: Columns 2 through 13, AID: columns 14 and 15, IBRD.

[a]All figures in millions of U.S. $.
[b]Includes $5.5 million for inter-American highways.
[c]Includes IFC: 0.4 (million U.S. $) in 1962–65.

TABLE B-47

JAMAICA[a]

Year	AID Loans	AID Grants	PL 480 I	PL 480 II	Peace Corps	MAP Grants	Ex.-Im. Bank	Other U.S. Govt.	IBRD	IFC	IDB	UN	Total All Sources	Debt Service	As % of Exp. Rev.
1953-61 MSA	--	2.2	--	4.6	--	--	--	--	--	0.2	--	0.7	7.7	--	--
1962-65 FAA	11.6	3.0	--	8.9	1.5	0.5	4.3	--	5.5	--	--	1.9	37.2	6.9	--
66	--	1.4	--	1.7	0.6	0.6	3.0	--	20.7	--	--	1.4	29.4	7.9	1.8
67	--	0.7	--	0.9	0.6	--	3.0	--	9.5	--	--	1.7	16.4	9.4	2.2
68	--	1.0	--	6.8	0.7	--	--	--	--	--	--	0.4	8.9	13.2	3.2
69	--	0.9	--	0.6	0.7	--	15.0	--	5.0	2.9	--	1.1	26.2	13.8	3.0
1970	--	0.8	--	0.4	0.9	--	7.0	--	2.0	--	--	1.4	12.5	16.5	3.2
71	20.0	0.9	--	1.1	1.1	--	0.9	--	17.2	--	16.9	1.8	59.9	21.7	3.9
72	--	1.2	--	3.9	1.0	--	16.7	0.8	--	--	3.0	1.3	27.9	--	5.3
73	4.4	1.2	--	1.4	1.0	--	7.3	0.4	9.3	--	7.9	0.7	33.6	--	--
74	9.1	0.8	0.8	1.0	1.0	--	15.9	0.5	20.5	--	22.9	0.9	73.4	--	--
Total 1953-74	45.1	14.1	0.8	31.3	9.1	1.1	73.1	1.7	89.7	3.1	50.7	13.3	333.1	--	--

Sources: Columns 2 through 14, AID; columns 15 and 16, IBRD.

[a]All figures in millions of U.S. $.

TABLE B-48

NICARAGUA[a]

Year		AID Loans	AID Grants	PL 480 II	Peace Corps	MAP Grants	Ex.-Im. Bank	Other[b] U.S. Govt.	IBRD[c]	IDA	IDB	UN	Total All Sources	Debt Service	As % of Exp. Rev.
1953-61	MSA	10.2	8.1	0.2	--	1.9	12.5	15.2	30.2	--	2.0	1.6	81.9	--	--
1962-65	FAA	17.9	9.5	5.2	--	5.7	--	18.1	0.1	3.0	8.9	4.7	73.1	7.3	--
66		14.3	2.0	1.2	--	1.3	2.8	--	--	--	15.7	0.5	37.8	9.6	4.3
67		9.2	2.2	0.8	--	1.1	--	--	5.0	--	7.0	1.0	26.3	11.5	5.6
68		23.7	1.8	0.2	--	1.1	4.9	--	21.3	--	2.2	1.5	56.7	14.4	6.4
69		--	1.8	0.3	0.2	0.8	--	--	--	--	12.2	0.4	15.7	19.1	7.6
1970		--	2.3	0.4	0.4	1.0	--	0.1	--	--	0.2	0.8	5.2	23.0	10.1
71		9.9	2.6	0.3	0.4	1.1	1.1	--	--	--	12.4	0.6	28.4	30.8	10.8
72		--	2.5	1.7	0.5	0.9	0.1	--	30.9	--	4.0	1.5	42.1	--	13.6
73		20.3	2.2	3.9	0.8	1.5	--	1.0	11.0	20.0	34.7	1.4	95.9	--	10.5
74		10.0	2.4	2.4	0.5	1.3	3.4	1.9	8.5	--	9.8	2.0	42.2	--	--
Total 1953-74		115.5	37.4	15.7	2.8	17.7	24.8	36.3	107.0	23.0	109.1	16.0	505.3	--	--

Sources: Columns 2 through 13, AID; columns 14 and 15, IBRD.

[a]All figures in millions of U.S. $.
[b]Includes $25.2 million for inter-American highways.
[c]Includes IFC: 2.1 (million U.S. $) in 1968.

TABLE B-49

PANAMA[a]

Year	AID Loans	AID Grants	PL 480 II	Peace Corps	MAP Grants	Ex.-Im. Bank	Other[b] U.S. Govt.	IBRD	IFC	IDB	UN	Total All Sources	Debt Service	As % Exp. Rev.
1953-61 MSA	14.8	12.8	5.7	--	0.1	13.0	21.6	14.0	--	--	1.4	83.4	--	--
1962-65 FAA	22.7	19.1	2.5	2.2	1.4	12.8	25.0	4.0	--	4.0	4.9	98.6	5.8	--
66	11.3	1.5	0.5	1.1	0.6	--	--	--	--	9.7	1.4	26.1	6.2	2.7
67	28.5	6.7	0.6	0.7	0.5	--	--	--	--	10.4	1.5	48.9	6.9	2.7
68	15.8	3.8	0.3	0.9	0.2	--	--	--	--	--	0.4	21.4	8.4	3.0
69	13.1	2.9	0.6	0.8	0.3	--	--	--	--	--	1.5	19.2	9.1	3.4
1970	8.5	3.3	1.0	0.7	0.9	2.5	--	42.0	--	9.8	1.2	69.9	28.1	7.8
71	7.0	4.1	0.6	0.5	1.2	2.7	4.7	--	1.5	19.1	3.1	44.5	36.2	9.4
72	19.1	3.7	1.2	--	0.5	30.1	9.8	23.4	--	--	2.2	90.0	--	11.0
73	3.8	3.3	0.5	--	0.6	45.6	7.9	4.7	--	15.7	2.2	84.3	--	--
74	8.3	2.5	0.7	--	0.6	2.8	16.4	30.0	--	21.5	0.1	82.9	--	--
Total 1953-74	152.9	63.7	14.2	6.9	6.9	109.5	85.4	118.1	1.5	90.2	19.9	669.2	--	--

Sources: Columns 2 through 13, AID; columns 14 and 15, IBRD.

[a] All figures in millions of U.S. $.
[b] Includes $56.8 million for inter-American highways and $12.9 million under Social Progress Trust Fund.

TABLE B-50

TRINIDAD–TOBAGO[a]

Year	AID Loans	AID Grants	PL 480 II	Peace Corps	Ex.-Im. Bank	IBRD	IDB	UN	Total All Sources	Debt Service	As % of Exp. Rev.
1953–61 MSA	--	7.5	0.4	--	--	--	--	0.4	8.3	--	--
1962–65 FAA	--	24.3	0.3	0.1	12.8	21.4	--	1.1	60.0	9.6	--
66	--	5.0	0.1	--	4.0	--	--	0.3	9.4	10.5	4.2
67	--	5.0	0.1	--	--	13.6	--	0.9	19.6	9.8	3.5
68	--	--	--	--	5.9	--	1.0	1.0	7.9	8.7	3.0
69	--	--	0.1	--	--	11.4	4.3	0.8	16.6	12.5	3.7
1970	--	--	--	--	--	--	3.6	0.3	3.9	11.9	3.8
71	--	--	0.1	--	2.1	3.0	--	0.8	6.0	11.2	3.3
72	--	--	0.1	--	6.5	2.0	7.6	0.7	16.9	--	3.0
73	--	--	--	--	--	21.3	13.1	0.9	35.3	--	--
74	--	--	--	--	8.3	18.0	2.4	1.5	30.2	--	--
Total 1953–74	--	41.8	1.2	0.1	39.6	90.7	32.0	8.7	214.1	--	--

Sources: Columns 2 through 10, AID; columns 11 and 12, IBRD.

[a]All figures in millions of U.S. $.

TABLE B-51

VENEZUELA[a]

Year	AID Loans	AID Grants	PL 480 II	Peace Corps	MAP Loans	MAP Grants	Ex.-Im. Bank	Other U.S. Govt.	IBRD	IFC	IDB	UN	Total All Sources	Debt Service	As % of Exp. Rev.
1953-61 MSA	15.0	1.3	--	--	31.2	0.1	51.2	--	--	3.2	9.2	2.9	114.1	--	--
1962-65 FAA	40.0	7.7	16.4	5.6	44.0	13.9	44.2	72.9	174.0	0.3	23.4	8.2	450.6	46.1	--
66	--	1.7	3.9	3.6	10.0	1.9	--	--	54.1	0.5	3.0	3.7	82.4	67.2	2.7
67	--	1.4	2.3	2.4	--	0.9	27.5	--	13.8	--	17.2	-0.6	66.1	53.1	2.0
68	--	1.4	1.5	2.1	--	1.0	61.2	--	--	2.5	23.5	2.4	95.6	55.5	2.1
69	--	1.0	0.6	1.6	--	0.8	1.3	--	51.0	2.1	32.2	0.8	91.4	54.2	2.0
1970	--	1.1	--	1.6	--	0.8	13.5	--	--	--	75.4	1.4	93.8	80.9	2.9
71	--	1.0	--	1.5	7.4	0.9	12.2	--	35.0	11.8	12.8	1.9	84.5	117.6	3.7
72	--	0.8	4.7	1.4	7.5	2.1	36.9	--	28.0	1.0	2.1	2.7	87.2	--	4.5
73	--	0.4	--	1.2	7.6	2.7	15.4	0.1	--	3.0	58.4	2.6	91.4	--	--
74	--	0.3	--	2.2	7.5	0.9	24.5	0.1	22.0	--	10.6	0.4	68.5	--	--
Total 1953-74	55.0	18.1	29.4	23.2	115.2	26.0	287.9	73.1	377.9	24.4	267.8	27.6	1325.6	--	--

Sources: Columns 2 through 14, AID; columns 15 and 16, IBRD.

[a]All figures in millions of U.S. $.

NOTES

NOTES

Chapter 2

1. Wilson, who hoped to "teach the Latin-American republics to elect good men," refused to recognize the Huerta government in Mexico because it had come to power through violence and because he regarded it as counterrevolutionary; he even sent U.S. troops to take Veracruz by storm (with 400 casualties).

Chapter 3

1. Over the years, the title of the State Department bureau that handles Latin American affairs has changed many times. We shall refer to it as the Bureau of American Republic Affairs—ARA—and to its leader as assistant secretary for ARA. Similarly, despite title changes, we shall refer to the congressional committees as the House Foreign Affairs Committee (and its Latin American Subcommittee) and as the Senate Foreign Relations Committee (and its Latin American Subcommittee).

Chapter 4

1. That marked the beginning of Kennedy's focus on internal security. Before long, Kennedy became infatuated with counterinsurgency ("the worst folly of his administration," Schlesinger concluded later) and created the Green Berets, sent military teams to train Latin American troops in guerrilla fighting, and sent AID public safety experts, sometimes with heavy CIA involvement, to train Latin American police in riot control.

2. This looked like a long-term financial commitment, anathema to the U.S. Congress. President Kennedy had specifically promised more than $1 billion in U.S. aid in the first year but had said nothing about future U.S. aid, and Secretary Dillon had gone to Punta del Este without instructions on that crucial point. Presumably, the administration did not want to name a figure while the foreign aid bill was making its way through Congress. But Dillon found the Latin American finance ministers concerned because nobody could tell them how much money they could expect from the United States, yet they were begin asked to go back home and ask their parliaments to enact exceedingly difficult reforms. Dillon, though uninstructed, on his own announced that Latin America "can reasonably expect" a ten-year capital inflow of "at least $20 billion" and estimated that U.S. government aid might come to an average of $1.1 billion a year for ten years.

3. Puerto Rico's per capita income exceeded $1,000 for the first time in 1967—$1,047 on July 1. The World Bank in its annual report reclassified Puerto Rico as a "rich nation," a little poorer than the Soviet Union but richer than Italy, Japan, Spain, Greece, and all of Latin America.

4. AD's name is Acción Democrática—"Democratic Action." COPEI's full name is Comité de Organización Política y Electoral Independiente—"Committee for Independent Political and Electoral Organization"; it was originally founded in 1946 as a church-oriented alternative to the anticlerical Venezuelan Student Federation and the AD. After spending years of exile in Europe, however, COPEI's leaders realigned COPEI with the Social Christian movement.

5. President Kennedy sent the author to the Dominican Republic on a fact-finding mission at the end of the summer of 1961; then in March 1962, he appointed him our ambassador. For a full account of those missions, see John Bartlow Martin, *Overtaken by Events* (New York: Doubleday, 1966).

6. Late in 1975, after a long investigation, a Senate Select Committee on U.S. intelligence activities, led by its chairman, Frank Church, published a report on U.S. involvement in the assassination plots against Trujillo, Lumumba, Castro, Diem, and a Chilean general. The committee said that as early as February 1960 the Eisenhower administration had given high-level consideration to covert aid to Dominican dissidents; President Eisenhower himself had approved a contingency plan providing that if the Dominican situation deteriorated further, the United States would "take political action to remove Trujillo" as soon as a suitable successor regime could be established with U.S. political, economic, and, if necessary, military support. That spring, the U.S. ambassador in Santo Domingo established contact with Dominican dissidents, who asked for sniper rifles. A recommendation to provide them was approved both by State and the

CIA, but they were never provided. After the OAS imposed sanctions on Trujillo, the United States closed its embassy in Santo Domingo but left the deputy chief of mission, Henry Dearborn, there as CIA station chief. Dearborn, who maintained contact with the oppositionists, came to believe that nothing short of assassination could remove Trujillo and so informed Washington. In January 1961, the Special Group that approved or disapproved covert CIA actions approved a State plan to use the CIA to provide "small arms and other matériel" to dissidents inside the Dominican Republic. After President Kennedy's inauguration, CIA officials met Dominican dissidents in New York; the latter requested equipment and help from the CIA. Nothing seems to have come of all this. In March 1961, a CIA station officer reported that Dearborn had requested three .38 caliber pistols. The CIA headquarters in Washington was authorized to put the three pistols in the sealed diplomatic pouch regularly sent to Santo Domingo. But Dearborn told the Senate Committee that he had requested only one pistol and that it was for purposes completely unrelated to any assassination attempt. The committee concluded that no direct evidence linked any of these pistols to the assassination itself.

On other occasions, CIA headquarters or the Special Group approved smuggling guns into the CIA station, but they did not approve passing them to Dominican dissidents. Headquarters was coming to feel that a precipitous assassination might only bring about a Castro-style regime in place of Trujillo. Secretary Rusk sent President Kennedy a memorandum concerning plans for an orderly takeover "should Trujillo fall" and told him that our men in Santo Domingo had, at considerable risk, established contact with underground leaders and that the CIA had recently been authorized to deliver small arms and sabotage equipment to them. The Senate committee concluded that by mid-Februray 1961 the senior members of the new Kennedy administration, including Kennedy, knew of Special Group's approval for passing arms and equipment to the Dominican opposition. After the Bay of Pigs failure, however, State and CIA men in the Dominican Republic tried to dissuade the Dominican underground from a precipitous assassination attempt, but the latter seemed determined to go ahead with or without U.S. help. On May 16, President Kennedy approved a National Security Council recommendation that the United States not initiate the overthrow of Trujillo until it was known what government would replace him. The day before Trujillo was assassinated, Dearborn received a cable of instructions and guidance from President Kennedy himself. It advised him that the United States must not run the risk of being associated with political assassination, since the United States, as a matter of general policy, could not condone assassination. The cable also told Dearborn to continue to hold open offers of material assistance to the dissidents and to tell them the United States would support them if they succeeded in overthrowing

Trujillo.

The Senate committee concluded that U.S. officials "clearly desired the overthrow of Trujillo" and offered both encouragement and guns. The committee said, "The Presidents and other senior officials in the Eisenhower and Kennedy Administration sought the overthrow of Trujillo and approved or condoned actions to obtain that end." It concluded that the assistant secretary for ARA knew fairly early that the dissidents intended to assassinate Trujillo, but it was not clear how soon before May higher officials, including President Kennedy, knew it. The committee said the president's cable could be construed in at least three ways—that he was clearly opposed to assassination "as a matter of general policy," that he was trying to lay the groundwork for denying U.S. responsibility for the murder, and that both such interpretations might be correct. It also concluded that high policymaking officials frequently were not well informed about what was going on and that, after the assassination occurred, neither the president nor the Special Group issued any instruction to subordinates criticizing any aspect of U.S. involvement or took action to prevent it from happening again elsewhere.

7. This practice has now been widely criticized. At that time, however, and in that place, such training seemed imperative. The police, trained under Trujillo, knew nothing but to shoot to kill. Teaching them how to control riots with means short of deadly force seemed humanitarian.

8. The group became known as the Executive Committee of the National Security Council. Its members were the attorney general, the president's brother, Robert F. Kennedy; Secretary of State Rusk; Secretary of Defense McNamara; the director of the CIA, John McCone; Secretary of the Treasury Dillon; Theodore Sorensen, the president's counsel; Under Secretary of State George Ball; Deputy Under Secretary of State U. Alexis Johnson; General Maxwell Taylor, chairman of the Joint Chiefs of Staff; Ed Martin, assistant secretary of state for ARA; Ambassador Chip Bohlen (he left after one day to become ambassador to France and his place as a Soviet specialist on Ex Comm was taken by Llewellyn Thompson); Roswell Gilpatric, deputy secretary of defense; and Paul Nitze, assistant secretary of defense. Meeting with them intermittently were Vice-President Lyndon Johnson; Dean Acheson; our ambassador to the UN, Adlai Stevenson; Kenneth O'Donnell, President Kennedy's appointments secretary; and Donald Wilson, deputy director of the United States Information Agency.

9. About two months before Kennedy's death, an African ambassador told William W. Attwood, an American ambassador temporarily assigned to the U.S. Mission to the United Nations, that Castro was looking for a way to end his status as a Soviet satellite. Since other sources indicated that Castro wanted accommodation with the United States, President Kennedy

approved Attwood's meeting with the Cuban ambassador to the UN. The Cuban indicated that a meeting with Castro or his personal envoy might be useful. Negotiations over the place of the meeting and its agenda were proving successful; then Kennedy was assassinated, and the plans came to an end. See William Attwood, *The Reds and the Blacks* (New York: Harper and Row, 1967), pp. 142-147.

Chapter 5

1. The literature about the Dominican intervention is extensive. For opposing accounts, see John Bartlow Martin, *Overtaken by Events*; and Theodore Draper, "The Dominican Crisis: A Case Study in American Policy," *Commentary* 40, no. 6 (December 1965).

2. Total U.S. commitments to Latin America between July 1, 1961, and June 29, 1962, totaled $1.10 billion, and actual disbursements by AID, Export-Import Bank, Social Progress Trust Fund, Food-for Peace, and the Peace Corps totaled $1.03 billion. Disbursements in the Caribbean were:

Costa Rica	$ 6.0 million
Dominican Republic	12.4
Guatemala	8.4
Haiti	9.9
Honduras	7.2
Nicaragua	9.7
Panama	7.9
Venezuela	76.0
	$137.5 million

3. Eric Williams, prime minister of Trinidad-Tobago, has traced the origin of such shipping legislation to the English Navigation Acts of the seventeenth century, which are held to be a prinicipal cause of the American colonies' revolution against Britain.

4. President Johnson did not include a piece of land to call his own among the benefits the Alliance offered the peasant; instead, he referred to "land reform aimed at increased production." Tom Mann said, "Archaic land tenure systems still exist which must be replaced *within the objective of increased productivity.*" At Punta del Este II in 1967, the Declaration of the Presidents emphasized production.

Chapter 6

1. The consensus said that obstacles to development were increasing, especially tariffs and other restrictions that impeded access to world markets "on favorable and equitable terms" for the manufactured and semimanufactured goods of the poor nations: AID was diminishing and the terms of AID were tightening; debt service virtually wiped out AID. The international monetary system placed the poor nations at a disadvantage as

did shipping arrangements and inadequate technological transfers. A
"reformulation" of inter-American cooperation and the reaffirmation of
such basic principles as sovereignty, nonintervention, and aid without
political or military strings were needed to overcome these problems.
Inter-American political and security solidarity must be extended to
economic and social fields. Latin Americans should work together in the
United Nations and the Organization of American States. The Consensus
then presented the United States with its proposals, including these: to
negotiate with the United States for the elimination of all restrictions on
trade in Latin American products; to press for a special round of GATT
negotiations for primary commodities not already covered; to press for
observance of the timetables fixed at the second UNCTAD on commodity
agreements; to demand effective consultative machinery to prevent the
distortions in Latin American trade that resulted from tied AID loans "and
the haphazard sale of surpluses"; to review bilateral and multilateral food
aid, with a view to expanding the multilateral programs; to seek the active
support of the United States for Latin America's position in world trade; and
promptly to establish a general, nonreciprocal, nondiscretionary system of
preferences for poor countries' manufactures and semimanufactures. The
ministers demanded freedom to use foreign aid as they saw fit, an end to tied
aid, "real multilateralization" of lending, liberalized interest rates, aid
"without strings" of any kind, reforms in private investments, and a bigger
role for Latin America in international monetary reform. (See Benjamin S.
Rosenthal, "Three Key Documents on Latin America," Speech to House of
Representatives, July 16, 1969.) There was more, much more.

2. Nixon said, "For years, we in the United States have pursued the
illusion that we alone could remake continents. Conscious of our wealth
and technology, seized by the force of good intentions, driven by habitual
impatience, remembering the dramatic success of the Marshall Plan in
postwar Europe, we have sometimes imagined that we knew what was best
for everyone else and that we could and should make it happen."

3. "Legitimate aspirations" is a curious piece of State Department
cant. Latin Americans can read it with gratification, for it seems to
acknowledge that their aspirations are legitimate; but State can interpret it
to a skeptical Congress to mean that we and we alone will determine which
of their many aspirations are legitimate.

4. Acheson said:

To be sure, *great decisions* are, for the most part, made at the top,
when they are not made by events. But, as for policy—the sum total
of many decisions—it must be said, as it has been said of sovereignty,
that its real sources are undiscoverable. One fact, however, is clear

to anyone with experience in government: the springs of policy bubble up; they do not trickle down.

When this upsurgence of information, ideas, and suggestions is vigorous, appreciated, and encouraged, strong, imaginative, and effective policies are most apt to result. When the whole function of determining what is what, and what to do about it, is gathered into one hand, or into a small group at the top, the resulting action may or may not be strong, but it is likely to be ill-adapted to reality and self-defeating. [Don K. Price, ed., *The Secretary of State* (Englewood Cliffs, N.J.: Prentice-Hall, 1960), p. 41.]

During the last eighteen months of the Johnson administration, "the essential element of government," as Kissinger later called it, was the weekly Tuesday lunch the president held, a meeting of which no record was kept. U.S., Congress, Senate, Committee on Foreign Relations, *Hearings on the Nomination of Henry Kissinger*, 93rd Cong., September 1973, p. 310.

5. Principal Caribbean trade routes have been estimated to carry cargo as follows (given in million long tons of cargo in 1969):

From Europe to the West Coast of the U.S. and Canada: 7.6.
From U.S. East Coast to Japan: 32.9.
From U.S. East Coast to Asia less Japan: 7.9.
From U.S. East Coast to West Coast South America: 7.3.
From Europe to West Coast South America: 5.6.
South American intercoastal: 4.0.

In addition, of course, trade moves in the Caribbean-Gulf from the mouth of the Mississippi to the U.S. East Coast and to the Caribbean and South America was well as from the Caribbean countries themselves to the United States, Europe, Asia, and inter-Caribbean. James D. Theberge, ed., *Russia in the Caribbean: Part II-A, Special Report* (Washington, D.C.: Center for Strategic and International Studies, 1973), pp. 1-3.

6. The doctrine of credibility has been widely discredited as it was applied to Vietnam. But the Caribbean is not Southeast Asia, and in the Caribbean the doctrine of credibility would appear to have its own credibility.

7. The details of the Soviet ship deployments to the Caribbean follow: In mid-June 1969, two FOXTROT-class diesel-powered attack submarines, a NOVEMBER-class nuclear-powered attack submarine, and an UGRA-class submarine tender were seen departing the White Sea base area and on June 18 rounding North Cape, headed south into the Norwegian Sea.

Simultaneously, a surface force including a KYNDA-class missile cruiser left its Black Sea base area, passed through the Turkish Straits into the Mediterranean on June 23, entered the Atlantic on June 28, and rendez-voused with the submarine group off the Azores on July 3. After refueling from two Soviet tankers, they crossed the Atlantic on separate courses and rendezvoused off Bermuda on July 9. The seven-ship flotilla with nuclear missiles that entered the Gulf of Mexico and Caribbean in mid-July and visited Cuba from July 20 to July 27 (helping to celebrate the 26th of July anniversary of the Castro revolution) consisted of a KYNDA-class guided missile cruiser, a KOSHIN-class guided missile frigate, a KILDEN-class missile destroyer, two FOXTROT-class diesel attack submarines, an UGRA-class tender and tanker. The flotilla stayed in the Caribbean area for about a month, conducting antisubmarine exercises in the Gulf of Mexico and other exercises in the Caribbean, then some of them visited Fort-de-France in Martinique August 5-8 and Bridgetown, Barbados, August 10-12, finally departing the Caribbean August 12. The NOVEM-BER-class nuclear attack submarine apparently did not put into Havana or any other port. The KYNDA-class missile cruiser has eight launchers for the SHADDOCK surface-to-surface missile, which has a range of about 200 miles with guidance from the launching ship (450 miles with guidance from another ship or aircraft). The KYNDA-class cruiser carries sixteen such missiles, each with a payload of about 2,000 pounds and capable of delivering a nuclear warhead.

The Soviet Union sent another group to the Caribbean in April and May 1970, during its worldwide naval maneuvers called OKEAN. Two TV20/95 BEAR-D naval long-range reconnaissance aircraft took off from a Northern Fleet base in the White Sea, flew around Norway, flew over the Soviet ships conducting OKEAN exercises near Iceland, and continued nonstop all the way to Cuba, landing on April 18, 1970, a flight of more than 5,000 nautical miles. It was the first time that BEAR aircraft had landed outside Soviet bloc nations. At the same time, a Soviet flotilla consisting of a KRESTA I-class missile cruiser and a KANIN-class missile destroyer broke off from the North Atlantic OKEAN exercises and, after being joined by an ECHO-II class submarine, two FOXTROT-class attack submarines, and an UGRA-class tender and a tanker, arrived at Havana on May 14. Thus, within a single year, the Soviet Union had sent a powerful multipurpose naval force into the Caribbean. The KRESTA I has only four SHADDOCK antiship missile launchers but carries powerful antiaircraft and anti-submarine equipment. The KANIN is an advanced antiaircraft missile ship. The ECHO-II nuclear submarine carries eight SHADDOCK Launching Tubes—the NOVEMBER-class submarine of the first visit had carried only torpedoes. For details, see Theberge, *Russia in the Caribbean.*

8. China, France, USSR, Guinea, India, Panama, Sudan, Yugoslavia, Australia, Austria, Indonesia, Kenya, and Peru.

9. The "principles for negotiation" were these: (1) The Treaty of 1903 would be abrogated and an entirely new one concluded. (2) The concept of "perpetuity" would be eliminated and a fixed termination date agreed to. (3) "Termination of United States jurisdiction over Panamanian territory" would take place "promptly" in accordance with terms specified in the new treaty. (4) The Panamanian territory where the Canal was situated would be returned to Panama's jurisdiction; Panama, in its sovereign capacity, would grant to the United States on the new treaty's terms the right to use the lands, waters, and airspace necessary for the operation, maintenance, protection, and defense of the Canal and the transit of ships. (5) Panama would have "a just and equitable share" of the benefits derived from Canal operation, since Panama's geographical position was its principal natural resource. (6) Panama would participate in the administration of the Canal, as the treaty would provide, and assume responsibilty for operating the Canal when the treaty terminated. Panama would grant to the United States the rights necessary to regulate the transit of ships and to operate, maintain, protect, and defend the Canal, as the treaty would set out. (7) Panama and the United States would protect and defend the Canal as agreed in the treaty. (8) The United States and Panama would agree bilaterally on provisions for new projects to enlarge the Canal's capacity. U.S., Department of State, *Bulletin,* February 25, 1974, pp. 184-185.

10. For a good analysis of this issue and of the problem of rationalizing the world sugar trade, see chapter 21 of Philip Bonsal's *Cuba, Castro, and the United States* (Pittsburgh: University of Pittsburgh Press, 1971).

11. Dominican Republic, Haiti, Jamaica, Barbados, Trinidad, Guyana, Belize, Venezuela, Panama, Costa Rica, Nicaragua, Honduras, and Guatemala.

12. U.S. investment (in millions of U.S. dollars) was distributed as follows:

	Bauxite Mining	Alumina Production	Total
Dominican Republic	25	—	25
Haiti	30	—	30
Guyana	30	—	30
Jamaica	100	560	660
Surinam	125	50, and aluminum 125	300

Source: Bureau of Mines.

13. In the first credit *tranche,* the IMF imposes few conditions before granting the loan. Conditions become increasingly stringent thereafter.

14. They say that to ensure success certain conditions are essential: (1) the

associated producers must control a significant portion of the production, exports, and reserves or stocks of the commodity; (2) they must be able to forego export earnings for considerable periods of time and be immune to retaliation on imports; (3) consumer demand must be relatively price inelastic; (4) substitute or alternative products must not be too readily available to the consumers; and (5) producers must share similar strongly held political and economic objectives.

15. See, for example, Elizabeth Drew, "The Energy Bazaar," *The New Yorker*, July 21, 1975.

16. For a decade, the shoe industry has been complaining that it is being injured by the import of non-rubber shoes made abroad. In 1976, the International Trade Commission finally decided unanimously that it had indeed been injured and was entitled to relief. But the commission split over the question of what kind of relief: three members favored a steep tariff increase, two favored a "tariff quota" (higher duty only on imports beyond a certain volume), and one favored "adjustment assistance" to domestic companies and workers. President Ford, exercising discretion under the Trade Act of 1974, chose "adjustment assistance." In doing so, he understandably, in an election year, emphasized not the need to open our market to foreign producers but the need to keep shoe prices in the U.S. down to mitigate inflation. No one could be sure what "adjustment assistance" would amount to. As for the workers, many shoe workers were already eligible for expanded unemployment compensation, and a small additional number probably would be eligible. As for the companies, until now the Commerce Department has had a small program providing for such things as aid loans, guaranteed loans, and technical assistance. Such programs are far short of the central planned arrangements suggested above. *New York Times*, April 17, 1976; *Wall Street Journal*, April 19, 1976.

17. United States intelligence sources believe that Cuba had troops operating in at least ten countries in Asia and Africa. Cuban troops formed part of President Sekou Touré's bodyguard in Guinea, Cuban bureaucrats served in Equatorial Guinea and Somalia, Cuban troops trained guerrillas in Tanzania to harass the Rhodesian government, Cuban troops in Brazzaville Congo supported native troops in Angola, Cuban guerrillas showed Guinea-Bissau rebels how to use the terrain against the Portuguese, Cuban troops trained guerrillas from the western Sahara in Algeria, MIG-flying Cuban pilots served South Yemen, and in Syria Cubans formed a full armored brigade with nearly one hundred Soviet T-62 tanks.

18. See next section.

19. Or at least it seemed in June 1976, when the situation was far from clear. Of course, if Angola means that Castro, in middle age with his revolution at home secure, has indeed made the short-term choice of

foregoing rapprochement with the United States to assume militant leadership of a worldwide revolutionary movement, he is likely to bring about a collision with the United States that may go beyond polemics. Since the Soviet navy is far stronger now than at the time of the missile crisis, and since Cuba and the Soviet Union have become even more closely linked than they were then, Cuban resistance of a U.S. blockade might lead to a U.S.-Soviet confrontation far more dangerous than that of 1962. Castro did, however, send word to us that he intended to withdraw his troops from Angola.

20. The resolution was adopted twelve to two with nine abstentions. Those in favor were Bulgaria, Chile, People's Republic of China, Congo, Czechoslovakia, India, Iraq, Mali, Syria, Tanzania, USSR, and Yugoslavia. Those opposed were Ethiopia and Iran. Those abstaining were Afghanistan, Australia, Fiji, Indonesia, Ivory Coast, Sweden, *Trinidad-Tobago,* Tunisia, and *Venezuela.* (Sierra Leone was absent).

21. In transmitting information to headquarters, the station chief evaluates his informant on a sliding scale ranging from "highly reliable" through "fairly reliable" to "untrustworthy" and evaluates the information itself on a scale running from "almost surely true" to "possibly true" to "almost surely false." Sometimes a station chief nearing retirement will play it safe and evaluate every piece of information and every informant in the middle of the scales. Such an operation is worse than useless; it is dangerous. An ambassador reviewing the CIA cables can make his own evaluation and dispute the station chief's.

22. Anti-multinational feelings are particularly strong where people remember United Fruit's (later United Brands) ruthless operations.

23. This opening discussion draws on a *New York Times* editorial of December 21, 1975.

24. British firms are involved in Mexico's steel industry. West Germany sold Brazil a nuclear energy plant. France is an arms supplier in the hemisphere.

25. In fairness to Kissinger, it should be noted again that he was preoccupied with Vietnam, the Middle East, and, later, Africa and that he was operating in the straitjacket of a sullen national mood, a deep recession, a disillusioned Congress, an economy-minded administration and Congress, and a White House in crisis.

Chapter 7

1. The Caribbean nations could be grouped thus: Venezuela and Trinidad-Tobago at over $1,200; Barbados and Panama in the $900-$1,000 range; Costa Rica and Jamaica between $700 and $900; Nicaragua and the Dominican Republic at $500 to $700; Guatemala and Guyana at $300 to $500;

and Honduras and Haiti below $300. The U.S. figure is $6,051.

2. The labor force engaged in agriculture ranges from 22 percent in Venezuela and Trinidad to 83 percent in Haiti, with most of the other countries in the 40-60 percent range.

3. The percentage of the total population under fifteen ranges from 37 percent in Barbados and Cuba to 47 percent in Honduras, Nicaragua, and the Dominican Republic, with the other countries falling between 41 percent and 46 percent. The U.S. figure is 27 percent.

4. Australia, Austria, Belgium, Canada, Denmark, France, Germany, Japan, Italy, the Netherlands, New Zealand, Norway, Portugal, Sweden, Switzerland, the United Kingdom, and the United States.

5. See the tables in Appendix B.

6. See p. 233ff.

7. See p. 232ff.

8. The Export-Import Bank operates on nearly commercial terms; in 1972, it provided loans of an average maturity of about six years at 6.14 percent interest. The multilateral agencies, which depend on bond issues for their capital, must lend at terms considerably harder than those of bilateral donors. In 1972, World Bank loans averaged sixteen years maturity with 4.8 years of grace and carried 7.25 percent interest. The World Bank's International Development Association, funded by periodic capital subscriptions, makes soft loans to poor countries—up to fifty years maturity, ten years grace, and 0.75 percent interest. (It accounts for about 25 percent of total World Bank lending.) In 1972 the IADB made loans averaging 19.3 years maturity, 6.3 years grace, and 5.1 percent interest.

9. When a commodity price drops steeply on world markets, countries depending on export of that commodity suffer temporary balance-of-payments difficulties. The IMF extends loans to help (but on banker's terms), and little use has been made of it.

10. The reader will find recent material on the economies and economic policies of Caribbean nations, country by country, in Appendix A.

11. See Appendix B.

12. For example, $2.9 million to Jamaica in 1969, $1.5 million to Panama in 1971, $21 million to the Dominican Republic in 1974. The Dominican Republic has adopted a grandiose scheme to add at least 15,000 rooms between 1976 and 1981.

13. Guatemala, Honduras, El Salvador, Nicaragua, and Costa Rica.

14. For detailed statistics, see Appendix B.

15. See pp. 370 regarding the recent shoe case.

Chapter 8

1. *Special relationship* is a much abused phrase. All to often it has been the rhetorical flourish that we have vouchsafed Latin Americans when we

had no intention of giving them anything real. What is proposed here is a genuine special relationship, one that is tangible and serious. It can never, of course, be as close as the special relationship we developed with Great Britain during World War II—clearly we have no intention of consulting Jamaica or Guyana, let alone Grenada, about our posture in the SALT talks. But it should nevertheless be a unique relationship appropriate to our interests and the Caribbean's.

2. Colombia, El Salvador, and Surinam, though not treated fully in this book, would have to be included in this new special relationship. Mexico, too, would have to be taken into account.

3. The reader will find material underlying the recommendations at the bracketed pages attached to most recommendations.

4. Bonsal, *Cuba, Castro, and the United States,* pp. 219-225.

BIBLIOGRAPHY

BIBLIOGRAPHY

Bibliographic Note

The material in this book is based on a large number of sources, among them the author's own experiences and his numerous interviews with embassy officials and diplomats from all the countries involved in the study, including the United States. Many of those interviewed were willing to discuss sensitive matters only after being assured that they would not be identified. The book is also the result of wide reading and research in the field. The following books, articles, and documents are the basic sources consulted.

Books

Abel, Elie. *The Missile Crisis.* Philadelphia: Lippincott, 1966.

Agee, Philip. *Inside the Company: CIA Diary.* New York: Stonehill, 1975.

Alba, Victor. *Alliance Without Allies: The Mythology of Progress in Latin America.* Translated by John Pearson. New York: Praeger, 1965.

Alexander, Robert J. *Communism in Latin America.* New Brunswick, N.J.: Rutgers University Press, 1957.

Allison, Graham T. *Essence of Decision: Explaining the Cuban Missile Crisis.* Boston: Little, Brown, 1971.

Andic, Fuat and Suphan, and Dosser, Douglas. *A Theory of Economic Integration for Developing Countries.* University of York Studies in Economics. London: Allen and Unwin, 1971.

Bailey, Thomas A. *A Diplomatic History of the American People.* 8th ed. New

New York: Meredith (Appleton-Century-Crofts Educational Division), 1969.

Baker, Ray Stannard. *Woodrow Wilson, Life and Letters.* Vol. 4, *President 1913-1914.* New York: Doubleday Doran, 1939.

Ball, M. Margaret. *The OAS in Transition.* Durham, N.C.: Duke University Press, 1969.

Beckford, George. *Persistent Poverty: Underdevelopment in Plantation Economies of the Third World.* New York: Oxford University Press, 1972.

Bemis, Samuel Flagg, ed. *The American Secretaries of State and Their Diplomacy.* 10 vols. in 5. 2d ed. New York: Pageant Book Company, 1958.

―――. *The Latin American Policy of the United States: An Historical Interpretation.* Yale University Institute of International Studies Publications. New York: Harcourt, Brace, 1943.

Berle, Beatrice B., and Jacobs, Travis B. *Navigating the Rapids, 1918-1971.* New York: Harcourt, 1973. (From the papers of Adolf A. Berle)

Bernstein, Harry. *Origins of Inter-American Interest 1700-1812.* Philadelphia: University of Pennsylvania Press, 1945.

Bonsal, Philip W. *Cuba, Castro, and the United States.* Pittsburgh: University of Pittsburgh Press, 1971.

Boyke, Roy, ed. *Patterns of Progress: Trinidad and Tobago.* Port-of-Spain, Trinidad: Key Caribbean Publications, 1972.

Bradford, Colin I., Jr., et al. *New Directions in Development: Latin America, Export Credit, Population Growth, and U.S. Attitudes.* Overseas Development Council Studies, no. 2. New York: Praeger, 1974.

Burnham, Forbes. *A Destiny To Mould: Selected Discourses by the Prime Minister of Guyana.* Edited by C. A. Nascimento and R. A. Burrowes. London: William Clowes & Sons, Ltd., 1970.

Burr, Robert. N. *Our Troubled Hemisphere: Perspectives on United States–Latin American Relations.* Washington: Brookings Institution, 1967.

Callcott, Wilfrid Hardy. *The Caribbean Policy of the United States, 1890-1920.* Baltimore: Johns Hopkins Press, 1942.

Calvert, Peter. *The Mexican Revolution, 1910-1914: The Diplomacy of Anglo-American Conflict.* New York: Cambridge University Press, 1968.

Chalmers, Douglas A., ed. *Changing Latin America: New Interpretations of Its Politics and Society.* Proceedings of the Academy of Political Science, Columbia University, vol. 30, no. 4. New York, 1972.

Checchi, Vincent, et al. *Honduras: A Problem in Economic Development.* New York: The Twentieth Century Fund, 1959.

Connell-Smith, G. *The Inter-American System.* London: Oxford University Press, 1966.

Co-operative Republic Guyana 1970. *A Study of Aspects of Our Way of Life.* Georgetown, June 1970.

Corkran, Herbert, Jr. *Patterns of International Cooperation in the Caribbean, 1942-1969.* Dallas: Southern Methodist University Press, 1970.

Cotler, Julio, and Fagen, Richard R., eds. *Latin America and the United States: The Changing Political Realities.* Stanford, Calif.: Stanford University Press, 1974.

Cox, Isaac Joslin. *Nicaragua and the United States, 1909-1927.* World Peace Foundation Pamphlets, vol. 10, no. 7. Boston, 1927.

Crassweller, Robert D. *The Caribbean Community: Changing Societies and United States Policy.* New York: Praeger, 1972.

De Conde, Alexander. *Herbert Hoover's Latin-American Policy.* Stanford, Calif.: Stanford University Press, 1951.

De Kadt, Emanuel, ed. *Patterns of Foreign Influence in the Caribbean.* London: Oxford University Press, 1972.

Denny, Harold Norman. *Dollars for Bullets: The Story of American Rule in Nicaragua.* New York: Deal Press, 1929.

Dinerstein, Herbert S. *Soviet Policy in Latin America.* Santa Monica: Rand Corporation, 1966.

Dozer, Donald Marquand. *Are We Good Neighbors? Three Decades of Inter-American Relations, 1930-1960.* New York: Johnson Reprint Corp., 1972. (Reprint of work published 1959 by the University of Florida Press, with a new introduction by the author.)

Dreier, John C., ed. *The Alliance for Progress: Problems and Perspectives.* Baltimore: Johns Hopkins Press, 1962.

Dubois, Jules. *Danger Over Panama.* Indianapolis: Bobbs-Merrill, 1964.

Einaudi, Luigi R., ed. *Beyond Cuba: Latin America Takes Charge of Its Future.* New York: Crane, Russak & Co., 1974.

―――. *Latin America in the 1970's.* Santa Monica, Calif.: Rand Corporation, 1972.

Eisenhower, Dwight D. *The White House Years.* Vol. 1, *Mandate for Change, 1953-1956.* New York: Doubleday, 1963.

Eisenhower, Milton. *The Wine Is Bitter: The United States and Latin America.* New York: Doubleday, 1963.

Fairlie, Henry. *The Kennedy Promise: The Politics of Expectation.* New York: Doubleday, 1973.

Ferguson, Yale H., ed. *Contemporary Inter-American Relations: A Reader in Theory and Issues.* Englewood Cliffs, N.J.: Prentice-Hall, 1972.

Ferguson, Yale H., and Weiker, Walter F., eds. *Continuing Issues in International Politics: A Reader.* Pacific Palisades, Calif.: Goodyear Publishing Co., 1973.

Gabbert, Jack B., ed. *American Foreign Policy and Revolutionary Change.* Pullman: Washington State University Press, 1968.

Gantenbein, James Watson. *The Evolution of Our Latin-American Policy: A Documentary Record.* New York: Columbia University Press, 1950.

Georgetown University. Center for Strategic and International Studies. *Panama: Canal Issues and Treaty Talks.* Special Report Series, no. 3. Washington: Georgetown University, 1967.

Girvan, Norman. *Foreign Capital and Economic Underdevelopment in Jamaica.* Institute of Social and Economic Research, University of the West Indies, Jamaica, 1971.

Goldhamer, Herbert. *The Foreign Powers in Latin America.* Princeton: Princeton University Press, 1972.

Gordon, Lincoln. *A New Deal for Latin America: The Alliance for Progress.* Cambridge, Mass.: Harvard University Press, 1963.

Gorshkov, Sergei G. *Red Star Rising in Sea.* Washington, D.C.: U.S. Naval Institute, 1974.

Green, David. *The Containment of Latin America: A History of the Myths and Realities of the Good Neighbor Policy.* Chicago: Quadrangle Books, 1971.

Guerrant, Edward O. *Roosevelt's Good Neighbor Policy.* Albuquerque: University of New Mexico Press, 1950.

Haley, P. Edward. *Revolution and Intervention: The Diplomacy of Taft and Wilson with Mexico, 1910-1917.* Cambridge, Mass.: Massachusetts Institute of Technology Press, 1970.

Hanson, Simon G. *Five Years of the Alliance for Progress: An Appraisal.* Washington: Inter-American Affairs Press, 1967.

Hellman, Ronald G., and Rosenbaum, H. Jon. *Latin America: The Search for a New International Role.* Latin American International Affairs Series, sponsored by the Center for Inter-American Relations, vol. 1. New York: John Wiley & Sons, 1975.

Hirschman, Albert O. *A Bias for Hope: Essays on Development and Latin America.* New Haven: Yale University Press, 1971.

————. *Journeys Toward Progress: Studies of Economic Policy-Making in Latin America.* New York: The Twentieth Century Fund, 1963.

————. *Latin American Issues: Essays and Comments.* New York: The Twentieth Century Fund, 1961.

Howarth, David A. *Panama: Four Hundred Years of Dreams and Cruelty.* New York: McGraw-Hill, 1966.

Huberman, Leo, and Sweezy, Paul M. *Cuba: Anatomy of a Revolution.* New York: Monthly Review Press, 1961.

International Bank for Reconstruction and Development. *The Economic Development of Venezuela.* Report of a mission organized by the International Bank for Reconstruction and Development at the request of the government of Venezuela. Baltimore: Johns Hopkins Press, 1961.

Irving, Brian, ed. *Guyana: A Composite Monograph.* Hato Rey, Puerto Rico: Inter American University Press, 1972.

Jacobson, Harold Kazan. "The Contemporary Arena." In *Foreign Policy in the Sixties: The Issues and the Instruments,* ed. Roger Hilsman and Robert C.

Good. Baltimore: The Johns Hopkins Press, 1970.

Jagan, Cheddi. *The West on Trial.* New York: International Publishers, 1967.

James, Daniel. *Red Design for the Americas: Guatemalan Prelude.* New York: Day, 1954.

Kennedy, Paul P. *The Middle Beat: A Correspondent's View of Mexico, Guatemala, and El Salvador.* Edited by Stanley R. Ross. New York: Teachers College Press, 1971.

Kirkpatrick, Lyman B., Jr. *The U.S. Intelligence Community: Foreign Policy and Domestic Activities.* New York: Hill and Wang, 1973.

Kolko, Gabriel. *The Roots of American Foreign Policy.* Boston: Beacon Press, 1969.

Langley, Lester D. *The Cuban Policy of the United States.* New York: Wiley, 1968.

Larson, Arthur. *Eisenhower, the President Nobody Knew.* New York: Scribner's, 1968.

Latané, John Holladay, and Wainhouse, David W. *A History of American Foreign Policy 1776-1940.* 2d rev. ed. New York: Doubleday, 1941.

Levinson, Jerome, and de Onís, Juan. *The Alliance That Lost Its Way: A Critical Report on the Alliance for Progress.* New York: The Twentieth Century Fund, 1970.

Lieuwen, Edwin. *Arms and Politics in Latin America.* Rev. ed. New York: Praeger, 1962.

————. *Petroleum in Venezuela: A History.* University of California Publications in History, vol. 47. Berkeley: University of California Press, 1954.

————. *Venezuela.* London: Oxford University Press, 1961.

Lineberry, William P. *The United States in World Affairs 1970.* New York: Simon & Schuster, 1971.

Link, Arthur S. *Wilson: The New Freedom.* Princeton, N.J.: Princeton University Press, 1956.

————. *Wilson: The Struggle for Neutrality 1914-1915.* Princeton, N.J.: Princeton University Press, 1960.

Liska, George. *The New Statecraft: Foreign Aid in American Foreign Policy.* Chicago: University of Chicago Press, 1960.

Lockey, Joseph B. *Pan-Americanism: Its Beginnings.* New York: Arno Press, 1970. (Reprint of 1920 edition)

Lowenthal, David. *West Indian Societies.* Published for the Institute of Race Relations, London, in collaboration with the American Geographical Society, New York. New York: Oxford University Press, 1972.

Madariaga, Salvador de. *Latin America Between the Eagle and the Bear.* New York: Praeger, 1962.

Mahan, Alfred Thayer. *The Influence of Sea Power Upon History, 1660-1783.* Boston: Little, Brown, 1890.

Martin, John Bartlow. *Overtaken by Events*. New York: Doubleday, 1966.

Martz, J. D. *Central America: The Crisis and the Challenge*. Chapel Hill: University of North Carolina Press, 1959.

Massachusetts Institute of Technology. Center for International Studies. *The Objectives of United States Economic Assistance Programs*. Washington: Government Printing Office, 1957.

May, Ernest R. *The Making of the Monroe Doctrine*. Cambridge, Mass.: Harvard University Press, 1975.

May, Robert E. *The Southern Dream of a Caribbean Empire, 1954-1961*. Baton Rouge: Louisiana State University Press, 1973.

May, Stacy, and Plaza, Galo. *The United Fruit Company in Latin America*. Seventh Case Study in National Planning Association Series on United States Business Performance Abroad, vols. 6-7, 1957-1958. Washington: National Planning Association, 1958.

Mayer, George H., and Förster, Walter O. *The United States and the Twentieth Century*. Boston: Houghton Mifflin, 1958.

Mazo, Earl. *Richard Nixon: A Political and Personal Portrait*. New York: Harper & Brothers, 1959.

Mecham, J. Lloyd. *A Survey of United States–Latin American Relations*. Boston: Houghton Mifflin, 1965.

————. *The United States and Inter-American Security, 1889-1960*. Austin: University of Texas Press, 1961.

Melville, Thomas and Marjorie. *Guatemala: The Politics of Land Ownership*. New York: Free Press, 1971.

Mesa-Lago, Carmelo, ed. *Revolutionary Change in Cuba*. Pittsburgh: University of Pittsburgh Press, 1971.

Miner, Dwight Carroll. *The Fight for the Panama Route*. New York: Octagon Books, 1966.

Mitchell, Sir Harold. *Caribbean Patterns: A Political and Economic Study of the Contemporary Caribbean*. 2d ed. New York: John Wiley & Sons, 1972.

Morrison, deLesseps S. *Latin American Mission: An Adventure in Hemisphere Diplomacy*. New York: Simon and Schuster, 1965.

Moss, Robert, ed. *The Stability of the Caribbean: Report of a Seminar Held at Ditchley Park, United Kingdom, May 18-20, 1973*. Washington, D.C.: Georgetown University, Center for Strategic and International Studies, 1973.

Mowry, George E. *The Era of Theodore Roosevelt, 1900-1912*. New York: Harper & Row, 1958.

Munro, Dana G. *Intervention and Dollar Diplomacy in the Caribbean: 1900-1921*. Princeton, N.J.: Princeton University Press, 1964.

————. *The United States and the Caribbean Republics, 1921-1933*. Princeton, N.J.: Princeton University Press, 1974.

Myrdal, Gunnar. *Asian Drama: An Inquiry Into the Poverty of Nations.* 3 vols. New York: The Twentieth Century Fund, 1968.

Nearing, Scott, and Freeman, Joseph. *Dollar Diplomacy: A Study in American Imperialism.* New York: Huebsch & Viking Press, 1926.

Needler, Martin C., ed. *Political Systems of Latin America.* 2d ed. New York: Van Nostrand Reinhold, 1970.

———. *The United States and the Latin American Revolution.* Boston: Allyn and Bacon, 1972.

Nicole, Christopher. *The West Indies, Their People and History.* London: Hutchinson, 1965.

Nixon, Richard M. *Six Crises.* New York: Doubleday, 1962.

Notter, Harley. *The Origins of the Foreign Policy of Woodrow Wilson.* New York: Russell & Russell, 1965. (Reprint of 1937 edition.)

Parker, Franklin. *The Central American Republics.* London: Oxford University Press, 1964.

Paul, R. A. *American Military Commitments Abroad.* New Brunswick, N.J.: Rutgers University Press, 1973

The People's National Congress. Thirteenth Annual Conference. *Policy for the New Co-op Republic (of Guyana).* Georgetown, Guyana: Daily Chronicle, Ltd., 1970.

Pérez, Carlos Andrés al Congreso Nacional. *Primer Mensaje: Del Ciudadano Presidente de la República,* 1975.

Perkins, Dexter. *A History of the Monroe Doctrine.* New revised edition. Boston: Little, Brown, 1963.

———. *The Monroe Doctrine 1823-1826.* Cambridge, Mass.: Harvard University Press, 1932.

———. *The Monroe Doctrine 1867-1907.* Baltimore: Johns Hopkins Press, 1937.

———. *The United States and the Caribbean.* Rev. ed. Cambridge, Mass.: Harvard University Press, 1966.

———. *The United States and Latin America.* Baton Rouge: Louisiana State University Press, 1961.

Plaza, Galo. *1968-1975: Seven Years of Change.* Washington, D.C.: General Secretariat of the Organization of American States, 1975.

Porter, Charles O., and Alexander, Robert J. *The Struggle for Democracy in Latin America.* New York: Macmillan, 1961.

Pratt, Julius W. *Expansionists of 1898: The Acquisition of Hawaii and the Spanish Islands.* New York: Peter Smith, 1951.

Preiswerk, Roy, ed. *Regionalism and the Commonwealth Caribbean.* Trinidad: Institute of International Relations, University of the West Indies, 1968.

Price, Don K., ed. *The Secretary of State.* Englewood Cliffs, N.J.: Prentice-Hall, 1960.

Pringle, Henry F. *Theodore Roosevelt: A Biography.* Rev. ed. New York: Harcourt, Brace & World, 1956.

Pusey, Merlo J. *The U.S.A. Astride the Globe.* Boston: Houghton Mifflin, 1971.

Reno, Philip. *The Ordeal of British Guiana.* New York: Monthly Review Press, 1964.

Rickards, Colin. *Caribbean Power.* London: Dennis Dobson, 1963.

Rippy, J. Fred. *The Caribbean Danger Zone.* New York: Putnam, 1940.

————. *Latin America: A Modern History.* New ed. Ann Arbor: University of Michigan Press, 1968.

————. *Rivalry of the United States and Great Britain over Latin America (1808-1830).* Baltimore: Johns Hopkins Press, 1929.

Rogers, William D. *The Twilight Struggle: The Alliance for Progress and the Politics of Development in Latin America.* New York: Random House, 1967.

Romualdi, Serafino. *Presidents and Peons: Recollections of a Labor Ambassador in Latin America.* New York: Funk & Wagnalls, 1967.

Ronning, Neale. *Punta del Este: The Limits of Collective Security in a Troubled Hemisphere.* New York: Carnegie Endowment for International Peace, 1962.

Rosenthal, Mario. *Guatemala: The Story of an Emergent Latin-American Democracy.* New York: Twayne Publishers, 1962.

Rotberg, Robert I., with Clague, Christopher K. *Haiti: The Politics of Squalor.* A Twentieth Century Fund Study. Boston: Houghton Mifflin, 1971.

Rubin, Vera, ed. *Caribbean Studies: A Symposium.* Jamaica: Institute of Social and Economic Research, University College of the West Indies, 1957.

Rubinstein, Alvin Z. *The Soviets in International Organizations: Changing Policy toward Developing Countries, 1953-1963.* Princeton, N.J.: Princeton University Press, 1964.

Ruiz, Ramón Eduardo. *Cuba: The Making of a Revolution.* New York: W. W. Norton, 1970.

Ryan, Selwyn D. *Race and Nationalism in Trinidad and Tobago: A Study of Decolonization in a Multiracial Society.* Toronto: University of Toronto Press, 1972.

Schlesinger, Arthur M., Jr. *The Alliance for Progress: A Retrospective.* New York: Center for Inter-American Relations, 1975.

————, ed. *The Dynamics of World Power: A Documentary History of United States Foreign Policy 1945-1973.* Vol. 3. *Latin America.* New York: Chelsea House Publishers, 1973.

————. *The Imperial Presidency.* Boston: Houghton Mifflin, 1973.

————. *A Thousand Days.* Boston: Houghton Mifflin, 1965.

Schmitt, Karl M., and Burks, D. C. *Evolution or Chaos: Dynamics of Latin American Government and Politics.* New York: Praeger, 1963.

Schneider, Ronald M. *Communism in Guatemala 1944-1954.* New York: Praeger, 1959.

Segal, Aaron Lee, ed. *Population Policies in the Caribbean.* Lexington, Mass.: D. C. Heath, 1975.

Simms, Peter. *Trouble in Guyana: An Account of People, Personalities and Politics as They Were in British Guiana.* London: Allen & Unwin, 1966.

Slater, Jerome. *The OAS and United States Foreign Policy.* Columbus: Ohio State University Press, 1967.

Smith, Raymond T. *British Guiana.* London: Oxford University Press, 1962.

Sorensen, Theodore C. *Kennedy.* New York: Harper-Row, 1965.

Stebbins, Richard P. *The United States in World Affairs.* New York: Harper, 1951-. (Annual volumes from 1951 published for the Council on Foreign Relations.)

————, and Adam, Elaine P., eds. *Documents on American Foreign Relations 1970.* New York: Council on Foreign Relations, Harper and Row, 1970.

Steel, Ronald. *Pax Americana.* New York: Viking Press, 1967.

Steinberg, Alfred. *Sam Johnson's Boy: A Close-up of the President from Texas.* New York: Macmillan, 1968.

Stimson, Henry L. *American Policy in Nicaragua.* New York: Charles Scribner's, 1927.

Stuart, Graham H. *The Department of State: A History of Its Organization, Procedure, and Personnel.* New York: Macmillan, 1949.

Stupak, Ronald J. *The Shaping of Foreign Policy: The Role of the Secretary of State as Seen by Dean Acheson.* Indianapolis: Odyssey Press, 1969.

Szulc, Tad, ed. *The United States and the Caribbean.* Englewood Cliffs, N.J.: Prentice-Hall, Inc., 1971.

Szulc, Tad. *The Winds of Revolution: Latin America Today—and Tomorrow.* New York: Praeger, 1963.

Tannenbaum, Frank. *Ten Keys to Latin America.* New York: Knopf, 1962.

Theberge, James D., ed. *Russia in the Caribbean: Part 11-A, Special Report.* Washington, D.C.: Georgetown University, Center for Strategic and International Studies, 1973.

Thomas, Hugh. *Cuba: The Pursuit of Freedom.* New York: Harper and Row, 1971.

Toriello Garrido, Guillermo. *La Batalla de Guatemala.* Mexico City: Ediciones Cuadernos Americanos, 1955.

Urquidi, Victor L. *The Challenge of Development in Latin America.* New York: Praeger, 1964.

Veliz, Claudio, ed. *Latin America and the Caribbean.* New York: Praeger, 1968.

Weintal, Edward, and Bartlett, Charles. *Facing the Brink: An Intimate Study of Crisis Diplomacy.* New York: Scribner's, 1967.

Welles, Sumner. *Naboth's Vineyard: The Dominican Republic, 1844-1924.* New York: Arno Press, 1972. (Reprint of 1928 ed., 2 vols. in one)

Wells, Henry. *The Modernization of Puerto Rico: A Political Study of Changing Values and Institutions.* Cambridge, Mass.: Harvard University Press, 1969.

Whetten, N. L. *Guatemala: The Land and the People.* Westport, Ct.: Greenwood Press, 1974. (Reprint of 1961 edition.)

Whitaker, Arthur Preston. *The United States and the Independence of Latin America, 1800-1830.* New York: Russell and Russell, 1962.

————. *The Western Hemisphere Idea: Its Rise and Decline.* Ithaca, N.Y.: Cornell University Press, 1954.

Wilgus, A. Curtis, ed. *The Caribbean: British, Dutch, French, United States.* Caribbean Conference Series, vol. 8. Gainesville: University Presses of Florida, 1958.

————, ed. *The Caribbean: Contemporary International Relations.* Gainesville: University Presses of Florida, 1957.

————, ed. *The Caribbean: Its Hemispheric Role.* Gainesville: University Presses of Florida, 1967.

————, ed. *The Caribbean: Its Political Problems.* Gainesville: University Presses of Florida, 1956.

Williams, Eric. *From Columbus to Castro: The History of the Caribbean 1492-1969.* London: Harper & Row Publishers, 1970.

————. *History of the People of Trinidad and Tobago.* Trinidad: PNM Publishing Company, Ltd., 1962.

Williams, William Appleman. *The United States, Cuba, and Castro: An Essay on the Dynamics of Revolution and the Dissolution of Empire.* New York: Monthly Review Press, 1962.

Wise, David, and Ross, Thomas B. *The Invisible Government.* New York: Random House, 1964.

Wood, Bryce. *The Making of the Good Neighbor Policy.* New York: Columbia University Press, 1961.

Ydígoras Fuentes, Miguel. *My War With Communism. As Told to Mario Rosenthal.* Englewood Cliffs, N.J.: Prentice-Hall, 1963.

Articles

Acheson, Dean G. "Homage to Plain Dumb Luck." *Esquire*, February 1969, pp. 76-77.

Adler, Selig. "Bryan and Wilsonian Caribbean Penetration." *Hispanic American Historical Review* 20 (May 1940):198-226.

Allan, Donald A., and Sherman, George. "Panama: Distrust and Delay."

Reporter, February 27, 1964, pp. 28-29.

Ameringer, Charles D. "The Panama Canal Lobby of Philippe Bunau-Varilla and William Nelson Cromwell." *American Historical Review* 68 (January 1963):346-363.

Bender, Lynn Darrell. "Contained Nationalism: The Mexican Foreign Policy Example." *Revista/Review Interamericana* 5 (Spring 1975).

Berle, A. A., Jr. "Our Role in Latin America." *Reporter*, November 9, 1961, pp. 30-33.

Bronheim, David. "Relations Between the United States and Latin America." *International Affairs* (London) 46 (July 1970):501-516.

Bundy, William P. "Dictatorships and American Foreign Policy." *Foreign Affairs* 54 (October 1975):51-60.

Cabranes, José A. "The Status of Puerto Rico." *International Comparative Law Quarterly*, April 1967, pp. 531-539.

Cater, Douglass. "The Lesson of Punta del Este." *Reporter*, March 1, 1962, pp. 19-22.

Cochrane, James D. "U.S. Policy towards Recognition of Governments and Promotion of Democracy in Latin America since 1963." *Journal of Latin American Studies* 4 (November 1972):275-291.

Cohen, Paul. "The Erosion of Surface Naval Power." *Foreign Affairs* 49 (January 1971):330-341.

Cox, Isaac J. "Pan-American Policy of Jefferson and Wilkinson." *Mississippi Valley Historical Review* 1 (September 1914):222-223.

Crassweller, Robert D. "Darkness in Haiti." *Foreign Affairs* 49 (January 1971):315-329.

Crossley, J. Colin. "Continuing Obstacles to Agricultural Development in Latin America." *Journal of Latin American Studies* 4 (November 1972): 293-305.

Dale, Edwin L., Jr. "Captain of Our Economic Campaign." *New York Times Magazine*, August 31, 1958.

Donelan, Michael. "The Ideas of United States Economic Aid." *The Year Book of World Affairs*, no. 20 (1966), pp. 106-142.

Dozer, Donald M. "Recognition in Contemporary Inter-American Relations." *Journal of Inter-American Studies* 8 (April 1966):318-335.

Draper, Theodore. "How Red is Guatemala?" *Reporter*, November 7, 1950, pp. 23-26.

————. "The Minutemen of Guatemala." *Reporter*, October 24, 1950, pp. 32-35.

Dreier, John C. "New Wine and Old Bottles: The Changing Inter-American System." *International Organization* 22 (Spring 1968):477-493.

Duggal, Ved Prakash. "Some Notes on International Divestment in Latin

America." *Revista/Review Interamericana* 2 (Fall 1972):388-395.

Eder, Richard. "Haiti, Land of the Big Tontons." *New York Times Magazine,* January 24, 1965.

Foner, Philip S. "Why the United States Went to War with Spain in 1898." *Science and Society* 32 (Winter 1968):39-65.

Frank, Richard A. "The Law At Sea." *New York Times Magazine*, May 18, 1975.

Frei Montalva, Eduardo. "The Alliance That Lost Its Way." *Foreign Affairs* 45 (April 1967):437-449.

————. "Latin America in the World of Today." *International Affairs* (London) 42 (July 1966):373-380.

Frei Montalva, Eduardo. "The Second Latin American Revolution." *Foreign Affairs* 50 (October 1971):83-96.

Friedenberg, Daniel M. "Can the Alliance for Progress Work?" *Commentary,* August 1962, pp. 93-101.

Galbraith, J. K. "Conditions for Economic Change in Underdeveloped Countries." *Journal of Farm Economics* 33 (November 1951):689-696.

Gall, Norman. "The Challenge of Venezuelan Oil." *Foreign Policy*, no. 18 (1975), pp. 44-67.

Geyelin, Philip. "The Irksome Panama Wrangle." *Reporter*, April 9, 1964, pp. 14-17.

Goebel, Dorothy Burne. "British Trade to the Spanish Colonies, 1796-1823." *American Historical Review* 43 (January 1938):288-320.

Goodwin, Richard N. "Our Stake in a Big Awakening." *Life*, April 14, 1967, pp. 66-83.

Gordon, Lincoln. "Punta del Este Revisited." *Foreign Affairs* 45 (July 1967):624-628.

Gordon, Max. "A Case History of U.S. Subversion: Guatemala, 1954." *Science and Society* 35 (Summer 1971):129-155.

Graham, David L. "Guatemala's Shrine of Blood." *Nation,* June 2, 1962, pp. 496-497.

Grayson, George W., Jr. "The Era of the Good Neighbor." *Current History* 56 (June 1969):327-332.

Greer, Virginia L. "State Department Policy in Regard to the Nicaraguan Election of 1924." *Hispanic American Historical Review* 34 (November 1954):445-467.

Hanson, Simon G. "Alliance for Progress: The Second Year." *Inter-American Economic Affairs* 17 (Winter 1963):3-101.

————. "The End of the Good-Neighbor Policy." *Inter-American Economic Affairs* 7 (Autumn 1953):3-49.

Haviland, H. Field, Jr. "Foreign Aid and the Policy Process: 1957." *American Political Science Review* 52 (September 1958):689-724.

Heinl, Robert Debs, Jr. "Bailing Out Duvalier." *New Republic*, January 14, 1967, pp. 15-16.

———. "Haiti. A Case Study in Freedom." *New Republic*, May 16, 1964, pp. 15-21.

Hollick, Ann L. "What To Expect From a Sea Treaty." *Foreign Policy*, no. 18 (Spring 1975), pp. 68-78.

Howard, Anthony. "Lurching into the Cannon's Mouth." *New Statesman*, January 31, 1969, pp. 144-145.

Huelin, David. "A New Latin America." *International Affairs* (London), special issue, November 1970, pp. 56-71.

Jagan, Cheddi. "From Guyana to Chile." *World Marxist Review* 17 (June 1974):101-104.

Johnson, Leland L. "U.S. Business Interests in Cuba and the Rise of Castro." *World Politics* 17 (April 1965):440-459.

Juárez, Joseph Robert. "United States Withdrawal from Santo Domingo." *Hispanic American Historical Review* 42 (May 1962):152-190.

Kahan, Jerome H., and Long, Anne K. "The Cuban Missile Crisis: A Study of Its Strategic Content." *Political Science Quarterly* 87 (December 1972):564-590.

Klare, Michael T. "Superpower Rivalry at Sea." *Foreign Policy*, no. 21 (1975).

Kling, Merle, "Towards a Theory of Power and Political Instability in Latin America." *Western Political Quarterly* 9 (March 1956):21-35.

Kramer, Jane. "Letter from Guyana." *New Yorker*, September 16, 1974, pp. 100-128.

Langley, Lester D. "Military Commitments in Latin America: 1960-1968." *Current History* 56 (June 1969):346-351.

Leuchtenburg, William E. "Progressivism and Imperialism: The Progressive Movement and American Foreign Policy, 1898-1916." *Mississippi Valley Historical Review* 39 (December 1952):483-504.

Lieuwen, Edwin. "Neo-Militarism in Latin America: The Kennedy Administration's Inadequate Response." *Inter-American Economic Affairs* 16 (Spring 1963):11-19.

Lillich, Richard B. "Economic Coercion and the International Legal Order." *International Affairs* (London) 51 (July 1975):358-371.

Litvak, Isaiah A., and Maule, Christopher J. "Nationalisation in the Caribbean Bauxite Industry." *International Affairs* (London) 51 (January 1975):43-59.

Lleras Camargo, Alberto. "The Alliance for Progress: Aims, Distortions, Obstacles." *Foreign Affairs* 42 (October 1963):25-37.

Logue, John J. "Coming Showdown: Ocean Nationalism." *America*, December 27, 1975, pp. 466-469.

Luard, Evan. "The Law of the Sea Conference." *International Affairs*

(London) 50 (April 1974):268-278.

Manger, William. "Reform of the OAS. The 1967 Buenos Aires Protocol of Amendment to the 1948 Charter of Bogotá: An Appraisal." *Journal of Inter-American Studies* 10 (January 1968):1-14.

Manley, Michael. "Overcoming Insularity in Jamaica." *Foreign Affairs* 49 (October 1970):100-110.

Meek, George. "U.S. Influence in the Organization of American States." *Journal of Inter-American Studies* 17 (August 1975):311-325.

Meisler, Stanley. "Meddling in Latin America: Dubious Role of AFL-CIO." *Nation,* February 10, 1964, pp. 133-138.

Mesa-Lago, Carmelo. "The Sovietization of the Cuban Revolution: Its Consequences for the Western Hemisphere." *World Affairs* 136 (Summer 1973):3-35.

Molineu, Harold. "The Concept of the Caribbean in the Latin American Policy of the United States." *Journal of Inter-American Studies* 15 (August 1973):285-307.

Monroe, Keith. "Guatemala: What the Reds Left Behind." *Harper's Magazine,* July 1955, pp. 60-65.

Montbrial, Thierry de. "For a New World Economic Order." *Foreign Affairs* 54 (October 1975):61-78.

Morrison, Thomas K. "Case Study of a 'Least Developed Country' Successfully Exporting Manufactures: Haiti." *Inter-American Economic Affairs* 29 (Summer 1975):21-31.

Myers, John J. "Sanity From the Sea?" *America,* October 24, 1970, pp. 318-319.

Nevins, Allan. "President Hoover's Record." *Current History* 36 (July 1932): 385-394.

Petras, James. "U.S.-Latin American Studies: A Critical Assessment." *Science and Society* 32 (Spring 1968):148-168.

Pike, Fredrick B. "Guatemala, the United States, and Communism in the Americas." *Review of Politics* 17 (April 1955):232-261.

Pringle, Robin. "Banking in the Land of Balboa." *The Banker,* October 1975.

Quester, George H. "Missiles in Cuba, 1970." *Foreign Affairs* 49 (April 1971):493-506.

Reichard Estevas, Herman. "The United States, Spain, and the *Maine,* or the Diplomacy of Frustration." *Revista/Review Interamericana* 3 (Winter 1973).

Richardson, Bonham C. "The Agricultural Dilemma of the Post-Plantation Caribbean." *Inter-American Economic Affairs* 26 (Summer 1972):59-70.

Rippy, J. Fred. "The Initiation of the Customs Receivership in the Dominican Republic." *Hispanic American Historical Review* 17 (1937): 419-457.

Romualdi, Serafino. "A U.S. Policy for the Hemisphere." *New Leader*, December 27, 1954.

Rosenfeld, Stephen S. "The Panama Negotiations—A Close-Run Thing." *Foreign Affairs* 54 (October 1975):1-13.

Schellenberg, T. R. "Jeffersonian Origins of the Monroe Doctrine." *Hispanic American Historical Review* 14 (1934):1-32.

Schlesinger, Arthur M., Jr. "Good Fences Make Good Neighbors." *Fortune*, August 1946, pp. 130-135.

Sloan, John W. "Three Views of Latin America: President Nixon, Governor Rockefeller and the Latin American Consensus of Viña del Mar." *Orbis* 14 (Winter 1971):934-950.

Smith, Daniel M. "Bainbridge Colby and the Good Neighbor Policy, 1920-1921." *Mississippi Valley Historical Review* 50 (June 1963):56-78.

Sterling, C. M. "Henry Clay: Forerunner of Pan-Americanism." *Américas* 16 (May 1964):1-6.

Sunkel, Osvaldo. "Big Business and 'Dependencia': A Latin American View." *Foreign Affairs* 50 (April 1972):517-531.

Swing, John Temple. "Who Will Own the Oceans?" *Foreign Affairs* 54 (April 1976):527-546.

Tannenbaum, Frank. "The Future of Democracy in Latin America." *Foreign Affairs* 33 (April 1955):429-444.

Taylor, Philip B., Jr. "The Guatemalan Affair: A Critique of United States Foreign Policy." *American Political Science Review* 50 (September 1956): 787-806.

Tierney, John J., Jr. "U.S. Intervention in Nicaragua, 1927-1933: Lessons for Today." *Orbis* 14 (Winter 1971):1012-1028.

Tomasek, Robert D. "Caribbean Exile Invasions: A Special Regional Type of Conflict." *Orbis* 17 (Winter 1974):1354-1382.

Tretiak, Daniel. "Cuba and the Communist System: The Politics of a Communist Independent, 1967-1969." *Orbis* 14 (Fall 1970):740-764.

Watson, G. Llewellyn. "Patterns of Black Protest in Jamaica: The Case of the Ras-Tafarians." *Journal of Black Studies* 4 (March 1974):329-343.

Welles, Sumner. "Pressure Groups and Foreign Policy." *Atlantic Monthly*, November 1947, pp. 63-67.

Williams, Eric. "The Foreign Policy of the Caribbean States." *The Round Table*, no. 249 (January 1973), pp. 77-88.

Wood, Bryce. "External Restraints on the Good Neighbor Policy." *Inter-American Economic Affairs* 16 (Autumn 1962):3-24.

Woodruff, William and Helga. "The Illusions about the Role of Integration in Latin America's Future." *Inter-American Economic Affairs* 22 (Spring 1969):69-79.

Yergin, Daniel. "Fulbright's Last Frustration." *New York Times Magazine* November 24, 1974.

Documents

Berriós, Rubén. *Independence, Socialism, and Democracy: The Only Solution.* Summary by the president of the Puerto Rican Independent Party of the Program of the Puerto Rican Independent Party as approved by the Program and Regulations Convention, May 29-30, 1971. San Juan, Puerto Rico, 1975.

Burnham, Forbes. *In the Cause of Humanity.* Address by prime minister of Guyana at Commonwealth heads of government meeting on the new international economic order, Kingston, Jamaica, May 1, 1975. Guyana Printers Ltd., 1975.

Caribbean Community Secretariat. *The Caribbean Community: A Guide.* Georgetown, Guyana: Caribbean Community Secretariat, 1973.

Commission on United States–Latin American Relations. *The Americas for a Changing World.* New York: Center for Inter-American Relations, 1974.

Del Mar, Roland H. *Strategic Characteristics of the Caribbean.* Report by major general delivered at the University of Florida, Gainesville, Florida, Seventeenth Annual Conference on the Caribbean, December 1-3, 1966.

Dunkley, Carlyle, ed. *The Aluminum Industry and the Caribbean Connexion.* Kingston, Jamaica: Caribbean Bauxite, Mine and Metalworkers' Federation, 1969.

General Secretariat of Organization of American States. Department of Information and Public Affairs. *Inside of Jamaica.* Washington, D.C.: Department of Information and Public Affairs, 1974.

Georgetown University. Center for Strategic and International Studies. Western Hemisphere Minerals: *As Goes Oil So Goes Other Minerals? A Review of Recent Development in Major Raw Materials and Energy, the Future Outlook and Economic Impact on Canada, Latin America and the United States.* Report of a conference on Western Hemisphere mineral problems held in Washington, D.C., March 27, 1974.

Jenkins, Brian; Sereseres, Cesar; and Einaudi, Luigi. *United States Military and Guatemalan Politics.* Paper presented to the California Arms Control and Foreign Policy Seminar, 1974.

Ministry of Information and Culture. *Toward a Balanced Economy in Guyana.* Ministry of Information and Culture, 1973.

Nixon, Richard. *United States Foreign Policy for the 1970s: Shaping a Durable Peace.* Report to Congress, May 3, 1973. Washington, D.C.: U.S. Government Printing Office, 1973.

Rosenthal, Benjamin S. "Three Key Documents on Latin America." Speech to House of Representatives, July 16, 1969. *Viña del Mar,* July 16, 1969, pp. 19840-19846.

U.S. Congress, House. Committee on Foreign Affairs, Hearings of the 91st (1970), 92nd (1971), and 93rd (1973, 1974) Congress.

U.S. Congress, Senate. Committee on Foreign Relations. Hearings of the 89th (1966), 91st (1969, 1970), 92nd (1972), 93rd (1973, 1974), and 94th (1975) Congress; Committee on Appropriations, Hearings of the 93rd Congress (1973).

U.S. State Department. *Bulletin.* Many volumes contain important documents, e.g., February 24, 1969, p. 159, carries the "Nixon News Conference of February 6, 1969: Latin America."

Tapia House Publishing Company, Ltd. *Tapia Says: Power to the People: Proposals for a New Constitution.* Tunafuna: Tapia House Printing Co., 1973.

Williams, Eric. *Economic Transformation and the Rule and Vision of the PNM.* Address by political leader to PNM's Sixteenth Annual Convention. Port-of-Spain, Trinidad: PNM Publishing Co., 1974.

————. *The International Significance of Asia and the Far East: From the Intellectual and Cultural Standpoint.* Address by political leader to the Chinese Association, December 9, 1974. Port-of-Spain, Trinidad: Key Caribbean Public, 1974.

Wilson, Harold. Speech on World Trade Commodities Delivered by the Prime Minister to the Commonwealth Heads of Government, Kingston, Jamaica, May 1, 1975. British Information Services, Policy and Reference Division, 1975.

INDEX

INDEX